Student-Involved
Assessment FOR Learning

Fourth Edition

RICHARD J. STIGGINS

Assessment Training Institute

PEARSON

Merrill
Prentice Hall

Upper Saddle River, New Jersey
Columbus, Ohio

Library of Congress Cataloging-in-Publication Data

Stiggins, Richard J.
   Student-involved assessment for learning/Richard J. Stiggins.—4th ed.
     p. cm
   Rev. ed. of: Student-involved classroom assessment. 3rd ed. c2001.
   Includes bibliographical references and index.
   ISBN 0-13-118349-4
    1. Educational tests and measurement—United States. 2. Examinations—United States.
  I. Stiggins, Richard J. Student-involved classroom assessment. II. Title.

LB3051.S8536 2005
371.26—dc22   2004044900

Vice President and Executive Publisher: Jeffery W. Johnston
Publisher: Kevin M. Davis
Development Editor: Autumn Crisp Benson
Editorial Assistant: Amanda King
Production Editor: Mary Harlan
Production Coordinator: Amy Gehl, Carlisle Publishers Services
Copy Editor: Robert L. Marcum
Design Coordinator: Diane C. Lorenzo
Text Design and Illustrations: Carlisle Publishers Services
Cover Design: Jeff Vanik
Cover Image: Index Stock
Production Manager: Laura Messerly
Director of Marketing: Ann Castel Davis
Marketing Manager: Autumn Purdy
Marketing Coordinator: Tyra Poole

This book was set in Garamond by Carlisle Communications, Ltd. and was printed and bound by R.R. Donnelley & Sons Company. The cover was printed by The Lehigh Press, Inc.

Pearson Education Ltd.   Pearson Education Australia PTY, Limited
Pearson Education Singapore, Pte. Ltd.   Pearson Education North Asia Ltd.
Pearson Education Canada, Ltd.   Pearson Educacíon de Mexico, S.A. de C.V.
Pearson Education—Japan   Pearson Education Malaysia, Pte. Ltd.

10 9 8 7 6 5 4 3 2
ISBN: 0-13-118349-4

I dedicate this fourth edition to my teammates at the Assessment Training Institute, as capable and dedicated a group of professionals as one could ever hope to be associated with:

Judy Arter
Laura Camacho
Barbara Carnegie
Jan Chappuis
Steve Chappuis
Mindy Dotson
Sharon Lippert

Acknowledgments

In this fourth edition of *Student-Involved Assessment FOR Learning,* the reader will see the continuing evolution of our understanding of how to use the classroom assessment and its results to benefit (not merely grade) student learning. The most exciting change reflected in this edition is our presentation of the distinction between assessment OF learning and assessment FOR learning—that is, assessment used in support of learning combined with assessment verifying that learning has been attained. For this distinction, we thank the team of educators who form the Assessment Reform Group in the United Kingdom, especially Paul Black of Kings College, London, from whom we all have learned so much.

The vision of sound assessment practice I offer here is not mine alone. Rather, it represents the collective wisdom of many. I claim only to be an able learner blessed with the opportunity to work with many outstanding teachers over the years. I refer specifically to the members of our team at the Assessment Training Institute, to whom this edition is dedicated. We test each other's ideas continuously and, in the process, promote increasing clarity in our collective vision of the right way to use classroom assessment for student well-being.

I also continue to learn from those teachers who provide us with guidance from afar. The distance over which wisdom travels does not diminish its brilliance. For lighting the way, I thank Anne Davies of British Columbia, Carol Commodore of Wisconsin, Ken O'Connor of Scarborough, Ontario, and Ruth Sutton of Manchester, England.

Thanks also to those who reviewed early drafts and provided such helpful suggestions for improvement: JoAnne Carter-Hauser, Cardinal Stritch University; Mark W. Conley, Michigan State University; Catherine Fallona, University of Southern Maine; Jarene Fluckiger, University of Nebraska at Omaha; Donald L. Haefele, Ohio State University; Eric Hampton, Indiana State University; and Charlotte Haselhuhn, University of Northern Iowa.

Kevin Davis, Publisher at Merrill/Prentice Hall, has guided the development, publication, and distribution of all editions of this text and has made it a success. He alone saw the potential when I proposed the first edition to him and has remained its champion ever since. For this fourth edition, Kevin has been ably assisted by Autumn Benson and Mary Harlan. Thanks to all.

All four editions have been copyedited by freelancer Robert L. Marcum, forever my director of "voice." From the outset 10 years ago, Robert has consistently heard and remained steadfastly committed to defending the nontraditional, nontechnical, and nonacademic voice that I use in this book. Under his guidance, we have achieved focus, clarity, and economy of communication—but always with a friendly, welcoming tone that is so essential for those new to the assessment.

Finally, thanks to my wife and partner, Nancy Bridgeford, who always knows how to offer the encouragement that not only keeps me going, but keeps me striving for excellence.

Thank you, everyone. We know more together than any one of us does alone. Let us continue to teach and learn from each other.

Rick Stiggins

About the Author

Richard J. Stiggins, B.S., M.A., Ph. D., is founder and president of the Assessment Training Institute, Inc., Portland, Oregon, a service agency devoted to supporting teachers as they face the day-to-day challenges of classroom assessment. He received his bachelor's degree in psychology from the State University of New York at Plattsburgh, master's degree in industrial psychology from Springfield (MA) College, and doctoral degree in education measurement from Michigan State University. Dr. Stiggins began his assessment work on the faculty of Michigan State before becoming director of research and evaluation for the Edina, Minnesota, Public Schools and a member of the faculty of educational foundations at the University of Minnesota. In addition, he has served as director of test development for the American College Testing Program, Iowa City, Iowa; as a visiting scholar at Stanford University; and as director of the Centers for Classroom Assessment and Performance Assessment at the Northwest Regional Educational Laboratory, Portland, Oregon.

Rick has turned two decades of classroom assessment research into a national movement to combat decades of assessment training neglect for teachers and administrators. He is helping colleges of education, states, and districts across the nation to launch the professional development needed to meet emerging classroom, school, district, and state assessment responsibilities. Rick coined the phrase *assessment literacy* to represent the standards of professional excellence to be attained and has pioneered the use of local learning teams as an effective means of low-cost, in-service assessment training.

Further, to achieve his vision of excellence in assessment, he has pioneered the design and development of print and video assessment training materials to promote practical understanding of sound assessment practice. His unique approach to turning *Student-Involved Assessment FOR Learning* into an immensely powerful motivator for students and a time-saver for teachers has turned this text into one of the most practical and widely used teacher guides in the country. In fact, the text has received the National Council on Measurement in Education annual award for outstanding dissemination of measurement concepts and the best professional publication award from the California County Superintendents Association. Rick's very popular interactive videos show teachers how to turn classroom assessment strategies into very engaging learning experiences for their students.

EDUCATOR LEARNING CENTER: AN INVALUABLE ONLINE RESOURCE

Merrill Education and the Association for Supervision and Curriculum Development (ASCD) invite you to take advantage of a new online resource, one that provides access to the top research and proven strategies associated with ASCD and Merrill— the Educator Learning Center. At **www.EducatorLearningCenter.com** you will find resources that will enhance your students' understanding of course topics and of current educational issues, in addition to being invaluable for further research.

How the Educator Learning Center Will Help Your Students Become Better Teachers

With the combined resources of Merrill Education and ASCD, you and your students will find a wealth of tools and materials to better prepare them for the classroom.

Research

- More than 600 articles from the ASCD journal *Educational Leadership* discuss everyday issues faced by practicing teachers.
- A direct link on the site to Research Navigator™ gives students access to many of the leading education journals, as well as extensive content detailing the research process.
- Excerpts from Merrill Education texts give your students insights on important topics of instructional methods, diverse populations, assessment, classroom management, technology, and refining classroom practice.

Classroom Practice

- Hundreds of lesson plans and teaching strategies are categorized by content area and age range.
- Case studies and classroom video footage provide virtual field experience for student reflection.
- Computer simulations and other electronic tools keep your students abreast of today's classrooms and current technologies.

Look into the Value of Educator Learning Center Yourself

A four-month subscription to Educator Learning Center is $25 but is **FREE** when used in conjunction with this text. To obtain free passcodes for your students, simply contact your local Merrill/Prentice Hall sales representative, and your representative will give you a special ISBN to give your bookstore when ordering your textbooks. To preview the value of this website to you and your students, please go to **www.EducatorLearningCenter.com** and click on "Demo."

Discover the Companion Website Accompanying This Book

The Prentice Hall Companion Website: A Virtual Learning Environment

Technology is a constantly growing and changing aspect of our field that is creating a need for content and resources. To address this emerging need, we have developed an online learning environment for students and professors alike—Companion Websites—to support our textbooks.

In creating a Companion Website, our goal is to build on and enhance what the textbook already offers. For this reason, the content for each user-friendly website is organized by chapter and provides the professor and student with a variety of meaningful resources. Common features of a Companion Website include:

For the Professor

Every Companion Website integrates **Syllabus Manager**™, an online syllabus creation and management utility.

- **Syllabus Manager**™ provides you, the instructor, with an easy, step-by-step process to create and revise syllabi, with direct links into Companion Website and other online content without having to learn HTML.

- Students may logon to your syllabus during any study session. All they need to know is the web address for the Companion Website, and the password you've assigned to your syllabus.

- After you have created a syllabus using **Syllabus Manager**™, students may enter the syllabus for their course section from any point in the Companion Website.

- Class dates are highlighted in white and assignment due dates appear in blue. Clicking on a date, the student is shown the list of activities for the assignment. The activities for each assignment are linked directly to actual content, saving time for students.

- Adding assignments consists of clicking on the desired due date, then filling in the details of the assignment—name of the assignment, instructions, and whether it is a one-time or repeating assignment.

- In addition, links to other activities can be created easily. If the activity is online, a URL can be entered in the space provided, and it will be linked automatically in the final syllabus.

- Your completed syllabus is hosted on our servers, allowing convenient updates from any computer on the Internet. Changes you make to your syllabus are immediately available to your students at their next login.

For the Student

- **Chapter Objectives**—outline key concepts from the text.
- **Interactive Self-quizzes**—complete with hints and automatic grading that provide immediate feedback for students. After students submit their answers for the interactive self-quizzes, the Companion Website Results Reporter computes a percentage grade, provides a graphic representation of how many questions were answered correctly and incorrectly, and gives a question-by-question analysis of the quiz. Students are given the option to send their quiz to up to four email addresses (professor, teaching assistant, study partner, etc.).
- **Message Board**—serves as a virtual bulletin board to post—or respond to—questions or comments to a national audience.
- **Chat**— real-time chat with anyone who is using the text anywhere in the country—ideal for discussion and study groups, class projects, etc.
- **Web Destinations**—links to www sites that relate to chapter content.
- **Additional Resources**—access to chapter-specific or general content that enhances material found in the text.

To take advantage of these resources, please visit the *Student-Involved Assessment FOR Learning* Companion Website at

www.prenhall.com/stiggins

Brief Contents

Contents

Note: Every effort has been made to provide accurate and current Internet information in this book. However, the Internet and information posted on it are constantly changing, so it is inevitable that some of the Internet addresses listed in this textbook will change.

Student-Involved
Assessment FOR Learning

PART I

Introduction to Student-Involved Assessment FOR Learning

In this book, we lay the foundation of professional competence you need to meet standards of excellence in classroom assessment. The presentation unfolds in three parts. We begin in Part 1 by articulating the *standards of good assessment practice* that are your responsibility as a classroom teacher. We continue in Part 2 with specific suggestions for how you can meet those standards by *accurately assessing* the achievement of your students and by using assessment and its results to benefit them, and we conclude in Part 3 with practical options for *communicating the assessment results,* once again, in ways that maximize student learning success.

As you study this text, you will see a very strong theme emerge around the use of classroom assessment as a confidence builder for your students, as a motivator to keep them striving to learn, and as a strong foundation for unprecedented achievement gains for them. You can use assessment to help your students become confident, motivated, and successful learners by involving them deeply in ongoing classroom assessment, record keeping, and communication.

The idea of student involvement in assessment deviates from the traditions of the American educational system. Those traditions have us using assessments to hold students accountable for learning. Assessment has provided an index of the amount learned. However, we also can use classroom assessment to support or cause learning. We achieve excellence in classroom assessment when we balance a continuous array of assessments used to help students learn (assessment FOR learning) with periodic assessments used to verify that they did, in fact, meet prescribed academic achievement standards (assessment OF learning).

The three chapters of Part 1 set the stage for sound assessment practices. Chapter 1 addresses the users and uses of assessment, including classroom, instructional support, and policy users. It makes the point that different decision makers need access to different information about student achievement in different forms at different times to do their jobs. Our assessments must meet those various information needs.

Chapter 2 defines the kinds of achievement expectations, contending that we can dependably assess only those targets that we have clearly and appropriately defined. We will examine several different kinds of achievement, starting with achievement standards, break those down into classroom-level achievement targets, and discuss the need for student-friendly versions of these expectations. Students can hit any target that they can see and that holds still for them. We'll see how to use classroom assessment to set them up for success in these terms.

Chapter 3 frames commonsense standards of classroom assessment quality, explaining how to select proper assessment methods, given particular users and achievement targets. Sometimes the situation demands a selected response (multiple-choice) test, other times an essay assessment. Still other times a performance assessment or simply a conversation with a student about achievement will meet your needs. The most unique feature of this chapter is the manner in which it connects these various methods to the various kinds of achievement discussed in Chapter 2.

Part 2 is about the effective use of different assessment methods. Our presentation takes you inside each of the four families of assessment methods one at a time: selected response (e.g., multiple-choice, true/false) assessments, essay assessments, performance assessments, and assessments based on direct personal communication with students. We will explore how to apply each method in appropriate contexts, detailing how to develop good ones, how to avoid biased results, and when and how to involve students in their use in ways that promote increased achievement.

In Part 3 we delve deeply into the alternative ways of managing assessment results and communicating to their many users, such as students, parents, other teachers, administrators, and so on, in timely and understandable terms. The communication vehicles we will explore include test scores, report card grades, standards-based report cards, portfolios, and conferences. We will explore the strengths and limitations each offers when it comes to using assessment to improve student learning.

Become a Reflective Learner

Be advised from the very beginning that you have much to learn to manage your classroom assessment environment efficiently and effectively. This is part of the reason many new and even most experienced teachers dread the assessment part of their jobs. It's hard work, often complex and confusing.

Besides, we all carry with us those emotional associations with assessment that we learned in our youth. Most of us grew up in classrooms in which our teachers believed that the way to maximize learning is to maximize anxiety, and assessment was always the great intimidator. Mention assessment, evaluation, or grading to adults and immediate feelings of anxiety, vulnerability, and frustration come to the fore. As a result the entire topic is one most of us would prefer to avoid.

My mission is to give you the information and tools you need to be *confident* in and *comfortable* with your assessment practices. Confident—knowing your practices are sound and they will support, not stifle, your students' learning. Comfortable—you have had enough opportunity to think about and try out practices so that you know them well.

How will we accomplish this? I have built a variety of interactive opportunities into the text, including times for your personal reflection during learning, practice exercises, and growth portfolio entries, each of which is designed to function as an integral part of your learning. These are designed to bring the book's ideas to life in your own context. They will serve to integrate your new learning about assessment into your existing structures of knowledge and under-standing. *If you merely read this book with the purpose of committing to short-term memory the parts you think will be on the midterm or final exam, you will finish neither confident in nor comfortable with your assessment practices.* You must practice applying the concepts and procedures as you learn about them. Only then can you develop the level of personal understanding needed to make them part of your teaching routine.

I plan to model in our relationship and in your learning the very relationship that must exist between you and your students. I want the work you do in conjunc-tion with this book to keep you in touch with, and therefore feeling in control of, your own ongoing professional development. Thus, this work models in your adult learning environment the very student-involved assessment, record-keeping, and communication tactics that have been demonstrated to yield unprecedented achieve-ment gains when used with students in classrooms.

Keep a Journal to Watch Yourself Grow

Extensive experience in helping teachers learn about classroom assessment leads me to suggest that you maintain a learning log, journal, or diary as you proceed. From time to time I will suggest entries that may be useful. Here are three for you to consider:

Times for Reflection

As you study, periodically you will encounter "Times for Reflection" asking you to relate an idea to your personal perceptions, to think about something in greater depth, or to write something down before moving on. These occur within and at the end of each chapter. These reflections will help you construct your own personal meaning of the material presented. Consider recording your written responses to each of these reflections in your learning log or journal. They will help you watch yourself grow.

Time and Energy Savers

It is most important that you understand why high-quality classroom assessment ef-fectively used to benefit student learning can become an immense time saver for you in the classroom. It can make everyone's job far easier—students, teachers, and par-ents. Periodically I will offer specific procedural suggestions that promise time and energy savings. They will be highlighted with a clock icon (shown in the margin). Consider keeping a list of these time savers somewhere in your learning log for easy reference and later review.

Practice Opportunities

To help you integrate the ideas presented herein into your teaching practices, I have woven in a variety of opportunities for you to practice applying student-involved classroom assessment strategies and methods. They appear within and at the end of chapters, and include the following:

- Case studies that ask you to confront real-world classroom assessment dilemmas and use what you are learning to find solutions
- Examples of unsound assessments that you can practice fixing
- Examples of high-quality assessments for you to study and learn from
- Projects that you can complete to meld these ideas directly into your classroom

Again, keep a record of your responses in your journal. Over time they will permit you to monitor your own growth.

Form a Learning Team or Study Group

It has been my experience that I learn more, faster, and with deeper understanding when I collaborate with like-minded learners. The research literature on adult learning and professional development backs me up in this contention. In fact, we rely exclusively on learning teams in our work at the Assessment Training Institute (ATI) to provide professional development experiences to practicing educators around the world. Teamwork works! For this reason, consider forming a team of classmates to help you learn about classroom assessment.

Use each meeting to talk about the big ideas, help each other through difficult parts, discuss applications relevant to each team member, or compare your responses to Times for Reflection and to the practice exercises. This "talking time" is very important to solidifying your understanding.

Companion Website

Pearson/Prentice Hall and ATI have teamed up to create a Companion Website (http://www.prenhall.com/stiggins). Among other features, this learning aid will provide opportunities for you to practice applying the standards of good practice described herein. This further study will support those seeking deeper understanding of key topics. For example, as the chapters unfold, we will build a comprehensive set of rubrics for evaluating classroom assessment quality. These rubrics appear in the Appendix. The website provides additional sample assessments for you to evaluate and revise for practice.

Chapter 1

Classroom Assessment for Student Success

CHAPTER FOCUS

This chapter answers the following guiding question:

> What are my classroom assessment responsibilities as a teacher and how can I fulfill them in ways that maximize the success of my students?

From your study of this chapter, you will understand the following:

1. How classroom assessment fits into the big picture of your job as a teacher.
2. What it means to develop and use assessments that are valid and reliable.
3. The relationship among assessment, student motivation, and student success at learning.
4. Four guiding principles that lead to sound classroom assessment practice.

Our Classroom Assessment Responsibilities

Assessment is the process of gathering evidence of student learning to inform instructional decisions. This process can be done well or poorly. To function effectively in the classroom, we all must be able to do it well. That means we must do both of the following:

- Gather *accurate information* about the achievement of our students.
- Weave classroom assessment and its results into instruction in ways that *benefit our students;* that is, not merely to grade them, but to enhance both their desire to learn and their achievement.

These two standards of professional practice are central to our effectiveness as teachers. Gather dependable information and use it well and our students can prosper. In short, we succeed. Gather inaccurate information or use it poorly and we will do severe and perhaps long-lasting damage to some (perhaps many) of our students.

5

Let me introduce you to Ms. Weathersby, a teacher who has mastered her classroom assessment responsibilities and who carries them out very effectively. She and her student, Emily, can teach us valuable lessons.

A Story of Assessment for Student Success

At a local school board meeting, the English department faculty from the high school presents the results of their evaluation of the new writing instruction program that they had implemented over the past year. The audience includes a young woman named Emily, a junior at the local high school, sitting in the back of the room with her parents. She knows she will be a big part of the presentation. She's only a little nervous. She understands how important her role is. It has been quite a year for her, unlike any she has ever experienced in school before. She also knows her parents and teacher are as proud of her as she is of herself.

As part of their preparation for this program, the faculty attended a summer institute on assessing writing proficiency and integrating these assessments into their teaching and their students' learning. The teachers were confident that this kind of professional development and their subsequent program revisions would produce much higher levels of writing proficiency.

As the first step in presenting program evaluation results, the English department chair, Ms. Weathersby, who also happens to be Emily's English teacher, distributes a sample of student writing to the board members (with the student's name removed), asking them to read and evaluate this writing. They do so, expressing their dismay aloud as they go. They are less than complimentary in their commentary on these samples of student work. One board member reports with some frustration that, if these represent the results of that new writing program, then clearly it is not working. The board member is right. This is, in fact, a pretty weak piece of work. Emily's mom puts her arm around her daughter's shoulder and hugs her.

But Ms. Weathersby urges patience and asks the board members to be very specific in stating what they don't like about this work. As the board registers its complaints, a faculty member records the criticisms on chart paper for all to see. The list is long, including everything from repetitiveness to disorganization to short, choppy sentences and disconnected ideas.

Next, Ms. Weathersby distributes another sample of student writing, asking the board to read and evaluate it. Ah, now this, they report, is more like it! This work is much better! But be specific, she demands. What do you like about this work? They list positive aspects: good choice of words, sound sentence structure, clever ideas, and so on. Emily is ready to burst! She squeezes her mom's hand.

The reason she's so full of pride at this moment is that this has been a special year for her and her classmates. For the first time ever, they became partners with their English teachers in managing their own improvement as writers. Early in the year, Ms. Weathersby ("Ms. W." they all call her) made it crystal clear to Emily that she was, in fact, not a very good writer and that just trying hard to get better was not going to be enough. She expected Emily to improve—nothing else would suffice.

Ms. W. started the year by working with students to implement new state writing standards, including understanding quality performance in word choice, sentence structure, organization, and voice, and by sharing some new "analytical scoring guides" written just for students. Each scoring guide explained the differences between good and poor-quality writing in understandable terms. When Emily and her teacher evaluated her first two pieces of writing using these standards, she received very low ratings. Not very good. . . .

But she also began to study samples of writing Ms. W. provided that Emily could see were very good. Slowly, she began to understand *why* they were good. The differences between these and her work started to become clear. Ms. W. began to share examples and strategies that would help her writing improve one step at a time. As she practiced and time passed, Emily and her classmates kept samples of their old writing to compare to their new writing, and they began to build portfolios. Thus, she literally began to watch her own writing skills improve before her very eyes. At midyear, her parents were invited in for a conference at which Emily, not Ms. Weathersby, shared the contents of her portfolio and discussed her emerging writing skills. Emily remembers sharing thoughts about some aspects of her writing that had become very strong and some examples of things she still needed to work on. Now, the year was at an end and here she sat waiting for her turn to speak to the school board about all of this. What a year!

Now, having set up the board by having them analyze, evaluate, and compare these two samples of student work, Ms. W. springs a surprise. The two pieces of writing they had just evaluated, one of relatively poor quality and one of outstanding quality, were produced by the same writer at the beginning and at the end of the school year! This, she reports, is evidence of the kind of impact the new writing program is having on student writing proficiency.

Needless to say, all are impressed. However, one board member wonders aloud, "Have all your students improved in this way?" Having anticipated the question, the rest of the English faculty joins the presentation and produces carefully prepared charts depicting dramatic changes in typical student performance over time on rating scales for each of six clearly articulated dimensions of good writing. They accompany their description of student performance on each scale with actual samples of student work illustrating various levels of proficiency.

Further, Ms. W. informs the board that the student whose improvement has been so dramatically illustrated with the work they have just analyzed is present at this meeting, along with her parents. This student is ready to talk with the board about the nature of her learning experience. Emily, you're on!

Interest among the board members runs high. Emily talks about how she has come to understand the truly important differences between good and bad writing. She refers to differences she had not understood before, how she has learned to assess her own writing and to fix it when it doesn't "work well," and how she and her classmates have learned to talk with her teacher and each other about what it means to write well. Ms. W. talks about the improved focus of writing instruction, increase in student motivation, and important positive changes in the very nature of the student–teacher relationship.

A board member asks Emily if she likes to write, and she answers, "I do now!" This board member turns to Emily's parents and asks their impression of all of this.

They report with pride that they had never before seen so much evidence of Emily's achievement and that most of it came from Emily herself. Emily had never been called on to lead the parent-teacher conference before. They had no idea she was so articulate. They loved it. Their daughter's pride in and accountability for her achievement has skyrocketed in the past year.

As the meeting ends, it is clear to all in attendance that evening that this application of student-involved classroom assessment had contributed to important learning. The English faculty accepted responsibility for student learning, shared that responsibility with their students, and everybody won. There are good feelings all around. One of the accountability demands of the community was satisfied with the presentation of credible evidence of student success, and the new writing program was the reason for improved student achievement. Obviously, this story has a happy ending.

Success from the Student's Point of View

The day after the board meeting, I interviewed Emily about the evening's events. As you read, think about how our conversation centers on what really works for Emily.

"You did a nice job at the school board meeting last night, Emily," I started.

"Thanks," she replied. "What's most exciting for me is that, last year, I could never have done it."

"What's changed from last year?"

"I guess I'm more confident. I knew what had happened for me in English class and I wanted to tell them my story."

"You became a confident writer."

"Yeah, but that's not what I mean. Last night at the board meeting I was more than a good writer. I felt good talking about my writing and how I'd improved. It's like, I understand what had happened to me and I have a way to describe it."

"Let's talk about Emily the confident writer. What were you thinking last night when the board members were reacting to your initial writing sample—you know, the one that wasn't very good? Still confident?"

"Mom helped. She squeezed my hand and I remember she whispered in my ear, 'You'll show 'em!' That helped me handle it. It's funny, I was listening to their comments to see if they knew anything about good writing. I wondered if they understood as much about it as I do—like, maybe they needed to take Ms. Weathersby's class."

"How did they do?" I asked, laughing.

"Pretty well, actually," Em replied. "They found some problems in my early work and described them pretty well. When I first started last fall, I wouldn't have been able to do that. I was a terrible writer."

"How do you know that, Em?"

"I understand where I was then, how little I could do. No organization. I didn't even know my own voice. No one had ever taken the time to show me the secrets. I'd never learned to analyze my writing. I wouldn't have known what to look for or how to describe it or how to change it. That's part of what Ms. W. taught us."

"How did she do that?"

"To begin with, she taught us to do what the board members did last night: analyze other people's writing. We looked at newspaper editorials, passages from books we were reading, letters friends had sent us. She wanted us to see what made those pieces work or not work. She would read a piece to us and then we'd brainstorm what made it good or bad. Pretty soon, we began to see patterns—things that worked or didn't work. She wanted us to begin to see and hear stuff as she read out loud."

"Like what?" I asked.

"Well, look, here's my early piece from the meeting last night. See, just read it!"

(Please read the Beginning of the Year Sample in Figure 1.1.)

"See, there are no grammar or usage mistakes. So it's 'correct' in that sense. But these short, choppy sentences just don't work. And it doesn't say anything or go anywhere. It's just a bunch of disconnected thoughts. It doesn't grab you and hold your attention. Then it stops. It just ends. Now look at my second piece to see the difference."

(Please read the End of the Year Sample in Figure 1.1.)

"In this one, I tried to tell about the feelings of frustration that happen when humans use machines. See, I think the voice in this piece comes from the feeling that 'We've all been there.' Everyone who works with computers has had this experience. A writer's tiny problem (not being able to find a good ending) turns into a major problem (losing the whole document). This idea makes the piece clear and organized. I think the reader can picture this poor, frustrated writer at her computer, wanting, trying to communicate in a human way—but finding that the computer is just as frustrated with her!"

"You sound just like you did last night at the board meeting."

"I'm always like this about my writing now. I know what works. Sentences are important. So is voice. So are organization and word choice—all that stuff. If you do it right, it works and you know it," she replied with a smile.

"What kinds of things did Ms. W. do in class that worked for you?"

"Well, like, when we were first getting started, Ms. Weathersby gave us a big stack of student papers she'd collected over the years—some good, some bad, and everything in between. Our assignment was to sort them into four stacks based on quality, from real good to real bad. When we were done, we compared who put what papers in which piles and then we talked about why. Sometimes, the discussions got pretty heated! Ms. W. wanted us to describe what we thought were the differences among the piles. Over time, we formed those differences into a set of rating scales that we used to analyze, evaluate, and improve our writing."

"Did you evaluate your own work or each other's?"

"Only our own to begin with. Ms. W. said she didn't want anyone being embarrassed. We all had a lot to learn. It was supposed to be private until we began to trust our own judgments. She kept saying, 'Trust me. You'll get better at this and then you can share.'"

"Did you ever move on to evaluating each other's work?"

"Yeah. After a while, we began to trust ourselves and each other. Then we were free to ask classmates for opinions. But Ms. W. said, no blanket judgments—no saying just, this is good or bad. And we were always supposed to be honest. If we couldn't see how to help someone improve a piece, we were supposed to say so."

Computers are a thing of the future. They help us in thousands of ways. Computers are a help to our lives. They make things easier. They help us to keep track of information.

Computers are simple to use. Anyone can learn how. You do not have to be a computer expert to operate a computer. You just need to know a few basic things.

Computers can be robots that will change our lives. Robots are really computers! Robots do a lot of the work that humans used to do. This makes our lives much easier. Robots build cars and do many other tasks that humans used to do. When robots learn to do more, they will take over most of our work. This will free humans to do other kinds of things. You can also communicate on computers. It is much faster than mail! You can look up information, too. You can find information on anything at all on a computer.

Computers are changing the work and changing the way we work and communicate. In many ways, computers are changing our lives and making our lives better and easier.

So there I was, my face aglow with the reflection on my computer screen, trying to come up with the next line for my essay. Writing it was akin to Chinese water torture, as I could never seem to end it. It dragged on and on, a never-ending babble of stuff.

Suddenly, unexpectedly—I felt an ending coming on. I could wrap this thing up in four or five sentences, and this dreadful assignment would be over. I'd be free.

I had not saved yet, and decided I would do so now. I clasped the slick, white mouse in my hand, slid it over the mouse pad, and watched as the black arrow progressed toward the "File" menu. By accident, I clicked the mouse button just to the left of paragraph 66. I saw a flash and the next thing I knew, I was back to square one. I stared at the blank screen for a moment in disbelief. Where was my essay? My ten-billion-page masterpiece? Gone?! No—that couldn't be! Not after all the work I had done! Would a computer be that unforgiving? That unfeeling? Didn't it care about me at all?

I decided not to give up hope just yet. The secret was to remain calm. After all, my file had to be somewhere—right? That's what all the manuals say—"It's in there *somewhere*." I went back to the "File" menu, much more carefully this time. First, I tried a friendly sounding category called "Find File." No luck there; I hadn't given the file a name.

Ah, then I had a brainstorm. I could simply go up to "Undo." Yes, that would be my savior! A simple click of a button and my problem would be solved! I went to Undo, but it looked a bit fuzzy. Not a good sign. That means there is nothing to undo. Don't panic ... don't panic ...

I decided to try to exit the program, not really knowing what I would accomplish by this but feeling more than a little desperate. Next, I clicked on the icon that would allow me back in to word processing. A small sign appeared, telling me that my program was being used by another user. Another user? What's it talking about? *I'm* the only user, you idiot! Or at least I'm trying to be a user! Give me my paper back! Right now!

I clicked on the icon again and again—to no avail. Click ... click ...clickclickclickCLICKCLICKCLICK!!!! Without warning, a thin cloud of smoke began to rise from the back of the computer. I didn't know whether to laugh or cry. Sighing, I opened my desk drawer, and pulled out a tablet and pen. It was going to be a long day.

Figure 1.1
Emily's writing samples
Source: Personal writing by Nikki Spandel. Reprinted by permission.

"Were you able to see improvement in your writing along the way?" I wondered.

"Yeah, see, Ms. W. said that was the whole idea. I've still got my writing portfolio full of practice, see? It starts out pretty bad back in the fall and slowly gets pretty good toward spring. This is where the two pieces came from that the board read last night. I picked them. I talk about the changes in my writing in the self-reflections in here. My portfolio tells the whole story. Want to look through it?"

"I sure do. What do you think Ms. Weathersby did that was right, Emily?"

"Nobody had ever been so clear with me before about what it took to be really good at school stuff. It's like, there's no mystery—no need to psych her out. She said, 'I won't ever surprise you, trust me. I'll show you what I want and I don't want any excuses. But you've got to deliver good writing in this class. You don't deliver, you don't succeed.'

"Every so often, she would give us something she had written, so we could rate and provide her with feedback on her work. She listened to our comments and said it really helped her improve her writing. All of a sudden, *we* became *her* teachers! That was so cool!

"You know, she was the first teacher ever to tell me that it was okay not to be very good at something at first, like, when you're trying to do something new. But we couldn't stay there. We had to get a little better each time. If we didn't, it was our own fault. She didn't want us to give up on ourselves. If we kept improving, over time, we could learn to write well. I wish every teacher would do that. She would say, 'There's no shortage of success around here. You learn to write well, you get an A. My goal is to have everyone learn to write well and deserve an A.'"

"Thanks for filling in the details, Em."

"Thank you for asking!"

The Keys to Success

Let's consider the conditions that needed to be in place in Ms. W.'s classroom for Emily and her classmates to have experienced such success. To begin with, Ms. W. understood who is in charge of whether or not learning happened—her students. Therefore, assessment was a student-involved activity *during the learning* in which Emily and her classmates assessed their own achievement repeatedly over time, so they and their parents could watch the improvement. To be sure, Ms. W. controlled the definition of good writing and the evaluation criteria. And clearly, she made important instructional decisions based on assessment results. But she also shared the wisdom and power that come from being able to assess the quality of writing. She showed her students the secrets to their own success.

In this way, Ms. W. used assessment and its results to build her students' confidence in themselves as writers. She wanted her students to continue to believe the target was within reach if they kept striving. Students who see the target as being beyond reach will give up in hopelessness.

Second, Ms. Weathersby wanted her students always to remain in touch with where they are currently in relation to an ultimate vision of success. She wanted her students to continually see the distance closing between their present position and their goal. This turned out to be incredibly empowering for them.

Third, Ms. W. and her colleagues knew that their assessments of student achievement had to be very accurate. Writing exercises had to elicit the right kinds of writing. Scoring procedures needed to focus on the important facets of good writing. As faculty members, they needed to train themselves to apply those scoring standards dependably—to avoid making biased judgments about student work.

But, just as importantly, Ms. W. understood that she also had to train her students to make dependable judgments about the quality of their own work. *This represents the heart of competence.* Any student who cannot evaluate the quality of her own writing and fix it when it isn't working cannot become an independent, life-long writer.

Another key to success was the great care taken to communicate effectively about student achievement. Whether Ms. W. was describing for Emily improvements needed or achieved in her work or sharing with the school board summary information about average student performance, she took pains to speak simply, to the point, and with examples to ensure that her meaning was clear.

Some Students Aren't So Lucky

Sadly, for every such positive story, in which sound assessment feeds into productive instruction and important learning, there may be another with a far less constructive, perhaps even painful, ending. For example, consider the story of our daughter Kristen Ann, when she was just beginning to learn to write:

Kristen arrived home one afternoon full of gloom when she was in third grade. She said she knew we were going to be angry with her. She presented us with a sheet of paper—the third-grade size with the wide lines. On it, she had written a story. Her assignment was to write about someone or something she cares about deeply. She wrote of Kelly, a tiny kitten who had come to be part of our family, but who had to return to the farm after two weeks because of allergies. Kelly's departure had been like the loss of a family member.

On the sheet of paper was an emergent writer's version of this story—not sophisticated, but poignant. Krissy's recounting of events was accurate and her story captured her very strong sadness and disappointment at losing her new little friend. She did a pretty darn good job of writing, for a beginner.

At the bottom of the page, below the story, was a big red circled "F"! We asked her why, and she told us that the teacher said she had better learn to do it right or she would fail. Questioning further, we found that her teacher had said that students were to fill the page with writing. Krissy had used only three-quarters of the page, so she hadn't followed directions and so deserved an F.

When she had finished telling us this story, Kristen Ann put the sheet of paper down on the kitchen table and, with a very discouraged look, said in an intimidated voice, "I'll never be a good writer anyway," and left the room. My recollection of that moment remains vivid after 20 years.

In fact, she had *succeeded* at hitting the achievement target. She produced some pretty good writing. But her confidence in herself as a writer was deeply shaken because her teacher failed to disentangle her expectation that students comply with directions with her expectation that they demonstrate the ability to write well. As a result, both the assessment and the feedback had a destructive impact on this student. Without question, it's quite easy to see if the page is full. But is that the point? It's somewhat more challenging to assess accurately and to formulate and deliver understandable and timely feedback that permits a student to write better the next time and to remain confident about her ability to continue to grow as a writer.

Please *never* underestimate the power of your evaluations of student performance and the impact of your feedback on your students. For we adults, it's a grade that goes in a gradebook or a score we average with other scores. But for students, it's always far more personal than that. It's how they decide how they fit into the world of people who do this thing called "writing," or "reading" or "math." Indeed, they interpret your feedback to decide whether they fit in at all. And depending on how they "come down" on this, we may or may not be able to influence their learning lives. Never lose sight of this very personal dimension of your classroom assessment processes.

Time for Reflection

Analyze and compare the assessments experienced by Emily and Kristen. Considering the keys to success discussed here, what were the essential differences? Why was one productive and the other not?

Other Potential Problems

Some unfortunate students may be mired in classrooms in which they are forced to try to guess the meaning of academic success. Their teachers may lack a vision of success or may focus on an incorrect one. Or they might choose to keep the secrets of success a mystery to retain power and control in the classroom. When their students guess at the valued target and guess wrong, they fail the assessment. Under these circumstances, they fail not from lack of motivation, but from lack of insight as to what they are supposed to achieve. This can be very discouraging. It destroys confidence. These students may well have succeeded had they been given the opportunity to strive for a clear objective.

Then there are those students who prepare well, master the required material, and fail anyway because the teacher prepares a poor-quality test, thus inaccurately measuring their achievement. Student achievement may also be mismeasured because a teacher places blind faith in the quality of the tests that accompanied the textbook, when in fact that confidence is misplaced. In addition, some students fail not because of low achievement, but because their teacher's subjective performance assessment judgments are riddled with the effects of unconscious bias.

When these and other such problems arise, an environment of assessment illiteracy dominates, assessments will be of poor quality, and students are placed directly in harm's way.

Anticipating and Avoiding Assessment Problems

Your job is to avoid problems like these by applying the basic principles of sound assessment. As you will see, assessments can serve many masters, take many different forms, reflect many different kinds of achievement, and fall prey to any of a variety of different problems that may lead to inaccurate results. When our journey together through the chapters of this book is complete you will have developed your own framework for understanding all of the options and for selecting from among them for each classroom assessment context. You will know what can go wrong and how to prevent assessment problems. In short, you will be prepared to assemble the parts of the classroom assessment puzzle as artfully as Ms. Weathersby does.

Understanding Assessment Validity

One way to think about the quality of an assessment is in terms of the fidelity of the results it produces. Just as we want our recorded music to provide an accurate representation of the real thing, so too do we want assessments to provide a high-fidelity reproduction of the desired learning. In the assessment realm, this is referred to as the *validity* of the test. All assessments results (scores, for example) provide outward indications of inner mental states. We must always seek assessment results that accurately represent student learning.

Another way to think about the validity of an assessment is in terms of the usefulness of its results. A valid, sound assessment serves the purpose for which it is developed and administered. For instance, a diagnostic test helps the user see and understand student needs. A college admission test leads to appropriate selection decisions among candidates. We always seek to develop assessments that fit the context at hand—that are valid for a specific purpose or set of purposes.

As we go, I will fill in details about this important concept of validity.

Understanding Assessment Reliability

Still another way to think about assessment quality is in terms of its ability to give us consistent results. Assume that, in the truth of the world, a student possesses a specific and stable level of proficiency in reading comprehension. So we know that achievement is not changing. A dependable or *reliable* assessment will reflect that stable level of achievement no matter how many times we measure it.

Additionally, as that proficiency improves, a reliable assessment will produce changing scores that track right along with that improvement. We will be able to count on this assessment to deliver dependable information about that student's evolving proficiency.

As we progress, you will come to see that factors other than students' actual level of reading comprehension proficiency can influence test scores—bad test items, test anxiety, distractions during testing, and the like. When this happens the score is muddled by these extraneous factors and is said to have become *unreliable*. This is a bad thing and we will discuss how to anticipate and avoid this kind of problem.

The Changing Role of Assessment

The faculty members of the high schools from which you and I graduated were evaluated in terms of their ability to sort us into a dependable rank order by graduation. Our schools were assigned the social mission of channeling graduates into the various segments of our social and economic system. Our entire classroom assessment and grading legacy was built around this mission.

In recent decades, however, society has come to realize the inadequacy of this mission for schools in today's increasingly complex world. The problem is that those who finish low in the rank order (along with those who give up in hopelessness and drop out before they are ever ranked!), fail to master the fundamental reading, writing, math problem-solving, and other proficiencies needed to survive in and contribute to an increasingly demanding and technical society. This is why, in the middle of the last century, scholars and policy makers began to conceive of a different social mission for schools. To meet society's needs, schools needed to ensure that all students reach a certain minimum level of academic competence in reading, writing, and math problem solving, for example.

This new vision of effective schools has continued to evolve over the decades, leading to today's dominant view that truly effective schools help all students meet specified academic achievement standards.

Virtually every state has developed its own standards defining the important academic learning that students are expected to master. Once articulated by experts in each academic field, these standards are translated into state assessments, and schools are accountable for student mastery of them. Thus, state policy makers have decreed that schools will be judged effective not merely in terms of their ability to rank students, but also on their ability to produce competent students. We have even witnessed federal educational policy rally around this definition of effective schools.

This shift in mission profoundly affects the role of assessment. Assessments must do far more for us than merely help us grade and rank students. They must help us accurately diagnose student needs, track and enhance student growth toward standards, motivate students to strive for academic excellence, and verify student mastery of required standards. This book will help you understand the role of classroom assessment in accomplishing these things.

Your Assignment in Standards-Driven Schools

In a standards-driven school, as a classroom teacher, your assignment is to maximize the number of students who meet standards; that is, who experience success—who become competent readers, writers, math problem solvers, or whatever version of academic success you choose for them. Therefore, in standards-driven schools, assessments must be far more than appendages connected to the end of teaching; they must do far more than merely gauge student success for grading or ranking purposes. Rather, you must use assessment to build student confidence and, indeed, to promote or cause greater student achievement. To do this, you must

- Understand the achievement targets you want your students to hit—what it means to succeed academically in your classroom.
- Transform your vision of academic success into assessment exercises and scoring procedures that provide accurate information about student achievement.
- Use both assessment and its results to help students both to believe in themselves as learners and to strive for academic success.

To be more specific, as a teacher, your job is to gather solid information about student achievement and feed it into your instructional decision making. You can do this only when you are able to do the following:

- *Anticipate the information needs* of those instructional decision makers who will use the assessment results. Your assessments must be designed specifically to meet those needs.
- *Identify the achievement targets* (goals, objectives, expectations, standards) that you expect your students to hit. These must be the focus of your assessment exercises and scoring procedures.
- *Select proper assessment methods* that accurately reflect your achievement expectations.
- *Assemble high-quality assessment exercises into an array (a sample)* that spans the full range of your expectations and thus leads you to confident conclusions about student achievement.
- *Anticipate and eliminate all sources of bias* that creep into your assessments.
- *Communicate assessment results* in a timely and understandable manner into the hands of their intended user(s).

These keys to success are presented graphically in Figure 1.2.

Important Benefits to You

There are three specific reasons why you must understand the principles of sound assessment. First, you will spend a quarter to a third of your available professional time involved in assessment-related activities. This includes designing and building them, selecting them from other sources, administering them, scoring them, and

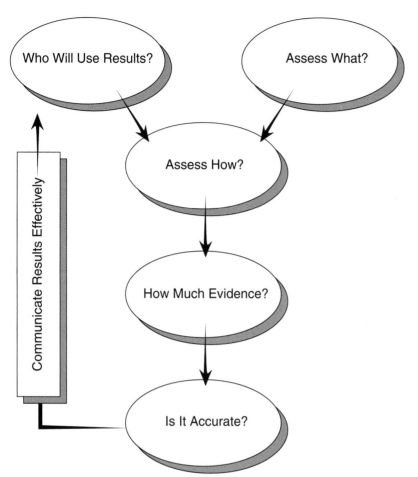

Figure 1.2
Keys to effective classroom assessment

managing and reporting results. It is hard work and can be tedious. The procedures described herein can *make that job MUCH easier.* The time savings detailed in the chapters that follow are legion. In fact, as noted previously, every time one appears, I will highlight it with a small clock icon (shown in the margin). Second, the routine application of the principles of sound assessment offered herein has been shown to *yield remarkable gains in student achievement* versus environments where they are missing (Black & Wiliam, 1998; Meisels, Atkins-Burnett, Xue, & Bickel, 2003). These gains accrue for all students, but especially for low achievers. In other words, the consistent application of these ideas can help you reduce achievement gaps between different subgroups of the student population.

Third, understanding the elements of sound classroom assessment will allow you to build a strong defense for their use in your classroom. The ideas presented herein run counter to decades of assessment traditions in schools. As a result, you will work with colleagues who will challenge you on them and try to draw you back into "conventional" practice. Chances are, you will encounter teachers who are more experienced than you whose assessment and grading fall short of the standards of sound practice you will learn here. If you master the principles of sound practice, you will be able to carry them out and help others understand why they should do the same.

A Fundamental Assessment Belief

Our assessment traditions are built on the belief that assessments serve us best when they inform the instructional decisions made by the adults who manage schools and classrooms (teachers, parents, principals, superintendents, etc). However, this book manifests a fundamentally different belief. The instructional decisions that contribute the most to student success are, in fact, not made by the adults. Rather, the decisions that contribute the most to determining student success or failure in learning are made by students themselves. We will consider those decisions in great depth later in the chapter. For now, suffice it to say that students decide whether the learning is worth the risk and effort required to acquire it. They decide if they believe they are smart enough to learn it. And they decide these things based on their own interpretation of their personal record of academic success.

Therefore, whatever else we do, we must help them believe that success in learning is possible for them and worthy of the effort. If we cannot do that, we cannot help them learn. This book is about how to use student involvement in classroom assessment in the service of that mission.

To make their decisions well, students need continuous access to understandable descriptive information about their own improvement as readers, writers, math problem solvers, and the like. When they are partners in that kind of assessment process, teachers tell me, it's almost shocking how fast they can grow. The purpose of this book is to enable you to join the ranks of these very strong teachers.

This is not to say that adult decision makers are unimportant. Indeed, they are crucial to student success. But the adults are not in charge of the learning. *Learners* are. If students don't want to learn or don't feel able to learn, there will be no learning. So as teachers, our fundamental driving questions must be, How can we help our students want to learn? How can we help them believe that they are capable learners?

This book is about all of the different ways you can use day-to-day classroom assessment, record keeping, and communication to answer these questions. It's about learners being in control of their own success. It's about avoiding circumstances in which assessments have the effect of destroying student confidence. This book is about using assessment in support of learning—not merely as a gauge of learning. It's about assessment without victims.

Assessment and Student Motivation

As I noted in the Introduction to Part 1, most of us grew up in classrooms in which our teachers believed that the way you maximize learning is by maximizing anxiety.

Assessment was always the great intimidator. Many of our teachers believed that if a little intimidation doesn't work, turn up the heat—try a lot of intimidation. This is why most adults today feel that being evaluated is a distinctly dangerous enterprise. It always left us feeling vulnerable.

Please understand that our teachers were *wrong* about this. Here is the fundamental problem with this way of thinking: Research on the biological functioning of the human brain during cognition tells us that, when the brain is in an anxious state of tension, it draws itself inward—it closes down—for protection. In this state, it becomes very difficult to see, understand, and learn new things. This research tells us that, if we wish to maximize learning, we must do just the opposite of what our teachers did—we must *drive out the fear* of failure. This runs exactly counter to our traditions. But the research results are ironclad. In this book, I will show you how to use classroom assessment in ways that drive out the fear of failure and maximize student success. We do this by involving students deeply in assessment, record keeping, and communication.

Consider the student as consumer of assessment results: Right from the time students arrive at school, they look to their teachers for evidence of their success. If that early evidence suggests that they are succeeding, what begins to grow in them is a sense of hopefulness and an expectation of more success in the future. This in turn fuels enthusiasm and the motivation to try hard, which fuels even more success. The basis of this upward spiral is the evidence of their own achievement, which students receive from their teachers based on ongoing classroom assessments. Thus, classroom assessment information is the essential fuel that powers the learning system for students.

However, when the evidence suggests to students that they are not succeeding, what can then begin to grow in them is a sense of hopelessness and an expectation of more failure in the future. This can rob them of the confidence they need to take the risk of trying to learn. So they stop trying and stop learning, which in turn leads to more failure. In this downward spiral, here again we see consequences of classroom assessment evidence, but this time it is evidence of failure that fuels frustration and discouragement.

Please understand, I do not mean to imply that all assessment results should be positive simply to keep students involved and motivated. On the contrary, if students are not meeting your standards, your assessments must accurately reflect that fact. But if those results reflect a lack of academic success, you must act to change your instructional approach to prevent the pattern of failure from becoming chronic. You must find a different formula that brings to students hope of future success. Ongoing student-involved classroom assessment is your best tool for revealing increments of improvement to your students and for keeping them believing that success is within reach if they keep trying.

As you will learn in the next section, there are many important assessment users at all levels of the educational system. However, students, who use the results to set expectations of themselves, are the most important. Students decide how high to aim based on their sense of the probability that they will succeed. They estimate the probability of future success based on their record of past success as reflected in their classroom assessment experience. *No single decision or combination of decisions made by any other party exerts such influence on student success.* For this reason, to be considered valid for this context, your classroom assessments must help both you and your students clearly understand the results of each individual assessment and track increments in their achievement over time.

A Note on Students with Learning Disabilities

When students are academically challenged, we and they face the constant danger that they will sense the slowness of their learning and develop a sense of futility in that regard. As we proceed, we will discuss specific ways to deal with this. But for now, suffice it to say that you must be aware of this danger and its origins. The achievement targets we set for them will be framed in their Individual Educational Plans (IEPs). We must be sure those are based on where they *really* are currently in the continuous-progress curriculum—that is, their level of achievement—not some "grade-level expectation." It is neither ethical nor pedagogically appropriate to hold students accountable for achievement targets they have no hope of hitting. This dooms them to inevitable failure and that is unacceptable. The effect of doing so will be the loss of student confidence in themselves as learners and the development of that sense of futility that leads to hopelessness.

On the other hand, if we manage their learning in a continuous-progress manner and at a rate appropriate for them, keeping them in touch with their own improvement through their involvement in assessment, we can keep them believing that success (as defined uniquely for them) is within reach.

Guides to Valid and Reliable Assessment

My job is to teach myself out of a job. In other words, my job is to help you reach a place where you no longer need me or your professor to tell you whether your assessments are valid and reliable. My mission is to help you know when you have done well because you know and understand *how to apply to your own work the criteria that define sound assessment.*

Your job is exactly the same: to take your students to a place where they no longer need you to tell them whether they have succeeded, but rather where they know this in their own minds because they understand the criteria that define high achievement—just as Ms. W. helped Emily and her classmates learn.

As we proceed toward this end, you will see (indeed, already have seen) repeated reference to a set of guiding principles. They are represented graphically in Figure 1.3. I highlight them with you here at the outset as interrelated themes that map the path to valid and reliable assessment. The order in which they are presented is immaterial; each principle is profoundly important. Together, they represent the concrete foundation on which we will build the structure of your understanding of how to assess well in your classroom.

As you read about these principles, keep Ms. W. and Emily in mind and you will see why I started our journey together with their story.

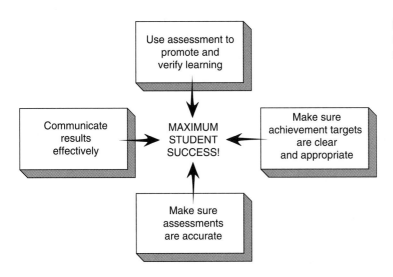

Figure 1.3
Guiding principles for effective classroom assessment

Guiding Principle 1: Classroom Assessments Can Both *Promote* and *Verify* Student Learning

To understand how to use assessment to support learning, first, we must see the big picture. A variety of different people use assessment results to inform a variety of instructional decisions—that is, to answer many different questions, as shown in Tables 1.1, 1.2, and 1.3. These tables illustrate how each assessment user's roles and responsibilities contribute to student success by depicting three levels at which assessment results can come into play.

Taken together, all three sets of assessment users make the decisions that determine whether schools work for any individual child, or for all children considered collectively. While I am of the opinion that decisions made at the classroom level contribute the most to student success, please understand that all parties listed make important decisions; their information needs deserve careful attention.

Column one of each table lists decision makers whose decisions are (or can be) informed by assessment results. Column two presents questions these decision makers ask whose answers are based at least in part on assessment results of some kind. These tables are not intended to be exhaustive but are rather samples from among the array of assessment users and uses. As you read on, bear in mind our *validity* concept: An assessment is valid only when it serves its intended purpose well.

Time for Reflection

Before continuing, please study Tables 1.1, 1.2, and 1.3 carefully. Based on the information provided in each, write down whatever insights or generalizations you can draw about assessment's role in promoting student success. When you have done this for all three tables, read on.

Classroom Users

The first level of use is in the classroom. Students, teachers, and parents gather and use the results of student assessments to inform a variety of decisions that influence both student motivation and their level of success. Some of these call for the formative use of assessment in support of learning: How can we help students improve? Others use assessment in a summative manner, checking achievement status for accountability purposes: Did the student learn enough?

After reflecting on the classroom-level questions listed in Table 1.1, can you imagine the dire consequences for student success if students, teachers, and parents

Table 1.1
Sample questions that we use assessment to answer at the classroom level

Assessment User	Sample Questions
Student	Am I succeeding?
	Am I improving over time?
	Do I know what it means to succeed here?
	What should I do next to succeed?
	What help do I need to succeed?
	Do I feel in control of my own success?
	Does my teacher think I'm capable of success?
	Do I think I'm capable of success?
	Is the learning worth the effort?
	How am I doing in relation to my classmates?
	Where do I want all of this to take me?
Teacher	Are my students improving?
	Is it because of me?
	What does this student need?
	Is this student capable of learning this?
	What do these students need?
	What are their strengths that we can build on?
	How should I group my students?
	Am I going too fast, too slow, too far, not far enough?
	Am I improving as a teacher?
	How can I improve?
	Did that teaching strategy work?
	What do I say at parent/teacher conferences?
	What grade do I put on the report card?
Parent	Is my child learning new things—growing?
	Is my child succeeding?
	Is my child keeping up?
	Are we doing enough at home to support the teacher?
	What does my child need to succeed?
	Does the teacher know what my child needs?
	Is this teacher doing a good job?
	Is this a good school? District?

were to try to answer them based on misinformation about student achievement due to inaccurate classroom assessment? What if students were not hitting the target, but the assessments said they were succeeding? What if they were succeeding, but the assessments said they were not?

Clearly, inaccurate assessments would lead to misdiagnosis of student needs on the part of the teacher, failure to understand which instructional strategies work and which do not, and communication of misinformation to parents, among other problems.

The point is that accurate information derived from quality classroom assessments is essential for instruction to work effectively and for students to learn. In addition, the following critically important generalizations are warranted on the basis of analyzing the questions in Table 1.1:

- Although we most often think of students as the examinees and not as examiners, they clearly are assessors of their own academic progress, and they use those results in compelling ways.
- Given the manner in which assessment results fit into day-to-day classroom decision making, assessment must be a regularly occurring process in all cases. These are continually recurring decisions. This is precisely why classroom assessment events are so much more frequent in a student's life than are annual, formal standardized tests.
- At this level, assessment virtually always focuses on individual students' mastery of specified material. You, the teacher, must set standards of acceptable achievement if your assessments are to show whether students have succeeded.

Instructional Support Users

The second level is that of instructional support. Decision makers at this level provide teachers with whatever backup they may need in the form of curricular, professional development, and/or resource support. Backup may come from the department, building, or district level, or beyond. In this case, formative applications examine assessment results to see what teachers may need to be more effective. Summative uses center on such questions as, Did the new reading program we purchased work effectively?

We can see the following patterns emerge from the information presented in Table 1.2:

- In every case, the decisions to be made focus on the instructional program or the teacher.
- Typically, the focus is not on the individual student but is rather on group performance.
- Decisions are made infrequently and thus assessment need only be periodic (typically once a year), not continuous.
- At this level, heavy reliance is placed on the use of assessment results in which assessment instruments or procedures must be held constant across classrooms. In other words, some standardization is required if sound information and good decisions are to result.

For all these reasons, this is the domain of the standardized test.

Table 1.2
Sample questions that we use assessment to answer at the instructional support level

Assessment User	Sample Questions
Principal	How do we define success in terms of student learning? Is this teacher producing results in the form of student learning? How can I help this teacher improve? Is instruction in our building producing results? Is instruction at each grade level producing results? Are our students qualifying for college? Are our students prepared for the workplace? Do we need professional development as a faculty to improve? How shall we allocate building resources to achieve success?
Mentor Teacher	Is this new teacher producing results? What does this new teacher need to improve?
Curriculum Director	How do we define success in terms of student achievement? Is our program of instruction working? What adjustments do we need to make in our curriculum?
Special Services	Who needs (qualifies for) special educational services? Is our program of services helping students? What assistance does this student need to succeed?

Policy-Level Users

The final level of assessment user is policy makers, including the superintendent, the school board, public officials (appointed and elected), and citizens of the community. They establish achievement standards to guide instruction in classrooms and then demand evidence of achievement to verify that students are meeting the standards. Based on the evidence they receive, they allocate district resources to overcome weaknesses, set personnel policies to regulate who gets to teach, and set procedural policies that guide teaching practices. Once again, we find both formative and summative applications.

We can make the following generalizations on the basis of the information in Table 1.3:

- The focus is on broad domains of achievement, not on specific objectives of instruction.
- As with the instructional support level, results summarized across students (group results) fill the need.
- As with the instructional support level, periodic assessment will suffice.
- At this level too, assessment procedures must be standardized across contexts and over time. The decisions to be made require it.

Again, this is the domain of the standardized test.

Table 1.3
Sample questions that we use assessment to answer at the policy-making level

Assessment User	Sample Questions
Superintendent	Are our programs of instruction producing results in terms of student learning? Is each building principal producing results? Which schools deserve or need more or fewer resources?
School Board	Are our students learning and succeeding? Is the superintendent producing results?
State Department of Education	Are programs across the state producing results? Are individual school districts producing results?
Citizen/Legislature	Are our students achieving in ways that prepare them to become productive citizens?

Generalizations About Users and Uses

Having reflected on these three tables, do any general conclusions come to your mind regarding the role of assessment in determining and enhancing the effectiveness of schools? Try the following and see if you agree:

- Obviously, assessment is intricately woven into the effectiveness of school functioning. Often the depth and complexity of the contributions of the various assessment levels are surprising to many educators. As teachers and instructional leaders, we must all face this complexity and come to terms with it.
- Students count on many people at all levels and in all decision-making contexts to use sound assessment results in productive ways. Every question listed in the tables is critical to student well-being. This is why we must continually strive for the most valid assessments—those that fit the purpose most closely. It is a moral, ethical, and professional imperative of the highest order.
- Considering the tables together, it is clear that both information gathered continuously on individual student mastery of specified material and information gathered periodically for the purpose of comparing students serve important roles. Different users need different information at different times in different forms to do their jobs.

Given this summary of all of the decision-oriented users and uses of assessment, it becomes clear that we need to maintain a balanced perspective about assessment's valuable role at all levels. High-quality classroom assessment serving its important users must be balanced with high-quality standardized assessment serving its important users.

Thought of in another way, purpose becomes a standard of assessment quality. Unless we begin development of any assessment with a clear sense of both the intended user and use, and thus the *user's information needs,* we cannot build an assessment that will accomplish its mission. A clear sense of purpose is essential.

Similarly, we can evaluate the quality of any assessment in retrospect in part by asking if the developer began with a clear sense of the user's information needs.

From now on, we will regard this as our first criterion by which to judge the quality of an assessment. High-quality assessments always begin with a clear purpose and the assurance that the assessment will be developed to serve it. Poor-quality assessments arise from contexts where (1) the purpose is missing, (2) there are so many purposes that the assessment could never serve them all, or (3) the evidence gathered cannot serve the intended user. This criterion is the first entry in a comprehensive set of rubrics for judging classroom assessment quality that appears in the Appendix. We will continue to build these criteria as we proceed and, as we go, you will practice applying them.

Therefore, the Principles of Assessment FOR Learning

This book is about how to use classroom assessment in the service of student success. We speak here, not merely of dependable assessment OF learning, but also of dependable assessment FOR learning. We seek to use assessment and its results, not merely to keep track of learning, but to help students learn more. The tools and strategies offered herein will permit you to help your students go on internal control and take responsibility for their own learning.

Both assessment of and for learning are important. In the case of the former, we use assessment to verify that students have met standards in an accountability sense. For instance, statewide standardized tests ask students to demonstrate that they have met required achievement standards. Or in the classroom, teachers administer final examinations to determine a student's report card grade. These are periodic events that happen after learning is supposed to have occurred in order to let others know if students have learned.

But assessment for learning is different. In this case, we rely on the process not merely to check for learning, but to increase the learning. These are the assessments that we use early in learning to diagnose student needs. These have no place in the gradebook. They are the assessments that we conduct while learning is happening to help students see and feel in control of their own ongoing growth. In short, these are continuous assessments that we use to inform students about themselves during learning. In between the periodic assessments of learning, we rely on a steady flow of assessments for learning. This is what Ms. W. did for Emily and her classmates.

In this sense, teachers who help students understand the learning targets, engage in self-assessment, watch themselves grow, talk about that growth, or anticipate next steps in learning are applying the principles of assessment for learning.

Following this line of reasoning, we at the Assessment Training Institute have developed a checklist of attributes of instruction that manifests the principles of assessment for learning (Figure 1.4). When teachers can say that these things are true about their instruction as a matter of routine, they are using assessment for learning—assessment in support of student success.

In the chapters that follow, I will show you the specifics of how to make these principles operational in your classroom through the use of student-involved classroom assessment, record keeping, and communication.

1. I understand and can articulate *in advance of teaching* the achievement targets that I want my students to hit.

2. I inform my students continuously about those targets *in terms that they can understand;* that is, in student-friendly language with illustrations.

3. I transform those targets into classroom assessments that I am certain *will yield accurate evidence* of student achievement.

4. I understand the relationship between assessment and student motivation and, in my classroom, we use assessment to *build (and not to destroy) student confidence.*

5. I consistently *act on classroom assessment results,* as needed, to revise instructional plans; that is, we go to where my students need to go, given their current achievement.

6. The feedback that my students receive is *frequent and descriptive* (versus infrequent or merely judgmental), providing a basis for improvement.

7. My students are actively involved in the *assessment of their own achievement.*

8. My students *actively communicate with others* about their achievement status and improvement over time.

9. My students *can describe the achievement targets* they are trying to hit, even though they can't hit them yet.

Figure 1.4

The Principles of Assessment *FOR* Learning

Source: Adapted From *Assessment* FOR *Learning: An Action Guide for School Leaders* (p. 35), by S. Chappuis, R. J. Stiggins, J. Arter, and J. Chappuis, 2004, Portland, OR: Assessment Training Institute. Adapted by permission.

Guiding Principle 2: Clear and Appropriate Achievement Targets Are Essential

The quality of any assessment depends on how clearly and appropriately you define the achievement target you are assessing. In our opening vignette, a breakthrough in student writing achievement occurred in part because the English department faculty returned from that summer institute with a shared vision of writing proficiency. They built their program, and thus the competence of their students, around that vision.

You cannot validly (accurately) assess academic achievement targets that you have not precisely and completely defined. There are many different kinds of valued achievement expectations within our educational system, from mastering content knowledge to complex problem solving, from performing a flute recital to speaking Spanish to writing a strong term paper. All are important. But to assess them well, you must ask yourself, Do I know what it means to do it well? Precisely what does it mean to succeed academically? You are ready to assess only when you can answer these questions with clarity and confidence.

If your job is to teach students to become better writers, you had better start with a highly refined vision of what good writing looks like and a sense of how to help your students meet that standard. If your mission is to promote math problem-solving proficiency, you had better be a confident, competent master of that performance domain yourself. Without a sense of final destination reflected in your standards, and signposts along the way against which to check students' progress, you will have difficulty being an effective teacher.

Guiding Principle 3: Accurate Classroom Assessment Is Essential

To be of high quality (that is, to produce accurate results), assessments need to satisfy five specific quality standards. They must

1. Serve a specific purpose—that is, meet specified user information needs.
2. Arise from clear and appropriate achievement targets.
3. Rely on a proper assessment method.
4. Sample student achievement appropriately.
5. Eliminate distortion of results due to bias.

Assessments that meet these standards are said to be *valid* and *reliable.* All assessments must meet these standards. No exceptions can be tolerated, because to violate any of them is to risk inaccuracy, placing student academic well-being in jeopardy. (Return to Figure 1.2 to see these five standards represented graphically.) This is the first of many discussions and illustrations of these quality standards that permeate this book. On this first pass, I intend only to give you a general sense of the meaning of *quality.*

Guiding Principle 4: Sound Assessments Require Effective Communication

Mention assessment and the first thoughts that come to mind are of scores, numbers, and grades attached to very briefly labeled forms of achievement such as *reading, writing, science, math,* and the like. The underlying meaning of these one-word labels is rarely explained. In contrast, in our opening vignette the English faculty started with a clear vision of the meaning of academic success in writing in their classrooms and communicated that meaning effectively to students, parents, and school board members. They accomplished this by thoughtfully using performance rating schemes combined with examples of student performance, both of which reflected their vision. Sound assessment requires clear thinking and effective communication, not merely the quantification of ill-defined achievement targets.

While many assessments do translate levels of achievement into scores, we have come to understand two important realities more and more clearly. First, numbers are not the only way to communicate about achievement. We can use words, pictures, illustrations, examples, and many other means to convey this information. Second, the symbols we use as the basis of our communication about student achievement are only as meaningful and useful as the definitions of achievement that underpin them and the quality of the assessments used to produce them.

Educators who are aware of sound practices and who are critical consumers of assessment information are constantly asking, "Precisely what is being assessed here, and do I know what the results mean?" They do not rest until they have good answers to these questions, and they certainly don't use the results to affect students until they have good aswers. They demand clear thinking about appropriate standards and effective communication, both in their own assessments and those of others.

The Power of Student Involvement

The guiding belief or value underpinning this book is that the greatest potential value of classroom assessment is realized when we open the process up and welcome students in as full partners. By now you understand that I do not simply mean having students trade test papers or homework assignments so they can grade each other's work. That's strictly clerical stuff. This concept of full partnership, as Emily and her classmates learned, goes far deeper.

Scriven (personal communication, 1995) provides a sense of the variable extent of student involvement in assessment. Starting with very superficial involvement, each level brings students further into the actual assessment equation. Students can do the following:

- Take the test and receive the grade.
- Be invited to offer the teacher comments on how to improve the test.
- Suggest possible assessment exercises.
- Actually develop assessment exercises.
- Assist the teacher in devising scoring criteria.
- Create the scoring criteria on their own.
- Apply scoring criteria to the evaluation of their own performance.
- Come to understand how assessment and evaluation affect their own academic success.
- Come to see how their own self-assessment relates to the teacher's assessment and to their own academic success.

Students who participate in the thoughtful analysis of quality work to identify its critical elements or to internalize valued achievement targets become better performers. When students learn to apply these standards so thoroughly that they can confidently and competently evaluate their own and each other's work, they are well on the road to becoming better performers in their own right. Consider Emily's case in our opening vignette. Ms. W. helped her to internalize key elements of good writing so she could understand the shortcomings of her own writing, take responsibility for improving them, and watch herself improve. Her confidence and competence as a partner in her classroom assessment came through loud and clear, both in the parent-teacher conference she led at midyear and in her commentary to the school board at the end of the year. I offer many specific suggestions for melding assessment and instruction in this way throughout this text.

Summary: The Importance of Sound Assessment

The guiding principles discussed in this chapter (and illustrated with Emily's experience) form the foundation of the assessment wisdom all educators must master in order to manage classroom assessment environments effectively.

Teachers who are prepared to meet the challenges of classroom assessment understand that they need to do their assessment homework and be ready to think clearly and to communicate effectively at assessment time. They understand why it is critical to be able to share their expectations with students and their families and why it is essential that they conduct high-quality assessments that accurately reflect achievement expectations.

Well-prepared teachers realize that they themselves lie at the heart of the assessment process in schools and they take that responsibility very seriously. Competent teachers understand the complexities of aligning a range of valued achievement targets with appropriate assessment methods so as to produce information on student achievement that both they and their

students can count on to be accurate. They understand the meaning of *valid assessment* and they know how to use all of the assessment tools at their disposal to produce valid information to serve intended purposes.

Effective classroom assessors/teachers understand the interpersonal dynamics of classroom assessment and know how to set students up for success, in part through using the appropriate assessment as a teaching tool. They know how to make students full partners in defining the valued targets of instruction and in transforming those definitions into quality assessments.

As teachers involve students in assessment, thus demystifying the meaning of success in the classroom, they acknowledge that students use assessment results to make the decisions that ultimately will determine if school does or does not work for them. Our collective classroom assessment responsibility is to be sure students have access to and understand the information they need to see themselves growing over time.

Final Chapter Reflection

Each chapter in this text will conclude with a brief and consistent set of questions for you to reflect on to solidify your understanding and ease your transition to subsequent chapters. Please take time to record your answers in your journal. They will help you make key connections as we continue our journey through the realm of classroom assessment.

1. *What are the three most important new insights to come to you as a result of your study of this chapter?*
2. *What questions come to mind now about classroom assessment that you hope to have answered in subsequent chapters?*

Practice with Chapter 1 Ideas

The following activities provide opportunities for your personal reflection on ideas presented in Chapter 1 and may serve as an excellent basis for discussion of those ideas among classmates:

1. Read the following classroom assessment scenarios. Is each likely to increase or decrease student confidence and motivation to learn? Why?

   Scenario

   - Alan is having his students score each other's quizzes and then call out the scores so he can enter them in his gradebook.
   - Students in Eileen's class are discussing some samples of anonymous science lab notes to decide which are great examples, which have some good points, and which don't tell the story of the lab at all well. They're gradually developing criteria for their own lab "learning logs."
   - Catherine has just received back a grade on a report she wrote for social studies. She got a D+. There were no other comments.
   - Students in Henry's basic writing class are there because they have failed to meet the state's writing competency requirements. Henry tells students that the year will be a time of learning to write. Competence at the end will be all that matters.
   - Jeremy's teacher tells him that his test scores have been so dismal so far that no matter what he does from then on he will fail the class.
   - Pat is reading her latest story aloud for the class to critique. Like each of her classmates, she's been asked to take notes during this "peer assessment" so that she can revise her work later.

2. Think of an assessment experience from your personal educational past that was a GOOD experience for you. What made it a productive experience? What emotional and learning impact did if have for you? Now think of one that was a BAD experience for you. What made it a counterproductive experience? What was its emotional and learning impact? What were the essential procedural differences between the two experiences? How do those differences related to the standards of sound classroom assessment practice described in this chapter?

Chapter 2

Defining Achievement Standards for Assessment

CHAPTER FOCUS

This chapter answers the following guiding question:

> What kinds of achievement must teachers be able to assess in the classroom?

From your study of this chapter, you will understand the following:

1. Clear and appropriate achievement standards and targets are central to sound assessment and student success.
2. Sound achievement standards and targets have clear, identifiable attributes.
3. Teachers must be prepared to assess in their classrooms four different, but interrelated, kinds of achievement targets, plus dispositions.

Validity from a Different Perspective

Chapter 1 was about one key to valid classroom assessment: sound assessments arise from a clear sense of purpose. We must know why we are conducting the assessment—exactly who will use the assessment and how. Different users need different information in different forms at different times to do their jobs. Every assessment must be valid for its intended purpose; that is, it must serve its intended user well. Sometimes the users are students themselves trying to decide if the learning is worth the risk of trying for it and the effort required to attain it. Sometimes the users are teachers trying to diagnose student needs. Other times users are principals, parents, school board members, and so on. Each brings different information needs to the assessment context.

In this chapter, we move on to the next key to excellence in classroom assessment: clear and appropriate achievement targets (Figure 2.1). What do we expect our students to achieve? Teachers who cannot define the student characteristic(s) that they wish to assess will have difficulty developing assessment exercises and scoring procedures that reflect their expectations. Further, they will find it impossible both to share a clear vision of success with their students and to select instructional strategies that promise and deliver student success.

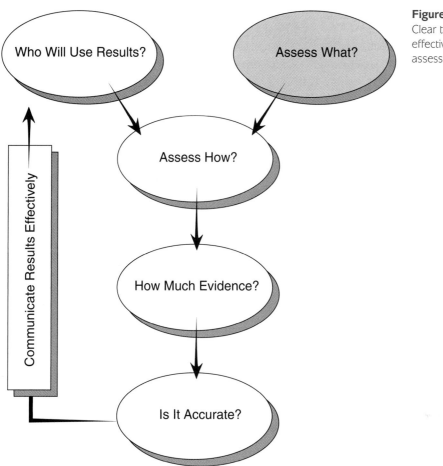

Figure 2.1
Clear targets: A key to effective classroom assessment

Only after clarifying the achievement target can the assessor pick an appropriate assessment method and develop and implement it properly so as to produce a high-fidelity representation of student achievement. Assessments that appropriately cover the material to be learned are said to meet standards of *content validity*.

Defining *Achievement Targets*

Achievement targets define academic success—what we want students to know and be able to do. Visualize a target with its concentric circles and a bull's-eye in the middle. The center circle defines the highest level of performance students can achieve; a very high-quality piece of writing, the most fluent oral reading, the highest possible score on a math problem-solving test. Each consecutive outside ring on the target defines a level of performance further from the highest level.

As students improve, they need to understand that they are progressing toward the bull's-eye.

Our mission as teachers in standards-driven schools is to help the largest possible percentage of our students to get there. To reach that goal, you must take charge of defining where "there" is. What are the attributes of a good piece of writing, such as Emily's end-of-year sample from Chapter 1? How does this level of performance differ from performance of lesser quality—that is, from the outer rings of the target? Ms. Weathersby knew, and gave Emily the insights she needed to understand as well.

I have adopted the target metaphor to permit me to point out now and repeatedly throughout this book that students can hit any target that they see and that holds still for them. But if they are guessing at what success looks like, in effect trying to learn while blindfolded, success will be a random event for them.

Schools use a variety of labels for their achievement expectations. Some call them *goals* and *objectives*. Others refer to *scope* and *sequence*. Still others label them *proficiencies* or *competencies*. More recently, we refer to *standards* and *benchmarks*. These terms all refer to the same basic thing: what we want students to know and be able to do.

I suggest that we think of them in this way: States and local school districts have developed academic achievement *standards*. These are the focus of state and district standardized tests. However, as teachers, we know that it is never the case that students attain mastery of standards in an instant. Rather, they progress through ascending levels of proficiency over time as they journey up to a place where they are ready to demonstrate that they have met the state standard. This is illustrated in Figure 2.2.

Figure 2.2

Relationship of standards to enabling classroom targets

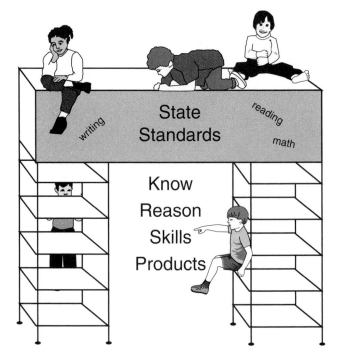

The scaffolding on which they climb during the process of becoming competent can be thought of as *enabling classroom-level achievement targets*. They must be the focus of classroom instruction and day-to-day classroom assessment if students ultimately are to arrive at success. Figure 2.3 provides two examples of state standards deconstructed into their enabling classroom-level achievement targets.

Our standards and achievement targets form a solid foundation for classroom assessment when they meet the following criteria:

1. *Are Clearly Stated*—Our achievement expectations must be written in clear language, offered in public, and include student-friendly versions. When achievement targets are clearly stated, all who read and paraphrase them

---

Sample State Standard

History: Students will evaluate different interpretations of historical events.

The teacher must translate this into relevant classroom targets:

Knowledge and Understanding: Students must know and understand each historical event, and must understand each of the alternative interpretations to be evaluated. The teacher must determine if students are to know those things outright or if they can use reference materials to retrieve the required knowledge.

Reasoning: Evaluative reasoning requires judgment about the quality of each interpretation. Thus students must demonstrate both an understanding of the criteria by which one judges the quality of an interpretation and the ability to apply these criteria.

Performance Skills: None required

Products: None required

Sample State Standard

Writing: Students will use styles appropriate for their audience and purpose, including proper use of voice, word choice, and sentence fluency.

The teacher must translate this into relevant classroom targets:

Knowledge and Understanding: Writers must possess appropriate understanding of the concept of style as evidenced in voice, word choice, and sentence structure. In addition, students must possess knowledge of the topic they are to write about.

Reasoning: Writers must be able to figure out how to make sound voice, word choice, and sentence construction decisions while composing original text. The assessment must provide evidence of this ability.

Performance Skills: One of two kinds of performance will be required. Either respondents will write longhand or will compose text on a keyboard. Each requires its own kind of skill competence.

Products: The final evidence of competence will be written products that present evidence of the ability to write effectively to different audiences.

Figure 2.3
Converting state standards to classroom achievement targets

interpret them to mean essentially the same thing. Similarly, one criterion by which we should judge the appropriateness of our achievement expectations is our ability to provide samples of student work to illustrate different levels of proficiency.

2. *Center on Important Learnings*—Academic achievement expectations cannot merely be a matter of local opinion. Rather, they must be steeped in the best thinking of leading experts in the field. We don't get to vote on what our local faculty means by "good writer." Those traits have been clearly defined in our professional literature. Nor is it merely a matter of individual teacher opinion of what it means to do good science or solve math problems appropriately. As teachers, it is our personal and collective responsibility to remain in touch with our professional literature and know the most current thinking in the fields we teach.

3. *Are Articulated Within and Across Grades*—The achievement expectations held as important in any particular classroom cannot be merely a matter of the judgment of teachers at that grade level. Rather, they must fit into a continuously progressing curriculum that guides instruction across grade levels in that school and district. The overall curriculum should define ascending levels of competence that spiral through grade levels, mapping a journey to academic excellence. Each teacher's goals and objectives, therefore, must arise directly from what has come before and lead to what will follow.

   Besides, because of differences in academic capabilities, students will ascend that continuous-progress curriculum at vastly different rates. Some will zoom, others will crawl very slowly. But please realize that the path to academic success doesn't change as a function of how fast they travel it. Prerequisites will remain foundations for what follows. They must be mapped to guide progressive learning—for students with learning disabilities, for midrange students, and for those who are gifted and talented.

4. *Are Manageable in Number and Scope*—It is always the case that time and resources available to promote student learning are limited. Similarly, students vary in the rate at which they are capable of learning. And achievement expectations vary in the demands they place on teacher and learner. It is essential that these variables be considered in defining each teacher's assigned responsibilities. In the productive classroom assessment environment, the amount to be learned fits within those limited resources. Too much overwhelms, too little frustrates. Both excesses discourage both teacher and learner.

5. *Fall Within the Teacher's Repertoire*—As a classroom teacher, it will fall to you to deliver instruction and to conduct classroom assessments that focus on an assigned set of achievement expectations. To fulfill this responsibility, you must become a confident, competent master of the achievement targets that you expect your students to hit. This doesn't mean, for example, that elementary teachers need to be masters of high school physics. But it does

---

WRITING

1. The student writes clearly and effectively.

   To meet this standard, the student will:

   1.1 develop concept and design

   develop a topic or theme; organize written thoughts with a clear beginning, middle, and end; use transitional sentences and phrases to connect related ideas; write coherently and effectively

   1.2 use style appropriate to the audience and purpose

   use voice, word choice, and sentence fluency for intended style and audience

   1.3 apply writing conventions

   know and apply correct spelling, grammar, sentence structure, punctuation, and capitalization

SCIENCE

1. The student understands and uses scientific concepts and principles

   To meet this standard, the student will:

   1.1 use properties to identify, describe, and categorize substances, materials, and objects, and use characteristics to categorize living things

   1.2 recognize the components, structure, and organization of systems and the interconnections within and among them

   1.3 understand how interactions within and among systems cause changes in matter and energy

---

Figure 2.4
Sample state of Washington learning requirements
Source: Washington State Office of Superintendent of Public Instruction. Reprinted by permission.

mean these teachers must thoroughly and completely understand those physics concepts that their students must master at this particular point on their journey toward high school physics and beyond. If they do not, then important prerequisites will be missing. This dooms students to inevitable later failure.

An Example

Figure 2.4 presents sample learning requirements for the state of Washington. These represent just a subset of the essential learning objectives that Washington educators feel are important for their students, and are stated at a general statewide level of specificity. But they are clearly stated and specific. Washington educators have developed benchmarks that define continuous progress in attainment through grades 4, 7, and 10. A sample of these is seen in Figure 2.5. It remains a local responsibility to be sure that each teacher is able to deliver them.

The student understands and uses different skills and strategies to read.

To meet this standard, the student will: ①

Components	Benchmark 1–Grade 4	Benchmark 2–Grade 7 ③	Benchmark 3 – Grade 10
1.1 use word recognition and word meaning skills ②	apply phonetic principles to read, including sounding out, using initial letters, and using common letter patterns to make sense of whole words	➡ apply phonetic principles to read, including sounding out initial letters and using common letter patterns to make sense of whole words ④	➡ apply phonetic principles to read, including sounding out, using initial letters, and using common letter patterns to make sense of whole words ④
	use language structure to understand reading materials, including sentence structure, prefixes, suffixes, contractions, and simple abbreviations ⑦	➡ use language structure to understand reading materials, including sentence structure, prefixes, suffixes, contractions, and simple abbreviations ⑦	➡ use language structure to understand reading materials, including sentence structure, prefixes, suffixes, contractions, and simple abbreviations ⑦
1.5 use features of non-fiction text and computer software ②	locate and use text organizers (title headings, ⑥ table of contents, index, captions, alphabetizing, numbering, glossaries, etc.)	use organizational features of printed text (titles, headings, table of contents, indexes, glossaries, prefaces, appendices, captions, etc.)	use complex organizational features of printed text (titles, headings, table of contents, indexes, glossaries, prefaces, appendices, captions, citations, endnotes, etc.)
	recognize organizational features of electronic ⑤ information such as *pull-down menus, key word searches, icons,* etc.	use organization features of electronic information microfiche headings and numberings, CD-ROMS, Internet, etc.	use features of electronic information (electronic bulletin boards and databases, e-mail, etc.)

① Essential Academic Learning Requirement: A statement of what students should know and be able to do at the completion of their K–12 education. These statements are purposefully broad and are intended to serve as guideposts to school districts and give teachers flexibility in designing curriculum, teaching strategies, and planning instruction.

② Components: The key components to each Essential Academic Learning Requirement. The components are intended to describe broad categories of student behaviors or actions.

③ Benchmark: A point in time that may be used to measure student progress. Designed to help educators organize and make sense of a complex process of interaction between the student, the teacher, and the learning process. TBD means "to be determined" in science, social studies, arts, and health and fitness.

④ ➡ The text repeats for each benchmark. The arrow means that the skills or materials used become increasingly complex.

⑤ Content *for example* or *such as* (italics): Provides examples of skills contained in the benchmarks so that parents and students can more clearly see the particular skills students are being asked to acquire.

⑥ Parentheses ( ) indicate material or types of material that are included in the test specifications for reading, writing, and communication.

⑦ Each set of indicators demonstrates the developmental, cumulative nature of learning. For example, young readers should be able to progress independently through the steps of the reading process but will read simpler materials than maturing learners.

Figure 2.5
Sample Washington learning requirements broken down into grade-level benchmarks
Source: Washington State Office of Superintendent of Public Instruction. Reprinted by permission.

The Benefits of Clear and Appropriate Targets

The energy you invest in becoming clear about your classroom targets will pay big dividends.

Control Over Your Professional Success

One major benefit of defining specific achievement targets is that you set the limits of your own professional responsibility. These limits provide you with a standard by which to gauge your own success as a teacher. In short, defining targets helps you control your own professional destiny. The better you become at bringing your students to mastery of your delimited learning outcomes, the more successful you become as a teacher. The thoughtful use of classroom assessment can help with this.

As a community of professionals, I think each of us must take responsibility for our own success. If I succeed as a teacher and my students hit the target, I want acknowledgement of that success. If my students fail to hit the target I want to know it, and I want to know why they failed.

I can think of at least five possible reasons why my students might not have learned:

1. They lacked the prerequisites needed to achieve what I expected of them.
2. I didn't understand the target to begin with, and so could not convey it appropriately.
3. My instructional methods, strategies, and materials were inappropriate or inadequate.
4. My students lacked the confidence to risk trying—the motivation to strive for success.
5. Some force(s) outside of school and beyond my control (death in the family, for example) interfered with and inhibited learning.

If I am a professional educator whose students failed to hit the target, I must know which problem(s) inhibited learning if I expect to remedy the situation. Only when I know what went wrong can I make the kinds of decisions and take the kinds of action that will promote success for me and my students next time.

For example, if my students lacked prerequisites (reason 1), I need to work with my colleagues in the lower grades to be sure our respective curricula mesh. If I lack mastery of the valued targets myself or fail to implement solid instruction (reasons 2 and 3), I have to take responsibility for some pretty serious professional development. Similarly, if my students lack confidence or motivation (reason 4), I may need to investigate with them the reasons for their lack of motivation and plan a course of action that will teach me new and better motivational tactics. And finally, if reason 5 applies, then I need to reach out into the community beyond school to seek solutions.

As a teacher employed in a school setting committed to helping all students meet state or local academic standards, my success hinges on my understanding the reasons for any lack of success.

Note that I can choose the proper corrective action if and only if I take the risks of (1) gathering dependable information about student success or failure using my own high-quality classroom assessments, and (2) becoming enough of a classroom researcher to uncover the causes of student failure. If I as a teacher simply bury my head in the sand and blame my students for not caring or not trying, I may doom them to long-term failure for reasons beyond their control. Thus, when they fail, I must risk finding out why. If it is my fault or if I can contribute to fixing the problem in any way, I must act accordingly.

I believe that the risk is greatly reduced when I start out with clear and specific targets. If I can share the vision with my students, they can hit it! If I have no target, how can they hit it?

Benefits in Student Motivation

Teachers must know which achievement targets they expect their students to hit if they are to share that meaning of success with them. If teachers can help students understand these expectations, they set them up to take responsibility for their own success. The motivational implications of this for students can be immense.

Personalize this! Say you are a student facing a big test. A great deal of material has been covered. You have no idea what will be emphasized on the test. You study your heart out but, alas, you concentrate on the wrong material. Nice try, but you fail. How do you feel when this happens? How are you likely to behave the next time a test comes up under these same circumstances?

Now, say you are facing another test. A great deal of material has been covered. But your teacher, who has a complete understanding of the field, points out the parts that are critical for you to know. The rest will always be there in the text for you to look up when you need it. Further, the teacher provides lots of practice in applying the knowledge in solving real-world problems and emphasizes that this is a second key target of the course. You study in a very focused manner, concentrating on the important material and its application. Your result is a high score on the test. Good effort—you succeed. Again, how do you feel? How are you likely to behave the next time a test comes up under these circumstances?

Given clear requirements for success, students are better able to gauge the appropriateness of their own preparation and thus gain control over their own academic well-being. Students who feel in control of their own chances for success are more likely to care and to strive for excellence.

Greater Efficiency

In our research on the task demands of classroom assessment, my colleagues and I determined that typical teachers can spend as much as one-third of their available professional time involved in assessment-related activities. That's a lot of time! In fact, in many classrooms it is too much time. Greater efficiency in assessment is possible.

Clear achievement targets can contribute to that greater efficiency. Here's why: Any assessment is a sample of all the questions we could have asked if the test were infinitely long. But because time is always limited, we can never probe all important dimensions of achievement. So we sample, asking as many questions as we can within the allotted time. A sound assessment asks a representative set of questions, allowing us to infer a student's performance on the entire domain of material from that student's performance on the shorter sample. If we have set clear limits on our valued target, then we have set a clear sampling frame. This allows us to sample with maximum efficiency and confidence; that is, to gather just enough information on student achievement without wasting time overtesting. When we have a clear sense of the desired ends, we can use the assessment methods that are most efficient for the situation.

Accurate Classroom Assessments

In Part 2 of this book I discuss several assessment methods in detail. I will argue that some methods work well with certain kinds of achievement targets but not with others. In that context, it also will become clear that some methods produce achievement information more efficiently than do others. Skillful classroom assessors match methods to targets so as to produce maximum information with minimum invested assessment time. This is part of the art of classroom assessment. Your skill as an artist increases with the clarity of your vision of important learning.

Sources of Information About Achievement Standards

You can search out, identify, come to understand, and even place limits around the achievement targets and thus your teaching responsibilities in three ways: analyzing state and local standards, studying your local written curriculum, and through interaction with professional colleagues. Let's explore each.

State and Local Standards

As noted earlier, our emergence into the era of standards-driven schools has spurred a great deal of high-powered reexamination of important achievement expectations. This is a boon to teachers because in virtually every field, we have at our disposal definitions of achievement success that hold the promise of allowing us to produce better achievers faster than ever before. This applies to reading, writing, science, math reasoning and problem solving, foreign languages, and many other subjects. Virtually every state and lots of local districts have standards of academic excellence, typically developed by teams of experienced teachers from within the state. In addition, states administer statewide assessments reflective of those standards and schools are held accountable for demonstrating student mastery of state standards by scoring high on these tests. Contact your district office or state department of education for information about them.

On investigation, you will find that standards identified in these contexts typically are articulated in the form of goals or objectives. Two examples appeared earlier in this chapter in Figure 2.3, one in history and the other in writing. As a classroom teacher, it is your responsibility to transform such objectives into the classroom-level achievement targets that your students must hit to build over time to a place where they are ready to demonstrate the required proficiency. To accomplish this, you must ask the following questions:

- What do students need to come to *know and understand* to be ready to demonstrate that they can meet this standard when the time comes to do so?
- What patterns of *reasoning* must they develop the ability to apply?
- What performance *skills,* if any, are called for as building blocks beneath this standard?
- What *products* must they be proficient at creating, if any?

Be advised that all standards arise from a foundation of knowledge. As the faculty, you and your colleagues must divide up responsibility for providing students with the opportunity to master it. Further, many standards expect mastery of specific reasoning patterns, while some also imply performance skill and product development capabilities. We will study these in depth in the next section. You must identify them, build instruction to focus on them, and transform them into accurate classroom assessments.

Your Local Written Curriculum

Every school district will take its state standards across subjects and grade levels and transform them into their own local written curriculum. This document will present achievement expectations in much greater detail, typically identifying how subjects will be articulated within and across grade levels. Specific topics to be covered will be described, revealing how they are woven together over time. The document also will state if teachers are to emphasize integration across subjects or grades, such as writing across the curriculum. For all of these reasons, you can turn to your local curriculum description for insights regarding your assigned achievement expectations.

Professional Networking

Besides consulting state standards and your local curriculum, the next most important source of insight into key achievement targets is your team of professional colleagues. This includes your principal, other teachers in your school and grade levels, and others with experience in teaching in your context. Besides these, another way to remain current and to grow as a teacher is to join the appropriate local and national professional associations of teachers. Most have assembled commissions of their members to translate current research into practical classroom guidelines, and many regularly publish journals to disseminate this research. Work with the resource personnel in your professional library if you have one. Often they can route special articles and information to you when they arrive. In addition, you can always search the Internet for information on valued achievement targets.

Types of Achievement Targets

All right, you might now ask, how do I make my targets clear? What is it that I must describe about them? The first step in answering these questions is to understand that we ask our students to learn a number of different kinds of things. Our challenge as teachers is to understand which of these is relevant for our particular students at any particular point in their academic development.

As my colleagues and I analyzed the task demands of classroom assessment, we tried to discern categories of targets that seemed to make sense to teachers (Stiggins & Conklin, 1992). We collected, studied, categorized, and tried to understand the various kinds of valued expectations reflected in teachers' classroom activities and assessments. The following categories or types of achievement targets emerged as important:

- *Knowledge*—mastery of substantive subject matter content, where mastery includes both knowing and understanding it
- *Reasoning*—the ability to use that knowledge and understanding to figure things out and to solve problems
- *Performance Skills*—the development of proficiency in doing something where it is the process that is important, such as playing a musical instrument, reading aloud, speaking in a second language, or using psychomotor skills
- *Products*—the ability to create tangible products, such as term papers, science fair models, and art products, that meet certain standards of quality and that present concrete evidence of academic proficiency
- *Dispositions*—the development of certain kinds of feelings, such as attitudes, interests, and motivational intentions

As you will see, these categories are quite useful to our thinking about classroom assessment because they subsume all possible targets, are easy to understand, relate to one another in significant ways, and (now here's the important part!) have clear links to different kinds of assessment. But before we discuss assessment, let's more thoroughly understand these categories of achievement targets.

Knowing and Understanding Targets

When we were growing up, we were asked to learn important content. What happened in 1066? Who signed the Declaration of Independence? Name the Presidents of the United States in order. What does the symbol "Au" refer to on the periodic table of elements? Learn this vocabulary for a quiz on Friday . . . Here is your spelling list for this week . . . Learn your multiplication tables.

We had to memorize these things by test time or fail. And, in fact, at least some of what we learned in this way was important. For example, we can communicate our ideas to others because we mastered a sufficient vocabulary. We may have attained proficiency in speaking a second language because we learned the vocabulary and syntax of that language. We would have remained incapable of reading and understanding our science text if we had not learned to understand at least some science content.

Such knowledge is prerequisite to more sophisticated achievements, so part of our jobs as teachers is to be sure our students gain control of that content. This is precisely why I have structured this book in part to help you know and understand the foundations of sound assessment. You cannot do the classroom assessment part of the teaching job well unless you know certain things. In that sense this knowledge represents a foundation of your teaching competence.

But remember three important things about mastery of content knowledge—all of which have direct implications for classroom assessment:

1. Knowing something is not the same as understanding it. To understand content, students need to see how it fits into the larger schema of the academic discipline they are studying.
2. In this information age, the world does not operate merely on facts stored in our brains. I am every bit as much a master of content if I know where to find it as if I know it outright. This way of knowing is becoming increasingly important as technology continues to permeate our society.
3. There are ways to come to know and understand something that do not rely on memorization. I can come to know because I figured it out and the resulting insight left an indelible impression. I can come to know because frequent use of certain knowledge leaves memories.

In short, mastering (meaning *gaining control over*) content knowledge is a complex enterprise. Let's consider these items in greater detail.

To Know and to Understand Are Not the Same

The world around me is full of wonderful things that I know but don't understand. For instance, the Golden Gate Bridge arches beautifully over San Francisco Bay. But I don't understand the structures that keep it from falling into the bay. I know that my computer will save the text that I am composing. But I don't understand how it does this. I know that $E = MC^2$. So if someone asked me what E equals, I can say, "MC^2." But I don't understand what it means, and can't use it to help me solve physics problems. Thus, for me these represent useless information.

On the other hand, the world is also full of things that I know and understand. Airplanes whisk me across the country and don't fall out of the sky. I understand that this is because of the vacuum formed over the wing when air accelerates over the top of that wing. I can say and spell the science word *watershed* and I understand what it means. I even understand what not to do in a watershed environment. I can read and understand guidebooks on fly fishing because I know and understand the physics of a fly line in motion. These represent elements of knowledge that are useful to me because I know and understand them.

I submit that merely knowing but not understanding leaves any learners unable to make use of what they have learned. Simply knowing that bridges don't fall down does not make that knowledge useful. Learning a few mathematical equations cannot by itself lead me to comprehend physics. But knowing and understanding the *meaning* of such equations will.

Therefore, as a classroom teacher/assessor, I must know and understand what I expect my students to master. Further, I must be prepared to assess my students' understanding of what they claim to know.

Two Ways of "Knowing"

When I was a student, consequences were dire if anyone was caught with a crib sheet in a test. We were expected to know the required material outright. We were expected to have burned the content into the neural connections of our brains by whatever means. Remember all the tricks? Color-coded flash cards. Repetition—over and over. Cramming. All nighters. Playing recordings repeatedly while sleeping. If we didn't memorize it, we failed. There can be no question, some of that stuff stuck and that's a good thing. Regardless of how one gets there, knowing something outright can be a powerful way of knowing. But this is not the only way of knowing.

The reason, as stated previously, is that I am every bit as much a master of content if I know where to find it as if I know it outright. In other words, the world does not operate solely on information retrieved only from memory. To see what I mean, just try to fill out your income tax return, operate a new computer, or use an unfamiliar transit system without referring to the appropriate (hopefully well written!) user's guide. When we confront such challenges in real adult life, we rely on what we know to help us find what we don't know.

In short, this "knowledge" category of achievement targets includes both those targets that students must learn outright to function within an academic discipline (core facts, principles, concepts, relationships within structures of knowledge, and accepted procedures) and those targets they tap as needed through their use of reference resources. Each presents its own unique classroom assessment challenges. And remember, each way of "knowing" must be accompanied by "understanding."

To help our students know and understand content, we ourselves must be masters of the disciplines we expect them to master. Thus, we must be prepared to share the topics, concepts, generalizations, and theories that hold facts together. We also must be ready to share with them our skills and methods of researching information. Further, as classroom teachers, part of our job is to devise assessment exercises that require students to demonstrate their understanding of those connections.

Ways of Coming to Know

I can think of at least three ways to come to "know" something. Give me a list to memorize and in the end I will know it. If that list bears useful information and knowing is accompanied by understanding, important learning has occurred. Put me in a situation where I must use the same body of knowledge repeatedly, and habits of use eventually will entitle me not to have to look it up every time. Present me with a novel problem whose solution forces me to put together two pieces of knowledge previously mastered, and once I figure it out, that solution becomes part of my knowledge.

Think about the assessments Ms. W. had Emily involved in as she was learning to write. What were the foundations of knowledge that Emily needed to master? Among these were the attributes of good writing: word choice, sentence structure, organization, and so on. How did Ms. W. help Emily to mastery? Did she give her definitions of the attributes and performance rating scales to memorize? I think not. She helped Em and her classmates figure out what it was they needed to know and then she provided lots of repetitive practice in applying those standards of good writing. Emily came to know and understand them.

Time for Reflection

Identify at least five achievement targets that take the form of knowledge that you would expect students to master at the grade level(s) and in the subject(s) you teach or plan to teach.

Relationship to Other Types of Achievement

The foundation of academic competence rests on knowledge and understanding. I know that, for some, it is not trendy today to value learning the content. We are supposed to be attending to "higher-order thinking" and process skills. I agree that these, too, are important. But there is a danger lurking here.

In our haste to embrace "higher-order thinking," we deemphasize what we have a tradition of calling "lower-order thinking." But what have we traditionally defined as "lower order"? The mastery of content knowledge. So by deemphasizing content mastery, we in effect deny our students access to the very content they need to solve the problems that we want them to solve. Does that make sense to you? This is why you will find no reference to higher- or lower-order thinking in this book. Rather, we will honor both the ability to retrieve useful knowledge and the ability to use it to reason and solve problems.

Time for Reflection

Identify the academic discipline you regard as your greatest strength. How strong is your underlying knowledge of facts, concepts, and generalizations in that area? Think about your weakest area of academic performance. How strong is your knowledge and understanding base there? From this two-part analysis, what inference would you draw about how much a part of academic success is a strong, basic understanding of facts, concepts, and generalizations?

Reasoning Targets

Having students master content merely for the sake of knowing it and for no other reason is a complete waste of their time and ours. It is virtually always the case that we want students to be able to use their knowledge and understanding to reason, to figure things out, to solve certain kinds of problems. For example, we want them to

- Analyze and solve story problems in math because those problems mimic life after school
- Compare current or past political events or leaders because they need to be active citizens
- Reason inductively and deductively in science to find solutions to everyday problems
- Evaluate opposing positions on social and scientific issues because life constantly requires critical thinking

If we hold such targets as valuable for students, it is incumbent on us to define precisely what we mean by *reasoning and problem-solving proficiency*. Exactly what does it mean to reason "analytically"? It means that we take things apart and see what's inside them. But what is the difference between doing it well and doing it poorly? That's the key question. What does it mean to reason "comparatively"? We do this when we think about similarities and differences. But when and how is that relevant? Another key question. What does it mean to categorize, synthesize, to reason inductively or deductively? What *is* critical thinking, anyway? Not only must we be clear about the underlying structure of these patterns of reasoning, but we must help students understand and take possession of them, too. And, of course, we must be ready to translate each pattern into classroom assessment exercises and scoring procedures.

Obviously, these patterns represent important forms of achievement. The key to our success in helping students master them is to understand that any form of reasoning can be done either well or poorly. Our assessment challenge lies in knowing the difference. Our success in helping students learn to monitor the quality of their own reasoning—a critical part of lifelong learning—is to *help them learn the difference*.

In the case of reasoning, as with the other kinds of achievement targets, we who presume to help students master effective reasoning must first ourselves become confident, competent masters of these patterns. In other words, we must strive to meet standards of intellectual rigor in our own reasoning if we are to make this vision come alive in our students' minds. If we do not, then we remain unprepared to devise assessments that reflect sound reasoning.

All Reasoning Arises from Knowledge

There is no such thing as "content-free" reasoning. My auto mechanic can diagnose the reason for my car problems in large part because he knows and understands the systems that make my car run. My attorney can help me with my legal problems because she has studied and learned the law. CPAs prepare taxes correctly because they know proper procedures. My physician can help me get well because she knows the human body and understands medical remedies. Chefs create culinary delights because they know and understand how ingredients blend to look and taste good. You will develop sound assessments in your classroom in part because of the knowledge and understanding you acquire from studying the *content* of this book.

Realize That Students Are Natural Thinkers

Virtually all students arrive at school from day one as natural thinkers. You don't have to teach them to "think." Rather, you must help them learn to focus and structure their thinking into reasoning. The vast majority of students possess those cognitive abilities they need to survive and even prosper in school and beyond. Hidden within them is the capacity to interact purposefully with their world, confronting problems, reflecting on solutions, solving problems, and deriving or constructing personal meaning from experience.

But there's a problem. According to critical thinking expert Richard Paul (1995), the unschooled human mind is a mixed bag of good and bad thinking, of sharp focus and fuzzy thinking, of ignorance and sound knowledge, of accurate conceptions and misconceptions, of misunderstanding and important insight, of open-mindedness and prejudice. Our challenge as teachers is to help students learn to clean out and organize their mental houses as needed, to clear out the garbage and let sound reasoning prevail.

Patterns of Reasoning

How then should we understand and help students learn what it means to reason effectively? The answer lies in understanding various ways to organize our thinking and how those ways must come together to solve problems. Let's start by exploring a few of the commonly referenced forms of reasoning. Then we'll explore their dynamic interrelationships.

In the real world, we frequently find instances of the need to see relationships by reasoning analytically, comparatively, or in an evaluative manner. Real-life thinkers need to be able to synthesize, classify, and reason inductively or deductively. Let's think together about what these inferring processes really mean.

As you read about these different ways of reasoning, you will see that each has its own definition. Each can be illustrated in understandable terms. Nevertheless, as the examples reveal, *reasoning patterns are rarely used independently of one another.* Rather, these patterns blend to bring us to problem solutions. For now, as you read about each pattern, take a few seconds to see if you can identify some of the ways they fit together. We'll discuss those connections later.

Just to be sure you see the path ahead, I intend to argue that students must know and understand these patterns if they are to be able to use them productively to reason and solve problems. Therefore, they have a place among our valued achievement targets. We need to be ready to teach and assess student mastery of each. But more important, *we must prepare our students to be lifelong assessors of the quality of their own reasoning.*

Analytical Reasoning.   Consider, for example, the performance arena of writing and the assessment of writing proficiency. Here we draw the distinction between holistic and analytical scoring. In *holistic* scoring we consider all aspects of the written piece together and base our judgments on overall impression, assigning one overall score. In *analytical* scoring, we break performance down into its component parts (word choice, organization, voice, and the like), evaluating and

Questions that help students reason *analytically*:
1. What is it that I wish to analyze?
2. Why is analysis relevant?
3. What are the relevant parts, subdivisions, or categories?
4. How do the parts relate to each other?
5. How do the parts come together to create the whole?

Key concepts that underpin *analytical* reasoning:
- Interrelated parts of a whole
- Components
- Ingredients

Graphic representation of an example:
Reasoning Task: Analyze the ingredients of assessment quality covered in this book:

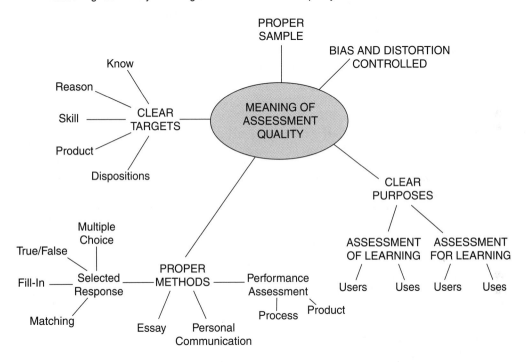

Figure 2.6
Understanding analytical reasoning

assigning a score to each part. It is this sense of the meaning of *analytical* that we are speaking of here.

When we reason analytically, we draw inferences about the component parts of something: its ingredients, how they fit together, and how they function as a whole. When good reporters do "news analysis" they go into a story in greater depth to study its parts. When we try to figure out how a machine works (to go inside and see how the pieces fit and work together) we are reasoning analytically. When we infer what goes into making something good, like food, a movie, or a teacher, we are involved in analytical reasoning. Figure 2.6 analyzes and presents a graphic representation of this pattern of reasoning, analyzing key assessment topics.

In this case, our instructional challenges are to be sure that students have access to whatever knowledge and understanding they need to analyze something and that they have guided practice in exercising their analytical thought processes.

Our assessment challenge is to ask them to tap into that knowledge base and apply their reasoning skills to a novel analytical task. For example, in literature, we might provide practice in character analysis by having students read a new story (gathering knowledge of a new character) and asking them to generate an original analysis of this character they have just "met."

As a teacher, I want my students to know exactly what is called for whenever I ask them to "analyze" something. I might even put a chart on the wall detailing the process and highlighting examples of analytical inferences. These might include character analyses from literature, storyline or plot analyses, breakdown diagrams of machines, or depictions of the subparts of a scientific process such as the water cycle. I want students to recognize when analysis is needed and to understand how to apply that pattern of reasoning in novel problem situations.

Synthesizing.   Let's say you have just finished helping students analyze the structure of two short stories. Then, you have them pool or synthesize these into a set of generalizations about the typical structure of a short story. Thus two different sources of knowledge and understanding about short stories are integrated. This is *synthesizing*. You then ask them to draw the following inference: How does the story you just read align with what you know about the typical structure that you just developed? Figure 2.7 presents a description of synthesis.

We find a great deal of interest being expressed these days in the development of "integrated" or "thematic" instruction or curricula. This often is described as being different from discipline-based instruction, in which students study separately math, science, writing skills, and so on. Thematic instruction encourages students to bring knowledge and productive patterns of reasoning together from several disciplines, as they explore their particular theme, whether it be the study of a particular culture, scientific problem, or social issue. Such curricula place a premium on synthesizing insights from divergent sources and present wonderfully rich opportunities to develop and assess student mastery of this pattern of reasoning.

Comparative Reasoning.   *Comparative reasoning* refers to the process of figuring out or inferring how things are either alike or different. Sometimes we compare in terms of similarities, other times we contrast in terms of differences, still other times we do both. To understand this kind of reasoning, we must see that those who are proficient begin with a clear understanding of the things they are to compare. Then they identify the dimensions of each that they will examine for similarities or differences. And finally, they detail the comparison, highlighting why those particular points are important. Here are simple examples: In what way are these two poems alike and different? Given this early and this late work by this particular author, how are they different in style? How are these insects alike and different? Figure 2.8 illustrates the structure.

Questions that help students *synthesize*:
1. What is the problem to be solved by combining ideas?
2. Why is synthesis relevant in this context?
3. What are the various understandings that can be combined to help?
4. How do those parts fit together to help us find a solution?

Key concepts:
- Convergence
- Generalization
- Whole is more than the sum of its parts

Example:
Understanding #1: My personal experience has shown me that students who are involved in the ongoing assessment of their own achievement are much more highly motivated to learn than are those who are not involved.

Understanding #2: The professional literature in both reading and writing instruction tells us that students must learn to monitor their own comprehension and the quality of their own writing to become independently literate adults.

Understanding #3: Research from around the world provides irrefutable evidence that students who are deeply involved in high-quality classroom assessment environments learn more.

Synthesis: It would be a very good idea for me, the teacher, to involve my students in assessment, record keeping, and communication to increase motivation.

Figure 2.7
Understanding synthesis as a pattern of reasoning

Classifying. Sometimes, life presents us with reasoning challenges that ask us to categorize, or *classify,* things. When we budget, we classify expenses. When we analyze how we use our time, we organize events into different categories. In science, we classify plants and animals. In politics, we categorize issues and candidates. To reason productively in this manner, we must first know the defining parameters of each category and the attributes of those things we are classifying. Then we can compare each item with the categorical options and infer its appropriate group (Figure 2.9).

Induction and Deduction. In the case of *inductive* reasoning, we reason productively when we can infer principles, draw conclusions, or glean generalizations from accumulated evidence. Induction results from synthesis. Reasoning travels from particular facts to a general rule or principle. Here are two examples:

- Now that you have read this story, what do you think is its general theme or message?
- Given the evidence provided in this article about the stock market [note that this is an example of using knowledge gained through reference], what is the relationship between interest rates and stock values?

Questions that help students *compare* and *contrast*:
1. What is to be compared?
2. Why is it relevant to draw the comparison?
3. Upon what basis will we compare them?
4. How are they alike?
5. How are they different?
6. What important lessons can we learn from this *comparison*?

Key concepts:
- Similar
- Different

Example:
Compare classroom and standardized assessment

Criterion	Classroom Assessment	Standardized Test
Focus	Narrow Targets	Broad Targets
Developer	Teacher	Test Publisher
Frequency	Continuous	Once a year
Users	Teacher Student Parent	Principal Curriculum Director Superintendent School Board Legislator

Figure 2.8
Understanding comparative reasoning

We help students gain control over their inductive reasoning proficiency when we make sure they have the opportunity to access the proper knowledge from which important rules or principles arise and when we provide guided practice in drawing inferences, conclusions, or generalizations.

We also reason when we apply a general rule or principle to find the solution to a problem. This is *deductive* reasoning. Here, reasoning travels from the general to the specific:

- Given your theory about criminal behavior, who did the killing?
- Given what you know about the role of a tragic hero in classic literature, if this character is a tragic hero, what do you think will happen next in the story?
- If the chemical test yields this result, what element is it?

Obviously, the key instructional challenge is to be sure students have the opportunity to learn and understand the rules, generalizations, or principles we want

Questions that can help students *classify:*
1. Classify what?
2. Into what categories?
3. Why is it relevant to do so?
4. What elements into what categories?
5. What is the basis of (our reasoning behind) each proper match?

Key concepts:
- Objects have characteristics
- Categories have characteristics
- Alignment in terms of characteristics

Example:
Classify each instructional objective on the left in terms of the kind of achievement target that it represents.

Objective	*Target*
Read aloud fluently	Understand content knowledge
Know the causes of the Great Depression	Pattern of reasoning
Speak a second language fluently	Performance skill
Predict the results of an experiment	Product development
Set up the science lab apparatus properly	
Learn a poem	
Create a model dwelling	
Compare two characteristics from literature	

Figure 2.9
Understanding the reasoning that underpins classification

them to apply. Then and only then can we assess their reasoning proficiency by presenting them with novel contexts within which to apply those rules.

Evaluative Reasoning.   We reason in an evaluative manner when we apply certain criteria to judge the value or appropriateness of something. The quality of the reasoning depends on our ability to logically or dependably apply proper judgmental criteria. Synonyms for this pattern of reasoning include *critical thinking* and *judgmental reasoning*.

Within the context of our journey together, the very process of evaluating the quality of student work in terms of some predetermined achievement standards, such as writing assessment, is a classic example of evaluative reasoning. When we express and defend a point of view or opinion, we reason in an evaluative manner. When we judge the quality of an assessment using our five standards of quality, we reason in an evaluative manner.

Our instructional task is to help students understand the criteria they should be applying when they defend their point of view on an issue. Who is the best candidate for mayor? That's a matter of opinion. What are the important characteristics of a good mayor? As we discuss these criteria in class, we must address how to apply these standards logically.

Our assessment challenge is to determine if students are able to apply those criteria appropriately, given a novel evaluative challenge. Students who are able to appropriately evaluate a piece of writing they have never seen before using a learned set of analytical rating scales are demonstrating proficiency in evaluative reasoning. It is in this sense that I say this entire book is about developing critical thinkers.

Why These Patterns?

Three reasons. First, I sought to describe what people normally think of as reasoning processes. I wanted as few patterns as possible that, at the same time, covered sufficient ground to provide the most commonsense meaning of *reasoning*. This would make the list comprehensive but manageable. It needed to be practical. These patterns are simple and understandable, and at the same time describe what happens in the real world.

Second, I finally realized that there is no final "truth" in the universe with respect to defining *reasoning*. As I studied the professional literature, I found a variety of labels for patterns. Classification systems abound. Every scholar has a different opinion about the truth. So I tried to glean from these various opinions the things they had in common. The patterns described here have a foundation in current thinking about reasoning.

Third, I wanted patterns that I could describe and illustrate in terms that students (including you!) could master. The fact that we can diagram each pattern and easily find examples makes them approachable by our students. That's a good thing.

But remember, after studying and reflecting on the reasoning targets that you want your students to master, you may find other classifications or definitions that work better for you. That's fine. Just be clear enough about your vision of excellence in reasoning that your definitions are practical, based on the best current understanding, and student friendly.

Relationships Among Patterns

As I wrote about these patterns of reasoning and their classroom applications, I tried to use descriptive vocabulary so you could see key connections. I hope that your study of and reflection on the six organizing structures permitted you to notice some important connections among them. I list some here to establish the dynamic nature of reasoning. Your own reasoning may be different. If you are seeing rich relationships, you are reasoning productively.

- All reasoning consists of seeing relationships among things.
- Synthesis requires inductive inference; that is, we do it well when we can infer or see the unity arising from divergent parts.
- Complex comparisons require a prior step of analyzing the things to be compared to infer or identify potential points of similarity and difference.
- Classification involves comparison of each item to be classified to the attributes of each category to infer which goes where.

- Inductive inference requires that we compare the pieces of evidence at hand to see what they have in common.
- Evaluation often requires analysis and comparison of different points of view before coming to judgment.
- Evaluative judgments about the quality of any reasoning can be made if we have standards for what it means to do it well.

So it is that different ways of reasoning form a puzzle whose pieces can fit together in various ways to permit you and your students to figure things out. It is appropriate to help students see and understand the different organizing structures.

Students who encounter a new math problem, debate a volatile social issue, or confront an unknown substance in a science lab bring all of these ways of reasoning into play in a rapid-fire manner, analyzing the problem to infer what knowledge bases they must bring to bear. Beyond school, when students are confronted with a drug pusher, make career choices, or deal with the demands of peer pressure, they must think clearly and select a proper course of action. Those who are masters of their own reasoning and who know how to use their minds effectively have a strong chance of generating productive responses to such circumstances.

Time for Reflection

Identify at least five reasoning or problem-solving achievement targets that might be relevant for students to master at the grade levels and in the subjects you teach or plan to teach.

Relationship to Other Targets

We can use our reasoning powers to generate new knowledge and understanding. When I combine two things that I knew before to derive an insight that I hadn't realized before, that insight can remain with me for future use. Further, my reasoning powers will come into play as I strive for skillful performance or product development—the next two kinds of targets. You'll see how as you read on.

Performance Skill Targets

In most classrooms, there are things teachers want their students to *be able to do,* instances for which the measure of attainment is students' ability to demonstrate that they can perform or behave in a certain way. For example, at the primary-grade level, a teacher might look for certain fundamental social interaction behaviors or oral reading fluency skills. At the elementary level, a teacher might observe student performance in cooperative group activities. In middle school or junior high, manipulation of a science lab apparatus might be important. And at the high school level, public speaking or the ability to converse in a second language might be a valued outcome.

In all of these cases, success lies in "actually *doing* it well." The assessment challenge lies in being able to define in clear terms, using words, examples, or both, what it *means* to do it well—to read or speak fluently, work productively as a team member, or carry out the steps in a lab experiment. To assess well, we must provide opportunities for students to show their skills, so we can observe and evaluate while they are performing.

Time for Reflection

Identify at least three achievement targets that take the form of performance skills that might be relevant for students to master at the grade levels and in the subjects you teach or plan to teach.

Relationship to Other Targets

To perform skillfully, one must possess the fundamental procedural knowledge and reasoning proficiency needed to figure out what skills are required. Further, skillful performance must combine with this knowledge and reasoning proficiency to create quality products (discussed in the next section). In this way, performance skills represent an end in and of themselves as well as a building block for other competencies. For example, I cannot produce a quality piece of writing (a product) unless I have handwriting or computer keyboarding proficiency (performance skills) *and* the ability to think about the topic in ways that permit me to write fluently and coherently. I cannot deliver an effective spontaneous speech (skill) unless I know something about the subject and can figure out what needs to be said about that topic at this moment. It is critical that we understand that, in this category, the student's performance objective is to integrate knowledge and reasoning proficiencies and to be skillful. This is precisely why achievement-related skills often represent complex targets requiring sophisticated assessments. Success in creating products—the next kind of target—virtually always hinges on the ability to perform some kinds of skills. Performance skills underpin product development.

Product Development Targets

Yet another way for students to succeed academically in some contexts is by developing the capacity to create products that meet certain standards of quality. These represent tangible entities that are created by the performer, and that present evidence in their quality that the student has mastered basic knowledge, requisite reasoning and problem-solving proficiencies, and specific production skills.

For example, a high school social studies teacher might have students prepare a term paper to gather evidence of writing proficiency. A technology teacher might ask students to repair a computer to judge job-related preparedness. An elementary school teacher might challenge students to create a model or diorama. A primary-grade teacher might collect samples of student artwork.

In all cases, student success lies in creating products that possess certain key attributes when completed. The assessment challenge is to be able to define clearly and understandably, in writing and/or through example, what those attributes are.

We must be able to specify exactly how high- and low-quality products differ and we must be prepared to express those differences in student-friendly language.

Time for Reflection

Identify at least two product development achievement targets that might be relevant for students to master at the grade levels and in the subjects you teach or plan to teach.

Relationship to Other Targets

Note once again that successful performance arises out of student mastery of prerequisite knowledge and through the application of appropriate reasoning strategies. In addition, students will probably need to perform certain predefined steps to create the desired product. Prerequisite achievement thus underpins the creation of quality products, but evidence of ultimate success resides in the product itself. Does it meet standards of quality?

Dispositional Targets

This final category of aspirations for our students is quite broad and complex. It includes those characteristics that go beyond academic achievement into the realms of affective and personal feeling states, such as attitudes, sense of academic self-confidence, or interest in something that motivationally predisposes a person to act or not act.

Many teachers set as goals, for example, that students will develop positive academic self-concepts or positive attitudes toward school subjects predisposing them to strive for excellence. Without question, we want our students to develop strong interests, as well as a strong sense of internal control over their own academic well-being. We may define each disposition in terms of three essential elements:

- It is focused on some specific thing.
- It varies along a continuum from positive to negative.
- It varies in intensity from strong to weak.

Examples of things about which we might have attitudes (feelings) include ourselves as learners, school in general, specific subjects, classmates, and teachers. Those feelings about things are positive, neutral, or negative. For instance, our academic self-concepts are positive or negative. We might hold positive or negative attitudes about math or English. And sometimes those feelings are very strong, other times very weak—we range from passionate to disinterested. In school, we seek to impart strong positive dispositions toward learning new things, among other attitudes.

Positive learning experiences can result when teachers are in touch with students' dispositions (either as individuals or as a group) and when teachers can put students in touch with their own feelings about important issues. Obviously, however, we cannot know students' feelings about things unless we ask. This requires assessment.

Because these affective and social dimensions are quite complex, thoughtful assessment is essential. We define success in assessing them exactly as we do success in assessing achievement: Sound assessment requires a crystal-clear vision or understanding of the characteristic(s) to be assessed. Only then can we select a proper assessment method, devise a sampling procedure, and control sources of bias and distortion so as to accurately assess direction and intensity of feelings about specified objects.

Time for Reflection

Identify at least three dispositional targets that might be relevant for students to master at the grade levels and in the subjects you teach or plan to teach.

Summary of Targets

We have discussed four different but interrelated visions of achievement plus the affective component of student learning. Knowledge and understanding are important. Reasoning and problem solving require applying that knowledge. Knowledge and reasoning are required for successful skill performance and/or product development. And dispositions very often result from success or lack of success in academic performance. But once again, remember that these can all grow and change in dynamic, interrelated ways within students. Figure 2.10 summarizes the kinds of targets we have discussed, and Table 2.1 presents sample achievement targets from various academic disciplines. Read down each column.

Time for Reflection

Let's say we wanted to extend Table 2.1 to include three more columns. Identify examples of knowledge, reasoning, skill, product, and dispositional targets that would be relevant for Foreign Language (spoken and written, separately) and for Social Studies.

Figure 2.10
An overview of kinds of achievement

- Master Content Knowledge
  - ✓ *Master* means know and understand
  - ✓ Things to know outright
  - ✓ Know where to find it
- Use Knowledge to Reason and Solve Problems
  - ✓ Analysis
  - ✓ Synthesis
  - ✓ Comparison
  - ✓ Classification
  - ✓ Inference
  - ✓ Evaluation
- Demonstrate Performance Skills
- Create Products
- Develop Attitudinal, Motivational Predispositions

Table 2.1
Sample achievement targets across school subjects

Achievement Target	Reading	Writing	Music	Science	Math
Know and Understand	Sight vocabulary Background knowledge required by text	Vocabulary needed to communicate Mechanics of usage Knowledge of topic	Instrument mechanics Musical notation	Science facts and concepts	Number meaning Math facts Numeration systems Algorithms
Reason	Decode the text and comprehend the meaning	Choose words and syntactic elements to convey message Evaluate text quality	Evaluate tonal quality	Hypotheses testing Classifying species	Formulate math problem from situation
Performance Skills	Oral reading fluency	Letter formation Keyboarding skills	Instrument fingering Breath control	Manipulate lab apparatus correctly	Use manipulatives while solving problem
Products	Diagram revealing comprehension	Samples of original text	Original composition written in musical notation	Written lab report Science fair model	Well-reasoned problem solution
Dispositions	"I like to read."	"I can write well."	"Music is important to me."	"Science is worth understanding."	"Math is useful in real life."

59

A critical step in planning instruction or designing classroom assessments is to specify the type(s) of target(s) students are to hit. As you will see later, once a target is defined, the process of designing assessments is quite easy. The toughest part by far is coming up with the clear and complete vision!

A Final Reminder: The Targets in Your Classroom Are Your Responsibility

As a teacher, you may or may not practice your profession in a district that engages in integrated planning. You may or may not practice in a school in which staff collaborate in articulating achievement targets across grade levels or subjects. In short, you may or may not receive the kind of school and community support needed to do a thorough job of generating a continuous-progress portrait of success for students.

Nevertheless, each of us has a responsibility to our particular students to be clear, specific, and correct about our achievement expectations. The point is that, regardless of what is going on around you, tomorrow or as soon as you enter a classroom a bunch students will show up wanting and needing to master content knowledge, learn to solve problems, master important performance skills, learn to create important products, and/or develop certain dispositions. They count on you to know what these things mean and to know how to teach and assess them. *When it comes to being clear about what it means to be successful in your classroom, the responsibility stops with you! Embrace this responsibility.*

Summary: Clear Targets Are Essential for Sound Assessment

In this part of our journey into the realm of classroom assessment, I have argued that the quality of any assessment rests on the clarity of the assessor's understanding of the achievement target(s) to be assessed. We strive for content-valid assessments, and they start with clear and appropriate targets.

We have identified five kinds of interrelated types of achievement expectations as useful in thinking about and planning for assessment and for integrating it into your instruction:

- Mastering content knowledge (including understanding)

- Using that knowledge to reason and solve problems
- Demonstrating certain kinds of performance skills
- Creating certain kinds of products
- Developing certain dispositions

Each teacher faces the challenge of specifying desired targets in the classroom, relying on a commitment to lifelong learning, strong professional preparation, community input, and collegial teamwork within the school to support this effort.

When we are clear, benefits accrue for all involved. Limits of teacher accountability are established, setting teachers up for time savings and greater success. Limits of student accountability are established, setting students up for success. And, the huge assessment workload faced by teachers becomes more manageable.

We will make this clarity the second criterion by which to judge classroom assessment quality. High-quality assessments arise from easily identified and clearly articulated learning targets. They reflect the best current thinking in the field and are obviously important—that is, they deserve instructional and assessment time and effort. Poor-quality achievement targets, on the other hand, either (1) are missing, (2) are too broad or vague to guide assessment development, (3) fail to link to important academic

standards, or (4) fail to reflect the wisdom of the field of study.

Thus, clarity and appropriateness will be the second entry in our set of comprehensive rubrics for judging classroom assessment quality (see the Appendix). You will have opportunities throughout your study to practice applying these standards of good practice.

I urge that you specify clear expectations in your classroom. Do so in writing and publish them for all to see. Eliminate the mystery surrounding the meaning of success in your classroom by letting your students see your vision. If they can see it, they can hit it. But if they cannot see it, their challenge turns into pin the tail on the donkey—blindfolded, of course. You will see in the next chapter how this triggers key decisions about how to assess the achievement of your students.

Final Chapter Reflection

1. *What are the three most important new insights to come to you as a result of your study of this chapter?*
2. *Which of your previous questions about assessment can you now answer based on your study of this chapter?*
3. *What new questions have come to mind as a result of your study of this chapter that you hope to have answered as your study continues?*

Practice with Chapter 2 Ideas

1. Engage your professor in a discussion of the intended standards and achievement targets of the course in which you are using this text. How do those expectations relate to the attributes and types of targets discussed in this chapter?

2. Here are several state standards. Deconstruct each into the enabling classroom-level knowledge, reasoning,

performance skill, or product achievement targets (as appropriate) that underpin it.

Reading—The student understands the meaning of what is read. Specifically, the student comprehends important ideas and details.

Writing—The student writes effectively. Specifically, the student uses style appropriate to the audience and purpose; uses voice, word choice, and sentence fluency for intended style and audience.

Mathematics—The student uses mathematical reasoning. Specifically, the student analyzes information from a variety of resources; uses models, known facts, patterns, and relationships to validate thinking.

Science—The student understands and uses scientific concepts and principles. Specifically, the student recognizes the components, structures, and organization of systems and the interaction within and among them.

Geography—The student understands the complex physical and human

characteristics of places and regions. Specifically, the student identifies the characteristics that define the regions within which she or he lives.

Civics—The student analyzes the purposes and organization of governments and laws. Specifically, the student compares and contrasts democracies with other forms to government.

3. Select three state achievement standards from a state in which you may teach—any grade level or content area—and analyze them in terms of the foundations of classroom targets that students must master on their journey up to each of those standards.

Chapter 3

Selecting Proper Assessment Methods

CHAPTER FOCUS

This chapter answers the following guiding question:

> As a classroom teacher, how should I assess the achievement of my students? What methods should I use?

From your study of this chapter, you will understand the following:

1. We have four categories of assessment methods from which to choose for any particular classroom assessment situation: selected response, essay, performance assessment, and personal communication.

2. The method of choice in any particular classroom assessment context is a function of the information needs of the user and the achievement target in question.

Selecting a Proper Assessment Method

Having introduced the idea that assessments must be valid for particular purposes (users and uses) and must be reflections of particular achievement targets, we now turn to our next validity issue: selecting proper assessment methods for a particular purpose and target. In this chapter, we explain how the various methods that we have at our disposal fit into the big picture of assessment quality (Figure 3.1).

We're going to study four basic assessment methods, all of which are familiar to you: selected response assessments, essay assessments, performance assessments, and assessments that rely on direct personal interaction or communication with students. Each provides its own special form of evidence of student proficiency. I introduce them in this chapter, and then in Part 2 devote an entire chapter to each method, studying it in depth in terms of advantages, disadvantages, its use to sample student achievement, principles of effective development, and keys to eliminating bias.

Figure 3.1
Proper method: one key to effective classroom assessment

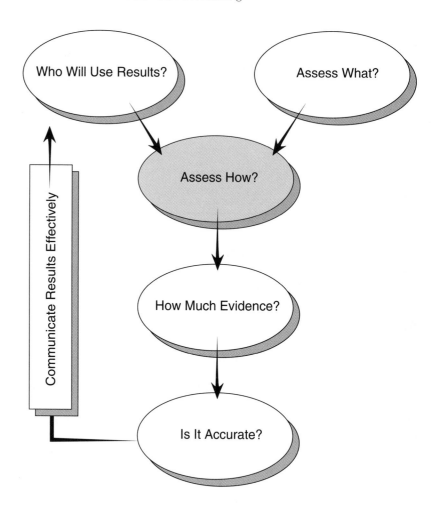

We will analyze how each of these four methods aligns with the four kinds of achievement targets plus dispositions discussed in Chapter 2. In essence, we will see which methods make sense with each target (can yield valid results) and which do not (will yield invalid results). We will do this by filling in the cells of Figure 3.2 with commentary on viable matches.

The Assessment Options

The artistry of classroom assessment emerges when teachers orchestrate a careful alignment among user information needs, achievement targets, and assessment methods. For example, an assessment of instrumental music proficiency is likely to look very different from an assessment of understanding of science knowledge. The former relies on the assessor to listen to and subjectively judge proficiency. The lat-

	Selected Response	Essay	Performance Assessment	Personal Communication
Know				
Reason				
Performance Skills				
Products				
Dispositions				

Figure 3.2
A plan for matching assessment methods with achievement targets

ter can be accomplished with a set of exercises scored correct or incorrect, yielding a score reflecting proficiency. Different targets, different assessment methods.

Note also that an assessment of instrumental music proficiency for the purpose of planning a student's next lesson demands a different kind of assessment from one designed to determine who receives a scholarship to the conservatory. The former requires a narrowly focused, brief assessment; the latter a much larger, more diverse sampling of proficiency. As purpose varies, so does the definition of sound assessment procedure.

In this chapter, we're going to study how to pick a method that truly reflects the target you wish to assess. We also will continue to fill in more details about the idea of student involvement with each assessment method.

Selected Response Assessment

This category includes all of the objectively scored paper and pencil test formats. Respondents are asked a series of questions, each of which is accompanied by a range of alternative responses. Their task is to select either the correct or the best answer from among the options. The index of achievement in this instance is the number or proportion of questions answered correctly. Format options within this category include the following:

- multiple-choice items
- true/false items
- matching exercises
- short answer fill-in items

I realize that fill-in-the-blank items do require a response originating from within a respondent's mind, but I include it in this category because it calls for a very brief answer that typically is counted right or wrong.

Essay Assessment

In this case, respondents are provided with exercises that call for them to prepare original written answers. Respondents might answer questions about content knowledge or provide an explanation of the solution to a complex problem. They might be asked to compare historical events, interpret scientific information, or solve open-ended math problems, where they must show and explain all their work. The examiner reads this original written response and evaluates it by applying specified scoring criteria.

Evidence of achievement is seen in the conceptual substance of the response (i.e., ideas expressed and the manner in which they are tied together). Once again, as with selected response, the student's score is determined by the number of points attained out of a total number of points possible.

Performance Assessment

In this case, respondents actually carry out a specified activity under the watchful eye of an evaluator, who observes their performance or its results and makes judgments as to the level of achievement demonstrated. Performance assessments can be based either on observations of respondents as they are demonstrating skills, or on the products created as a result of performing. In this sense, as with essay assessments, performance assessments consist of two parts: a performance task or assignment and a set of scoring guides.

Respondents may evidence achievement by carrying out a proper sequence of activities or by doing something in the appropriate manner. Examples include musical performance, reading aloud, communicating conversationally in a second language, or carrying out some motor activity, as in the case of physical education or dance. In this case, it is the doing that counts. The index of achievement typically is a performance rating or profile of ratings reflecting levels of quality in the performance.

Alternatively, respondents may demonstrate proficiency by creating complex achievement-related products intended to meet certain standards of quality. The product resulting from performance must exist as an entity separate from the performer, as in the case of term papers, science fair exhibits, or art and craft creations. The assessor examines the tangible product to see if those attributes of quality are indeed present. In this instance, it is not so much the process of creating that counts (although that may be evaluated, too) but rather the characteristics of the creation itself. Again in this case, the index of achievement is the rating(s) of product quality.

Personal Communication as Assessment

One of the most common ways teachers gather information about day-to-day student achievement in the classroom is to talk with them! We typically don't think of this as assessment in the same sense as a multiple-choice test or a performance assessment. But on reflection, it will become clear to you that certain forms of personal communication definitely do provide evidence of the level of student achievement.

These forms of personal communication include questions posed and answered during instruction, interviews, conferences, conversations, listening during class discussions, and oral examinations. The examiner listens to responses and either (1) judges them right or wrong if correctness is the criterion, or (2) makes subjective judgments according to some continuum of quality. Personal communication is a very flexible means of assessment that we can bring into play literally at a moment's notice. While it certainly is not as efficient as some other options when we must assess many students, it can probe achievement far more deeply than can the other alternatives.

Time for Reflection

Think about the assessments you have experienced in the classroom, either as a student or as a teacher, and identify two specific examples from your personal experience of each of the four assessment methods described.

Keep the Options in Balance

As you assess in your classroom, strive to maintain a balanced perspective regarding the viability of these assessment options. For decades, one method dominated in the United States, the objectively scored multiple-choice (selected response) test. As a result, some very important achievement targets that cannot be translated into this method simply were not assessed. This was especially true in the context of standardized testing, where selected response methods have been used extensively.

As we moved through the 1980s, however, we began to experience a shift in our values regarding the dominant method. As we began to embrace a more complex array of valued achievement expectations, including direct assessment of writing proficiency and some relatively more complex patterns of reasoning, we began to make more extensive use of such alternatives as extended written response and performance assessment.

As a result of this swing in values, however, if we aren't careful we may go out of balance in the other direction. By this, I mean we risk trading our prior obsession with multiple-choice tests for a new obsession with performance assessments. Neither method is inherently superior to the other. We can prevent this problem only by knowing what method to use and when and how to use each of them well.

Matching Methods with Targets

Note that three of the four assessment methods described call for students to develop complex original responses. They require extended written responses, demonstrate complex performance skills, create multidimensional products, or participate in one-on-one communication, all of which take more time to administer and certainly more time to score than, say, true/false test items. Thus, if the amount of assessment time is held constant, selected response assessments can provide a much larger sample of performance per unit of assessment time.

Given this fact, you might ask, why not just use the most efficient option all the time, selected response? The reason is that selected response assessment formats cannot validly depict all of the kinds of achievement we expect of our students. Different kinds of assessment methods align well with different kinds of achievement targets. We explore these relationships next.

Your objective, given a choice of methods, is to identify the most efficient (most valid evidence per unit of time) for your specific context. As it turns out, the recipes for creating these blends are not complicated.

As you saw in Figure 3.2, we visualize this blending by crossing the five kinds of outcomes with the four methods to create a table depicting the various matches of targets to methods. We may then explore the nature and practicality of the match within each cell of this table. The result, though not a simple picture, is both understandable and practical. Table 3.1 presents brief descriptions of the various matches.

Important Things to Remember

As you read Table 3.1, please keep the following key points in mind:

Know Your Targets

Remember that assessments provide us with external indicators of the learner's internal mental states *(achievements)*. These indicators take the form of visible manifestations that we can see and count or evaluate, such as correct or incorrect responses to test items or ratings of a performance skill. In other words, because we can't just lift the tops off students' heads and look inside to see if math problem-solving proficiency is in there, we administer an assessment in the form of several math problems to gather evidence of proficiency from which we infer mastery of the desired achievement. Your job in selecting a method for any particular form of achievement is to choose the method that permits you to draw the most valid (defensible) inference about student learning. For this reason, I reiterate yet again, you must be a master of the targets your students are expected to hit if you are to select, develop, and use sound assessments of those targets.

Remember, We Sample Achievement to Generalize About Student Learning

Any assessment will represent a sample of all the exercises we could have posed if the assessment were infinitely long. A sound assessment relies on a sample that is

Table 3.1
Links between achievement targets and assessment methods

		ASSESSMENT METHOD		
TARGET TO BE ASSESSED	**Selected Response**	**Essay**	**Performance Assessment**	**Personal Communication**
Knowledge & Understanding	Multiple choice, true/false, matching, and fill-in can sample mastery of elements of knowledge	Essay exercises can tap understanding of relationships among elements of knowledge	Not a good choice for this target—three other options preferred	Can ask questions, evaluate answers, and infer mastery, but a time-consuming option
Reasoning Proficiency	Can assess application of some patterns of reasoning	Written descriptions of complex problem solutions can provide a window into reasoning proficiency	Can watch students solve some problems or examine some products and infer about reasoning proficiency	Can ask student to "think aloud" or can ask followup questions to probe reasoning
Performance Skills	Can assess mastery of understandings prerequisite to skillful performance, but cannot rely on these to tap the skill itself	Can assess mastery of understandings prerequisite to skillful performance, but cannot rely on these to	Can observe and evaluate skills as they are being performed	Strong match when skill is oral communication proficiency; also can assess mastery of knowledge prerequisite to skillful performance
Ability to Create Products	Can only assess mastery of the under-standings prerequisite to the ability to create quality products	Can assess mastery of knowledge prerequisite to product develop-ment; brief essays can provide evidence of writing proficiency	Can assess (1) proficiency in carrying out steps in product development, and (2) attributes of the product itself	Can probe procedural knowledge and knowledge of attributes of quality products, but not product quality
Dispositions	Selected response questionnaire items can tap student feelings	Open-ended questionnaire items can probe dispositions	Can infer dispositions from behavior and products	Can talk with students about their feelings

systematically representative of the possibilities. We use performance on the sample to infer how much of the target students have mastered.

Our goal in assessment design is to use the most powerful assessment option we can. Power derives from the accuracy and efficiency with which a method can represent our valued standard. We always want the highest-resolution picture of that valued target we can get using the smallest possible sample of student performance; maximum information for minimum cost.

As you read Table 3.1, I hope you can see more clearly why it is crucial to understand the achievement target in order to select a proper assessment method. This cannot be overstated: *Different targets require different methods.*

Remember Too, This Is Just Your First Pass

This plan for aligning achievement targets and assessment methods is going to sound somewhat complex to you the first time through it. Just remember that this is *only* our first time! The remainder of the book is about how to make these matches work to your benefit and to the benefit of your students. All I hope for here is that the alignments described make sense to you. More practice in later chapters will help you become comfortable with these procedures.

Time for Reflection

Please take a few minutes now to study Table 3.1 and then read on. Do not read on without reading through the table.

Assessing Knowledge and Understanding

Here is how our four assessment methods align with knowledge and understanding targets.

Selected Response

We all know that we can use selected response, objective paper and pencil tests to measure student mastery of facts, concepts, and even generalizations. Typically, these assessments tend to rely on independent items to test mastery of disconnected elements of knowledge, such as knowledge of United States history, spelling, vocabulary, earth science, and the like.

These tests are efficient in that we can administer large numbers of multiple-choice or true/false test items per unit of testing time. Thus, they permit us to sample widely and draw relatively confident generalizations from the content sampled. For this reason, when the target is knowledge mastery, selected response formats fit nicely into the resource realities of most classrooms.

But remember, even with this most traditional of all assessment methods, things can go wrong. For instance, what if respondents confronted with a multiple-choice test can't read? A nonreader or a student who is still learning English might actually know the material but score low because of poor reading proficiency. If we conclude that their low score means a lack of knowledge, we would be wrong. We'll explore these and other potential sources of mismeasurement in later chapters.

Essay

When the domain of knowledge is defined not as elements in isolation but rather as important relationships among elements, larger concepts, and important generalizations—in other words, where the knowledge to be mastered is organized in complex ways—we can test student mastery by having them portray their knowledge using an extended written essay format. Examples of larger information chunks we might ask students to know are the causes of westward migration in U.S. history or differences among igneous, metamorphic, and sedimentary rocks.

In this case, we sample with fewer exercises, because each exercise requires longer response times, and each provides us with relatively more information than any single selected response item would.

Further, essay assessments present us with a more complex scoring challenge, and not just in terms of the time it takes. Because we must subjectively judge response quality, not just count it right or wrong, bias can creep in if we are not cautious. This requires developing and using carefully developed scoring guidelines. And remember, in this case, students also must bring writing proficiency into the assessment context. We must remain aware of the danger that students might know and understand the material but be unable to communicate it in this manner.

Performance Assessment

When it comes to the use of performance assessment to detect mastery of content knowledge, things quickly become complicated. This match is not always a strong one. To see why, consider a brief example.

Let's say we ask a student to complete a rather complex repair of a piece of technical equipment to determine if the student understands the equipment. If the student succeeds, the equipment will work properly. So this is an instance of product-based performance assessment. Success turns on attributes of the final product. If the student successfully completes the repair and the piece works properly, then we know that she possesses the prerequisite knowledge of equipment assembly and operations needed to both identify and solve the problem. In this case, the match between performance assessment and assessment of mastery of knowledge is a strong one.

However, to understand the potential problem with this match, consider the instance in which the student failed to produce functioning equipment. Was her failure due to lack of knowledge? Or did she possess the required knowledge but not use it properly to identify the problem (a flaw in reasoning)? Or did the student possess the knowledge and reason productively, but fail because of inept use of repair tools (a performance skill problem)? At the time the student fails to perform successfully, we just don't know.

In fact, we cannot know the real reason for failure unless and until we follow up the performance assessment by asking some questions to find out the cause; in short, unless we turn to one of the other assessment methods to gather more evidence. But if our initial goal simply was to determine if she had mastery of that prerequisite content knowledge, why go through all this hassle? Why not just ask—that is, turn to one of the other three options from the outset?

Also understand that the purpose of the assessment represents an important consideration here. If my reason for assessing is to certify repair technicians, I don't care why the student failed. But if I am a teacher whose job is to help students learn to perform, unless I know why this student failed, I have no way to help her perform better in the future.

Personal Communication

The final option for assessing mastery of knowledge is direct personal communication with students; for example, by asking questions and evaluating answers. This is a good match across all grade levels, especially with limited amounts of knowledge to be mastered, few students to be assessed, and in contexts where we need not store records of performance for long periods of time.

The reason I impose these conditions is that this obviously is a time- and labor-intensive assessment method. So if our domain of knowledge to assess is large, we are faced with the need to ask a large number of questions to cover it well. That just doesn't fit the resource realities in most classrooms. Further, if the number of students to be assessed is large, this option may not allow enough time to sample each student's achievement representatively. And, if we must store records of performance over an extended period of time, written records will be needed for each student over a broad sample of questions. This, too, eats up a lot of time and energy.

Assessment via personal communication works best in those situations when teachers are checking student mastery of critical content during instruction in order to make quick, ongoing adjustments. Further, sometimes with some students in some contexts, it is the only method that will yield accurate information. For various reasons, some students just cannot or will not participate in the other forms of assessment, such as those who experience debilitating evaluation anxiety, have difficulty reading English, have severe learning or communication disabilities, or simply refuse to "test."

Assessing Reasoning Proficiency

It is virtually always the case that we want students to be able to use their knowledge to reason and solve problems. In the previous chapter, we described several valued patterns of reasoning. For example, one is *evaluative* or *critical thinking,* the ability to make judgments and defend them through application of standards or criteria. In newspapers, movie or restaurant critics evaluate based on their standards of quality. So, too, can students evaluate the quality of a piece of literature or the strength of a scientific argument by learning to apply certain criteria of quality or standards of excellence. This is evaluative reasoning in action.

Another commonly valued pattern is *analytical* reasoning, the ability to break things down into component parts and to see how the parts work together. Yet another pattern involves using knowledge to *compare and contrast* things, to infer similarities and differences.

How does one assess these kinds of reasoning targets? Our four methodological choices all provide excellent options when we possess both a clear vision of what we wish to assess and sufficient craft knowledge of the assessment methods.

Selected Response

For example, we can use selected response exercises to determine if students can reason well. We can use them to see if students who have read a story can analyze its elements, compare them, or draw inferences or conclusions. Consider the following examples of questions from a reading test:

- *Analytical reasoning*—Which of the following sequences of plot elements properly depicts the order of events in the story we read today? (Offer alternative orderings, only one of which is correct.)
- *Comparative reasoning*—What is one essential difference between the story we read today and the one we read yesterday? (Offer alternative differences, only one of which is correct.)
- *Drawing conclusions*—If you had to choose a theme from among those listed for the story we read today, which would be best? (Offer response options, one of which is best.)

Assuming that these are novel questions posed immediately after reading the story, so students had no opportunity to memorize the answers, they ask students to dip into their knowledge base (about the story) and use it to reason. Students who see themselves becoming increasingly proficient at responding to questions like these become increasingly confident readers. This can be powerful.

I continue to be surprised by how many educators believe that selected response exercises can test only recall of content knowledge. While multiple-choice formats certainly can do this very well, they also can tap important reasoning proficiencies.

There are limits, however. *Evaluative reasoning*—the ability to express and defend a judgment, opinion, or point of view—cannot be tested using multiple-choice or true/false items because this kind of reasoning requires at least a presentation of the defense. Answers are not merely right or wrong—they vary in quality. Essay, performance assessment, or personal communication are needed to present that defense.

In a similar sense, problems that are multifaceted and complex, involving several steps, the application of several different patterns of reasoning, and/or several problem solvers working together, as real-world problems often do, demand more complex assessment methods.

But, nevertheless, for some relatively simple, straightforward patterns of reasoning, such as analysis, comparison, classification, and the like, selected response can work. Be advised also that we can provide students with sharply focused practice in mastering valued patterns of reasoning by having them practice writing sample test items that require them to properly reason out the answer. This is assessment *for* learning in action.

Essay

This represents an excellent way to assess student reasoning and problem solving. Student writing provides an ideal window into student thinking. Teachers can devise highly challenging exercises that ask students to analyze, compare, draw complex inferences, evaluate, or use some combination of these proficiencies, depicting their reasoning in written form.

Of course, the key to evaluating the quality of student responses to such exercises is for the assessor to understand the pattern of reasoning required and be able to detect its presence in student writing. This calls for exercises that really do ask students to reason through an issue or figure something out, not just regurgitate something that they learned earlier. And these exercises must be accompanied by clear and appropriate scoring criteria that reflect sound reasoning, not just content mastery.

Very often, we can help our students become confident masters of various patterns of reasoning by providing them with the opportunity to assess their own reasoning and problem solving during learning. In this assessment *for* learning context, we might, for example, engage them as partners in creating student-friendly versions of scoring criteria for evaluating the quality of their analytical reasoning.

Performance Assessment

Once again, here we have an excellent option that is applicable across all grade levels. We can watch students in the act of problem solving in a science lab, for example, and draw inferences about their proficiency. To the extent that they carry out proper procedures or find solutions when stymied, they reveal their ability to carry out a pattern of reasoning. When we watch students work with math manipulatives to demonstrate a problem solution or figure out how to manipulate computer software to accomplish something that they haven't done before, we can literally see their reasoning unfolding in their actions.

However, again, drawing conclusions about reasoning proficiency on the basis of the quality of student products can be risky. If performance is weak, did the student fail to perform because of a lack of basic knowledge, failure to reason productively, or lack of motivation? As previously stated, without followup assessment by other means, we just don't know. If we don't follow up with supplemental assessment, and thereby infer the wrong cause of failure, at the very least our remedy is likely to be inefficient. We may waste valuable time reteaching material already mastered or teaching reasoning skills already developed.

Personal Communication

One of the strongest matches between target and assessment method in Table 3.1 is the use of personal communication to evaluate student reasoning. Teachers can do any or all of the following:

- Ask questions that probe the clarity, accuracy, relevance, depth, and breadth of reasoning.
- Have students ask each other questions and listen for evidence of sound reasoning.
- Have students reason out loud, describing their thinking as they confront a problem.
- Have students recount their reasoning processes.
- Ask students to evaluate each other's reasoning.
- Simply listen attentively during class discussions for evidence of sound, appropriate reasoning.

Just talking informally with students can reveal so much, when we know what we're looking for! However, with this method, it will always take time to carry out the assessment and to keep accurate records of results.

Assessing Mastery of Performance Skills

When our assessment goal is to find out if students can demonstrate performance skills, such as play a role in a dramatic performance, fluently speak in a second language, effectively give a formal speech, or interact with classmates in socially acceptable ways, then there is only one way to assess. We must observe them while they are exhibiting the desired behaviors and make judgments as to their quality. This calls for performance assessment. There is no other choice. Each of the other options falls short for this kind of target.

But sometimes limited resources make it impossible to assess the actual skill. At those times, we may need to go for second best and come as close to the real target as we can. We have several options when we need to trade high fidelity for greater efficiency in skills assessment. We can use selected response test items to determine whether students can recognize high-level achievement. For example, given a number of performance demonstrations (on video, perhaps), can respondents identify the best? Or, we may use a multiple-choice format to see if students know the proper sequence of activities to carry out when that is relevant to the outcome. Given several descriptions of a procedure, can respondents identify the correct one? We can also use this method to ask if students have mastered the vocabulary needed to communicate about desired skills.

Realize, however, that such tests assess only prerequisite knowledge underpinning effective performance—important building blocks to competence, to be sure. But they will not assess examinees' actual levels of skill in performing.

With this same limitation, we could have students write essays about the criteria they might use to evaluate performance in a vocal music competition, knowledge that might well represent an important foundation for performing well in such a competition. But, of course, this will fall short of a real test of performance. Only performance assessment will suffice.

Finally, personal communication represents an excellent means of skills assessment when the skills in question have to do with oral communication proficiency, such as speaking a foreign language. For such an outcome, this is the highest-fidelity assessment option. For other kinds of performance skills, however, personal communication falls short of providing direct data on students' abilities.

Assessing Proficiency at Creating Products

The same limitations discussed for performance skills assessment apply here. If our assessment goal is to determine whether students can create a certain kind of achievement-related product, there is no other way to assess than to have them actually create one. In fact, performance assessment represents the *only* means of *direct* assessment. The best test of the ability to throw a ceramic pot is the quality of the finished pot. The best test of the ability to set up a scientific apparatus is the completed arrangement. The best test of the ability to write a term paper is the finished paper.

Again, we could use selected response assessment to see if students can pick out a quality product from among several choices. Or, we could test knowledge of a quality product's key attributes. But these are limited substitutes for assessment that actually asks students to create the product.

It is also possible to have students answer questions, write brief essays, or just discuss informally the key attributes of a carefully crafted object, such as a cabinet in shop class (personal communication). In this way, we can be sure they start with the key understandings they need—a necessary, but not sufficient, condition for success. Then students won't waste valuable time working on projects they are not prepared to succeed on.

But ultimately the real issue is whether students can create a carefully crafted cabinet. When that is the question, product-based performance assessment is the method of choice.

When we wish to assess writing proficiency by judging the quality of students' written products, we have two methodological choices. One is to have them write brief essays. The other is to have them produce much longer performance assessment products, such as term or research papers. Both are acceptable when accompanied by high-quality scoring criteria reflecting attributes of good writing.

Assessing Dispositions

Let's take a minute to review some of the student characteristics that fall under this heading. Affective dimensions of individuals that might be the object of classroom assessment include attitudes, values, interests, self-concept, and motivation. Remember, as stated earlier, the focus of assessment in this case is to determine the direction and intensity of student feelings about different school-related issues. When it comes to dispositions, we typically seek strong positive affect: positive attitudes about school, subjects, classmates, and so on; strong values about hard work; a strong positive academic self-concept; and strong positive motivation or seriousness of purpose. But negative attitudes—about drugs, for example—are important, too.

The key to success in assessing these things, as usual, is a clear and appropriate definition of the characteristic to be assessed. Given a clear understanding, could we translate such targets into selected response questions? You bet! But our collection of such items won't be a test per se, it would more properly be considered a *questionnaire.*

Selected Response Questionnaire

Many selected response formats are very useful for such highly structured questionnaires. For instance, we could offer students statements and ask if they agree, disagree, or are undecided. Or, we could ask them to select from among a list of adjectives those that most accurately apply to themselves or to some other object. This assessment realm is rich with useful options.

Written Response Questionnaire

Essay questions are another viable option for tapping dispositions. We can write open-ended questionnaire items that ask students to describe both the direction and intensity of their feelings about any particular object. After more than 20 years of in-school and in-classroom research on classroom assessment practices, one of the most startling realizations for me has been how rarely teachers use questionnaires to gather affective information from their students, information that could make everyone's job much easier. In fact, the act of seeking student opinion can yield its own very positive impact on student dispositions. They may be honored to know that you care what they feel about aspects of the classroom.

Performance Observations

The match between dispositions and performance assessment is a bit more complex, however, because of the nature of the inferences we must draw. In this case, I urge caution. It certainly is possible to look at samples of student performance or at student-created products and draw conclusions about attitudes, values, and motivational dispositions with respect to that particular project. If students demonstrate high levels of achievement, their attitude was probably strongly positive, they probably valued the project and their work, and they probably were disposed to work hard to perform well. Just remember, such inferences on your part can be wrong. There is also some chance that such students are just coping well with a frustrating academic challenge, are angry about the project, in fact, and just don't want you to know it.

Care must be exercised at the low end of the performance continuum, too. When performance is poor, there are many possible explanations, only one of which is a poor attitude and lack of motivation. Only additional followup assessment will reveal the real reason for failure to perform.

Personal Communication

One excellent way to conduct such a follow up is direct personal communication with students. In the right atmosphere, students will talk openly and honestly about the strength and direction of their dispositions. The keys to success, of course, are to be able to establish that open, trusting environment and to know what kinds of questions to ask to tap important affect.

Time for Reflection

To review, please create your own version of the matrix crossing achievement targets with assessment methods (Table 3.1). Fill in the cells that describe the matches and mismatches in your own words. These connections are critical to your success as a classroom assessor.

Assessment *for* Learning

If our goal in classroom assessment is to gather valid and reliable evidence of student achievement, then we must know why we are assessing, we must clearly define the achievement targets we wish to assess, and we must be sure we select an assessment method capable of reflecting the valued achievement. Different assessment contexts (purposes and targets) afford us opportunities to use different assessment methods. Valid assessments rely on proper methods—methods capable of tapping the learning in question.

Once we select an assessment method, we need to use that method in a manner calculated to present us with an accurate portrait of achievement. This means two things. First, we must assemble enough of the right kinds of high-quality exercises (test items, if you will) to representatively sample student performance. We need enough evidence to lead us to a confident conclusion about each student's achievement without wasting time gathering too much. This is how we devise assessments that produce consistent results—reliable results.

Further, we must understand that each method carries with it a list of things that can go wrong—that can yield misleading information about student achievement. As it turns out, distortions in assessment results can creep in from many sources, including the assessment itself, the evaluator, the students, and the test administration environment. Part of assessment literacy is understanding those potential sources of bias and knowing what to do by way of assessment development and implementation to prevent such problems. In Part 2, I discuss how to sample achievement appropriately with high-quality exercises and how to avoid bias so as to maximize assessment accuracy.

However, before we turn to that, as you know, the basic premise of this book is that we can involve students actively in classroom assessment and derive great motivational and learning benefits for them. Here are more suggestions for how you can assess *for* learning:

- Develop a pretest version of a multiple-choice final exam, have students take it early in the unit of study, and help them analyze their results by item focus—knowledge or reasoning—so they can see their own strengths and weaknesses from the beginning of the learning.
- Have students work in teams to draft practice essay exercises. Then have teams trade exercises and develop scoring criteria for each other's exercises. This can go even further, if you want. Have students try to respond to each other's exercises and practice applying the scoring criteria. Then engage everyone in a discussion of the experience.
- How about providing students with a sample of your writing—a piece that you have not finished yet—so they can give you some feedback? Then revise your work based on their feedback and show them their impact on your work.
- Have your students themselves create their own performance assessment exercises that tap performance skill and product targets that you establish as important for them to master. In addition, have them develop scoring guides for evaluating their own performance.

Sprinkled throughout the remaining chapters are suggestions of ways to involve students to unlock for them the secrets of their own academic success. All four assessment formats welcome student involvement during learning.

Summary: A Vision of Excellence in Classroom Assessment

In this chapter, we made some crucial connections: we connected the *why, what* and *how* of assessment into one unified picture. Sound classroom assessments arise from a clear sense of purpose, clear and appropriate targets, and reliance on a proper assessment method. A proper method is one that provides the most direct view of student performance, permitting the strongest inferences from the assessment results to the actual status of the achievement target.

We have established four assessment methods: selected response tests, essay exercises, performance assessments, and direct personal communication with students. We discussed how we might use them selectively to tap student achievement on a range of kinds of

achievement. Given the range of our valued achievement targets, we will need to apply all of the assessment tools we have at our disposal—no single method can serve all of our assessment needs at all grade levels. We must learn to use all available methods. If we do, the results will be better information about student success gathered in less time.

Therefore, selecting a proper assessment method becomes our third criterion, and thus the third entry in our set of comprehensive rubrics for evaluating classroom assessment quality (see the Appendix). Assessments are ready to go when the method matches the target. They still need work when there is an obvious mismatch.

In the chapters that follow, we provide the instruction and practice needed to become assessment literate. We'll address the sampling and quality-control guidelines needed to use each assessment method well. We also will explore using student-involved assessment as a motivational and teaching tool.

Final Chapter Reflection

1. *What are the three most important new insights to come to you as a result of your study of this chapter?*
2. *Which of your previous questions about assessment can you now answer based on your study of this chapter?*
3. *What new questions have come to mind as a result of your study of this chapter that you hope to have answered as your study continues?*

Practicing with Chapter 3 Ideas

1. If your supervisor's objective is to evaluate your teaching proficiency, what assessment method(s) should be employed and why? (Be careful here! Pause to reflect on the active ingredients of good teaching before answering.)

2. When you took your driver's test, what achievement targets were covered and why? What assessment methods did they use and why?

3. What assessment method did Ms. Weathersby use to determine Emily's writing proficiency and that of her classmates and why?

4. Create a blank version of Table 3.1. In each cell of the table, insert an example of an achievement target from a subject you will teach that might be assessed with that method. For primary-grade teachers (before students have reading or writing proficiencies), fill in only the performance assessment and personal communication columns.

PART II

Understanding Assessment Methods

The fabric of your classroom assessment environment must be woven from four basic assessment methods: selected response, essay, performance assessment, and personal communication. Each is the focus of its own chapter in Part 2. Your challenge is to use these methods to create a continuously evolving portrait of each student's achievement, keeping your students in touch with and feeling in control of their own growth, and encouraging them to continue to believe in themselves as learners.

Chapter 4 describes selected response methods of assessment: multiple choice, true/false, matching, and short answer fill-in. Their power lies in their great efficiency.

Chapter 5 offers guidance in developing and using essay assessments. In this case, students construct brief written responses to questions, which you then read and score.

Chapter 6 explores the basics of currently popular performance assessment methods, based on teacher observation and professional judgment. This option offers a variety of ways to evaluate students' performance skills and the products they create.

Chapter 7 details a set of assessment options not normally thought of as part of classroom assessment: direct personal interaction or personal communication with students. Teachers can and often do learn a great deal about achievement by talking to their students. We will explore how to do this well.

None of these assessment methods is inherently superior to the others. Each is capable of providing vivid insights into student learning in certain contexts, when in the hands of a competent user. At the same time, however, each also can be done poorly. An assessment-literate classroom teacher knows the difference and is committed to carrying out sound assessment practices.

In Chapter 8, we turn to assessment methods used to help us determine student dispositions. Sometimes it is useful to explore student attitudes, values, interests, and motivations in order to support achievement. When this is the goal, then questionnaires, interviews and careful observations become useful.

Remember as you study Part 2 that you can apply the tactics and strategies presented both when you develop and refine your own assessments and when you evaluate assessments developed by others. Never trust that a test is of good quality merely because it is published along with a good textbook. Always check for and verify quality. These chapters will help you do this.

As you study each chapter, keep our big picture in mind as reflected in the accompanying illustration. In Part 1, we addressed the need to be clear about each user's information needs, to identify clear and appropriate achievement targets, and to select a proper assessment method for each context: In Part 2, we move to the next set of quality control issues, as shaded below: How much evidence of learning do I need to gather? How can I ensure that bias doesn't sneak into my assessment, distorting results? The chapters of Part 2 answer these questions for each assessment method.

Keys to Effective Classroom Assessment

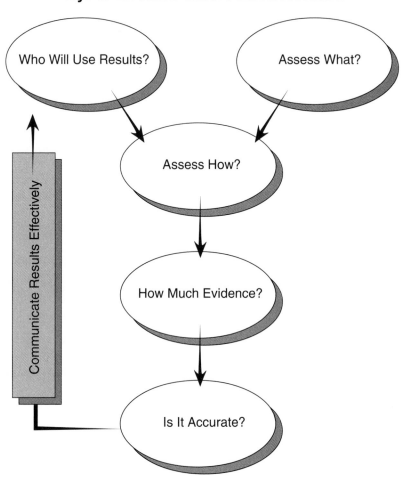

Chapter 4

Selected Response Assessment

CHAPTER FOCUS

This chapter answers the following guiding question:

> When and how do I use selected response methods of assessment most effectively?

From your study of this chapter, you will understand the following:

1. Selected response assessments align well with knowledge and understanding targets, as well as with some patterns of reasoning.
2. We can efficiently develop these assessments in three steps: blueprinting, focusing, and item writing.
3. This method can fall prey to avoidable sources of bias that can distort results if users are not careful.
4. By involving our students in developing and using selected response assessments, we can set them up for confident, energetic, and successful learning.

As you study this chapter, keep our big picture in mind. Figure 4.1 crosses the various kinds of achievement targets with the four methods of assessment. In this chapter, we will be dealing in depth with the shaded areas.

The Most Traditional Assessment Methods

Consider multiple-choice, true/false, matching, and fill-in tests. These represent what many people think of as the "real" tests—the kind we've all come to know and love or hate depending on our personal experiences as we were growing up. Have you ever noticed how many people contend that they were never "good test takers" in school? These usually are the kinds of tests to which they refer.

Nevertheless, these remain very powerful assessment *for* learning tools when put into operation by thoughtful users who understand how to sample student

	SELECTED RESPONSE	ESSAY	PERFORMANCE ASSESSMENT	PERSONAL COMMUNICATION
Know				
Reason				
Performance Skills				
Products				
Dispositions				

Figure 4.1
Aligning achievement targets and assessment methods

achievement efficiently by means of test items and how to control for those bedeviling sources of bias that can creep into these assessments.

Know When to Use Selected Response Formats

It is appropriate to consider using selected response formats in a written form only when you are absolutely certain students have a sufficiently high level of reading proficiency to be able to understand the test items. With selected response formats, students' mastery of the material being assessed is always confounded with their ability to read. Therefore, this is not an appropriate method, for example, for primary-grade nonreaders. If you are administering a selected response test of knowledge mastery or reasoning proficiency to poor readers, nonreaders, or students who are still learning English, you must help them overcome their reading difficulty by reading the questions to them. It is only through such adjustments that you can disentangle content mastery from reading proficiency and obtain an accurate estimate of achievement of the knowledge and reasoning in question.

Obviously, however, if you are conducting an assessment of reading proficiency per se, such a remedy would be inappropriate. In this case, if students can't read, a valid and reliable assessment will, indeed must, reflect that fact.

From a different perspective, it is possible to use a selected response format in primary grades when you, the teacher, read the question and provide students with pictorial response options, one of which is the correct or best. For example, you might pose the following questions:

Which of these pictures shows what this story is about?
Which set of pictures tells the story in the right order?

It is particularly appropriate to use selected response assessments when you need efficiency. Once developed, you can administer them to large numbers of students at the same time and score them very quickly.

These days, it is common for schools to have access to computer support for this kind of assessment that includes software that can assist teachers with banks of previously written items, test printing, and optical scan scoring. Any teacher who is using selected response assessments and is scoring by hand is wasting valuable time. Optical scan scoring technology can do it faster and more accurately.

The Myth of Objectivity

I have chosen the label *selected response assessment* rather than the more traditional label *objective test* because the latter connotes an absence of subjectivity in development or use. Almost from the time of their first appearance on the educational scene in the 1920s, selected response assessments have carried an air of objectivity or scientific precision—an apparent freedom from the fallibility of human judgment—that belies the underlying reality. In truth, subjectivity—that is, matters of teacher/assessor judgment—permeate all facets of selected response assessment. In fact, whenever we use selected response assessments, if we are not careful, there is the danger that subjectivity can render the assessment undependable and place students directly in harm's way. You need to understand how to prevent such occurrences, and please be advised that we know how to do so. But it requires attention to detail.

All assessments are made up of the following:

- Exercises designed to elicit some response from students
- An evaluation scheme that allows the user to interpret the quality of that response

Let's be very clear about the fact that the renowned "objectivity" in selected response assessment applies *only* to the scoring system. It has nothing to do with the exercise side of the equation.

Well-written multiple-choice test items, for example, allow for just one best answer or a limited set of acceptable answers. This leads to the "objective" scoring of responses. No judgment required. Students' answers are either right or wrong.

However, developing exercises that form the basis of this kind of test involves a major helping of the test author's subjective professional judgment. The developer decides what learnings to transform into exercises, how many questions to pose on a test, how to word each question, what the best or correct answers will be, and which incorrect answers to offer as choices, if needed.

All assessments, regardless of method, arise from the assessor's professional judgment. So we will address this matter again in each of the following chapters. All assessments reflect the assessor's biases or perspectives. The key to your effective use of sound classroom assessment as a part of instruction is to make sure that your perspectives or instructional priorities are clear and public for your students from the outset. This way, they have a chance to see and understand what it means to be successful.

Matching Method to Targets

In Chapter 3, we touched on strategies for aligning the various assessment methods with the different kinds of achievement targets. Let's continue that discussion now by examining the kinds of targets that we can effectively translate into selected response formats. Select the best answer for the following question:

Which of the following test item formats can be used to assess both students' mastery of content knowledge and their abilities to use that knowledge to reason and solve problems?
1. Multiple choice
2. True/false
3. Matching
4. Short answer fill-in
5. All of the above

The best answer is *5,* all of the above. All four formats can tap both knowledge mastery and reasoning, two of the four basic kinds of achievement targets discussed in earlier chapters.

Assessing Knowledge Mastery

We can use selected response test items to assess student mastery of subject matter knowledge. But remember from Chapter 3, students can know things but not understand them. If we wish to assess understanding, we need to weave it into test items. Shepard (1997) provides us with a classic illustration.* When students were presented with the following problem, 86 percent of them answered it correctly:

$$\begin{array}{r} 4 \\ \times 3 \\ \hline \end{array}$$
   A. 9
   B. 12
   C. 15
   D. 18

---

*From *Measuring Achievement: What Does It Mean to Test for Robust Understanding?* (n.p.) by L. A. Shepard, 1997. Princeton, NJ: Educational Testing Service. Copyright 1997 by ETS Policy Information Center. Reprinted by permission of Educational Testing Service.

But when confronted with the same problem in a manner that requires conceptual understanding the results were quite different. Here's an example:

Which choice goes with:

X	X	X	X
X	X	X	X
X	X	X	X

A. $3 \times 4 =$
B. $3 + 4 =$
C. $3 \times 12 =$

This time, only 55 percent of those same students were able to answer correctly. For many, rote learning of the answer (first problem) did not result in conceptual understanding of the mathematics involved (second problem).

If we expect students to know and understand, we must teach for and assess knowing and understanding. Selected response assessment formats can help us with this.

Assessing Reasoning

When we ask students to dip into their knowledge and understanding and to use what they know in novel ways to figure something out, we ask them to *reason*. To assess this well, at testing time we must present them with new test items that they have not seen before to see if they can reason their way through the problems we present. For example, we might ask students to demonstrate proficiency in figuring out one or more of the following:

- How things are alike or different (comparative reasoning)
- How something can be subdivided into its component parts or how the parts work together (analytical reasoning)
- The main idea or theme of a story just read (inductive inference)
- The insights that can be derived from a provided data chart (deductive inference)

In this case, our teaching challenges are to (1) make sure students have the opportunity to master the knowledge they need to solve such problems, and (2) provide them with lots of guided practice in applying specified patterns of reasoning. But at assessment time, we must leave them alone to see if they can combine the two successfully. In other words, assessments of reasoning proficiency must ask novel questions that require new applications of available knowledge. They cannot ask students merely to regurgitate solutions figured out previously and then memorized.

Skillful selected response test item writers can use multiple-choice, true/false, matching, and fill-in test items to tap the various other forms of student reasoning included in their curriculum. Examples of such questions appear in Figure 4.2. But again, to do so, these items must present students with novel problems.

Reasoning	Illustration
Analysis	Of the four laboratory apparatus setups illustrated below, which will permit the user to carry out a distillation? (Offer four diagrams, one of which is correct.)
Synthesis	If we combine what we know about the likely impact of strong differences in barometric pressure and in temperature, what weather prediction would you make from this map? (Accompany the exercise with a map and several predictions, one of which is most likely.)
Comparison	What is one important difference between igneous and sedimentary rocks? (Offer several differences, only one of which is correct.)
Classification	Given what you know about animal life of the arid, temperate, and arctic regions, if you found an animal with the following characteristics, in which region would you expect it to live? (Describe the case and offer regions as choices.)
Inference	From the evidence provided to you in the graph, if water temperature were to go up, what would happen to the oxygen content of that water? (Provide a graph depicting the relationship between the two and offer conclusions as choices.)

Figure 4.2
Sample selected response exercises that require reasoning

Assessing Performance Skills

We cannot use selected response test formats to assess student mastery of performance skills such as speaking, drama, physical education, interacting socially, tuning an automobile engine, and the like. But we can use them to assess mastery of at least some of the procedural knowledge and understanding prerequisite to being able to demonstrate such skills.

For instance, if we use a performance assessment to determine that students are unable to communicate effectively in a second language, we might follow up with another assessment method to see if they know the vocabulary. Or, if students are unable to adequately solve a math problem, we might diagnose why by assessing their mastery of prerequisite procedural knowledge. If students fail to carry out a science lab procedure correctly, we can use selected response formats to ask whether they understand the science knowledge to which the experiment relates or if they know and understand the steps in the lab process.

Assessing Products

Selected response exercises cannot help us determine if students can create quality products. They cannot tap proficiency in building a structurally sound model bridge, creating an authentic model of a native village, or producing an artistic creation that meets specified standards of quality. But they can test students' prerequisite knowledge of the attributes of a quality product. Students who don't know the attributes of a sound bridge are unlikely to be able to make the right kind of model. Students who cannot distinguish a quality product from an inferior one are unlikely to be able to produce quality. Selected response assessments can test these prerequisites.

Please understand that such fundamental knowledge is only a prerequisite to success. It is never sufficient merely to know and understand, but it is *always* essential.

Assessing Dispositions

In a different vein, we can develop questionnaire items to tap student attitudes, values, motivational dispositions, and other affective states, items that ask students to select from among a limited number of response options. Questions inquiring about preferred extracurricular activities, for example, might offer a series of choices. Attitude scales might offer a statement about a particular feeling, such as, "Our school meets my academic needs"; the responses might ask students if they agree, disagree, or are undecided. These formats can be excellent ways to tap both the direction and intensity of student feelings about important aspects of school or classroom life.

The remainder of this chapter deals only with the design of selected response assessments of student achievement. In Chapter 8, we will discuss in depth the assessment of dispositions.

Summary of Target Matches

While we certainly can't reach all of the achievement targets we value with selected response exercises, we can tap parts of many of them. We can test student mastery of content knowledge, including what they learn outright and what they learn to retrieve through effective use of reference materials. In addition, we can tap a variety of kinds of reasoning and problem solving, including analytical, comparative, and other kinds of inferential reasoning proficiencies. And we can get at some of the underpinnings of successful performance in more complex arenas, assessing knowledge of appropriate procedures, and/or understanding of the key attributes of quality products. Table 4.1 summarizes the Selected Response column of our comprehensive targets-by-methods chart.

The Steps in Assessment Development

Described in its simplest form, the selected response assessment is developed in three steps, each of which requires the application of special professional competence:

1. Develop an assessment plan or blueprint that identifies an appropriate sample of achievement.
2. Identify the specific elements of knowledge, understanding, and reasoning to be assessed.
3. Transform those elements into test items.

Table 4.1
Selected response: Assessment of achievement targets

Target to Be Assessed	Selected Response
Knowledge & Understanding	Multiple choice, true/false, matching, and fill-in can sample mastery of elements of knowledge
Reasoning Proficiency	Can assess application of some patterns of reasoning
Performance Skills	Can assess mastery of the knowledge prerequisite to skillful performance, but cannot rely on these to tap the skill itself
Ability to Create Products	Can assess mastery of the knowledge prerequisite to the ability to create quality products, but cannot assess the quality of products themselves
Dispositions	Selected response questionnaire items can tap student feelings

The steps of test planning and identifying elements to be assessed are the same for all four test item formats, so we will deal with those together. Then we will discuss how to write quality test items using each individual format.

Step 1: Preparing a Blueprint

Building a test without a plan is like building a house without a blueprint. Two things are going to happen and both are bad. Construction is going to take much longer than you want and the final product is not going to meet your standards. Plan well and the test will almost automatically develop itself. Fail to plan and you will struggle. In fact, the practice of test blueprinting will save you more time than any other single idea offered in this text.

Besides making test development easier and more efficient, test blueprinting offers an opportunity for teachers and students to clarify achievement expectations, to sharpen their vision of what it means to be successful. But to work well, as you will see, this kind of planning absolutely requires that the test developer understand both the underlying structure of the knowledge students are to master and the nuances of reasoning, if that is part of the focus of the assessment. Without this clarity and depth of vision, it will be impossible to develop sound assessments.

In the classroom, teachers have two types of test blueprints to choose from. One is called a *table of test specifications,* the other a list of *instructional objectives.* Choose whichever you like, both work. They are essentially equally effective as test planning devices, as you shall see.

Table of Specifications as a Blueprint
To explain how the table of test specifications works, we must first consider the individual assessment exercise or test question. Any question requires respondents to do two things: (1) gain access to a specific piece of information (either from memory or reference materials), and (2) use that knowledge to carry out a cognitive operation (i.e., to solve some kind of problem).

Table 4.2
Sample table of test specifications

Content	Know & Understand	Comparative Reasoning	Classification Reasoning	Total
Alternative Forms of Government	9 questions	5	1	15
Structure of U.S. Government	4	5	1	10
Rights and Responsibilities of Citizens	7	5	3	15
Total	20	15	5	40

For example, you might construct a test item based on knowledge of a piece of literature and ask respondents simply to demonstrate the ability to retrieve it from memory:

Who were the main characters in the story?

Or, you might ask respondents to recall two elements of content knowledge from literature and relate one to the other, as in this comparison item:

What is one similarity between two leading characters in this story?

In this case, respondents must dip into their reservoir of knowledge about the two characters (prerequisite knowledge), understand the various facets of each, and find elements that are similar (comparative reasoning). So it is in the case of all such test questions: Elements of knowledge are carried into some reasoning process.

The table of test specifications takes advantage of this combination of knowledge retrieval and its application to permit you to develop a plan that promises to sample both in a predetermined manner. Table 4.2 is a simple example of such a table. For our example, pretend that you are teaching a class in Government. In this table, we find your plan for a unit test. The test is to include 40 questions worth one point each. You choose this number because you feel (a) you need this many questions to adequately sample the knowledge and reasoning students need to master, and (b) your students can attempt all 40 in the available time.

On the left, you subdivide the content into three basic categories: Alternative Forms of Government, Structure of U.S. Government, and Rights and Responsibilities of Citizens. Each category contains many elements of knowledge within it, some of which you regard as sufficiently important to be tested—to transform into test items later. But for now, note in the last column that you have decided to include 15 questions covering knowledge of Forms, 10 on structure, and 15 on

Responsibilities. These numbers reflect your sense of the relative importance of these three categories of material.

Time for Reflection

Before reading on, think about how a teacher might establish sampling priorities. Why might some categories in a blueprint receive more questions than others? How have you set these priorities in the past, if you are now a classroom teacher? What important factors must a teacher consider in making these decisions?

The difference in the number of items assigned to each category might reflect any or all of the following:

- Amount of instructional time spent on each
- Amount of material in each category
- Relative importance of material in each category for later learning
- Important relationships among various ideas

This is an important part of the art of classroom assessment: As a teacher, your special insights about the nature and capabilities of your students and the nature and amount of material you want them to master must guide you in setting these priorities. Given this particular body of material, as a teacher/test developer, you must ask, What should be my areas of greatest emphasis now if I am to prepare students for important concepts and general principles they will confront later in their education?

Now let's continue with your table of specifications. Notice the columns in Table 4.2. Three patterns of reasoning appear, representing three different kinds of cognitive actions required of respondents: demonstrate understanding of the content, reason comparatively using elements of content, and use knowledge and reason to classify elements of content. As with the content categories, these are patterns you have emphasized during this unit of study. It might be that they are patterns that you have decided are sufficiently important to be covered across all or several units or just for this one, because they bond well with the content to be learned. In any event, your target priorities are reflected at the bottom of each column: 20 understanding items, 15 comparison items, and 5 items requiring classification.

Remember, if the test and your instruction are to align well—that is, if the test is to reflect the results of instruction accurately and fairly—then students need to have been provided with opportunities to (1) master the essential content and (2) practice with the valued patterns of reasoning. This is the kind of instruction that sets them up for success.

Once you have defined categories and specified row and column totals (which does not take long when *you* understand the material), you need only spread the numbers of questions into the cells of the table so that they add up to the row and column totals. This will generate a plan to guide you in writing a set of test questions that will systematically sample both content and reasoning priorities as established.

How do you decide how many and what rows and columns to include in a table of test specifications? There are no rigid rules. You can include as many rows and columns as make sense for your particular unit and test. This aspect of test development is as much art as science. You should consider the following factors with respect to blueprint categories for content:

1. In Chapter 2, we discussed how to deconstruct state standards into the classroom-level achievement targets that set students up for success on state assessments. Those standards should go a long way toward identifying the knowledge and reasoning foundations of student success in your state and, therefore, in your classroom.
2. Look for natural subdivisions in the material presented in a text, such as chapters or major sections within chapters. These are likely to reflect natural subdivisions of material generally accepted by experts in the field. Each chapter or section might become a row in your table of specifications.
3. Use subdivisions of content that are likely to make sense to students as a result of their studies. Ultimately, you want them to see the vision, too.

The patterns of reasoning (columns) in your test blueprint should have the following characteristics:

1. Patterns should have clear labels and underlying meanings, both for you and your students.
2. Again, patterns taught and learned should relate to those specified in state and local achievement standards.
3. Categories should be so familiar and comfortable to you that you can almost automatically pose questions that demand student thinking in those terms.
4. Each category should represent kinds of reasoning and problem solving that occur in the real world.
5. All categories should translate into student-friendly terms, including description and examples.

Published text materials may supply the content categories for you, but you probably will have to establish the patterns of reasoning. The bottom line is this: The categories of content, kinds of reasoning tested, and proportion of items assigned to each should reflect the target priorities communicated to students from the very beginning. *Students can hit any target they can see and that holds still for them!* Do not leave them guessing.

Instructional Objectives as Plans for Assessment

You also may build your assessment from a list of instructional objectives. To accomplish this, understand that objectives, like each cell in your table of specifications, specify the knowledge students must bring to bear and the action they must take (recall it, analyze it, compare it, and so on). Following are examples of such objectives:

> *Students will be able to compare and contrast different forms of government.*
> *Students will understand a citizen's voting rights and responsibilities.*

Note that you need not write each objective so as to define targets at a high level of specific detail. Rather, like cells in a table of specifications, they can set frames around categories that contain many possible test items within them. Sound objectives answer the question, What knowledge must respondents use to perform what cognitive activity? Later, you can prepare test items that ask students to retrieve required knowledge and use it to figure out the right answer.

Blueprints Really Help

The limits you place on content and reasoning by devising tables of specifications or lists of instructional objectives are very important for three reasons. First and foremost, they define success for students, giving them more control over their own fate. So be sure to share your expectations with them. Turn the spotlight on your expectations so all can see them.

Second, clearly written expectations in the form of tables of test specifications and lists of objectives set limits on your accountability for your students' learning. With thoughtful plans in place, you are no longer responsible for seeing to it that every student knows every single fact about the subject. Rather, students need to know and understand specific parts and know how to reason using that information. When your students can hit such a complex target, you are a supreme success as a teacher, and there can be no question about it.

Third, once your overall plan is assembled, it becomes possible for you to develop more than one form of the same test. This can be very useful when you need to protect test security, such as when you need another form for students who were absent or who must retake the test for some reason. You can develop two tests (or more, if you like) made up of different items that you know sample the same content and reasoning patterns. This means that you provide all students with the same chance of success regardless of when they take the test.

Think Assessment *for* Learning

Remember how Ms. Weathersby involved Emily and her classmates in the process of figuring out the important attributes of good writing? Then she involved them in learning to build those attributes into their own work. She revealed her definition of success at the outset and then provided an environment that entitled them to master that vision.

That same kind of thinking can play out with selected response modes of assessment. What if a teacher develops the table of test specifications for a unit final exam before she begins teaching the unit? And what if she provides a copy of the test plan to every student on *day one* of the unit? This establishes a contract between teacher and student saying that, our collective goal is to maximize your performance down the road on an assessment of these priorities. Let's go to work. No surprises, no excuses.

Time for Reflection

Let's say you have developed a table of test specifications and two forms of your test. You need to keep one secure for administration as your final exam. This leaves you a "spare test" to use as you see fit to maximize student learning. How might you involve your students during instruction in productive ways with that table of specs and the "spare" assessment?

Summary of Step 1
The first step in selected response assessment development is to formulate a plan or blueprint. Sound plans can be developed only when you yourself have attained complete mastery of the material (knowledge and reasoning) that you expect your students to master. Given that foundation, you can either (1) design a table of test specifications, or (2) prepare a list of instructional objectives. Any cell of the table or any objective will represent the union of two essential elements: some content knowledge students must retrieve via memory or reference and some cognitive act they must carry out using that material. These plans permit you to reveal the meaning of success to your students, giving them a visible target to shoot for.

Step 2: Selecting Material to Assess

After developing your table of specifications or list of objectives, you must select the specific and individual elements of knowledge and reasoning around which you will create test items. In Table 4.2, the cell crossing Alternative Forms of Government with Know & Understand requires the construction of nine test questions. Your next key test development question is, Can these nine questions test any facts or concepts that I wish? How do I decide which of the huge number of facts, concepts, and general principles about alternative forms of government to include in the assessment?

There are two factors to consider in answering such a question: (1) coverage of the full range of material in the unit, and (2) the relative importance of the elements within. Let me explain how these come into play.

Coverage of Material
As previously stated, any set of assessment exercises really only represents a sample of all of the questions you could ask if the assessment were infinitely long. Clearly, if you were to test student mastery of every aspect of government, we'd be talking about an impossibly long test! The most efficient way to prevent this problem (and to create tests that fit into reasonable time limits) is to include questions that cover as much of the *important* material as time will permit. Then infer that each student's score on the sample also reflects level of mastery of the entire domain of knowledge and understanding sampled. A student who answers 80 percent of the questions on the assessment correctly probably has mastered about 80 percent of the material in the entire domain sampled.

To understand this, think about commonly used polling techniques. Pollsters cannot afford to ask every citizen's opinion. So they select a sample of voters, ask them to express their opinions, and then estimate from this carefully selected sample how the general population probably feels on key issues.

In test development, we do exactly the same thing with assessment questions. If we thoughtfully sample larger bodies of content and reasoning, then the percentage of questions students answer correctly on the test will let us estimate the proportion of the larger body of knowledge that they have mastered.

But precisely what portion of the larger domain do we sample on our test? Can we pick just any set of facts, test them, and then generalize? The answer is No. Here is another place where classroom assessment becomes an art. We must select a sample (a subset) of all possible *important elements* of knowledge and understanding.

Who decides what is important, and how do they do it? If you are to develop the assessment, you do! If the textbook publisher developed the test and you are considering using it, you must establish your classroom achievement standards and must evaluate the text-embedded test to see if it accurately represents them. If the book covers more than students can master during your time with them, you must select from among the array of possibilities what to emphasize. This is yet another reason why you must have immersed yourself in your subject(s), so you know what is important.

But there are other places to turn to for advice in determining which material is important. For example, the textbook's author will highlight and emphasize the most important material in lists of objectives and chapter summaries, as will any accompanying teacher's guides. In addition, state, district, building, and/or department curriculum guidelines typically spell out priorities at some level. Sometimes, just taking time to talk with colleagues about instructional priorities can help.

Other valuable sources of guidance in articulating valued knowledge and reasoning targets are the various national and state professional associations of teachers, such as science, mathematics, English, and so on. Nearly every such association has assembled a commission within the recent past to identify and publish standards of excellence for student achievement in their domain. You should be familiar with any national standards of student performance held as valuable by teachers in your field.

But even with all of this help, in the end, you must decide what is important to test within each cell of your table of specifications or within each instructional objective you specify in your classroom. And so it is that, even though you might use an "objective test" format, the material tested is very much a matter of your professional judgment.

Please understand that this subjectivity is not a problem as long as you (1) are a master of the achievement targets that make up the school subject(s) you teach, (2) specify your valued achievement targets carefully, and (3) communicate them to your students. No one can do this work for you. You must possess the vision, and it must be a sound and appropriate one, given the students you teach and the latest thinking about the disciplines you teach and assess.

Identifying Important Elements

In this section, I offer a practical and efficient means of transforming your vision, whether expressed in a table of specifications or a list of objectives, into quality test questions. Here is another strategy that promises to save you immense amounts of test development time while improving the quality of your tests.

 Capture the elements you wish to test in the form of clearly stated sentences that reflect important elements of content and stipulate the kind of cognitive operation respondents must carry out. In the test development field, such statements are called *propositions*. As you shall see, propositions save you time in assessment development.

But before I illustrate them, I need to ask you to accept something on faith now, which I will verify for you later through example: When you have identified and listed all of the propositions that form the basis of your test, that test is 95 percent developed! While the work remaining is not trivial, I promise you that it will go so fast it will make your head spin. If you invest your time up front in identifying those things students should know and be able to do, the rest of your test development will be almost automatic.

To collect these propositions, or basic units of test items, begin by reviewing the material you will sample on the test, keeping your table of specifications or instructional objectives close at hand.

Refer to Table 4.2 once again. You need a total of 20 Knowledge & Understanding test items (bottom of column 1). Nine of these must arise from content related to Alternative Forms of Government. So as you review this material, you seek out and write down, say, 15 to 20 statements that capture important facts, concepts, or enduring understandings about Alternative Forms of Government that you think every student should know and understand. I recommend collecting about twice as many propositions as you will need to fill your final quota of test items. That way, if you need to replace some later or if you want to develop two parallel forms of the same test, you have your active ingredients (that is, additional propositions) ready to go. Remember, those collected must reflect the most important material. As you collect propositions, use clearly stated sentences like these:

> *Three common forms of government are monarchies, dictatorships, and democracies.*
>
> *In democracies, the power to govern is secured by vote of the people.*

And by the way, item writing is easier when you state propositions in your own words. That process forces you to understand what it is you are going for in the questions. Don't lift them verbatim from the text.

Likewise, your table of specifications calls for four questions in the Know and Understand/Structure of U.S. Government cell. Here are two sample propositions:

> *The three branches of U.S. government are legislative, judicial, and executive.*
>
> *Under the system of checks and balances, the executive branch balances the legislative branch through its ability to veto legislation.*

Once you have written your propositions for the cell of the first column of Table 4.2, move on to the next column, this time crossing the content categories with Comparative Reasoning. Note from the blueprint that you need 5 of these in each cell, for a total of 15. Given this expectation, try to identify and state 10 important propositions for each cell. Here's an example from the row on Structure of U.S. Government:

> *A difference between the U.S. Senate and House of Representatives is the term of office.*

And so you proceed through all nine cells of the table, seeking out and writing down more propositions than you will need. In effect, you are creating a list of elements of the material that it is important for students to learn. Note that you have not yet attempted to write any test questions.

Remember our general sampling goal: For any given body of material, we must collect enough test propositions to confidently generalize from students' perform-ance on the sample (score on the test) to their proportional mastery of the whole. We know we can't ask everything. But we need to be sure to ask enough. It's a mat-ter of judgment and, as the test creator, you are the judge.

A Note on Propositions Focused on Student Reasoning

When you wish to assess your students' ability to use their knowledge to figure things out—that is, to *reason*—your challenge is to state propositions reflecting im-portant learning that you may not have explicitly covered in class. That is, they may represent the kinds of comparative inferences you want them to be able to draw us-ing their own knowledge of government and their understanding of comparison—they apply the concepts of similarity and difference. To test their ability to reason on their feet, then, you must present cognitive challenges at assessment time that de-mand more than mastery of fundamental knowledge.

To reach this goal, a very special relationship must exist between the questions that appear on the test and your preceding instruction: The item must present a problem for which students (1) have had the opportunity to master appropriate prerequisite knowl-edge but (2) have not had the opportunity to use it to solve this particular problem. The assessment exercise challenges them to reason it out right there on the spot.

Certainly, students must dip into their reservoir of available knowledge. That is, they must retrieve the requisite information if they are to reason productively. But the aim of these propositions is to convey more than retrieval from memory, when the goal of instruction is more than just knowing. If you want students to make the leap, for example, from just knowing something to analyzing or comparing (that is, to reasoning), you must write propositions representing inferences you expect them to make. It is not acceptable for them to have solved the problem before and mem-orized the answer for later regurgitation. You want them to be able to use their knowledge to figure things out at assessment time. Otherwise, you have not assessed their reasoning powers.

Completing Step 2

Once you have completed your collection of propositions tapping critically impor-tant learnings to be assessed—remember, you have been writing twice as many as you need—you must make the final cut. At this time, it is wise to step back from this list of propositions, review them one more time, and ask yourself, Do these really provide a composite picture of what I think are the important knowledge and rea-soning targets of this unit? If you really know and understand the material and know how it relates to what students will confront in the future, weak propositions will jump out at you. If you find weak entries, remove them. When the list meets your highest standards of coverage, you are ready to select the specific number needed to actually fill the cells of the table.

Just remember to keep those that do not make the final cut. They will come in very handy during instruction, as you will see.

Additional Thoughts on Steps 1 and 2

Without question, these are not simple test development steps. At this point, you may be asking, How does he expect me to find time to do all of this and teach, too? Stick with me through the third and final test development step and it will become apparent why all of this planning saves you a great deal of time and effort.

Also, this kind of test development quickly becomes second nature to those who practice and master it. I promise you, if you are not confident that you have mastered all of the content or reasoning targets that you value when you start test development, by the time you finish designing some tests in this way, you will have a much stronger handle on them. In this sense, the very act of developing tests is an excellent professional growth experience.

Continue to Think Assessment *for* Learning

Just as it is possible to connect students to a vision of their own success by sharing a table of test specifications with them at the beginning of learning, so too is it possible to involve students with propositions in ways that promote their success:

- During instruction, have students jot down and share propositions they think are important.
- At the end of a day of instruction, engage students as partners in listing the important propositions of the day.
- Provide students with some sample propositions (perhaps some they developed), along with the table of test specifications, and have them practice fitting each proposition into its proper cell in the table.

All of these provide students with focused practice.

Time for Reflection

Can you think of other specific ways to involve students with the combined ideas of test blueprints and propositions in ways that set them up for success in learning content and patterns of reasoning?

Step 3: Building Test Items from Propositions

Previously, I noted that developing a high-quality test plan and specifying propositions represent 95 percent of the work in selected response test development. Complete the list of propositions and the test will almost develop itself from that point on. The reason lies in the fact that each proposition captures a complete and coherent thought. Professional test developers understand that the key to fast and effective item writing is to be sure to start with a complete and coherent thought about each fact, concept, general principle, or matter of inference that you intend to test.

Once you have a proposition in hand, you can spin any kind of selected response item out of it that you wish. Let me illustrate with the following proposition from the cell in Table 4.2 that crosses Alternative Forms of Government with Know & Understand:

In a monarchy, the right to govern is secured through birth.

To generate a true/false item out of this proposition that is true, you can simply include the proposition on the test as stated! The proposition is a true true/false test item as written. This is always the case with well-stated propositions.

If you want a false true/false item, simply make one part of the proposition false:

> *In a monarchy, the right to govern is secured through the approval of those governed.*

To convert this proposition to a fill-in item, simply leave out the phrase dealing with the effect and ask a question:

> *How is the right to govern secured in a monarchy?*

If you desire a multiple-choice item, add a number of response options, only one of which is correct.

> *How is the right to govern secured in a monarchy?*
> a. *With military power*
> b. *Through birth*
> c. *By popular vote*
> d. *Through purchase*

Mark my words: Every well-conceived and clearly stated proposition, whether requiring retrieval of knowledge or its application in a reasoning context, is an automatic source of test questions.

Here's another example, this time requiring Comparative Reasoning using an understanding of Structure of U.S. Government. In its initial statement, it is a true true/false question:

> *The executive and legislative branches of U.S. government differ in that the latter is elected directly by the people.*

As a false true/false question:

> *Members of executive and legislative branches are both elected directly by the people.*

As a fill-in item:

> *Election of members of the executive and legislative branches differs in what way?*

As a multiple-choice item:

> *Election of members of the executive and legislative branches differs in what way?*
> a. *Legislators are restricted by term limits; presidents are not*
> b. *Legislators are elected directly; presidents are not*
> c. *One must register to vote for legislators; not for president*

Invest your time and effort up front by learning the underlying structure of the material you teach, and finding the important propositions. These are the keys to the rapid development of sound selected response assessments.

Once you have identified the format(s) you plan to use, a few simple keys will aid you in developing sound test items. Some of these guidelines apply to all formats; others are unique to each particular format. They all have the effect of helping respondents understand exactly what you, the item writer, are going for in posing the exercise.

General Item Writing Guidelines

These tend to focus on the form of the item. The simplicity of their advice belies their power to improve your tests, believe me.

1. *Write clearly in a sharply focused manner.*   Good selected response assessment development is first and foremost an exercise in clear communication. Follow the rules of grammar—tests are as much a public reflection of your professional standards as any other product you create. Include only material essential to framing the question. Be brief and clear. Your goal is to test mastery of the material, not students' ability to figure out what you're asking!

Not this:

When scientists rely on magnets in the development of electric motors they need to know about the poles, which are?

*But this:**

What are the poles of a magnet called?

    a. Anode and cathode   c. Strong and weak
    b. North and south   d. Attract and repel

2. *Ask a question.*   When using multiple-choice and fill-in formats, minimize the use of incomplete statements as exercises. When you force yourself to ask a question, you force yourself to express a complete thought in the stem or trigger part of the question, which usually promotes respondents' clear understanding.

Not this:

Between 1950 and 1965

    a. Interest rates increased.   c. Interest rates fluctuated greatly.
    b. Interest rates decreased.   d. Interest rates did not change.

But this:

What was the trend in interest rates between 1950 and 1965?

    a. Increased only   c. Increased, then decreased
    b. Decreased only   d. Remained unchanged

3. *Aim for the lowest possible reading level.*   This is an attempt to control for the inevitable confounding of reading proficiency and mastery of the material in students' scores. You do not want to let students' reading proficiency prevent them from demonstrating that they really know the material. Minimize sentence length

---

*Item adapted from *Handbook on formative and summative evaluation of student learning* (p. 592, item A.4-n-2.211) by B. S. Bloom, J. T. Hastings, and G. F. Madaus, 1971, New York: McGraw-Hill. Copyright 1971 by McGraw-Hill, Inc. Adapted by permission of the publisher.

and syntactic complexity and eliminate unnecessarily difficult or unfamiliar vocabulary. For an example, see the previous magnet questions.

   4. *Eliminate clues to the correct answer either within the question or across questions within a test.*   When grammatical clues within items or material presented in other items give away the correct answer, students get items right for the wrong reasons. The result is misinformation about their true achievement.

Not this:

All of these are examples of a bird that flies, except an
   a. Ostrich
   b. Falcon
   c. Cormorant
   d. Robin

(The article *an* at the end of the stem requires a response beginning with a vowel. As only one is offered, it must be correct.)

Not this either:

Which of the following are examples of birds that do not fly?
   a. Falcon
   b. Ostrich and penguin
   c. Cormorant
   d. Robin

(The question calls for a plural response. As only one is offered, it must be correct.)

   5. *Have a qualified colleague read your items to ensure their appropriateness.* This is especially true of your relatively more important tests, such as big unit tests and final exams. No one is perfect. We all overlook simple mistakes. Having a willing colleague review your work takes just a few minutes and can save a great deal of time and assure accuracy of results.

   6. *Double check the scoring key for accuracy before scoring.*

Guidelines for Multiple-Choice Items

When developing multiple-choice test items, keep these few simple, yet powerful, guidelines in mind:

   1. *Ask a complete question to get the item started, if you can.*   I repeat this for emphasis. This has the effect of placing the item's focus in the stem, not in the response options.

   2. *Don't repeat the same words within each response option; rather, reword the item stem to move the repetitive material up there.*   This will clarify the problem and make it more efficient for respondents to read. (See the previous "interest rate" example.)

   3. *Be sure there is only one correct or best answer.*   This is where that colleague's independent review can help. Remember, it is acceptable to ask respondents to se-

lect a best answer from among a set of answers, all of which are correct. Just be sure to word the question so as to make it clear that they are to find the "best answer."

4. *Word response options as briefly as possible and be sure they are grammatically parallel.* This has two desirable effects. First, it makes items easier to read. Second, it helps eliminate grammatical clues to the correct answer. (See the second bird example.)

Not this:

Why did colonists come to the United States?
    a. To escape heavy taxation by their native governments
    b. Religion
    c. They sought the adventure of living among Native Americans in the new land
    d. There was the promise of great wealth in the new world
    e. More than one of the above answers

But this:

Why did colonists migrate to the United States?
    a. To escape taxation
    b. For religious freedom
    c. For adventure
    d. More than one of the above

5. *Vary the number of response options presented as appropriate to pose the problem you want your students to solve.* While it is best to design multiple-choice questions around three, four, or five response options, it is permissible to vary the number of response options offered across items within the same test. Please try not to use "all of the above" or "none of the above" merely to fill up spaces just because you can't think of other incorrect answers. In fact, sound practice suggests limiting their use to those few times when they fit comfortably into the context of the question.

Some teachers find it useful to include more than one correct answer and ask the student to find them all, when appropriate. Of course, this means those questions should be worth more than one point. They need to count for as many points as there are correct answers. For example:

Which of the labels provided represents a classification category for types of rocks? (Identify all correct answers[*])
    a. Geologic
    b. Metamorphic*
    c. Sandstone
    d. Igneous*

By the way, here's a simple, yet very effective, multiple-choice test item writing tip: If you compose a multiple-choice item and find that you cannot think of enough plausible incorrect responses, include the item on a test the first time as a fill-in question.

As your students respond, those who get it wrong will provide you with the full range of viable incorrect responses you need the next time you use it.

Guidelines for True/False Exercises

You have only one simple guideline to follow here: Make the item *entirely* true or false *as stated*. Complex "idea salads" including some truth and some falsehood just confuse the issue. Precisely what is the proposition you are testing? State it and move on to the next one.

Not this:

> From the Continental Divide, located in the Appalachian Mountains, water flows into either the Pacific Ocean or the Mississippi River.

But this:

> The Continental Divide is located in the Appalachian Mountains.

Guidelines for Matching Items

When developing matching exercises, which are really complex multiple-choice items with a number of stems offered along with a number of response options, follow all of the multiple-choice guidelines offered previously. In addition, observe the following guidelines:

1. *Provide clear and concise directions for making the match.*

2. *Keep the list of things to be matched short.*   The maximum number of options is 10. Fewer is better. This minimizes the information processing and idea juggling respondents must do to be successful.

3. *Keep the list of things to be matched homogeneous.*   Don't mix events with dates or with names. Again, idea salads confuse the issue. Focus the exercise. Figure 4.3 offers a list of alignments that work well.

Figure 4.3
Relationships that can provide a basis for strong matching exercises
Source: From *Measurement and Assessment in Teaching.* 8th ed. (p. 167) by R. L. Linn and N. E. Gronlund, 2000, Upper Saddle River, NJ: Merrill/Prentice Hall. Reprinted by permission.

Persons	Achievements
Dates	Events
Terms	Definitions
Rules	Examples
Symbols	Concepts
Authors	Book titles
Foreign words	English equivalents
Machines	Uses
Plants/animals	Classifications
Principles	Illustrations
Objects	Names of objects
Parts	Functions

4. Keep the list of response options brief in their wording and parallel in construction.   Pose the matching challenge in clear, straightforward language.

5. Include more response options than stems and permit students to use response options more than once.   This has the effect of making it impossible for students to arrive at the correct response purely through a process of elimination. If students answer correctly using elimination and you infer that they have mastered the material, you will be wrong.

Not this:

_____ 1. Texas	A. $7,200,000	
_____ 2. Hawaii	B. Chicago	
_____ 3. New York	C. Liberty Bell	
_____ 4. Illinois	D. Augusta	
_____ 5. Louisiana	E. Cornhusker	
_____ 6. Florida	F. Mardi Gras	
_____ 7. Massachusetts	G. 50th State	
_____ 8. Alaska	H. Austin	
_____ 9. Maine	I. Everglades	
_____10. California	J. 1066	
_____11. Nebraska	K. Dover	
_____12. Pennsylvania	L. San Andreas Fault	
	M. Salem	
	N. 1620	
	O. Statue of Liberty	

But this:

Directions: The New England states are listed in the left-hand column and capital cities in the right-hand column. Place the letter corresponding to the capital city in the space next to the state in which that city is located. Responses may be used only once.

States

_____ 1. Connecticut
_____ 2. Maine
_____ 3. Massachusetts
_____ 4. New Hampshire
_____ 5. Rhode Island
_____ 6. Vermont

Capital Cities

A. Augusta
B. Boston
C. Brunswick
D. Concord
E. Hartford
F. Montpelier
G. New Haven
H. Providence

Guidelines for Fill-in Items

Here are three simple guidelines to follow:

1. *Ask respondents a question and provide space for an answer.*   This forces you to express a complete thought. The use of incomplete statements as item stems

is acceptable. But if you use them, be sure to capture the essence of the problem in that stem.

2. *Try to stick to one blank per item.*   Come to the point. Ask one question, get one answer, and move on to the next question. Simple language, complete communication, clear conclusions. Does the student know the answer or not?

Not this:

In the percussion section of the orchestra are located _____,
_____, _____, and _____.

But this:

In what section of the orchestra is the kettle drum found?

_____

3. *Don't let the length of the line to be filled in be a clue as to the length or nature of the correct response.*   This may seem elementary, but it happens. Again, this can misinform you about students' real levels of achievement.

Assessment *for* Learning Ideas

Consider the possibility of engaging students as partners in developing practice items reflecting the important knowledge and reasoning proficiencies as given in a table of test specifications and set of propositions. This can turn into sharply focused instruction in the form of guided practice. They must begin to tune into the important content and become so comfortable with your valued reasoning patterns that they can pose questions of their classmates that require their application. Just remember, these activities are for practice only—they are assessments *for* learning. It is not acceptable for students to develop their own assessments *of* learning—those you use to verify learning for grading, for example. When it comes time for accountability, the assessment must be yours, seen by your students only at the proper time.

Summary of Step 3

In this step, you transformed propositions into assessment questions. This can be very quick and easy. Regardless of the item format, however, clarity and focused simplicity must be hallmarks of your exercises. Always try to ask questions. Strive to eliminate inappropriate clues to the correct answer, seek one clearly correct answer whenever possible and appropriate, ask a colleague to review important tests, and follow just a few simple format-specific guidelines for item construction. Figure 4.4 presents a summary of these guidelines collected for your convenient use.

Further, remember to help students perform up to their potential by providing clear and complete instructions, letting students know how each exercise contributes to the total test score, starting with easy items, and making sure the test is readable.

General guidelines for all formats

_____ Items clearly written and focused

_____ Question posed

_____ Lowest possible reading level

_____ Irrelevant clues eliminated

_____ Items reviewed by colleague

_____ Scoring key double checked

Guidelines for multiple-choice items

_____ Item stem poses a direct question

_____ Repetition eliminated from response options

_____ One best or correct answer

_____ Response options are brief and parallel

_____ Number of response options offered fits item context

Guideline for true/false items

_____ Statement is entirely true or false as presented

Guidelines for matching exercises

_____ Clear directions given

_____ List of items to be matched is brief

_____ List consists of homogeneous entries

_____ Response options are brief and parallel

_____ Extra response options offered

Guidelines for fill-in items

_____ A direct question is posed

_____ One blank is needed to respond

_____ Length of blank is not a clue

Figure 4.4
Test item quality checklist

Fine Tuning Assessment Applications

Consider the following suggestions as you develop your selected response assessments.

Mix Formats Together

The creative assessment developer also can generate some interesting and useful assessment exercises by mixing the various formats. For example, mix true/false and multiple-choice formats to create exercises in which respondents must label a statement true or false and select the response option that gives the proper reason it is so. For example:

As employment increases, the danger of inflation increases.
   a. True, because consumers are willing to pay higher prices
   b. True, because the money supply increases
   c. False, because wages and inflation are statistically unrelated to one another
   d. False, because the government controls inflation

Or, mix multiple-choice or true/false questions with the fill-in format by asking students to select the correct response and fill in the reason it is correct. As a variation, ask why incorrect responses are incorrect, too.

Time for Reflection

Can you think of combinations of these formats that might be useful?

Use Interpretive Exercises

Here's another simple but effective assessment development idea: Let's say you wish to use selected response formats to assess student reasoning and problem-solving proficiency. But let's also say you are not sure all of your students have the same solid background in the content, or you want to see them apply content you don't expect them to know outright. In these contexts, you can turn to what is called an *interpretive exercise.* With this format, you provide information to respondents in the form of a brief passage, chart, table, or figure and then ask a series of questions calling for them to interpret or apply that material. For example:*

1. Here is a graph of Bill's weekly allowance distribution. What is the ratio of the amount Bill spends for school supplies to the amount he spends for movies?
   a. 7:2
   b. 1:3
   c. 2:7
   d. 3:1

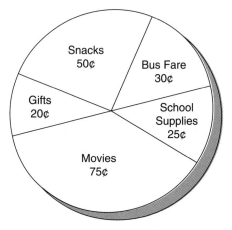

---

*Reprinted from "Measuring Complex Achievement: The Interpretive Exercise" (pp. 222-223, Example III) in *Measurement and Evaluation in Teaching,* 8th ed. by R. L. Linn and N. E. Gronlund, 2000, Upper Saddle River, NJ: Merrill/Prentice Hall. Copyright 2000 by Prentice-Hall, Inc. Reprinted by permission of the publisher.

2. What would be the best title for this graph?
    a. Bill's weekly allowance
    b. Bill's money graph
    c. Bill's weekly expenditures
    d. Bill's money planning

Format the Test Carefully

Finally, here are a few simple guidelines for setting up your test as a whole that will maximize the accuracy of the results:

1. Make sure your students know the point value for each assessment exercise. This helps them use their time wisely.
2. Start each test with relatively easy items. This will give students a chance to get test anxiety under control.
3. Present all questions of like format together (all multiple choice together, all fill-in, etc.)
4. Be sure all parts of a question appear on the same page of the test.
5. Make sure all copies are clear and readable.

Work Backwards to Verify Test Quality

You can reverse the three-step test development process described to evaluate existing tests, such as those that come with a textbook or those you have developed in previous years. To do this, begin at the test item level: Do the items themselves adhere to the few critical guidelines presented previously? If they do not, there is obvious reason for concern about test quality. If they do, proceed to the next level of evaluation.

At this level, you can transform the items into the propositions that they reflect. You accomplish this by doing the following:

- Combine the multiple-choice item stem with the correct response.
- Check that true true/false items already are propositions.
- Make false true/false items true to derive the proposition.
- Match up elements in matching exercises.
- Fill in the blanks of short answer items.

Then, analyze the resulting list of propositions, asking, Do these reflect the priorities in my instruction? Next, collect the propositions into like groups to determine the instructional objectives they represent or to create a table of specifications depicting the overall picture of the test, including the proportional representation of content and thinking. Again, ask, Do these reflect priorities as I see them?

This kind of reverse process can both reveal the flaws in previously developed tests and help you understand the nature of the revisions needed to bring the test up to your standards of quality.

Some Final Issues and Reminders

As you plan your development and use of selected response assessments, attend carefully to the following issues:

- Be sure time and test length permit students to attempt all test items. If a student doesn't get to try an item because time runs out, how can you know if that student has mastered the material tested? You cannot automatically assume they would get it wrong. They might not—you don't know. To avoid the problem, give everyone every chance. If that means extending test time for some, extend it.
- Remember, as mentioned previously, do not hand score unless absolutely necessary. It's a huge waste of time.
- Use fill-in exercises when you wish to control for guessing. And make no mistake about it, guessing can be an issue. If a student guesses an item right and you infer that the right answer means the student has mastered the material, you will be wrong. You have mismeasured that student's real achievement.
- Use multiple-choice items when you can identify one correct or best answer and a number of viable incorrect responses (also known as *distracters*). On its surface, this might sound obvious. But think about it. If you formulate your distracters carefully, you can use multiple-choice items to uncover common misunderstandings and to diagnose students' needs.

Barriers to Sound Selected Response Assessment

Recall that, in earlier chapters, we listed five key attributes of a sound assessment:

- Clear targets
- Clear purposes
- Proper method
- Appropriate sampling
- Control of bias

These also reflect the things that can go wrong—that can keep a student's test score from being an accurate reflection of that student's real level of achievement. Listed in Figure 4.5, by way of summary, are many of the sources of mismeasurement touched on in this chapter, together with actions you can take to prevent these problems. These remedies can help you develop sound selected response assessments.

Student Involvement in Selected Response Assessment

I have said from the outset that classroom assessment can serve two important purposes. One is to provide information for teacher, student, and parent to use in informing the various decisions they must make. The other is as a highly motivational teaching tool. Figure 4.6 reviews and expands our list of ways to weave selected re-

Potential Sources of Problems	Suggested Remedies
Lack of vision of the priority target(s)	Carefully analyze the material to be tested to find the knowledge and reasoning targets.
	Find truly important learning propositions.
Wrong method for the target	Use selected response methods to assess mastery of knowledge and appropriate kinds of reasoning only.
	Selected response can test prerequisites of effective skill and product performance, but not performance itself.
Inappropriate sampling:	
• Not representative of important propositions	Know the material and plan the test to thoroughly cover the target(s).
• Sample too small	Include enough items to cover key concepts.
• Sample too large for time available	Shorten cautiously so as to maintain enough to support confident student learning conclusions.
Sources of bias:	
• Student-centered problems	
• Cannot read well enough to respond	Lower reading level of test or offer reading support.
• Insufficient time to respond	Shorten test or allow more time.
• Poor-quality test items	Learn and follow both general and format-specific guidelines for writing quality items.
	Seek review by a colleague.
• Scoring errors	Double check answer key; use it carefully.

Figure 4.5
Avoiding problems with selected response tests and quizzes

sponse assessment development and use into the very fabric of your teaching and learning environment through student involvement. Remember when I asked you who else might become involved in your assessment development and use in order to lighten your classroom assessment workload? The coworkers to whom I referred are your students.

- Develop a table of test specifications for a final unit test *before* ever teaching the unit. A clear vision of the valued outcomes will result and you can tailor instruction to promote student success.
- Share a copy of that plan with every student. Review it carefully at the beginning of the unit and explain your expectations at that time. Now students and teacher share the same vision.
- Involve students in the process of devising the test plan, or involve them from time to time in checking back to the blueprint (1) to see together—as partners—if you might need to make adjustments in the test plan and/or (2) to chart your progress together.
- Once you have the test plan completed, develop a few test items each day as the unit unfolds. Such items certainly would reflect timely instructional priorities. Further, at the end of the unit, the final exam would be all done and ready to go! This eliminates the last-minute anxiety of test development and improves test quality.
- Involve students in writing practice test items. Think of the benefits: students will have to evaluate the importance of the various elements of content, and they will have to become proficient in using the kinds of reasoning and problem solving valued in your classroom. Developing sample test items provides high-fidelity practice in doing these things.
- As a variation on that theme, provide unlabeled exercises and have students practice (1) placing them in the proper cell of the test blueprint, and (2) answering them.
- As another variation, have students evaluate the quality of the tests that came with the textbook— do they match your plan developed for instruction?
- Have students use the test blueprint to predict how they are going to do on each part of the test before they take it. Then have them analyze how they did, part by part, after taking it. If the first test is for practice, such an analysis will provide valuable information to help them plan their preparation for the real thing.
- Have students work in teams, with each team given responsibility for finding ways to help everyone in class score high in one cell, row, or column of a table of specifications or one objective.
- Use lists of unit objectives and tables of test specifications to communicate among teachers about instructional priorities, so as to arrive at a clearer understanding of how those priorities fit together across instructional levels or school buildings.
- Store test items by content and reasoning category for reuse. If your item record also includes information on how students did on each item (say, the percentage that got it right), you could revise instruction next time for items students had trouble with. Incidentally, this represents an excellent place to use your personal computer to advantage as a test item storage and retrieval system.

Figure 4.6
Ideas for student-involved assessment

Summary: Productive Selected Response Assessment

We established at the beginning of the chapter that these options often are labeled "objective" tests because of the manner in which they are scored. When test items are carefully developed, there is only one clearly best answer. No judgment is involved. However, the teacher's professional judgment does play a major role in all other facets of this kind of assessment, from test planning to selecting material to test to writing the test items. For this reason, it is essential that all selected response test developers closely follow procedures for creating sound tests. Those procedures were the topic of this chapter.

We discussed the match between selected response assessment methods and the four basic kinds of achievement targets plus dispositions that are serving as signposts for our journey. These selected response formats can serve to assess students' mastery of content knowledge and understanding, ability to reason in important ways, and mastery of some of the procedural knowledge that underpins both the development of performance skills and the creation of complex products.

As we examined the test development process itself, we explored several context factors that extend beyond just the consideration of match to target that must be taken into account in choosing selected response assessment. These included factors related to students' reading abilities and to the kinds of support services available to the user.

Also under the heading of test development, we explored a three-step developmental sequence: test planning, identifying propositions to test, and test item writing. In each case, we touched on specific ideas for involving students in selected response assessment to extend their learning. We reviewed a limited number of specific item and test development tactics within each step that promise to decrease test development time and increase test quality. These tactics hold the promise of saving teachers immense amounts of time in test development. Not only do they result in quick and easy test item development, but teachers can store both test blueprints and items on their personal computer for convenient reuse later.

Final Chapter Reflection

---

1. What are the three most important new insights to come to you as a result of your study of this chapter?

2. Which of your previous questions about assessment can you now answer based on your study of this chapter?

3. What new questions have come to mind as a result of your study of this chapter that you hope to have answered as your study continues?

Practicing with Chapter 4 Ideas

1. Make up a simple table of test specifications for a 10-item selected response assessment of the content priorities presented in this chapter.

2. Transform each of the following test items into its basic proposition:
   - True T/F: One reason for declining numbers of Pacific salmon is the destruction of salmon habitat.
   - False T/F: A tariff is a tax on real estate.
   - Fill in: If we increase the radius of a ball by 3 inches, what will be the effect on its circumference?
   - Multiple choice: Which of the following is an example of a tariff?
     a. Income tax
     b. Tax on Chinese imports
     c. Real estate tax
     d. All of the above

3. Transform the following propositions into test items:
   - Automobiles and factories are the largest sources of air pollution.
   - The water cycle depends on evaporation and condensation.
   - In the United States, we have a bicameral legislature.
   - Our free market economic system is based on the law of supply and demand.

4. Write the 10 propositions that will fill in the table of test specifications for this chapter that you designed for Practice item 1. Then write the test items. Exchange work with a classmate, if possible, and evaluate each other's work.

5. Secure a copy of a selected response test that you have taken in the recent past and do the following:
   - Transform its items into propositions and summarize them into a table of test specifications.
   - Rate the quality of this assessment using the rubrics for evaluating assessment quality found in the Appendix along with the more specific guidelines presented in this chapter.
   - If you cannot obtain your own assessment, you will find sample assessments at this text's Companion Website (http://www.prenhall.com/stiggins).

Chapter 5

Essay Assessment

CHAPTER FOCUS

This chapter answers the following guiding question:

> When and how do I most effectively use assessments that ask students to construct original written responses?

From your study of this chapter, you will understand the following:

1. Essay assessment aligns well with knowledge and understanding targets, as well as with various patterns of reasoning.

2. It can be efficiently developed in three steps: assessment planning, exercise development, and preparation to score student responses.

3. This method can fall prey to avoidable sources of bias that can distort results if users are not careful.

4. By involving your students in essay assessment development and use, you can set them up for energetic and successful learning.

As we start this part of our journey, keep the big picture in mind. In this chapter, we deal with the shaded areas of Figure 5.1.

Assessment Based on Subjective Judgment

In recent years, our increasingly complex society has asked schools to help students master increasingly complex forms of achievement. These more sophisticated reasoning and writing achievement standards have heightened interest in assessment methods able to probe student learning more deeply than can be tapped using selected response assessment. One result has been renewed interest in essay assessment—the method, by the way, that dominated student evaluation until the appearance of the multiple-choice format in the 1920s.

	SELECTED RESPONSE	ESSAY	PERFORMANCE ASSESSMENT	PERSONAL COMMUNICATION
Know				
Reason				
Performance Skills				
Products				
Dispositions				

Figure 5.1
Aligning achievement targets and assessment methods

This chapter explores the potential of the essay assessment to tap achievement targets that do not translate into selected response formats, such as students' understanding of connections among elements of knowledge. As you will see, this method also can be integrated very productively into teaching and learning through student involvement, while at the same time saving teachers a great deal of scoring time.

As with all assessment methods, however, if we are not careful, problems can crop up. For instance, we are likely to inaccurately assess student achievement if we

- Lack a sufficiently clear vision of the learning targets.
- Rely on the essay format when it doesn't fit the achievement target.
- Use this method with students who lack sufficient writing skills to convey their achievement of content or reasoning skills.
- Do not sample the achievement target with enough high-quality essay exercises.
- Disregard the many sources of bias that can invade subjective assessments, especially during scoring.

This chapter is about how to avoid these problems. Let's start with an example.

An Example of Essay Assessment at Work in the Classroom

A professor acquaintance of mine uses essay exercises exclusively for his final examinations in the classroom assessment course that he teaches for teachers and school administrators. His students are like you—they're learning to assess effectively in their own classrooms. He reports that he likes the essay method in this context because it allows him to do the following:

1. Present exercises that depict relatively complex real-world classroom assessment dilemmas or problems to teacher candidates.
2. Ask them to use their assessment methodology knowledge, understanding, and reasoning abilities to describe how they would resolve each dilemma if confronted with it in their classroom.

Obviously, he could obtain a more "authentic" assessment of their proficiency if he could place his students in a real classroom and observe them solving real classroom assessment problems. But this kind of authenticity is beyond reach. So he turns to an essay test as a high-fidelity (meaning *valid*) approximation of reality and thus effectively gains insight into their achievement.

As you read, keep our standards of good practice in mind. Ask the following questions of this assessment plan:

- Can the essay format accurately reflect the professor's intended achievement targets?
- Does he sample student achievement appropriately with what appear to be high-quality exercises?
- Does the scoring process account for the problems that can lead to biased assessment?
- Does he rely on student involvement in assessment during learning in ways that motivate learning?

The Assessment

The professor samples the achievement of his students using 10 essay exercises on each final exam. He chooses them from a pool of exercises that he and his students have devised over the years to represent an array of classroom assessment challenges teachers face in real classrooms. He feels 10 exercises sample broadly enough to permit him to generalize to the examinees' overall competence.

For practice, this professor regularly involves his students in developing practice exercises and scoring criteria similar, but not identical, to those that will appear on the exam. He has students respond to each other's practice exercises and apply scoring guides to evaluating each other's work. Remember, this is for practice only—to help them track and manage their own growth. These scores play no role in determining their grades. The exercises that appear on the "official" final exam ask students to use their knowledge to solve novel problems presented at that time.

For each exercise on the actual final exam, he establishes performance expectations in advance by specifying either one best solution or a set of acceptable solutions to the classroom assessment problem presented. The professor carefully translates these expectations into predetermined scoring guides for each exercise.

Sample Essay Exercise:

Assume you are a French teacher with many years of teaching experience. You place great value on the development of speaking proficiency as an outcome of your instruction. Therefore, you rely heavily on assessments where you listen to and evaluate performance. But a problem has arisen. Parents of students who attained very high scores on your written tests are complaining that their children are receiving lower grades on their report cards. The principal wants to be sure your judgments of student proficiency are sound and so has asked you to explain and defend your procedures. Describe at least three specific quality standards that your oral proficiency exams would need to meet for you to be confident that your exams truly reflect what students can do; provide the rationale for each. (2 points for each procedure and rationale, total = 6 points.)

Score Responses as Follows:

2 points if the student's response lists any of these six procedures and defends each as a key to conducting sound performance assessments:

- Specify clear performance criteria
- Sample performance over several exercises
- Apply systematic rating procedures
- Maintain complete and accurate records
- Use published performance assessments to verify results of classroom assessments
- Use multiple observers to corroborate

Also award 2 points if the response lists any of the following and defends them as attributes of sound assessments:

- Specifies a clear instructional objective
- Relies on a proper assessment method
- Samples performance well
- Controls for sources of rater bias

All other responses receive no points.

Figure 5.2
Sample essay exercise and scoring guide

He tells students up front how many points are associated with each exercise, and they strive to attain as many of those points as they can.

Figure 5.2 provides a sample of one of his exercises, along with its scoring criteria. It reveals the kind of real-world complexity that the professor can attain with the essay mode of assessment. The professor states that, over the years, these final exams have become very much a part of his classroom routine. Let's explore why this might be the case.

The Assessment–Learning Relationship

The professor conducts this as a take-home exam, so as to maximize the amount of time students can spend reflecting and responding. He regards this as sharply focused learning time. His students report that they do, in fact, spend a considerable amount of time preparing their responses. Further, students receive the exercises a few at a time throughout the term, as the professor covers the material needed to address the various problems. This has the effect of making the achievement targets perfectly clear to the students, thus helping them focus their learning and reduce test anxiety. It also spreads the extra learning time and effort over the entire term.

As take-home exams, these obviously are open-book exams. The professor covers a great deal of material about assessment in this course and reports that he does not expect students to memorize it all, any more than he expects his physician to memorize all of the treatment options she has at her disposal.

Rather, each student receives a text and a parallel set of resource materials. Over the course, students learn how to use these reference materials. Hopefully, after the course is over, they will keep their "library" of assessment ideas handy for classroom use. The open-book exam format encourages them to learn the overall organizational structure of these materials for both present and later use.

The Scoring

At the end of the term, when students hand in their final exam for scoring (all 10 exercises come in together), the professor applies the predeveloped scoring guides in evaluating each response to each exercise. Because enrollment can exceed 50 students per class, he has had to find ways to maximize scoring efficiency. The single biggest time saver, he reports, is to have the scoring criteria clearly in mind before beginning. Next is to score all responses to one exercise at one time and then move on to the next exercise.

The Feedback

Students receive feedback on their performance in the following forms:

- Points assigned to each part of each response
- Brief written rationale for the score derived from the scoring guides, suggesting factors they might have overlooked
- The total number of points summed over all exercises
- A grade based on comparing the total score to a predetermined set of cutoff scores for each grade

Students who attain grades that are lower than they like can rework their response to any exercise(s) any time and resubmit their exam for reevaluation. If reevaluation of their written work and a personal discussion with the professor reveals that they have completed more productive study and have attained a higher level of proficiency, the professor submits a change of grade at once. This procedure has the effect of extending the learning time beyond the limits of a single term when necessary. However, the professor accepts resubmissions for one subsequent term only.

Time for Reflection

Is this an assessment of learning or an assessment for learning? How do you know?

The Impact

The professor reports that scoring all responses to a single exercise together helps him to integrate assessment into instruction in another important way. After reading 50 attempts to solve a relatively complex classroom assessment problem, he assures me that he knows which facets of his instruction were effective and which were not. When his students successfully resolve the classroom assessment dilemma presented in an exercise, he reports, he uses this as evidence of his instruction's effectiveness. But when the professor has failed to set his students up for success in solving some kind of classroom assessment problem, it becomes painfully obvious in paper after paper. He knows without question which phase of instruction did not work. Next term, he revises instruction in the hope that his students will perform better on similar exercises.

The impact on students is clear, too. A high percentage of them do very well on these exams. They report that they spend more time on these exercises than on other exams, and that they truly must study, analyze, and reflect deeply on the material covered in class and required readings to find solutions to the problems presented. In addition, they welcome the opportunity to rework the material when necessary to score higher.

Without question, this particular professor's assessment and grading procedures will not work in all contexts. In a very real sense, he works in what most teachers would regard as an ideal world: a manageable number of students and few preparations.

However, my point in telling you this story is not to convince you to adopt his procedures. Rather, it is to make the point that *essay assessment can contribute to the effectiveness of a learning community in which teacher and students enter into a partnership with a mutual goal of maximum achievement.*

Now let's explore how you might do this in your classroom, given your realities.

The Foundations of Assessment Quality

To begin with, we need to think about two quality control factors that form the foundation of the appropriate use of essay assessment. First, certain realities of life in classrooms can and should contribute to your decision about when to use this option. You must know that the context is right.

Second, written response assessments represent the first of three assessment methods we will discuss over the next few chapters that are subjective, not just in their development, but this time, also in their scoring.

Context Factors

Essay assessment is not for every teacher and every classroom. First and most importantly, this method cannot work in situations where students are not proficient in the English language (if that is the language of instruction) or as writers. The problem is very clear in this case.

In the primary grades, when dealing with students with learning disabilities, or when students are not yet comfortable writing in English, for example, they will not be able to let you know whether they have mastered the material using this format. Let's say a student has mastered the material but can't write well. You would read their poorly written essays and judge the student's achievement to be low and you would be wrong. Your assessment would be inaccurate, and would provide biased results. To gain access to accurate information, you would need to change to another assessment method.

The other context factor to consider in applying essay assessment is time. Essay exercises are relatively easy to develop, as are scoring guides. But scoring takes time. In general, the smaller the number of students involved and the number of exercises needed to sample achievement, the less time will be required. So, consider these factors in test planning.

Further, the more scorers involved, the easier it is to apply this method. This becomes a factor in assessment *for* learning contexts, where you can enlist your students as scorers. Of course, they must be trained to score accurately, but that is no problem if that training helps them center on your valued achievement targets. Their involvement represents excellent instruction.

But at assessment *of* learning time, such as when a report card grade is involved, this is not time for student involvement. You, or another qualified teacher, must be the rater.

Understanding Reliability: The Role of Teacher Judgment in Scoring

You will recall that reliable assessments produce consistent results. The danger here is that two teachers subjectively judging the same piece of student work can assign different scores. This is evidence of inconsistency, of unreliability.

We all have heard stories of studies in which student essays are scored by many different teachers and are assigned vastly different scores. Often this is used as an indictment of this method of assessment as producing unreliable results. Be advised that such condemnation is unjust. What these stories actually depict is a shoddy application of a potentially solid assessment option.

The unreliability revealed here can be eliminated if the researchers had helped the scorers achieve consistency by developing and using essay assessments appropriately. In this case, that would have meant creating clear and appropriate scoring guidelines and training the teachers to apply those criteria consistently. When scorers are prepared properly, scoring can be very reliable.

Perhaps the most important quality control message of this book is this: *Assessments that rely on teachers' professional judgments to evaluate student achievement can produce valid and reliable results leading to effective instruction if we anticipate potential problems and work to eliminate them.* In other words, subjectivity of assessment need not be a source of inaccuracy.

In the case of essay assessment, as with any form of assessment, the responsibility for avoiding problems and for ensuring quality rests squarely with you, the teacher! Those who thoroughly comprehend the content and patterns of reasoning to be assessed are in an excellent position to plan exercises and scoring procedures that fit the valued learning targets. It is only through developing and using strong exercises and appropriate scoring criteria that you may avoid errors of measurement attributable to evaluator or rater bias. This chapter is about how to accomplish this.

Understanding Validity: Matching Method to Target

Remember, a valid assessment accurately reflects the desired learning. Essay assessments have a potential contribution to make in assessing key dimensions of student learning in all five categories of valued targets, knowledge, reasoning, skills, products, and dispositions (affect).

Assessing Knowledge and Understanding

Most experts advise caution in using essay responses to assess student mastery of subject matter knowledge; that is, when the targets are specific facts or concepts students are to learn. The primary reason is that we have better options at our disposal for tapping this kind of target. Selected response assessment formats provide a more efficient means of assessment that, at the same time, allow for a more precise sampling of the achievement domain.

Selected response test formats are more efficient than essays in this case for two reasons. First, you can ask more multiple-choice questions than essay questions per unit of testing time because multiple-choice response time is so much shorter. So, you can provide a broader sample of performance per unit of time with selected response items than with essay exercises. Second, scoring selected response items is much faster than scoring essays.

Nevertheless, you can use the essay format for assessing student mastery of content knowledge in certain contexts. Let me explain.

In discussing the design and development of selected response items, I described planning that began with a broad domain of content, divided into categories for the table of specifications. Then I suggested further subdividing these into collections of important propositions, any one of which might be transformed into a specifically focused test item. In such test development, elements of knowledge become quite narrow and disconnected from one another.

However, this is not the only sort of knowledge we want our students to master. Sometimes, we may conceive of larger units of knowledge, each containing numerous important smaller elements within it that all relate to one another in some important way. For example, we might want students to know all of the parts of a particular ecosystem in science and to understand how they are related to one another. It is the *relationships among ideas* that are key. An essay assessment can help us evaluate student attainment of this depth of mastery.

Following is an example of such an exercise that a science teacher might use on a final exam in a biology course to find out if students know and understand the water cycle:

> *Describe how evaporation and condensation operate in the context of the water cycle. Be sure to include all key elements in the cycle and how they relate to one another. (20 points)*

We can use such exercises in an open-book exam, too, if we wish to assess mastery of such complex understanding through the use of reference materials. With essay assessments, we are seeking a readout of the more complex cognitive map of the learner. One of the most common complaints against the selected response form of assessment is that it compartmentalizes learning too much—students demonstrate mastery of discrete bits of knowledge but need not integrate them into a larger whole. Students familiar with and expecting essay assessments know that such integration is important.

Assessing Reasoning

A real strength of written responses resides in their ability to provide windows into student reasoning proficiency. At assessment time, we can present complex problems that ask learners to bring together their subject matter knowledge, understanding, and reasoning skills to find a solution. In instances where we cannot directly observe knowledge application or can't see the mental process of reasoning unfold, we can ask students to describe the results of their reasoning in their essays. From this, we infer the state of their understanding and their ability to use it in problem-solving contexts.

We can ask them to analyze, compare, draw inferences, and/or think critically in virtually any subject matter area. Furthermore, we can pose problems that require integrating material from two or more subjects and/or applying more than one pattern of reasoning. The key question here would be, Do students know how and when to use the knowledge they have at their disposal to reason and solve problems? Here is an example from a "science, technology, and society" course taught by a middle school teacher:

> *Using what you know about the causes of air pollution in cities, propose two potentially useful solutions. Analyze each in terms of its strengths and weaknesses. (20 points)*

Remember, however, the keys to success in assessing student reasoning with essays are the same as the keys to success with selected response:

1. Assessors must possess a highly refined vision of each relevant reasoning pattern.
2. Assessors must know how to translate that vision into clear, focused essay exercises and proper scoring criteria.
3. The exercises must present problems to students that are new at the time of the assessment (i.e., problems for which students must figure out a response on the spot).

Assessing Performance Skills

If our valued achievement target holds that students become proficient in demonstrating specific performance skills, then there is only one acceptable way to assess proficiency: we must observe actual performance and judge its quality. For instance, say we want to find out if students can perform certain complex behaviors, such as participating collaboratively in a group, communicating orally in a second language, debating a controversial issue in social studies, or carrying out the steps in a science experiment. In these cases, standards of sound assessment require that we give students the opportunity to demonstrate group participation skills, speak the language, debate, or conduct an actual lab experiment.

There is no way to use essay responses to tap these kinds of performances. However, there are some related targets that we can tap with the essay format. For instance, we can use the essay to assess mastery of some of the complex knowledge, understanding, and even problem-solving proficiencies prerequisite to performing the skill in question.

For example, if students do not know and understand the functions of different pieces of science lab equipment, there is no way that they will successfully complete the lab work. We could devise an essay question to see if they have mastered that prerequisite knowledge and understanding. Thus, we could use the written response format to assess student attainment of some of the building blocks of performance skill competence.

Assessing Product Development Capabilities

In this case, if we wish to infer students' level of achievement based on the attributes of a complex achievement-related product that they create, the only high-fidelity way to assess the outcome is to have them actually create the product. Only then can we determine if it meets established standards of quality. This requires a product-based performance assessment.

However, during learning, essays can provide insights into student mastery of prerequisite knowledge and reasoning targets that underpin the ability to create quality products. For instance, they can tell us whether students know and understand the attributes of or steps in the process of creating a quality product—fundamental knowledge. The results of such an essay assessment will be useful in a classroom context where we are working on building the foundations of competence. We can use essay assessments in these contexts, however, only if we remain constantly aware of the fact that being able to write about the attributes of a good product and the ability actually to create that product are different proficiencies. My point is that knowledge of attributes represents an essential building block of ultimate competence—it is necessary but not sufficient for success. As such, along the way to success, as a classroom teacher I might want to know the prerequisites are being put in place.

Assessing Writing as a Product

One kind of product we often ask students to create is samples of their writing. Without question, student responses to essay exercises do represent original written constructions, and we therefore can evaluate them in terms of the demonstrated writing proficiency. However, in this context, we must be sure not to confound matters of the content of a student's response with their ability to write well. They are not the same.

When we evaluate writing proficiency we center on matters of *form*. Our criteria reflect standards related to word choice, sentence fluency, organization, mechanics and the like. These are important, to be sure.

However, in the essay assessment context, it is the expression of ideas, the *content* of the response that comes under the microscope. We establish exercise-specific criteria that reflect the students' demonstration of content mastery and the quality of the reasoning presented.

In any essay context, you can evaluate either or both form and content. Just realize that they are different. Always make sure that students know and understand which will come into play in all essay applications. Make sure instruction helps them understand and learn to apply the standards of essay quality that they will be expected to meet.

Assessing Dispositions

Students' writing can also provide a window into their motivations or attitudes. When we ask them specific questions about the direction and intensity of their feelings about focused aspects of their schooling, in an environment where honesty is accepted, students can and will inform us about their attitudes, interests, and levels of motivation. Questionnaires containing open-ended questions can produce student responses that are full of profoundly important insights into the affective and social climate of a school or classroom.

Chapter 8 deals in detail with issues and procedures related to assessing dispositions using this and other methods.

Summary of Target Matches

On the whole, essay assessment is a very flexible option. It can provide useful information on a variety of targets. We can use it to evaluate student mastery of larger

Table 5.1
Essay: Assessment of achievement targets

Target to Be Assessed	Essay
Knowledge & Understanding	Essay exercises can tap understanding of relationships among elements of knowledge
Reasoning Proficiency	Written descriptions of complex problem solutions can provide a window into reasoning proficiency
Performance Skills	Can assess mastery of the knowledge prerequisites to skillful performance, but cannot rely on these to tap the skill itself
Ability to Create Products	Can assess writing proficiency and mastery of the knowledge necessary to create other products
Dispositions	Open-ended questionnaire items can probe dispositions

structures of knowledge, whether learned outright or mastered through the use of reference materials. We certainly can tap student reasoning and problem-solving skills. We can assess mastery of the complex procedural knowledge that is prerequisite to skilled performance and/or the creation of quality products. And finally, we also can explore student motivations and attitudes in rich and useful ways through student writing. Table 5.1 provides a quick summary.

Developing Essay Assessments

Practice Exercise

We are beginning the section on designing and developing sound essay exercises and scoring criteria. Before we do, please draft an essay exercise that could appear on a final exam on this chapter of this book that asks respondents to describe the relationships among essay assessment and the various achievement targets: knowledge, problem solving, and so on. Also, draft a scoring guide for your exercise. Be sure both your exercise and scoring guide are as complete as you can make them.

Keep these drafts handy, and refer to them as we discuss procedures for developing and scoring essay assessments. If you try this before learning some of the intricacies of essay development, it will provide you with an experience base from which to understand the design suggestions offered.

Designing and developing these assessments involves three steps:

1. Assessment planning
2. Exercise development
3. Scoring guides

Test planning for this form of assessment is very much like planning selected response assessments. While exercise development is a bit easier, scoring preparation is much more challenging.

Assessment Planning

The challenge, as always, is to begin with clearly articulated achievement targets. In this case, the target will reflect both the components of knowledge and the patterns of reasoning respondents must master. Consequently, once again we have the option of starting with either a table of test specifications or a list of instructional objectives.

Tables of specifications for essay tests are like those used for selected response assessments in some ways, and different in others. The similarities lie in the basic framework. Table 5.2 is an example of such a table for an essay test covering material on a series of short stories read in class. As the developer of such a table, I must specify the categories of knowledge respondents will use on one axis and the patterns of reasoning I expect on the other. Row and column totals, and therefore entries in the cells of the table, once again represent the relative emphasis assigned to each.

However, with the essay table of specifications, cells each contain the number of points on the test that I have assigned to that content-reasoning combination, not the number of individual test items, as was the case with selected response. When I actually construct the test, I might spread those points over one or more exercises associated with each cell.

Given 100 points for the entire exam, this plan obviously emphasizes the understanding of characters relative to the other two categories, requiring that respondents rely on that understanding to compare and evaluate. If I were to use exercises valued at 10 points each, I would need 10 exercises distributed so as to reflect these priorities.

I could translate these same values into instructional objectives, if I wish, as shown in the following list. I list these sample objectives simply to illustrate a second way of capturing and communicating the meaning of academic success reflected in the cells of the table. I need not do both the table and the objectives, but may select one or the other as a means of reflecting my valued outcomes.

- Students will be able to describe the settings, characters, and plots of the stories.
- Students will be able to find similarities and differences in settings, plots, and characters.
- Students will be able to carry out a systematic evaluation of the quality of the stories.

Table 5.2
Sample table of test specifications

	NUMBER OF POINTS			
Content	**Know**	**Compare**	**Evaluate**	**Total**
Setting	5	15	10	30
Plot	10	10	10	30
Characters	0	20	20	40
Total	15	45	40	100

Think Assessment *for* Learning

As with selected response specification tables, essay test plans can help focus students from the beginning of learning. The simplest version of this is to share the test blueprint at the outset. But beyond this, you might engage them as partners in creating the table itself by discussing what facets of the topic of study they think they might like to learn the most about. Be careful here, however. As a master of the domain to be learned as described in the district's curriculum, you are expected to know what is important to learn. But within this responsibility, if you have room for a bit of flexibility, weave in student interests. The motivational benefits can be helpful.

Exercise Development

One of my graduate students once described an exercise he received on a final exam at the end of his undergraduate studies. He had majored for four years in Spanish language, literature, and culture. His last final was an in-class essay exam with a 3-hour time limit. The entire exam consisted of one exercise, which posed the challenge in only two words: "Discuss Spain."

Haven't we all had experiences like this? One of the advantages often listed for essay tests relative to other test formats is that exercises are much easier and take less time to develop. I submit that many users turn that advantage into a liability by assuming that "easier to develop" means they don't have to put much thought into it, as evidenced in the previous example.

Another common mistake teachers make is trying to turn an essay exercise into a demonstration of their creativity as a test developer. A scientist friend offered an example from his experience as a college student: "Take a walk through a late Mesozoic forest and tell me what you see." This is better than "Discuss Spain." However, even more specification is needed to set respondents up for success.

To succeed with this assessment format, we must invest thoughtful preparation time in writing exercises that challenge respondents by describing a single complete and novel task. Sound exercises do three things:

1. Specify the knowledge students are supposed to command in preparing a response. For example:

During the term, we have discussed both the evolution of Spanish literature and the changing political climate in Spain during the twentieth century.

2. Specify the kind(s) of reasoning or problem solving respondents are to carry out. Be clear about what respondents are to write about. For example:

During the term, we have discussed both the evolution of Spanish literature and the changing political climate in Spain during the twentieth century. Analyze these two dimensions of life in Spain, citing three instances where literature and politics may have influenced each other. Describe the mutual influences in specific terms.

3. Point the direction to an appropriate response without giving away the answer. Good exercises literally list the key elements of a good response without cueing the unprepared examinee on how to succeed. For example:

> *During the term, we have discussed both the evolution of Spanish literature and the changing political climate in Spain during the twentieth century. Analyze these two dimensions of life in Spain, citing three instances where you think literature and politics may have influenced each other. Describe the mutual influences in specific terms. In planning your response, think about what we learned about prominent novelists, political satirists, and prominent political figures of Spain. (5 points per instance, total = 15 points.)*

Let's analyze the content of the example given in Figure 5.2, reproduced here.

Assume you are a French teacher with many years of teaching experience. You place great value on the development of speaking proficiency as an outcome of your instruction. Therefore, you rely heavily on assessments where you listen to and evaluate performance. But a problem has arisen. Parents of students who attained very high scores on your written tests are complaining that their children are receiving lower grades on their report cards. The principal wants to be sure your judgments of student proficiency are sound and so has asked you to explain and defend your procedures. Describe at least three specific quality standards that your oral proficiency exams would need to meet for you to be confident that your exams truly reflect what students can do; provide the rationale for each. (2 points for each procedure and rationale, total = 6 points.)

Here's the challenge to respondents in a nutshell:

Demonstrate understanding of:	Performance assessment methodology
By using it to figure out:	Proper applications of the method in a specific context
Adhering to these standards:	Include three appropriate procedures and defend them

Time for Reflection

Please return to the essay exercise you developed at the beginning of this section of the chapter. Did you specify the knowledge respondents must use, kinds(s) of reasoning they must employ, and standards they must apply? Adjust your exercise as needed to meet these standards.

Another excellent way to check the quality of your essay exercises is to try to write or outline a high-quality response yourself. If you can, you probably have a properly focused exercise. If you cannot, it needs work. Besides, this process will serve you well in your next step, devising scoring criteria.

Incidentally, when I use essays, I like to make it clear to my students that I care far more about the content of their answer than its form. I urge them to communicate their understanding and problem solutions to me as efficiently as they can, so I

Figure 5.3

Factors to consider when devising essay exercises

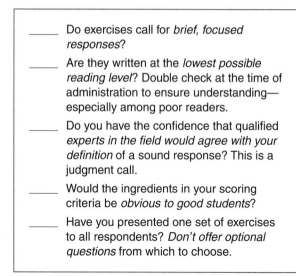

_____ Do exercises call for *brief, focused responses*?

_____ Are they written at the *lowest possible reading level*? Double check at the time of administration to ensure understanding—especially among poor readers.

_____ Do you have the confidence that qualified *experts in the field would agree with your definition* of a sound response? This is a judgment call.

_____ Would the ingredients in your scoring criteria be *obvious to good students*?

_____ Have you presented one set of exercises to all respondents? *Don't offer optional questions* from which to choose.

can read and score their responses as fast as possible. I urge them to use outlines and lists of ideas, examples, illustrations, charts, whatever it takes to come to the point quickly and clearly. I do not always require the use of connected discourse unless it is needed to communicate their solution to the problem. I explain that I do not want them beating around the bush in the hope that somewhere, somehow, they say something worth a point or two. Believe me, this suggestion makes scoring so much easier!

Figure 5.3 presents a checklist of factors to think about as you devise essay exercises. Answering these questions should assist you in constructing effective, high-quality essay exercises—those that avoid bias and distortion.

In regard to the last point in Figure 5.3, don't offer choices: The assessment question should always be, "Can you hit the agreed-on target?" It should never be, "Which part of the agreed-on target are you most confident that you can hit?" This latter question creates a sampling problem. It will always leave you uncertain about whether students have in fact mastered the material covered in exercises not selected, some of which may be crucial to later learning. When students select their own sample of performance, it can be a biased one.

I have one final idea to offer for exercise development. Let's say you wish to use the essay format to assess reasoning skills, but you do not expect your students to learn the content outright. Turn to the interpretive exercise format here. Provide the knowledge needed to solve the problem as part of the exercise (as a chart, graph, table, or paragraph of connected discourse) and then see if they can use it appropriately by spinning an essay or essays out of the material presented, as shown in the following example:

Map Skills: The Compromise of 1820

Study the map. Then decide whether these statements are true or false. In each case, explain your choice in a brief essay.

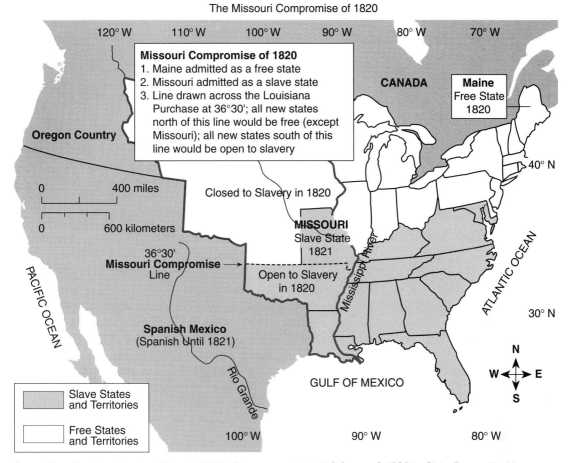

The Missouri Compromise of 1820

Missouri Compromise of 1820
1. Maine admitted as a free state
2. Missouri admitted as a slave state
3. Line drawn across the Louisiana Purchase at 36°30'; all new states north of this line would be free (except Missouri); all new states south of this line would be open to slavery

Source: From *Exploring American History* by Melvin Schwartz and John R. O'Connor. © 1986 by Globe Fearon. Used by permission of Pearson Education, Inc.

1. Most of the Louisiana Purchase was open to slavery.
2. Missouri was south of the line marked at 36 degrees, 30 minutes.
3. Missouri was admitted to the United States as a slave state.
4. The Mississippi River divided the free and slave territories.
5. The southwest boundary of the United States in 1820 was the Rio Grande.

Note here that "brief" essays are requested. These require only the most efficient explanation of the respondent's defense. If it's true, state why in the simplest possible terms. If it's false, again, defend your position. In some contexts extended responses are not needed to present convincing evidence of competence.

But whether we seek extended or short answers to essay exercises, we must conduct our scoring with clearly articulated evaluative criteria in mind. We go there next.

Think Assessment *for* Learning

But before we do, remember, you can engage students in devising practice essay exercises like those that will appear on a future examination. This will help them learn to center on important content and will require that they become sufficiently comfortable with your valued patterns of reasoning so that they can build them into practice exercises. If they write such exercises, and trade with classmates and write practice responses, both you and they gain access to useful information on what they are and are not mastering on their journey to meeting standards.

As a simpler variation of the theme, provide students with practice exercises and see if they can place them in the proper cells of the table of test specifications. Then have them defend their placement—good, focused practice. And remember, all the essay assessment work your students do during learning saves you valuable time.

Developing Essay Scoring Procedures

Many teachers score written responses by applying what I call "floating standards," in which you wait to see what responses you get to decide what you wanted. This represents the ultimate in unsound assessment practice, because it destroys both the validity and reliability of the assessment.

In that regard, I hope you will adhere to the instructional and assessment philosophy that has guided everything we have discussed up to this point: *Students can succeed if they know what it means to succeed.* State the meaning of success up front, design instruction to help students succeed, and devise and use assessments that reflect that vision of success. That includes formulating essay scoring criteria in advance and holding yourself and your students accountable for attaining those standards.

The scoring of an essay response represents a classic example of one of the most important reasoning patterns that we discussed in Chapter 2: evaluative reasoning. In evaluative reasoning, you will recall, one makes a judgment about something and defends it through the logical application of specified criteria. Theater critics evaluate plays according to certain (rarely agreed-on!) criteria and publish their reviews in the newspaper. Movie critics give thumbs up or down (an evaluative judgment) and use their criteria to explain why.

These are exactly the kinds of evaluative judgments teachers must make about responses to essay exercises. In all cases, the key to success is the clear articulation of appropriate evaluation criteria.

First, Evaluate What, Exactly?

When a student writes an essay, we can judge three different qualities of that work. We can evaluate whether the work conveys accurate knowledge and understanding, uses that knowledge in a manner that represents sound reasoning, or manifests the characteristics of effective written communication. The first two focus on substance, while the latter centers on matters of form. In this chapter, I will describe how one goes about evaluating the substance or content of essays: accuracy of knowledge and quality of reasoning. A rubric for evaluating the writing quality is provided in Chapter 6.

The key to student success is to be sure they know which set of criteria will come into play in any particular assessment and that they be provided with lots of guided practice in hitting those targets during instruction leading up to the final assessment *of* learning.

Scoring Options

Typically, we convey evaluative judgments about essay quality in terms of the number of points students attain. Here are two acceptable ways to do this, the checklist and scoring rubrics. Please note that scoring guides in essay assessment are exercise specific. That is, you create a separate and specific scoring guide for each new exercise, being sure to focus on keys to success in that specific context.

The Checklist.   We award points when specific ingredients appear in students' answers. The French teacher example (see Figure 5.2) provides an example of this kind of scoring. The scoring guide calls for respondents to cover certain material. They receive points for each key point they cover. Here is the scoring guide again:

2 points if the student's response lists any of these six procedures and defends each as a key to conducting sound performance assessments:

- Specify clear performance criteria
- Sample performance over several exercises
- Apply systematic rating procedures
- Maintain complete and accurate records
- Use published performance assessments to verify results of classroom assessments
- Use multiple observers to corroborate

Also award 2 points if the response lists any of the following and defends them as attributes of sound assessments:

- Specifies a clear instructional objective
- Relies on a proper assessment method
- Samples performance well
- Controls for sources of rater bias

All other responses receive no points.

Essay Scoring Rubrics.   In this case, we define achievement in terms of one or more performance continua. For example, a three-point rating scale might define three levels of mastery of the required material and we would apply that scale to each student's response. Here's an example:

3   The response is clear, focused, and accurate. Relevant points are made (in terms of the content expectations or kinds of reasoning sought by the exercise) with good support (derived from the content to be used, again as spelled out in the exercise). Good connections are drawn and important insights are evident.

2   The answer is clear and somewhat focused, but not compelling. Support of points made is limited. Connections are fuzzy, leading to few important insights.

1   The response either misses the point, contains inaccurate information, or otherwise demonstrates lack of mastery of the material. Points are unclear, support is missing, and/or no insights are included.

Some teachers devise such scoring rubrics to apply in a "holistic" manner, like this example. In this case, one overall judgment captures the teacher's evaluation of the essay. Other times teachers devise multiple "analytical" scales for the same essay, permitting them to evaluate the content coverage of the response separately from other important features. The idea is to develop as many such scales as needed to evaluate the particular material you are rating. Criteria for ratings, for example, might include these factors:

- Demonstrated mastery of content
- Organization of ideas
- Soundness of the reasoning demonstrated

Whether using holistic or analytical rubrics, however, the more specific and focused the criteria, the more dependable will be the results.

In addition to these essay scoring guidelines, experts urge that you adhere to the additional principles outlined in Figure 5.4 as you develop and apply scoring procedures.

Time for Reflection

Please return to the scoring plan you developed for your exercise at the beginning of this discussion. Did you devise a clear and appropriate set of standards? Adjust them as needed.

Think Assessment *for* Learning

Since scoring guides for essays are unique to each exercise, it is impossible to provide students with practice in applying them in advance of a final exam that is an assessment *of* learning—that is, where you are holding students accountable for having mastered the required material. In that case, they can't see the exercises until the time of that exam and you must do the scoring, not them.

However, you can involve them with designing sample scoring guides for practice exercises they developed above. Or, you can provide sample exercises and have students practice developing scoring guides for them. Further, they can practice scoring each other's practice responses to those exercises. By repeating this process as you proceed through a unit of study, you can provide students with opportunities to watch themselves improving. By the time they get to that final exam, they will know and will be ready to apply the secrets to their own success. Then this represents sharply focused instruction and a basis for very strong achievement.

- Set *realistic expectations and performance standards* that are consistent with instruction and that promise students some measure of success if they are prepared.
- Check scoring guides against a few real responses to see if any *last-minute adjustments* are needed.
- *Refer back to scoring guidelines* regularly during scoring to maintain consistency.
- *Score all responses to one exercise* before moving on to the next exercise. This does two things: It promotes consistency in your application of standards, and speeds up the scoring process.
- Score all responses to one exercise *in one sitting without interruption* to keep a clear focus on standards.
- Evaluate responses *separately for matters of content (knowledge mastery and reasoning) and matters of form (i.e., writing proficiency).* They require the application of different criteria.
- Provide feedback in the form of *points and written commentary* if possible.
- If possible, keep the *identity of the respondent anonymous* when scoring. This keeps your knowledge of their prior performance from influencing current judgments.
- Although it is often difficult to arrange, try to have *two independent qualified readers score* the papers. In a sense, this represents the litmus test of the quality of your scoring scheme. If two readers generally agree on the level of proficiency demonstrated by the respondent, then you have evidence of relatively objective or dependable subjective scoring. But if you and a colleague disagree on the level of performance demonstrated, you have uncovered evidence of problems in the appropriateness of the criteria or the process used to train raters, and some additional work is in order. When very important decisions rest on a student's score on an essay assessment, such as promotion or graduation, double scoring is absolutely essential.

Figure 5.4
Guidelines for essay scoring

Barriers to Sound Essay Assessment

To summarize, you can do many things to cause a student's score on an essay test to represent that student's real level of achievement with a high degree of accuracy. Potential sources of mismeasurement appear in Figure 5.5, along with action you can take to prevent or remedy them.

Student Involvement in Essay Assessment

With all assessment methods, the first and most obvious way to integrate assessment into teaching and learning is to match assessment to instruction by being sure that what you assess is what you teach, and what your students (hopefully) learn. In the

Potential Sources of Problems	Counteraction
Lack of target clarity:	
• Underlying knowledge unclear	Carefully study the material to be mastered and outline the knowledge structures to assess.
• Patterns of reasoning unspecified	Define forms of reasoning to be assessed in clear terms (see Chapter 9 for examples).
Wrong target for essay	Limit use to assessing mastery of larger knowledge structures (where several parts must fit together) and complex reasoning.
Lack of writing proficiency on part of respondents	Select another assessment method or help them become proficient writers.
Inadequate sample of exercises	Select a representative sample of sufficient length to give you confidence, given your table of specifications.
Poor-quality exercises	Follow guidelines specified above.
Poor-quality scoring:	
• Inappropriate criteria	Redefine criteria to fit the content and reasoning expected.
• Unclear criteria	Prepare explicit expectations—in writing.
• Untrained rater	All who are to apply the scoring criteria must be prepared to do so.
• Insufficient time to read and rate	Find more raters (see Figure 5.6 for ideas), or use another method.

Figure 5.5
Anticipating and countering sources of invalidity and unreliability

context of standards-based education, students deserve practice hitting the very targets for which you and they will be held accountable.

Beyond this essential perspective, Figure 5.6 summarizes and supplements our list of ways to integrate assessment with instruction by involving students as partners in assessing their own and each other's achievement. *Please study this list very carefully!*

It is intended merely to present enough ideas to prime your mental pump. It is only a start. The list of ways to bring students into the assessment equation is as limitless as your imagination. Please reflect and experiment, and find more ways. These uses of essay assessment development all contribute to that huge key to student success: making the target crystal clear for them to see and hit. These strategies serve to remove the mystery surrounding the meaning of good performance on an essay and in the classroom. They put students in control of their own academic well-being.

- As with selected response assessment, develop a blueprint for an essay test before ever teaching a unit, share that plan with students, and keep track of how well instruction is preparing them to succeed on the exam.
- Present students with unlabeled essay exercises and have them practice fitting them into the content and reasoning cells of the table of specifications.
- Have students join in on the process of writing sample exercises. To do so, they will need to begin to sharpen their focus on the intended knowledge and reasoning targets—as they do this, good teaching is happening! Be careful, though, these might best be used as examples for practice. Remember, to assess student reasoning, the exercises that actually appear on a test must present novel problems.
- Give students some sample exercises and have them evaluate their quality as test exercises, given the test blueprint.
- Have students play a role in developing the scoring criteria for some sample exercises. Give them, for example, an excellent response and a poor-quality response to a past essay exercise and have them figure out the differences.
- Bring students into the actual scoring process, thus spreading the work over more shoulders! Form scoring teams, one for each exercise on a test. Have them develop scoring criteria under your watchful eye. Offer them advice as needed to generate appropriate criteria. Then have them actually score some essays, which you double check. Discuss differences in scores assigned. Students find this kind of workshop format very engaging.
- Have students predict their performance in each cell in the table of specifications or objectives and then compare their prediction with the actual score. Were they in touch with their own achievement?
- Save essays and scoring criteria for reuse. A personal computer can help with this. If you keep information on student performance on each exercise (say, average score), you can adjust instruction next time to try to improve learning.
- Exchange, trade, or compare tables of specifications and/or exercises and scoring criteria with other teachers to ease the workload associated with assessment development.

Figure 5.6
Ideas for student-involved assessment

Summary: Tapping the Potential of Essay Assessment

In this chapter, we have explored ways to tap the considerable power of essay assessment. We must prevent validity and reliability problems that can arise with naïve use. We began by exploring the prominent roles subjectivity and professional judgment play in essay assessment. This method carries with it dangers of bias. We studied specific ways to prevent these dangers from becoming re-

alities. One is to connect essay assessment to appropriate kinds of achievement targets. These include mastery of complex structures of knowledge, complex reasoning processes, some of the knowledge foundations of skill and product proficiencies, and affective outcomes.

However, the heart of the matter with respect to valid and reliable assessment is adherence to specific assessment development procedures. We studied these in three parts: assessment planning, exercise development, and preparation to score. In each case, we reviewed specific procedural guidelines.

In addition, we considered an array of strategies to engage students as full partners in assessment, from design and development of exercises, to scoring, to interpreting and using essay assessment results. These strategies connect assessment to teaching and learning in ways that can maximize both students' motivation to learn and their actual achievement.

Final Chapter Reflection

1. *What are the three most important new insights to come to you as a result of your study of this chapter?*
2. *Which of your previous questions about assessment can you now answer based on your study of this chapter?*
3. *What new questions have come to mind as a result of your study of this chapter that you hope to have answered as your study continues?*

Practice with Chapter 5 Ideas

1. Critique for quality the following three brief descriptions of real essay contexts.

   Essay #1   Label the Graph.

   This question is intended for grades 3–12. It is one of six exercises using different content to assess problem solving in mathematics. Results will be used to track individual student progress toward mastery of state content standards. The scoring criteria have four traits, each scored separately by trained raters—conceptual understanding, mathematical procedures, strategic reasoning, and communication in mathematics. Students may or may not see the criteria depending on the teacher.

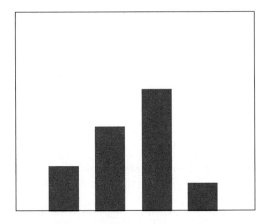

1. What might this be the graph of? Put titles and numbers on the graph to show what you mean.
2. Write down everything you know from your graph.

*Essay #2   Day and Night.**

The following task is intended for grade 2 to assess science understanding.

"Everyone knows about day and night. Write what you think makes day and night."

*Essay #3   Emerson Quiz.***

This quiz is intended for grades 10–12 to assess mastery of content knowledge (knowledge of Emerson) and reasoning in literature. Results will be used as 10 percent of the final grade in a literature class. [One of the essay questions follows. No scoring mechanism is described.]

"Read each of the statements below and put a check if Emerson would most likely complete the activity or put an X if he would disagree or not do the listed activity. For each answer, find a statement from Emerson's work to support your check or X. Be sure to quote the statement directly and give the page number in parentheses. Use the introduction to Emerson, *Nature,* and 'Self Reliance.'

1. _____ reject organized religion
2. _____ look to the past for guidance
3. _____ claim that religious truth comes from intuition
4. _____ rely on others for his success and happiness
5. _____ join a popular "civic organization"

2. Select a body of content you are learning as a student in another class or use the content of this chapter. Write three essay exercises that tap key content or reasoning dimensions of that material. When you have done so, review the list and defend your judgment that these represent the most important learnings from this chapter.

3. Devise scoring guides for each exercise, being sure they adhere to guidelines presented in this chapter.

4. Secure an example of an assessment that you have taken in the past that includes essay tasks. If you have no such assessment available, you can find samples at the Companion Website for this text http://www.prenhall.com/stiggins. Using the rubric found in the Appendix, along with the more specific guidelines provided in this chapter, evaluate the assessment for quality. Write a focused critique.

---

*Australian Council for Educational Research Ltd., *Exemplary Assessment Materials—Science,* 1996, p. 15. Available from The Board of Studies, 15 Pelham St., Carlton, Victoria 3053.

**From Thomas Mavor, 1999, Brother Martin High School, 4401 Elysian Fields Ave., New Orleans, LA 70122.

Chapter 6

Performance Assessment

CHAPTER FOCUS

This chapter answers the following guiding question:

> When and how do I use performance assessment most effectively to help my students succeed?

From your study of this chapter, you will understand the following:

1. Performance assessments permit you to rely on professional judgment to gather evidence of student reasoning proficiency, performance skills, and product development capabilities.
2. You can effectively develop performance assessments in two steps: (1) defining performance criteria; and (2) developing performance tasks or exercises.
3. This method can fall prey to problematic sources of bias that can distort results if users are not careful.
4. By involving your students in developing and using performance assessments, you can set them up for energetic and successful learning.

As we start this part of our journey, keep our big picture in mind. Figure 6.1 crosses our achievement targets with the four modes of assessment. In this chapter, we will be dealing in depth with the shaded areas.

Assessment Based on Observation and Professional Judgment

Performance assessments involve students in activities that require them actually to demonstrate performance of certain skills or to create products that meet certain standards of quality. In this case, we directly observe and judge their performance while it happens.

	SELECTED RESPONSE	ESSAY	PERFORMANCE ASSESSMENT	PERSONAL COMMUNICATION
Know				
Reason				
Performance Skills				
Products				
Dispositions				

Figure 6.1
Aligning achievement targets and assessment methods

As with essay assessments, we judge level of achievement by comparing each student's performance to predetermined levels of proficiency. Our goal is to make these subjective judgments as objective (free of bias and distortion) as they can be. We accomplish this by devising and learning to apply clear and appropriate performance criteria and gathering enough evidence (including enough performance tasks to sample adequately).

Table 6.1 lists examples of achievement targets that lend themselves to performance assessment. Notice that nearly all academic disciplines include both skills and products for which we might establish performance criteria in order to observe and judge proficiency. But to assess them accurately, we must be careful to zero in on the right standards of excellent performance. This chapter is about how to do this.

My goals for this chapter are to describe and illustrate a basic performance assessment design structure and process and to reveal the power of student involvement in their use. In later chapters, we will explore many more classroom applications.

The Promise and Perils of Performance Assessment

When we want to hear music in its truest form, we go to where it is being performed live. When we cannot do that, we revert to CDs or DVDs, seeking the highest-fidelity reproduction of the actual music we can obtain.

Table 6.1
Achievement targets for performance assessment

Focus of Assessment	Process or Skill Target	Product Target
Reading	Oral reading fluency	
Writing	Cursive writing skill; keyboarding	Samples of writing
Mathematics	Manipulate objects to form sets	Model depicting math principle
Science	Lab safety procedures	Lab research report
Social Studies	Debate	Term paper
Foreign Language	Oral fluency	Sample of writing
Art	Use of materials	Artistic creation
Physical Education	Athletic performance	
Technical Education	Computer operation	Software system designed
Vocational Education	Following prescribed procedures	Effectively repaired machine
Teamwork	Each member's contribution	
Early Childhood	Social interaction skill	Artistic creation

So it is with performance assessment. If we want to evaluate achievement in its truest form, we go to where it is being done live and we observe and judge the actual performance. We do this when we evaluate public speaking proficiency, oral proficiency with a foreign language, musical performance, or writing proficiency, for example. However, there are times when actual performance may be unsafe during learning or beyond reach in the classroom. For example, in driver education we might use a simulator to replicate driving performance before placing students behind the wheel for real. Or in engineering, we have the student build a bridge to test its strength, not actual bridges. In performance assessment sometimes we must approximate actual performance. But under any circumstances we seek high-resolution representations of those forms of achievement we can obtain.

We observe and we subjectively judge. But remember, as with essay assessment, subjectivity brings the risk of biased judgments. So we must be careful. It takes thorough preparation and attention to detail to attain appropriate levels of performance assessment rigor.

Adhere to the standards of assessment quality spelled out in earlier chapters when developing performance assessment and you can add immensely to the quality and utility of your classroom assessments. Always remember that you must begin assessment development with a clear purpose and a focused vision of the achievement you are assessing. Then you must select a proper target, devise a proper sample of performance tasks and scoring rubrics, and attend to all relevant sources of bias.

Time for Reflection

Can you think of instances in everyday life (outside of the school setting) where per-formance assessment comes into play as a matter of routine? For example, we observe and even try out automobiles to evaluate them, as we prepare to purchase one. We evaluate restaurants. Can you think of other examples?

The Foundations of Quality

Once again in this case, as with selected response and essay assessment, we begin by identifying certain realities of life in classrooms that can and should contribute to your decision about when to use this option. The context must be right for appro-priate application and we must understand the role of professional judgment in cre-ating and using performance assessments.

Understand When to Use Performance Assessment

By now it is clear to you that you will want to turn to performance assessment for certain kinds of achievement targets. We will review those connections in greater de-tail in the next section.

But there are other considerations in selecting this method. For instance, you must be sure all students have equal access to the resources and equipment needed to succeed. This may mean that each student has access to necessary materials pro-vided at school or at home. If circumstances beyond their control keep them from succeeding, that's not fair.

Consider performance assessment only when there is time to conduct it. It is a labor-intensive method. The more performance tasks you need to administer, the longer the per student time cost will be and the less feasible this method will be. One solution to a time crunch is to involve more observers and evaluators; such as, for example, (dare I say?) your students. We must think assessment *for* learning—student involvement.

Use performance assessment when you need an active, hands-on way to engage your students in learning. This may be the most powerful application of this method. Student-involved performance assessment can take your students right inside their learning so they can self-assess and remain aware of and in control of their own progress over time. As this chapter unfolds, I will offer several specific suggestions for how to do this.

Performance Assessment Is a Matter of Professional Judgment

Professional judgment guides every aspect of performance assessment design, de-velopment, and use. These judgments must be made carefully if assessment results are to be reliable.

For instance, as the developer or user of this method, you establish the achievement target you will assess based on priorities expressed in state and local achievement standards and benchmarks, your text materials, and the opinions of experts in the field. You devise the performance criteria, formulate performance tasks, and observe and evaluate student proficiency. Every step is a matter of your professional and subjective judgment. Just be sure your decisions are based on the best current thinking of experts in the subjects you teach.

Over the past decade, we have come to understand that carefully trained performance assessors—those who invest the clear thinking and developmental resources needed to do a good job—can use this subjective assessment methodology very effectively.

Understanding Reliability: Inter-Rater Agreement

Because of the subjective nature of performance assessment, you, the rater, become a potential source of bias. If the performance criteria you apply in evaluating student work are incorrect, imprecise, or influenced by factors unrelated to the student's actual achievement (such as gender, prior performance, etc.), the filters through which you see and evaluate that work can lead you to inaccurate judgments about proficiency. For example, if Ms. Weathersby had evaluated Emily's work with the prejudiced perspective that Emily would never be capable of improving her writing, her judgments of Emily's work would have been biased and inaccurate.

To prevent such occurrences, we must do our homework: establish sound performance criteria and learn to apply them consistently. The gauge of consistency that we apply in such assessment contexts is that of *inter-rater agreement*. Performance criteria are being applied consistently when two raters evaluate the same piece of work using the same criteria and, without conversing about it, draw the same conclusion about the level of proficiency demonstrated in that work. Surely you can see that, if they disagree, the judgment of student proficiency would be a function of who does the judging, not the actual level of achievement. That would be patently unfair. Our goal always is to be so clear about the attributes of good performance and so crisp and clean in our description of levels of proficiency in the performance continuum that consistency in judgement will always be within reach. This theme of inter-rater reliability will come up repeatedly through the rest of the chapter.

Understanding Validity: Matching Method to Target

Performance assessment can provide dependable information about student achievement of some, but not all, kinds of valued targets. Let's examine the matches and mismatches with our targets: knowledge, reasoning, skills, products, and dispositions.

Assessing Knowledge

If the objective of our instruction is to have students master content knowledge, observing and judging performance or products may not be the best way to find out if they have learned the material. It's not that we can't assess knowledge and understanding with this method. Under certain conditions, we can. But other times we cannot.

In this case, we always face a potential sampling problem. For example, you might ask students to participate in a group discussion in Spanish so you can assess their mastery of Spanish vocabulary and grammar. Although this is an apparently authentic performance assessment, it might lead you to incorrect conclusions about students' language mastery. They will choose to use only vocabulary and syntax with which they are most comfortable and confident, avoiding vocabulary and constructions unfamiliar to them. Thus, you will see a biased sample of their content mastery.

When assessing student mastery of content knowledge, whether learned outright or retrieved through the use of references, selected response or essay formats are usually better choices. These can be developed to include exercises that make sure students address all key elements of knowledge, not just the ones they choose.

Assessing Reasoning

Performance assessment can provide a means of assessing student reasoning and problem-solving proficiency. Remember that the challenge here is that we cannot lift off the top of students' heads and directly view their reasoning. So we rely on outward manifestations of sound reasoning to help us infer proficiency. Such inferences can arise from cognitive indicators, such as when students offer correct answers to a multiple-choice problem-solving question. Or they can spring from behavioral indicators, such as when students demonstrate actions or create products indicative of sound reasoning.

For example, you might give chemistry students unidentified substances to identify and watch how they go about setting up the apparatus and carrying out the study. The performance criteria would have to reflect the proper order of activities for conducting such experiments—an example of analytical reasoning. Those who reason well will follow the proper sequence and succeed. In this case, the process is as important as getting the right answer—the process is what you're trying to assess.

Performance assessments structured around the products students create also can provide insight into their reasoning proficiency. Consider the example in which students are to carry out a science experiment. One facet of your evaluation might center on their research report. You would evaluate these reports in terms of the standards of a good report, if those criteria have been clearly and completely articulated. But in addition, the resulting products could provide evidence of students' scientific reasoning while conducting the experiment and writing the report itself. You would need two sets of criteria, one reflecting the proper structure of a lab report and the other reflecting the reasoning requirements of the experiment.

Assessing Performance Skills

We also can use performance assessment to evaluate proficiencies beyond proper reasoning. The great strength of this methodology lies in its ability to provide a dependable means of evaluating skills as students are doing the things that reflect certain forms of achievement. Communication skills such as speaking and oral reading fall in this category, as do the performing and industrial arts, physical education, and oral proficiency in speaking a foreign language. Observing students in action can be a rich and useful source of information about their attainment of very important forms of skill achievement.

Assessing Products

Herein lies the other great strength of performance assessment. There are occasions when we ask students to create complex achievement-related products. The quality of those products indicates the creator's level of achievement. If we develop sound performance criteria that reflect the key attributes of these products and learn to apply those criteria well, performance assessment can serve us as both an efficient and effective tool. We may evaluate in this way everything from written products, such as term papers and research reports, to the many forms of art and craft products, and science exhibitions and models.

Assessing Dispositions

To the extent that we can draw inferences about positive attitudes, strong interests, motivational dispositions, and/or academic self-concept based either on students' actions or on what we see in the products they create, then performance assessment can assist us here as well. Chapter 8 will provide details.

However, I urge caution. Remember, sound performance assessment (like all other assessment methods!) requires strict adherence to an established set of rules of evidence. Each assessment must do the following:

- *Reflect a clear target*—We must thoroughly understand and develop sound definitions of the dispositions we are assessing.
- *Serve a clearly articulated purpose*—We must know precisely why we are assessing and what we intend to do with the results, especially tricky in the case of dispositions.
- *Rely on a proper method*—Our performance criteria must map a clear and complete continuum, each point on which corresponds to a different level of the disposition in question.
- *Sample the target appropriately*—We must collect enough evidence to give us confidence in our conclusions about student dispositions.
- *Control for key sources of bias*—We must understand the potential sources of bias in our judgments about student attitudes, values, interests, and so on and neutralize them in the context of our assessments.

Table 6.2
Performance: Assessment of achievement targets

Target to Be Assessed	Performance
Knowledge & Understanding	Not a good choice for this target—three other options preferred
Reasoning Proficiency	Can watch students solve some problems or examine some products and infer about reasoning proficiency
Performance Skills	Can observe and evaluate skills as they are being performed
Ability to Create Products	Can assess: (1) proficiency in carrying out steps in product development, and (2) attributes of the product itself
Dispositions	Can infer dispositions from behavior and products

Summary of Target–Performance Assessment Matches

Table 6.2 provides a simple summary of the alignments among performance assessment and the various kinds of achievement that we expect of our students.

Developing Performance Assessments

We initiate our creation of performance assessments just as we initiated the development of paper and pencil tests in the previous two chapters: with a plan or blueprint. The performance assessment plan includes just two specific parts. Each part asks the developer to make several specific design decisions.

We start by defining the performance(s) we wish to evaluate. Then we prepare tasks or assignments that we will use to elicit student performance so we may evaluate it. Figure 6.2 presents an overview of the design decisions we must make as performance assessment developers. The immense potential of this form of assessment becomes apparent when we consider all of the design combinations available within this structure.

As we explore, we will examine how one group of teachers selected from among the array of possibilities to find the design they needed to serve their purposes. Remember Emily, the high school English student in the school board meeting that opened Chapter 1? We will explore the assessment challenges that her English teachers faced as they endeavored to put her and her classmates in touch with their emerging proficiency as writers.

Remember Your Purpose

Remember, regardless of the assessment method, you must begin any developmental sequence with a clear sense of why you are assessing. Different assessment users need different information in different forms at different times to make informed decisions.

Design Ingredient	Options
Remember to articulate your purpose: Specify user(s) and use(s). Then:	
Design Step 1: Define Performance	
A. Type of performance	Skill target, product, or both
	Individual, group achievement, or both
B. Develop performance criteria	Articulate the keys to successful performance
	Score holistically, analytically, or a combination
Design Step 2: Develop Performance Tasks	
A. Task specification	Define target, conditions, criteria
B. Selecting a sample	Decide how many tasks are needed to cover the terrain

Figure 6.2
Performance assessment design framework

For example, as we discuss how Ms. Weathersby and Emily's other teachers used performance assessments of writing proficiency, bear in mind that they assessed for two reasons, or to serve two purposes:

1. To help their students become better writers (assessment *for* learning: students and teacher are users; they seek to understand strengths and weaknesses)
2. To gather information on improvement in student writing as part of the faculty's evaluation of the impact of their new instructional program (assessment *of* learning: verify achievement for accountability purposes)

Defining Performance

The first challenge we face as performance assessment developers is that of defining our vision of academic success. Ms. W. and the English faculty at Emily's high school, for example, needed to stipulate what it meant to be a "good writer" within their program. In specifying the target, we must make two design decisions: What type of performance are we assessing? Specifically, what does good performance look like? Let's consider these in a bit more detail.

Selecting the Type of Performance
This design decision asks us to answer the basic questions: How will successful achievement manifest itself? Where will we most easily find evidence of proficiency? That evidence might take the form of a particular set of performance skills—behaviors that students must demonstrate. Examples include working well with

classmates in the primary grades, development of motor skills in physical education, or proficiency at public speaking. In all these instances, success manifests itself in student actions.

Or, will we observe and judge something students have created to determine their proficiency? In this case, we ask students to create a particular kind of product, which we then examine to find evidence of achievement. Consider, for example, art or craft products, term papers, models, or effectively repaired machines.

Note also, that some performance assessments might focus both on skills and products that result, such as when we first assess a student's skill at writing a computer program and then assess the quality of the resulting program as it runs.

The English faculty in Emily's school wanted to evaluate their students' writing proficiency, so they needed to see and make judgments about the quality of actual samples of student writing (products).

Developing Rubrics

This is the part of the performance assessment design where we describe what "counts." The challenge is to not only describe what "outstanding" performance looks like, but also to map each of the different levels of performance leading up to the highest levels. We strive to do this with both descriptive language and examples of student work illustrating each level of proficiency. In this sense, rubrics provide the vocabulary needed to communicate with our students about the path to successful performance.

In one sense, accomplished teachers are connoisseurs of good performance, but in another sense, they are far more than that. Connoisseurs can recognize outstanding performance when they see it. They know a good restaurant when they find it. They can select a fine wine. They know which movies deserve a thumbs-up and which Broadway plays are worth their ticket price. Connoisseurs also can describe why they believe something is outstanding or not. However, because the evaluation criteria may vary somewhat from reviewer to reviewer, their judgments may not always agree. For restaurants, wines, movies, and plays, the standards of quality may be a matter of opinion. But, that's what makes interesting reading in newspapers and magazines.

Teachers are very much like these connoisseurs in that they too must be able to recognize and describe outstanding performance. But for accomplished teachers, there is more. Not only can well-prepared teachers visualize and explain the meaning of success, but they also can impart that meaning to others so as to help them become outstanding performers. *In short, they don't just criticize—they inspire improvement.*

In most disciplines, the standards of excellence that characterize high-quality performance are always those held by experts in the field of study in question. Outstanding teachers/classroom assessors are those who have immersed themselves in understanding those discipline-based meanings of proficiency. It is this depth of understanding that we must capture in our performance expectations so we can convey it to students through instruction, illustration, and practice. Our rubrics cannot exist only in our minds. We must translate them into student-friendly language, with examples, for our students to see and understand.

Many fields of study already have developed outstanding examples of sound rubrics for critical performances. Examples include writing proficiency, foreign language, mathematics, and physical education, and I use these as illustrations throughout this text.

As it turns out, the vision of good writing—the rubrics or scoring criteria— adopted by the English faculty at Emily's high school came from the summer professional development session they attended and included a set of rating scales reflecting six dimensions of effective writing. The faculty's first challenge was to understand these standards of writing excellence themselves. Then they had to transform the performance criteria into student-friendly language. They elected to bring their students in as partners. I'll explain later how they did that. But in the meantime, their transformation appears in Figure 6.3. Please read it.

Developing Performance Criteria (Think Assessment *for* Learning)

To develop your own rubrics, you will need to carry out a thoughtful analysis of the performance skill or product you wish to evaluate. That means you must look inside the skills or products of interest to find the active ingredients. In most cases, this is not complicated. Do it on your own, work with colleagues, or partner up with your students—it's all the same.

To illustrate, consider how Emily and her classmates worked with Ms. W. to learn the attributes of good writing through developing student-friendly rubrics. As you follow the steps described, consider other contexts where this process might come into play in your classroom. How might you use these steps to help your students understand rubrics for some form of their achievement you are evaluating? I once watched a class of third graders go through this same process to clarify criteria for assessing upcoming dramatic presentations of historical characters they were planning for their parents. A middle school social studies teacher I know used these steps to help his students see how to improve the research reports they were about to write. As you read on, see if you can see applications of this five-step process that might be relevant in your classroom.

Step 1: Discover.   The goal in this initial step is to help students begin to discover the keys to their own success. This requires that they become partners in the task or product analysis that will identify the active ingredients contributing to different levels of proficiency. As their teacher, you engage students in answering the question, How does a good task or product differ from a poor-quality one? To answer, students must have the opportunity to see examples. Regard Emily's experience as she describes it here.

But before you do, keep this key point in mind: This story is not about students determining the attributes of good writing. Ms. W. started with a clear vision of success. Hers is the vision that holds sway here. But note how she drew her students to her vision in ways that promoted ownership on their part:

"Ms. Weathersby gave us a writing assignment to complete on the first day of class. She said we were to write an essay about someone or something that we care deeply about. I wrote about my Mom. When we were done, she gave us each a folder and told us to put it in there and put the folder away.

Ideas

5. My paper is clear, focused, and filled with details not everybody knows.
   - You can tell I know a lot about this topic.
   - My writing is full of interesting tidbits, but it doesn't overwhelm you.
   - I can sum up my main point in one clear sentence: _____
   - You can picture what I'm talking about. I *show* things happening *(Fred squinted)*; I don't just *tell* about them *(Fred couldn't read the small print).*

3. Even though my writing grabs your attention here and there, it could use some spicy details.
   - I know *just* enough about this topic—but more information would make it more interesting.
   - Some "details" are things most people probably already know.
   - My topic is too big. I'm trying to tell too much. Or else it's too skimpy.
   - It might be hard to picture what I'm talking about. Not enough *showing.*
   - I'm afraid my reader will get bored and go raid the refrigerator.

1. I'm just figuring out what I want to say.
   - I need a LOT more information before I'm really ready to write.
   - I'm still thinking on paper. What's my main idea?
   - I'm not sure *anyone* reading this could picture *anything.*
   - I wouldn't want to share this aloud. It's not ready.
   - Could I sum it up in one clear sentence? No way! It's a list of stuff.

Organization

5. My paper is as clear as a good road map. It takes readers by the hand and guides them along every step.
   - My beginning hints at what's coming, and makes you want to read on.
   - Every detail falls in just the right place.
   - Nothing seems out of order.
   - You never feel lost or confused; however, there could be a surprise or two.
   - Everything connects to my main point or main story.
   - My paper ends at just the right spot, and ties everything together.

3. You can begin to see where I'm headed. If you pay attention, you can follow along pretty well.
   - I have a beginning. Will my reader be completely hooked, though?
   - Most things fit where I have put them. I might move *some* things around.
   - Usually, you can see how one idea links to another.
   - I guess everything should lead up to the most important part. Let's see, *where* would that *be?*
   - My paper has an ending. But does it tie up loose ends?

1. Where are we headed? I'm lost myself.
   - A beginning? Well, I might have just repeated the assignment . . .
   - I didn't know where to go next, so I wrote the first thing that came to me.
   - I'm not really sure which things to include—or what order to put them in.
   - It's a collection of stuff—kind of like a messy closet!
   - An ending? I just stopped when I ran out of things to say.

(continued)

Figure 6.3

Analytical writing assessment rating scales

Source: Reprinted from *Creating Writers,* 3d ed. (pp. 144–149) by V. Spandel, 2001, New York: Addison-Wesley Longman. Reprinted by permission.

Voice

5. I have put my personal, recognizable stamp on this paper.
   - You can hear my voice *booming* through. It's *me.*
   - I care about this topic—and it shows.
   - I speak right to my audience, always thinking of questions they may have.
   - I wrote to please myself, too.
   - My writing rings with confidence.

3. What I truly think and feel shows up sometimes.
   - You might not laugh or cry when you read this, but you'll hang in there and finish reading.
   - I'm right on the edge of finding my own voice—so *close!*
   - My personality pokes out here and there. You *might* guess this was my writing.
   - It's pleasant and friendly enough, but I didn't think about my audience *all* the time. Sometimes I just wanted to *get it over with!*

1. I did not put too much energy or personality into this writing.
   - It could be hard to tell who wrote this. It could be anybody's.
   - I kept my feelings in check.
   - If I liked this topic better or knew more, I could put more life into it.
   - Audience? *What* audience? I wrote to get it done.

Word Choice

5. I picked *just* the right words to express my ideas and feelings.
   - The words and phrases I've used seem *exactly* right.
   - My phrases are colorful and lively, yet nothing's overdone.
   - I've used some everyday words in new ways. Expect a few surprises.
   - Do you have a favorite phrase or two in here? I do.
   - Every word is accurate. You won't find yourself wondering what I mean.
   - Verbs carry the meaning. I don't bury my reader in adjectives.

3. It might not tweak your imagination, but hey, it gets the basic meaning across.
   - It's functional and it gets the job done, but I can't honestly say I stretched.
   - O.K., so there are some cliches hiding in the corners.
   - I've also got a favorite phrase lurking around here *someplace.*
   - Verbs? What's wrong with a good old *is, are, was, were…?*
   - I might have overutilized the functionality of my thesaurus.
   - You can understand it, though, right? Like, nothing's really wrong.

1. My reader might go, "Huh?"
   - See, I'm like this victim of vague wording and fuzzy phrasing.
   - It's, you know, kind of hard to get what I'm talking about. *I* don't even remember what I meant and *I wrote this stuff.*
   - Maybe I misutilized a word or two.
   - Some redundant phrases might be redundant.
   - I need verby power.

Figure 6.3

Analytical writing assessment rating scales *(continued)*

Sentence Fluency

5. My sentences are clear and varied—a treat to read aloud.
   - Go ahead—read it aloud. You won't need to practice.
   - Sentence variety is my middle name.
   - Hear the rhythm? Smooth, huh?
   - Deadwood has been cut. Every word counts.

3. My sentences are clear and readable.
   - My writing is *pretty* smooth and natural—you can get through it all right.
   - Some sentences should be joined together. Others might be cut in two.
   - There's a little deadwood, sure, but it doesn't bury the good ideas too badly under extra verbiage, even though I must say it won't hurt to cut some unneeded words here and there and shorten things up just a bit.
   - I guess I did get into a rut with sentence beginnings. I guess I could use more variety. I guess I'll fix that.

1. I admit it's a challenge to read aloud (even for me).
   - You might have to stop or reread now and then it just feels like one sentence picked up right in the middle of another a new sentence begins and, oh boy, I'm lost…Help! Untangle me!
   - My sentences all begin the same way. My sentences are all alike. My sentences need variety. My sentences need work.
   - Some sentences are too short. They're too short. They're really short. Way short. Short.
   - Reading this is like trying to skate on cardboard. Tough going!

Conventions

5. An editor would fall asleep looking for mistakes in this paper.
   - Capitals are all in the right places.
   - Paragraphs begin at the right spots.
   - Great punctuation—grammar, too.
   - My spelling (even of difficult words) would knock your socks off.
   - I made so few errors, it would be a snap getting this ready to publish.

3. Some bothersome mistakes show up when I read carefully.
   - Spelling is correct on simple words.
   - Capitals are O.k. maybe I should look again, Though.
   - The grammar might be a little informal, but it's OK for everyday writing.
   - A few pronouns do not match what IT refers to.
   - You might stumble over my innovative! Punctuation.
   - It reads like a first draft, all right.
   - I'd definitely need to do some editing to get this ready to publish.

1. Better read it once to decode, then once again for meaning.
   - Lotsuv errers Mak? The going ruf.
   - I've forgotten some CAPS—otherS aren't Needed.
   - Look out four speling mysteaks.
   - To tell the truth, I didn't spend much time editing.
   - I'll really have to roll up my sleeves to get this ready for publishing.

Figure 6.3

Analytical writing assessment rating scales *(continued)*

"Then she gave us all copies of an essay that she had just written for a magazine. Our homework assignment was to read it and try to decide if it was any good. The tough part was that she said she didn't want us to try to please her. She wanted our honest reaction. If it's good, what makes it good? Be specific, she said. If it's not very good, tell me why.

"Some kids noticed some bad things. But mostly we just thought it was real good. I mean, she's a professional writer. What do we know? Besides who wants to tick off the grade giver?"

"But then she did something very interesting. She gave us a copy of an essay that she had saved from her high school years, when she was first learning to write. She told us to read that one as our next homework assignment. Same deal: Come to class the next day ready to evaluate it. We all hoped that she meant it when she said that it's okay to be critical. We were! But she was cool. She made us be real specific about the problems we saw in that essay. She made us write 'em down, too. Then she took us back to her first essay—the real good one—and made us do the same thing. We brainstormed another list, this time of all the things that we thought made it good. We had to write those down, too, to take with us. This time our homework assignment was to study both essays and try to figure out the 10 most important differences between them. What are the things that one essay does well that are missing or done badly in the other? Then she told us to put our lists of differences in our folders along with the essay we had written. We'd return to them later.

"The next day, she gave us each a stack of essays—like, ten or so. Our job was to tell the good from the not-so-good. She had us work in teams to sort them into four piles: Very Good, Good, So-so, and Pretty Bad. In my group, we each read each paper and then voted on which pile. Sometimes we disagreed. But not much—just about two or three. Our homework that night was to get together to finish up the sorting if we didn't get done during class.

"The next day in class, she had us compare the Pretty Bad and So-so papers to figure out what made them different. Then we compared the So-so and Good papers, and then the Good and Very Good. Once again, we brainstormed lists of important differences. As I look back now, I see that she had us discovering how the quality of writing differs. When we finished figuring out the essential differences among those four stacks of papers, Ms. W. referred us back to our comparison of what was good and bad about her essays—you know, the list in our folders. The two lists were almost exactly alike!"

We'll return to our conversation with Emily. But first, notice the power of asking students to contrast examples of vastly different samples of performance. It virtually always helps them zero in on how to describe performance, good and poor, in their own clear and understandable language.

Step 2: Condense.   Next you help students build a vocabulary that both you and they can use to converse with each other about performance. This is why it is important to engage students in learning the rubric. When you share the stage with your students and involve them in defining success by having them analyze examples and choose the language to describe achievement, in effect you begin to connect them to their target. Emily continues:

"So now we're beginning to understand different levels of writing quality. Now Ms. Weathersby had us take our initial essays out of our folders and evaluate them. Which pile is our essay most like: Very Good, Good, So-so, or Pretty Bad? You know where mine was—thumbs down!! It was pretty bad. But she said, 'Just be patient. Improvement will come pretty quickly.' Since there wasn't a pile lower than the one my paper was in, I had to believe her.

"Ms. W. said that we had to start getting specific. We had long lists of attributes of different levels of performance, like 20 ingredients. We had to start boiling them down. We had to get to the important stuff. She asked things like, Can any of these be combined? Are some a lot more important than others? We actually read Ms. W.'s good essay again, this time out loud in class to see if it helped us zero in on keys to success. I don't remember all of our steps along the way. But this was when we had our first experience with the BIG SIX! Look! I put them on the cover of my writing portfolio:

Ideas and Content—you got something to say?

Organization—you have to have a plan

Sentence Fluency—rhythm, rhythm, rhythm

Word Choice—accurate and precise, always the right word, that's me!

Voice—speak right to your reader

Conventions—don't let errors distract your reader"

Step 3: Define.   In this step, it is crucial to remember that the job is not merely to define successful, or high-level, performance. Rather, you seek to describe the full range of performance, so each performer can come to understand where they are now in relation to where you want them to be down the road. Only with that roadmap in hand can they watch themselves travel their own personal journey to excellence, feeling in complete control all along the way.

"Ms. Weathersby divided us up into collaborative teams—six teams. Then she placed the labels for our six categories in a hat and each team had to draw one out. Each team was to take the lead in helping the rest of the class learn to master their element of good writing.

"Each team had to write a definition of their element. But we couldn't just make it up. We had to go to the library and check in the dictionary and other reference materials. And we needed to review the essays we had been analyzing to find examples of strong and weak performance of our element. Then we had to prepare a presentation for the rest of the class to show them what we had learned—using the overhead projector and all! Ms. W. encouraged us to question and argue with each other to be sure we all agreed on the final definitions. We really had good discussions. The illustrations really helped.

"As our next assignment, Ms. W. had us divide a piece of paper into three columns, labeled 'high,' 'middle,' and 'low.' Under the high column, we were to develop a list of words or phrases that we believed describe a piece of writing when it is of outstanding quality with respect to our particular element. Then under low, we were to describe a paper that is of poor quality on our assigned attribute. And finally, we were to describe the midrange, too. And once again, we had to find examples to illustrate different levels of writing and make a class presentation.

"Each team presented and we listened and questioned. Ms. W. asked the best questions—really challenged us to see if we knew what we were talking about. She also showed us how to stretch our rating scales from three to five points. When we were all done, Ms. W. told us how proud she was of us and how much we had learned. She collected the results of each team's work and overnight put all of the rating scales on her computer and printed copies for all of us to use with our next assignments."

Please refer to Figure 6.3 to see the results of the work of Emily and her classmates.

Step 4: Learn to Apply the Rubric.   The next step is to help your students learn to apply their performance criteria through practice. You accomplish this most effectively by providing them with varied examples of performance so they can analyze and judge quality. As this process unfolds, you can start your students down the road of discovering their own current level of performance using agreed-on rubrics. (When your students become trained raters, the workload spreads over many shoulders.) In this way, you show them where they are now in relation to where you want them to be, so they can begin to take charge of their journey to excellence. Here's how Ms. W. did this, as Emily recounts it:

"First, she returned us to the stack of papers that we had sorted into piles. You know, Very Good, So-so, and so on. Then she had us pick one paper from each pile and rate it using our six five-point performance criteria. We all rated the same four papers. Then using a show of hands, she asked us how many of us rated each paper on each criterion at each level. We didn't all agree with each other exactly. But we were pretty close. And boy, those profiles sure revealed why we had put each paper in each pile originally. They were really different.

"Next, Ms. W. had us go to our files and pull out the essay that we had written at the very beginning and rate it using our scales. Mine was terrible. But she said that was okay. Low ratings are not a bad thing when you're first getting started. Low ratings don't mean you've failed. They only mean you're just starting to learn about something. But, you have to start improving.

"Then she gave us another writing assignment, promising that even now we probably would see improvement in the quality of our writing. As I wrote that night, I found myself thinking, Ideas and Content—Have I got anything to say?; Organization—I gotta have a plan; Sentence Fluency—rhythm, rhythm, rhythm; Word Choice—Am I telling my story accurately and precisely?; Voice—Am I speaking to my reader?; and Conventions—Don't let errors interfere.

"The next day in class, we worked in teams to read and evaluate each other's essays and we all found that this second effort was much better! Ms. W. was right.

"From then on we did more and more of the same. She shared samples of writing that she had found that did or didn't do something well. We dug up some, too, and shared them. We wrote a lot. Sometimes we just evaluated one or two of the six criteria. Ms. W. said, when we're working on Organization, that's what we evaluate. But, she said, eventually all of the pieces have to come together."

Step 5: Refine.   Revising and refining performance criteria never stops. By evaluating lots of student work over time, you tune into the keys to success with increasing focus and precision. As new insights arise, revise your criteria to reflect your best current thinking. And remember, it is not uncommon for students who are involved in the process to "out think" their teachers and come up with criteria of excellence that you have not seen. When they do, honor their good thinking! Never regard performance criteria as "finished." Rather, always see them as works in progress.

Summary: Step by Step.   When it comes down to devising your own performance assessment rubrics, do what Ms. Weathersby did. Her steps are listed in Table 6.3.

And remember, when students are partners in carrying out these steps, you and they join together to become a learning community. Together, you open windows to the meaning of academic success, providing your students with the words and examples they need to see that vision.

The Attributes of Good Rubrics

So how do we know if the performance criteria that make up your rubric are any good? Interestingly enough, we need a rubric for rubrics! Good rubrics for evaluating student proficiency in a performance assessment context specify the *important content* (what counts) with sharp *clarity* (everyone understands) in terms that are *practical* (easy to use) and that are *fair* (are valid and can be reliably judged). Let's look inside each.

Rubrics rate high in *content* when everything of importance is included— nothing of importance is left out. But they do leave out things that are regarded as unimportant—tangential to student success.

Table 6.3
Steps in devising performance criteria

Step	Activity
Discover	Analyze examples of performance to uncover keys to success
Condense	Pool the resulting ideas into a coherent but concise and original set of key attributes
Define	Develop simple definitions of the key to success and devise performance continuums for each
Apply	Practice applying performance evaluation procedures until you can do so with consistency
Refine	Always remain open to the possibility that criteria might need to be revised

They rate high in *clarity* when it's easy for everyone involved (student and teacher alike) to understand what is meant. Terms are defined, as is each level of proficiency. Samples of student work have been collected to illustrate the various levels of performance.

Rubrics are *practical,* again, when everything is easy to understand and apply. Students can use the criteria for self-assessment. The information provided from rating is useful for deciding what to learn next. The number of ingredients evaluated is manageable, given the reality of life in classrooms.

And finally, they are dependable, or *fair,* when the ratings of student performance actually depict what students can do and how well—the results are valid. They are of high quality when independent raters agree on the level of proficiency demonstrated. Each level of proficiency is described in ways that apply equally well to all students, regardless of gender, or cultural or ethnic background.

Figure 6.4 provides a performance rating scale (rubrics) for each of the four attributes just described. Activities are provided at the end of the chapter for you to practice applying these criteria in evaluating some sample scoring guides.

Devising Performance Tasks

Performance assessment tasks, like selected response test items and essay exercises, frame the challenge for students. Thus, performance assessment tasks clearly and explicitly reflect the achievement target(s).

We face two basic design considerations when dealing with tasks in the context of performance assessment. We must determine the following:

- The specific ingredients of the task, defining what performers are to do
- The number of tasks needed to sample performance

Let's delve into each in some detail.

Developing the Performance Task

Like well-developed essay exercises, sound structured performance assessment tasks specify and explain the challenge to respondents, while setting them up to succeed if they can, by doing the following:

- Identifying the specific kind(s) of performance to demonstrate
- Detailing the context and conditions within which proficiency will be demonstrated
- Reminding students of the criteria applied in evaluating performance

Following is a simple example of a performance task that frames clear and specific problems to solve in all three terms:

- *Identify Achievement*—You are to use your knowledge and understanding of how to convert energy into motion, along with your understanding of the principles of mechanics, to reason through the design for a mousetrap car. A mousetrap car converts one snap of the trap into forward motion. Then you are to build and demonstrate your car.

Characteristic 1: Content

This refers to the aspects of student work we look for to determine its quality. It includes everything that is truly important about performance and leaves out things that we know are not important.

Ready for Use

- Everything included has clear justification in terms of the current thinking of the field; that is, it aligns with relevant standards.
- Informed users would generally agree that the performance continuum "makes sense" in terms of student performance—teachers are left with no questions unanswered.
- Description of keys to success reflects proper emphasis—more important things receive greater emphasis, yet nothing is overloaded.

Needs Revision

- Much of the content is directly relevant, but you can think of important things that have been left out; some important standards need more attention.
- While headed in the right direction, the rubric addresses some features incorrectly.
- Although the continuum seems reasonable, it includes some irrelevant features.

Don't Use

- You can think of major features of performance that are overlooked; some performance standards are completely omitted.
- Irrelevant features abound.
- Definitions are incorrect.
- The rubric is endless in its scope and coverage, including too much detail regarding content.

Characteristic 2: Clarity

The rubric describes performance in clear and appropriate language that everyone is likely to understand and interpret to mean the same thing. It is easy to think of examples to illustrate each point on the performance continuum.

Ready for Use

- Different teachers, working independently, are likely to rate the same piece of work at the same level.
- It would be easy to use the rubric consistently over time, once mastered.
- Everything is defined with specific and accurate terminology, and with sufficient detail.

Needs Revision

- The fuzzy language used might make it difficult to make the proper and consistent ratings.
- Sometimes clear definitions and descriptive detail are missing, making it hard for two teachers to agree on the proper rating.

Do Not Use

- Vague language promotes confusion about scale meaning.
- Definitions are missing or incorrect.
- Few descriptors leave levels of proficiency impossible to differentiate.
- Different interpretations make agreement among raters unlikely.

(continued)

Figure 6.4
Standards for evaluating rubrics

Characteristic 3: Practicality

Here we refer to ease of application. The ratings that result from the rubric must connect to specific instructional decisions—ways to help students improve.

Ready for Use

- The number of facets of performance to be evaluated is manageable in number—both teachers and students can understand and apply them.
- Assessment ratings can be transformed easily into instruction; that is, it's easy to see what to do next based on results.
- There is a student-friendly version—students can see how to revise their work to improve it.
- The rubric is of general value; that is, it is not task specific, it can be used to evaluate performance in response to a number of different tasks.

Needs Revision

- It provides good information but may be somewhat difficult to apply.
- A bit more detail would connect the rubric to the specifics of student work.
- Students can rate their work, but have some difficulty seeing how to improve it.

Do Not Use

- There is no apparent connection between ratings and specific action to help students improve.
- The need for rating efficiency seems to have overwhelmed the need for practical utility.
- There are too many things or not enough things to rate to make the rubric useful; the user is under- or overwhelmed.

Characteristic 4: Dependability

Ready for Use

- Given its focus and clarity, independent raters would probably agree on the level of proficiency demonstrated in any particular piece of student work.
- The language used to describe performance is appropriate for the diversity of students found in the classroom—wording is supportive of the learning of all students.
- There has been an independent evaluation of the rubric by a qualified colleague to maximize quality.

Needs Revision

- Issues of focus and clarity create some uncertainty about the expected degree of agreement among raters.
- The rubric is inconsistent in its appropriateness for diverse student populations, but it could be easily adjusted to be supportive of the learning of all students.

Do Not Use

- Due to lack of focus and clarity, independent raters would not be expected to agree on the level of proficiency demonstrated.
- The language reflects stereotypic thinking, an insensitivity to some cultures, and might be hurtful to some students.
- There has been no review of the rubric by a qualified colleague to assure fairness.

Figure 6.4
Standards for evaluating rubrics *(continued)*

- *Specify Conditions*—Using materials provided in class and within the time limits of four class periods, design and diagram your plan, construct the car itself, and prepare to explain why you included your key design features.
- *Establish Criteria*—Your performance will be evaluated in terms of the specific standards we set in class, including the clarity and completeness of your diagrammed plan, the match between your plan and the actual quality of your car, and the quality of your presentation explaining its design features. Scoring guides are attached.

The Attributes of Truly Effective Tasks.   The bottom line for performance tasks is that they have to elicit from students the kind of response that will permit you to dependably assess proficiency. That means that each task must be on target.

Quality tasks address the right *content*. They elicit the correct response—a performance that reveals the proper proficiency. In other words, it is obvious that the response can be effectively evaluated using the scoring criteria or rubric. The two align. When the achievement target is simple in nature, the task reflects that simplicity: to assess oral reading fluency, have students read. When the target is more complex, so is the task: to assess ability to proficiency in preparing a science research paper, create the paper.

Quality tasks are *clear* and specific in their instructions to students. There is no confusion—each student knows exactly what to do. Further, that description reminds students about the performance criteria you will apply when evaluating the quality of their response.

Quality tasks are *feasible* for use in the classroom. It is practical given the realities of the context. Students have enough time to respond. Proper materials and equipment are readily available for all respondents. Time is available to examine and evaluate performance using the previously developed scoring criteria.

There is nothing about the task set in its context that will give rise to an inaccurate picture of any student's proficiency. In this sense, it provides for a *fair and accurate* assessment of achievement.

In Figure 6.5, you will find a set of rating scales or rubrics you can use to judge the quality of your performance tasks. Are yours "Ready to Use," do they "Needs Revision," or are they "Do Not Use?" Activities provided at the end of the chapter allow you to practice applying these criteria in evaluating some sample performance tasks.

Selecting a Sample

The final dimension of performance tasks in Figure 6.5, Dependability, includes the admonition that all tasks tap the key facets of the same standard. In other words, they must sample performance appropriately. How do you know how many such exercises to include within any particular assessment to give you confidence that you are drawing dependable conclusions about student proficiency? In terms of our example, how many samples of Emily's writing must Ms. W. see to draw a dependable conclusion about her proficiency?

This can be a little tricky with performance assessments, because it can take quite a bit of time to develop, administer, observe, and score any single exercise. In a half-hour of testing time you can administer lots of multiple-choice test items, and thus cover much

Characteristic 1: Content

This dimension of the task spells out what the student is expected to do. It lays out the requirement of the task to be completed.

Ready to Use

- It aligns with the desired achievement target in that if the student performs, evidence of the desired proficiency will result.
- The task communicates all relevant expectations to the student.
- It is engaging in that it is likely to motivate students to do their best.

Needs Revision

- The alignment to the important standards or key aspects of performance could be improved.
- It might be made more engaging for students.

Do Not Use

- The task clearly doesn't fit the standard to be assessed.
- It is not clear what the student is expected to do or create.
- Students probably will not find the task engaging.

Characteristic 2: Clarity

There should be no ambiguity in the mind of the user regarding the details of what is expected.

Ready to Use

- Instructions are clear and unambiguous to all who read or hear them.
- Achievement expectations (kind of performance, target to hit) are clearly stated in the form of explicit performance criteria.
- The conditions governing performance are clearly stated (timing, resources to be used, etc.).

Needs Revision

- Instructions could be clearer; some meaning is ambiguous to you or your students.
- The performance expectations are not as clearly stated as they could be, so you or your students might be confused.
- Governing conditions are incomplete or confusing, but fixable.

Do Not Use

- Instructions are not offered or are unclear.
- Key terms are undefined.
- There is no reminder of performance criteria to be applied.
- No governing conditions are mentioned, or they are confusing.

Characteristic 3: Feasibility

Just as performance rubrics must be practical to use, so too must tasks fit into the practicalities of classroom operations.

Ready to Use

- The respondent has enough time and materials to do the job.
- There are no dangers to the student or others inherent in the task.

Figure 6.5
Rubric for evaluating performance tasks

- All necessary resources are ready and available.
- The information that will result is clearly worthy of the time required for task completion and observation.

Needs Revision

- It is uncertain if the respondent can complete the task within available resources; apparent adjustments can provide that assurance.
- The efficiency of the assessment could be increased with some adjustment in the assigned task.

Do Not Use

- Completion of the task represents a danger to the student or others.
- The demands of the task clearly outstrip the resources available to complete it.
- The resulting insights about student achievement are not worth the time and effort required to attain them.

Characteristic 4: Dependability

There must be nothing in the task that will cause it to yield an inaccurate picture of student achievement. All students have an equal chance to perform well.

Ready to Use

- If multiple tasks make up the assessment, they all tap appropriate dimensions of the same standard.
- There is no undue pressure or anxiety due to public demonstration of proficiency when that can distort student performance.
- Accommodations are made for students challenged by learning disabilities or language difficulties.
- The task includes or implies no cultural or language expectations that would place any subgroup of students at a disadvantage.

Needs Revision

- Adjustments can be made to align multiple tasks within the same assessment.
- Accommodations can easily be made to reduce evaluation anxiety or challenges due to learning disabilities or language proficiencies; that is, students can be presented with equal opportunities to perform well.

Do Not Use

- Multiple tasks seem to sample different achievements.
- Performance anxiety is likely to distort results.
- Those with learning disabilities or lacking language proficiencies are likely to be assessed inaccurately.
- Some subgroups of students will be placed at systematic disadvantage.

Figure 6.5
Rubric for evaluating performance tasks *(continued)*

territory with your sample, because each item demands so little response time. But what if the performance assessment exercise, which typically requires a more complex demonstration, takes 15 minutes? Clearly you cannot administer as many per unit of testing time. As a result, sometimes it can be very difficult to sample performance adequately using a number of different exercises, given your classroom workload and time constraints.

Consider the specific sampling challenges of writing assessment, for example. Because writing takes so many forms (narrative, expository, persuasive) and takes place in so many different contexts (for different audiences), assessing overall writing proficiency would be very complex if you were to sample them all. This would take time. This is the performance assessment sampling challenge.

Some Practical Guidance.   Sampling student performance with assessment tasks always involves tradeoffs between quality of resulting information and the cost of collecting it. Few have the resources needed to gather the perfect sample of student achievement. We all compromise. The good news for you as a teacher is that you must compromise less than the large-scale assessor, primarily because you get to have more time with your students. This is precisely why I feel that the great strength and future of performance assessment lies in the classroom more than in large-scale standardized testing.

Let's define *sampling* here as we have for the other assessment methods. You need to assemble tasks into a collection sufficient in coverage to support conclusions about student achievement. In the classroom, often you have the luxury of being able to gather that information strategically in bits and pieces over time. If you plan and administer assessment tasks carefully, these bits can form into a representative sample of performance that is broad enough in its coverage to lead to confident generalizations about student achievement.

An Illustration.   Let's explore an assessment situation from the adult world to see sampling in action. Then we can explore implications for the classroom.

Let's say we are members of a licensing board charged with responsibility for certifying the competence of commercial airline pilots. One specific skill we want them to demonstrate, among others, is the ability to land the plane safely. So we take candidates up on a bright, sunny, calm day and ask them to land the plane, clearly an authentic performance assessment. And let's say the first pilot does an excellent job of landing. Are you ready to certify?

If your answer is Yes, I don't want you screening the pilots hired by the airlines on which I fly! Our assessment reflected only one narrow set of circumstances within which we expect our pilots to be competent. What if it's night, not a bright, clear daylight? A strange airport? Windy? Raining? An emergency? These represent realities within which pilots must operate routinely. So the proper course of action in certifying competence is to see each pilot land under various conditions, so we can ensure safe landings on all occasions. To achieve this, we hang out at the airport waiting for the weather to change, permitting us to quickly take off in the plane so we can watch our candidates land under those conditions. And over the next year we exhaust the landing condition possibilities, right?

Of course not. Obviously, I'm being silly here. We have neither the time nor the patience to go through all of that with every candidate. So what do we do? We compromise. We operate within our existing resources and sample pilot performance. We have each candidate land the plane under several different conditions. And at some point, the array of instances of landing proficiency (gathered under strategically selected conditions) combine to lead us to a conclusion that each pilot has or has not mastered the skill of landing safely.

This example frames the performance assessment sampling challenge in a real-world situation that applies just as well in your classroom. How many "landings" must you see under what kinds of conditions to feel confident your students can perform according to your criteria? The science of such sampling is to have thought through the important conditions within which you will sample performance. The art is to use your resources creatively to gather enough different instances under varying conditions to bring you and your students to a confident conclusion about proficiency.

You must consider the decision to be made in planning the size of your sample. Some decisions are very important, like promotion to the next grade, high school graduation, or becoming licensed to practice a profession. These demand assessments that sample both more deeply and more broadly to give all users confidence in the decision that results. An incorrect decision based on poor-quality assessment would have dire consequences for students.

But other decisions are not so momentous. They allow you to reconsider the decision tomorrow, if necessary, at no cost to the student. For example, if you mismeasure a student's ability to craft a complete sentence during a lesson on sentence construction, you are likely to discover your error in later assessments and take proper action. When the target is narrow and the time frame brief, you can sample more narrowly and not do great harm.

Figure 6.6 identifies six factors to take into account when making sampling decisions in any particular performance assessment context. Your professional challenge is to follow the rules of sound assessment and gather enough information to minimize the chance that your conclusions are wrong. The conservative position to take in this case is to err in the direction of oversampling to increase your level of confidence in the inferences you draw about student competence. If you feel at all uncertain about the conclusion you might draw regarding the achievement of a particular student, you have no choice but to gather more information. To do otherwise is to place that student's well-being in jeopardy.

Fine Tuning Your Use of Performance Assessments

Clearly, your prime consideration in selecting an assessment method is the match of performance assessment methodology to your target. In addition, however, it is prudent to consider other practical questions when deciding if or how to use performance assessment in your classroom.

- *The Reason for the Assessment*—The more important the decision, the more sure you must be about the student's proficiency. The more sure you must be, the bigger should be your sample. Greater coverage leads to more confident conclusions about achievement.
- *The Scope of the Target*—The more narrowly focused the valued achievement target, the easier it is to cover it with a small sample. Targets broad in their scope require more exercises to cover enough material to yield confident conclusions.
- *The Coverage of Any One Exercise*—If the student's response is likely to provide a great deal of evidence of proficiency, you need not administer many such exercises. How many term papers must a student prepare to demonstrate that he or she can do it?
- *Time Available to Assess*—If you must draw conclusions about proficiency tomorrow, you have too little time to sample broadly. But as the time available to assess increases, so can the scope of your sample.
- *Consistency of Performance*—If a student demonstrates consistently very high or very low proficiency in the first few exercises, it may be safe to draw a conclusion even before you have administered all the exercises you had intended.
- *Proximity to the Standard*—If a student's performance is right on the borderline between being judged as competent or incompetent, you might need to extend the sample to be sure you know which conclusion to draw.

Figure 6.6
Practical considerations in performance assessment sampling

Checking for Bias or Errors in Judgment

As we have established, subjective scoring is the hallmark of performance assessment. We already have discussed many ways to ensure that your subjective assessment is as objective as it can be:

- Be mindful of the purpose for assessing—who needs to understand and act on the results?
- Be crystal clear about the target—align tasks and rubrics precisely to it.
- Articulate the key elements of good performance in explicit performance criteria within the rubric.
- Share those criteria with students in terms they understand—provide practice in applying those criteria if they are to be among the judges.
- Everyone who is to use them must learn to apply the rubrics in a consistent manner; remember the need for inter-rater agreement.
- Double check to be sure that inappropriate filters (factors unrelated to the achievement in question, your own biases) are not creeping into the evaluation, thus distorting assessment results.

There is a simple way to check for bias in your performance evaluations. Remember, bias occurs when factors other than the kind of achievement being assessed begin to influence rater judgment, such as examinees' gender, age, ethnic heritage, appearance, or prior academic record. We already have established that you can determine the degree of objectivity of your ratings by comparing them with the judgments of another trained and qualified evaluator who independently observes and evaluates the same student performance with the intent of applying the same criteria.

Now, you may be saying, it's just not practical to determine inter-rater agreement in the classroom. It'll take too much time. Besides, where do I find a qualified second rater? And how do I determine if the other rater and I agree in our judgments?

In fact, evaluating consistency among raters need not take much time. You need not find corroboration for every performance judgment you make. Just checking a few for consistency often will suffice. Perhaps a qualified colleague could double check a select few of your performance ratings to see if they are on target.

Further, it doesn't take a high degree of technical skill to do this. Have someone who is qualified rate some student performances you already have rated, and then sit down for a few minutes and talk about any differences in your ratings. If the performance in question is a product that students created, have your colleague evaluate a few. If it's a skill, videotape a few examples. Both you and your colleague apply your criteria to one performance and check for agreement. Do you both see it about the same way? If so, go on to the next one. If not, try to resolve differences, adjusting your performance criteria as needed.

Please understand that my goal here is not to have you carry out this test of objectivity every time you conduct a performance assessment. Rather, try to understand the spirit of my point. An important part of the art of classroom performance assessment is the ability to sense when your performance criteria are sufficiently explicit that another judge would be able to use them effectively, if called on to do so. Therefore, from time to time it is a good idea to actually check whether you and another rater really do agree in applying your criteria.

The more important the performance assessment (that is, the greater its potential impact on students, such as when it is used for promotion decisions, graduation decisions, and the like), the more important it becomes that you verify inter-rater agreement.

Barriers to Sound Performance Assessment

By way of summary, many things in the design and development of performance assessments can cause a student's real achievement to be misrepresented. Many of the potential problems and remedies are summarized in Figure 6.7.

Potential Sources of Problems	Recommended Remedy
Inadequate vision of the achievement target	Seek training and advice or consult the professional literature to sharpen your focus; work with colleagues in this process
Mismatch of target and method	Performance assessment aligns well with complex reasoning, performance skills, and product assessments; use it only for these
Unclear performance criteria	Analyze samples of performance very carefully, working with qualified experts, if necessary, to sharpen your focus
Incorrect performance criteria	Compare and contrast samples of performance of vastly different quality for real keys to success; consult the professional literature for advice; work with qualified colleagues in the process of identifying criteria
Unfocused tasks	Seek help from qualified colleagues in task development
Biased tasks	Understand the social and linguistic backgrounds of your students; seek advice of qualified reviewers in revising and selecting tasks
Insufficient sample of tasks	Start with a clear definition of the desired achievement target; work with a team of qualified colleagues to devise new tasks and determine how many would be enough
Too little time to assess	Add trained raters ... such as your students
Untrained raters	Train them and provide them with practice in applying criteria

Figure 6.7
Avoiding problems

Think Assessment *for* Learning: Involve Students in Performance Assessment

The purpose of the assessment drives the selection of observers and evaluators. When the goal is to certify that students have met performance standards for important grading, promotion, or graduation decisions, then you, the teacher, must be the assessor. These are assessment *of* learning contexts. The only acceptable alternative in these contexts is for you to bring into the classroom another adult rater (a qualified outside expert). Schools that ask students to do exhibitions and demonstrations, such as senior projects, science fairs, and music competitions, routinely do this. In all cases, it is essential that raters be fully trained and qualified to apply the performance criteria that underpin the evaluation. High-stakes decisions hang in the balance. So you must do it right.

On the other hand, as we have established, you can use assessments as far more than simply sources of scores for accountability. You can use them as teaching tools,

- Share the performance criteria with students at the beginning of the unit of instruction.
- Collaborate with students in keeping track of which criteria have been covered in class and which are yet to come.
- Involve students in creating prominent visual displays of important performance criteria for bulletin boards.
- Engage students in the actual development of performance exercises.
- Engage students in comparing and contrasting examples of performance, some of which reflect high-quality work and some of which do not (perhaps as part of a process of developing performance criteria).
- Involve students in the process of transforming performance criteria into checklists, rating scales, and other recording methods.
- Have students evaluate their own and each other's performance, one-on-one and/or in cooperative groups.
- Have students rate performance and then conduct studies of how much agreement (i.e., objectivity) there was among student judges; see if degree of agreement increases as students become more proficient as performers and as judges.
- Have students write about their own growth over time with respect to specified criteria.
- Have students set specific achievement goals in terms of the criteria and then keep track of their own progress.
- Store several samples of each student's performance over time, either as a portfolio or on videotape, if appropriate, and have students compare old performance to new, discussing their own growth.
- Have students predict their performance criterion-by-criterion, and then check actual evaluations to see if their predictions are accurate.

Figure 6.8
Ideas for student-involved assessment

as assessment *for* learning. You can accomplish this in one way by using performance assessments to teach students to evaluate their own and each other's performance. The very process of learning to dependably apply performance criteria helps students become better performers, as it helps them to learn and understand key elements of sound performance. So when the assessment is to serve instructional purposes, students can be raters, too. Figure 6.8 summarizes assessment *for* learning ideas mentioned in the chapter, adding a few new suggestions here at the end.

Summary: Thoughtful Development Yields Sound Assessments and Energized Students

This chapter has been about the great potential of performance assessment, with its array of design possibilities. Please refer to Table 6.1 and consider once again the variety of classroom applications. However, we have tempered the presentation with the admonition to develop and use this assessment method cautiously. Performance assessment, like other methods, brings with it specific rules of evidence. We must all strive to meet those rigorous quality control standards.

To ensure quality, we discussed the conditions that must be present for performance assessment to be used effectively. We also discussed the need to understand the role of subjectivity. We analyzed the matches between performance assessment and the various kinds of achievement targets, concluding that strong matches can be developed for reasoning, skills, and products. We discussed key context factors to consider when selecting this methodology for use in the classroom, centering mostly on the importance of having in place the necessary expertise and resources.

Clearly, the heart of this chapter was our exploration of the two basic steps in developing performance assessments:

- Clarifying performance (dealing with the nature and focus of the achievement being assessed)
- Developing performance tasks (dealing with the way we elicit performance for observation and judgment)

As we covered each step, we framed the possibilities available to you as a classroom teacher, establishing standards for sound performance criteria and performance tasks. We will return to both of these in Part 3 of this book, where we study examples of each.

In my opinion, the most practical part of the presentation in this chapter occurred when we devised five steps for formulating your own sound performance criteria, urging collaboration with students and/or colleagues. This is most practical because it affords you the best opportunities for bringing students into your performance assessment development and for teaching them the most valuable lessons. We began by comparing and contrasting examples of performance to discover the active ingredients of quality. From there, we began to boil those ingredients down to their essence: concise statements of the meaning of academic excellence. Once you and your students learn to apply those standards to evaluating student work, you are on the road to success.

As schools continue to evolve, I predict that we will come to rely increasingly on performance assessment as part of the basis for our evaluation of student achievement. Hopefully, we will find even more and better ways of integrating performance assessment and instruction. I feel strongly that, whatever those better ways are, they will have their foundation in student involvement. Let us strive for the highest-quality, most rigorous assessments our resources will allow.

Final Chapter Reflection

1. *What are the three most important new insights to come to you as a result of your study of this chapter?*
2. *Which of your previous questions about assessment can you now answer based on your study of this chapter?*
3. *What new questions have come to mind as a result of your study of this chapter that you hope to have answered as your study continues?*

Practice with Chapter 6 Ideas

1. Two teachers fundamentally disagree on the performance criteria to apply to evaluating a particular kind of student work. How should they resolve their difference of opinion?

2. A student and a teacher have a legitimate difference of opinion about the standards of excellence to apply to evaluating a particular kind of student work. What should happen then? Should the teacher simply assert ultimate authority and conduct the evaluation anyway? What are the alternatives?

3. Following are four sample performance assessments. Evaluate them using the rubrics shown in this chapter, as appropriate for each example.

Example 1: Camping Trip—Grade 5

"Eight people are going camping for 3 days and need to carry their own water. They read in a guidebook that 12.5 liters are needed for a party of 5 people for 1 day. Based on the guidebook, what is the minimum amount of water the 8 people should carry all together? Explain your answer."

Responses were assessed using a rubric with three traits: conceptual understanding, problem solving, and communication in math. Each trait was scored on a five-point scale with points 1, 3, and 5 defined (Figure 6.9). Students received student-friendly versions early in the school year and practiced using the rubrics on many other problems.

Example 2: Tall Tales and Fables—Grade 2

The learning targets emphasized in this unit of instruction, as listed by the teacher, were "language arts, writing, reading, and spelling." The performance task and associated performance criteria were described in the following manner. (Students did not see the rubric or criteria ahead of time.)

Unit Assessment List: Writing or retelling a tall tale or fable.

Activity/Assessment Descriptions: Develop and write a tall tale or fable.

Performance Criteria:
- Handwriting or word processing is neat and legible.
- Spelling on all core words is correct, and most other words are correct.
- Sentence structure—The student uses complete sentences.
- Capital letters are used appropriately to begin sentences and for proper names.
- Punctuation is used correctly.
- Understanding—The student demonstrates an understanding of the exaggeration and fictitious characters found in tall tales or fables.

Rubric:
- *Distinguished*—Writing shows creativity in plot and character development. Tall tale or fable uses exaggeration appropriately. Writing is correct in all mechanics.
- *Proficient*—Tall tale or fable correctly uses plot and exaggeration. Characters may not be well developed. Few errors in mechanics are apparent.
- *Apprentice*—Tall tale or fable does not show exaggeration or fictitious

Definitions

Mathematical Concepts and Procedures. A student demonstrates a grasp of the mathematical concepts, chooses and performs the appropriate mathematical operations, and performs computations correctly.

Problem Solving. A student demonstrates problem-solving skills and comprehension by framing the problem so that appropriate mathematical process(es) can be selected and used, by developing or selecting and implementing a strategy to find a solution, and by checking the solution for reasonableness.

Mathematics Communication. A student demonstrates communication skills in mathematics by explaining the steps and reasoning used in a solution with words, numbers, and diagrams.

Adult Rubric

Mathematical Concepts and Procedures

5 A strong performance occurs when the student demonstrates extensive understanding of the mathematical concepts and related procedures and uses them correctly. The student
- Understands mathematical concepts and related procedures.
- Uses all necessary information from the problem.
- Performs computation(s) accurately or with only minor errors.

3 A developing performance occurs when the student demonstrates general understanding of the mathematical concepts and related procedures, but there may be some gaps or misapplication. The student
- Partially understands mathematical concepts and related procedures.
- Uses some necessary information from the problem.
- May make some computational errors.

1 A weak performance occurs when the student demonstrates little or no understanding of mathematical concepts and related procedures. Application, if attempted, is incorrect. The student
- Does not appear to understand mathematical concepts and related procedures.
- Does not use information from the problem or uses irrelevant information.
- Does no computation, or does computation that is unrelated to the problem.

Problem Solving

5 A strong performance occurs when the student selects or devises and uses an efficient, elegant, or sophisticated strategy to solve the problem.
- The student translates the problem into a useful mathematical form.
- The student applies the selected plan(s) or strategy(-ies) through to completion; no pieces are missing.
- The plan or strategy may incorporate multiple approaches.
- Pictures, models, diagrams, and symbols (if used) enhance the strategy.
- The solution is reasonable and consistent with the context of the problem.

3 A developing performance occurs when the student selects or devises a plan or strategy, but it is partially unworkable.
- The student leaves gaps in framing or carrying out the strategy.
- The strategy may work in some parts of the problem, but not in others.
- The strategy is appropriate but incomplete in development or application.
- Results of computation, even if correct, may not fit the context of the problem.

Figure 6.9
Rubric for camping trip problem

1 A weak performance occurs when the student shows no evidence of a strategy or has attempted to use a completely inappropriate strategy.
  - The student shows no attempt to frame the problem or translates the problem into an unrelated mathematical form.
  - The strategy is inappropriate, misapplied, or disconnected.
  - Pictures, models, diagrams, and symbols, if used, may bear some relationship to the problem.
  - The solution is not reasonable and/or does not fit the context of the problem.

Mathematical Communication

5 A strong performance occurs when a student clearly explains in words, numbers, and diagrams both the strategy used to solve the problem and the solution itself.
  - The problem could be solved following the explanation. It is clearly explained and organized.
  - The explanation is coherent and complete. There are no gaps in reasoning. Nothing is left out.
  - The student presents logical arguments to justify strategy or solution.
  - The explanations may include examples and/or counterexamples.
  - Charts, pictures, symbols, and diagrams, when used, enhance the reader's understanding of what was done and why it was done.
  - Few inferences are required to figure out what the student did and why.
  - Correct mathematical language is used.

3 A developing performance occurs when the student's problem solving is partially explained, but requires some inferences to figure out completely.
  - The student attempts to use mathematical language, but may not have used all terms correctly.
  - Some key elements are included in the explanation.
  - The student explains the answer but not the reasoning, or explains the process but not the solution.
  - Charts, pictures, symbols, and diagrams, if used, provide some explanation of the major elements of the solution.

1 A weak performance occurs when the student's explanation does not describe the process used or the solution to the problem.
  - Charts, pictures, symbols, and diagrams, when used, interfere with the reader's understanding of what was done and why it was done.
  - The explanation appears to be unrelated to the problem.
  - The reader cannot follow the student's explanation.
  - Little or no explanation of the thinking/reasoning is shown.
  - The explanation only restates the problem.
  - Many inferences are required to follow the student's work.
  - Incorrect or misapplied mathematical language interferes with the reader's ability to understand the explanation.

Student-Friendly Rubric

Mathematical Concepts and Procedures

5 I completely understand the appropriate mathematical operation and use it correctly.
  - I understand which math operations are needed.
  - I have used all of the important information.
  - I did all of my calculations correctly.

Figure 6.9
Rubric for camping trip problem *(continued)*

(continued)

3 I think I understand most of the mathematical operations and how to use them.
- I know which operations to use for some of the problem, but not for all of it.
- I have an idea about where to start.
- I know what operations I need to use, but I'm not sure where the numbers go.
- I picked out some of the important information, but I might have missed some.
- I did the simple calculations right, but I had trouble with the tougher ones.

1 I wasn't sure which mathematical operation(s) to use or how to use the ones I picked.
- I don't know where to start.
- I'm not sure which information to use.
- I don't know which operations would help me solve the problem.
- I don't think my calculations are correct.

Problem Solving

5 I came up with and used a strategy that really fits and makes it easy to solve this problem.
- I knew what to do to set up and solve this problem.
- I knew what math operations to use.
- I followed through with my strategy from beginning to end.
- The way I worked the problem makes sense and is easy to follow.
- I may have shown more than one way to solve the problem.
- I checked to make sure my solution makes sense in the original problem.

3 I came up with and used a strategy, but it doesn't seem to fit the problem as well as it should.
- I think I know what the problem is about, but I might have a hard time explaining it.
- I arrived at a solution even though I had problems with my strategy at some point.
- My strategy seemed to work at the beginning, but did not work well for the whole problem.
- I checked my solution and it seems to fit the problem.

1 I didn't have a plan that worked.
- I tried several things, but didn't get anywhere.
- I didn't know which strategy to use.
- I didn't know how to begin.
- I didn't check to see if my solution makes sense.
- I'm not sure what the problem asks me to do.
- I'm not sure I have enough information to solve the problem.

Mathematical Communication

5 I clearly explained the process I used and my solution to the problem using numbers, words, pictures, or diagrams.
- My explanation makes sense.
- I used mathematical terms correctly.
- My work shows what I did and what I was thinking while I worked the problem.
- I've explained why my answer makes sense.
- I used pictures, symbols, and/or diagrams when they made my explanation clearer.
- My explanation was clear and organized.
- My explanation includes just the right amount of detail, not too much or too little.

Figure 6.9
Rubric for camping trip problem *(continued)*

---

3 I explained only part of the process I used, or I only explained my answer.
  - I explained some of my steps in solving the problem.
  - Someone might have to add some information for my explanation to be easy to follow.
  - Some of the mathematical terms I used make sense and help in my explanation.
  - I explained my answer, but not my thinking.
  - My explanation started out well, but bogged down in the middle.
  - When I used pictures, symbols, and/or diagrams, they were incomplete or only helped my explanation a little bit.
  - I'm not sure how much detail I need to help someone understand what I did.

1 I did not explain my thinking or my answer, or I am confused about how my explanation relates to the problem.
  - I don't know what to write.
  - I can't figure out how to get my ideas in order.
  - I'm not sure I used math terms correctly.
  - My explanation is mostly copying the original problem.
  - The pictures, symbols, and/or diagrams I used would not help somebody understand what I did.

Figure 6.9
Rubric for camping trip problem *(continued)*

characters. Errors in mechanics are common.

  - *Novice*—Tall tale or fable is begun but not concluded. Writing shows lack of understanding of exaggeration. Several errors in mechanics are found.

Example 3: Three-Minute Persuasive Speech—High School

The intent was to assess how well students can handle public speaking demands:

"In five minutes, you will be asked to stand at the front of the room and give a 3-minute persuasive talk on a topic of your choice. You may choose any topic you wish, something with which you are familiar, or you may choose a topic from the list provided. You have five minutes to think about what you will say before your speech begins. If you desire, you may make some notes for yourself to use during the speech." (The scoring rubric appears in Table 6.4.)

Gun control

Nuclear disarmament

Doctor-assisted suicide

Equal rights for women

National health insurance

Abortion laws and practices

High school sports programs

Effectiveness of the United Nations

Use of nuclear power in the United States

Methods of conserving energy in the United States

Parents' control of children's television viewing habits

Example 4: Math Portfolio—Grades 4 and 8

Students were asked to assemble a portfolio that demonstrated their

Table 6.4
Scoring rubric

Score	Language	Delivery	Organization
A = 5	Correct grammar and pronunciation are used. Word choice is interesting and appropriate. Unfamiliar terms are defined in the context of the speech.	The voice demonstrates control with few distractions. The presentation holds the listener's attention. The volume and rate are at acceptable levels. Eye contact with the audience is maintained.	The message is organized. The speaker sticks to the topic. The main points are developed. It is easy to summarize the content of the speech.
B = 4 C = 3	Correct grammar and pronunciation are used. Word choice is adequate and understandable. Unfamiliar terms are not explained in the context of the speech. There is a heavy reliance on the listener's prior knowledge.	The voice is generally under control. The speaker can be heard and understood. The speaker generally maintains eye contact with the audience.	The organization is understandable. Main points may be underdeveloped. The speaker may shift unexpectedly from one point to another, but the message remains comprehensible. The speech can be summarized.
D = 2 F = 1	Errors in grammar and pronunciation occur. Word choice lacks clarity. The speaker puts the responsibility for understanding on the listener.	The student's voice is poor. The volume may be too low and the rate too fast. There may be frequent pauses. Nonverbal behaviors tend to interfere with the message.	Ideas are listed without logical sequence. The relationships between ideas are not clear. The student strays from the stated topic. It is difficult to summarize the speech.

Source: Reprinted from Toolkit98: Chapter 3, Activity 3.3—Performance Criteria, Keys to Success. Reprinted by permission of Northwest Regional Educational Laboratory, Portland, Oregon.

mathematical problem-solving ability. Each portfolio was to contain 10–20 selections.

- 5–7 of these should be "best pieces" and must include: 1 puzzle, 1 investigation, 1 application, and no more than 2 pieces of group work.
- The student can select other pieces that demonstrate ability.
- The student should write a letter to the evaluator that describes what he or she has chosen for his or her portfolio and what it shows about the student.

The portfolios are assessed using this rubric:

Problem Solving: How well does the student understand the problem, how does the student solve the problem, why does the student solve it the way she or he did, and what observations, connections, and generalizations does the student make about the problem?

Communication: What terminology, notation, or symbols does the student use to communicate his or her math thinking, what representations (graphs, charts, tables, models, diagrams, pictures, manipulatives) does the student use, and how clear is the student's communication of mathematical thinking and problem solving?

Chapter 7

Personal Communication as Assessment

CHAPTER FOCUS

This chapter answers the following guiding question:

> How can I best use my direct personal interaction with my students during instruction to provide information about their achievement?

From your study of this chapter, you will understand the following:

1. Use personal communication-based assessments to tap knowledge and understanding, as well as reasoning and verbal performance skills.

2. This kind of assessment can take a variety of forms, including instructional questions and answers, class discussions, conferences and interviews, oral exams, conversations with others about students, and student journals.

3. Using personal communication in conjunction with other methods can deepen our understanding of student learning.

4. As with the other methods, this one can fall prey to avoidable sources of bias that can distort results if we are not careful.

5. By involving our students in assessments that rely on personal communication, we can set them up for energetic and successful learning.

As we start this part of our journey, keep our big picture in mind. Look at Figure 7.1. Once again, we will be dealing in depth with the shaded areas.

Classroom Interaction as Evidence of Learning

Teachers gather a great deal of valuable information about student achievement by talking with them. We seldom think of this personal interaction as "assessment," but it often is. At different times during teaching and learning, we ask questions, listen to answers, and evaluate achievement. Or we conduct conferences with students that, in effect, serve as interviews that yield information about achievement. These kinds of assessments are the focus of this chapter.

	SELECTED RESPONSE	ESSAY	PERFORMANCE ASSESSMENT	PERSONAL COMMUNICATION
Know				
Reason				
Performance Skills				
Products				
Dispositions				

Figure 7.1
Aligning achievement targets and assessment methods

When we use this method to gather evidence of learning, matters of validity and reliability are every bit as important as with the other methods of assessment. Assessments must arise from and serve specific purposes (i.e., meet users' information needs), accurately reflect intended achievement targets, and produce consistent information about that achievement.

You will find that the tenor of this chapter is somewhat different from that of the three previous methodology chapters. My intent is not so much to provide precise detail on procedures as it is to describe the factors to be aware of in drawing inferences about students' achievement based on what they say. If our interactions are focused, characterized by active listening, and lead to cautious conclusions, personal communications with and among students can provide a valid and reliable window into learning. We can engage in the following forms of interpersonal communication with students, all of which can provide valuable information:

- Questions and answers during instruction
- Conferences with students
- Student contributions during class discussions
- Oral examinations
- Journals, diaries, and learning logs

When we use these forms of assessment with care, we can tap dimensions of achievement not easily accessed through other means. For example, an effective questioner can use properly sequenced questions to probe deeply into students' reasoning to help them tune in to and understand their own problem-solving approaches. Further, thoughtful questioners can effectively link assessment to instruction by using questions to uncover and immediately correct students' misconceptions or faulty reasoning.

By the same token, if we are not careful in our use of personal communication as assessment, as with other modes, we can mismeasure students' achievement. As you shall see, the list of potential pitfalls is as long as that for performance or for paper and pencil assessments. In fact, in some senses, the list of challenges to the effective use of personal communication assessment is even longer than those of other modes because we often communicate casually in an informal context, where bias can creep in without our noticing it. The good news is that we know how to overcome these potential problems.

Nowhere is classroom assessment more of an art than when using personal communication to track student growth and development. Typically, there is no table of test specifications to match against our intended target. There are no test items to check for quality, no score results. We can't check for agreement among observers to see if judgments are consistent. Personal communication is more spontaneous, more personal.

Nevertheless, you must understand and appreciate the fact that this mode of assessment carries with it specific rules of evidence for effective use. Understand and adhere to those rules and you can derive valuable information about the attainments of your students. Disregard those rules and, just as with other forms of assessment, you can do great harm. With this form of assessment, just as with the others, you must vigilantly pursue quality.

This chapter will cover the context factors to consider when selecting this mode of assessment and the role of subjective teacher judgment. We will explore alignment to achievement targets and the various types of personal communication available for teacher use.

The Unique Power of Personal Communication

Even as learning is progressing, a few strategically placed questions can help you to monitor and adjust your teaching. But even beyond this, personal communication affords you some special opportunities. For example, unlike some other forms of assessment, if you are startled, puzzled, or pleased by a student's response, you can ask followup questions to dig more deeply to reveal student thinking. In other words, you can get beyond a particular response to explore its origins. If you find misconceptions, you can take immediate action to correct them.

If we vary that theme just a bit, we come upon another power of personal communication. You can attach those followup questions to any other mode of assessment to gain deeper understanding of student achievement. For instance, let's say a student fails a performance assessment and you wish to discover why in order to help that student find success. You can follow up the failure with a few carefully phrased questions to see if it was due to a lack of prerequisite knowledge or to poor-quality reasoning on the student's part.

To the attentive user, students' nonverbal reactions can provide valuable insights into achievement and feelings about the material learned (or not learned). These indicators of confidence or uncertainty, excitement or boredom, and comfort or anxiety can lead you to probe more deeply into the underlying causes. This kind of perception checking can result in levels of student–teacher communication not achievable through other assessment means.

The Foundations of Ensuring Quality Assessment

As with the other three assessment methods we have studied, the validity and reliability of a personal communication-based assessment relies on its use in appropriate contexts and on your ability to manage effectively the subjectivity inherent in this method.

Context Factors

There are several contextual pitfalls to sound assessment using personal communication about which you must remain constantly aware.

Common Language and Cultural Awareness Are Fundamental

Teacher and student must share a common language for this mode of assessment to work effectively, for in its absence bias can creep in, rendering the evidence undependable. This factor has become more and more critical through the new millennium, as ethnic and cultural diversity have increased markedly in our schools.

By common language, I don't just mean a shared vocabulary and grammar, although these obviously are critical to sound assessment. I also mean a common sense of the manner in which a culture shares meaning through verbal and nonverbal cues. Ethnicity and cultural heritage may differ between student and teacher. For example, we must realize that, in some cultures where social emphasis is placed on the collective good, it is unseemly for a student to hold him or herself up as appearing to know more than others. This can give rise to a reluctance to answer questions in class. Thus, the student may know the material but not be willing to demonstrate that fact in this manner. Or similarly, in some cultures it is a sign of disrespect to one's elders (e.g., their teacher) for children to make eye contact with those of older generations. But sometimes, as teachers, we draw inferences about student learning based on such nonverbal signs. Just be sure you understand the social environment from which your students come before doing so. When you lack that understanding, you ensure mismeasurement.

Personality Is Important as Well

Shy, withdrawn students simply may not perform well in this kind of assessment context, regardless of their real achievement. To make these methods work, two people must connect in an open, communicative manner. For some students, this simply is too risky, often for reasons beyond your control.

This coin has two sides: There also is the danger that students with very outgoing, aggressive personalities will try to lay down a "smoke screen" to mislead you with respect to their real achievement. But, this works only with assessors who have not prepared carefully, and who cannot stay focused. You fall prey to the dangers of bias in assessment when you allow yourself to be distracted by irrelevant factors.

Create a Safe Environment

Personal communication works best as assessment when students feel they are in a safe learning environment. There are many ways to interpret this.

In its most general connotation, we create safe learning environments when we make it clear to our students that they are successful when they meet standards—when we tell them that we know they will grow at different rates, that it's okay, and that they will have time to grow at their own effective rate.

When considered in the context of personal communication-based assessment, we promote safety when we permit our students to succeed or fail in private, without an embarrassing public spotlight. As mentioned above, in some cultures, it is unseemly to make public displays of competence—to call attention to one's self as standing above others. On the other side, it is always more embarrassing to fail in public than in private, especially for those students who lack social confidence. A safe environment provides private ways to excel or to grow.

Another kind of safety takes the form of a humane peer environment sensitive to the plight of those who perform less well and supportive of their attempts to grow. Still another kind of safety comes from having the opportunity to learn more and perform again later with the promise of a higher level of success. Nowhere is personal safety more important to sound assessment than when that assessment is conducted through public personal communication.

Students Must Understand the Need for Honesty

Personal communication works best as assessment when students understand that sometimes as their teacher you need an honest answer, not their attempt at a best possible answer or the answer they think will please you. This mode of assessment provides its best information most efficiently when a sound interpersonal relationship exists between you and your students. Again, the key is trust. Students must know that if they give you the "socially desirable" response to a question, a response that misrepresents the truth about their achievement or feelings, then you will be less able to help them.

This may be trickier than it first appears, especially when considered in light of our distinction between assessment *of* and *for* learning. In all cases of assessment *for* learning, our students need to know that, unless they can help us see and understand the real status of their current learning, we will have difficulty identifying their needs and we will have trouble finding ways to help them learn. In this case, when we ask them a question, they need to understand that it's okay to say, "I don't know." It is not a sign of weakness, indeed, it is a sign of willingness to learn.

This is precisely why our students need to know in all instances whether we are assessing to support or to verify their learning.

Accurate Records Are Key

Because, very often, there are no tangible results from assessments conducted via personal communication, such as a grade or score, records of achievement must be managed carefully. Sometimes information management is not a problem. Over a span of a few moments or hours when the communication focuses on narrow targets for a few students and the evidence is used to serve its intended purposes, extended record keeping is unneccessary. Just rely on memory. But when the context includes many students, complex targets, and a requirement of later use, and you absolutely must maintain tangible evidence, then written or taped records of some kind will be needed. Often, modern handheld digital technology can help with this. If you have no means or hope of securing such assistance, do not rely on your memory alone. Rather, revise your assessment plans to rely on another assessment method.

Context Summary

Figure 7.2 summarizes these practical keys to the effective use of assessment by means of personal communication by transforming them into seven quality control questions that you can ask about your assessments (the language/culture key is subdivided into its three aspects).

Understanding Validity and Reliability Issues

Professional judgment, and therefore subjectivity, permeates all aspects of assessments that rely on personal communication:

- Achievement targets we set for students
- Questions we pose (and sometimes generate on the spot)

Things to investigate:

- Do teacher and students share a common language?
- Have students attained a sufficiently high level of verbal fluency to interact effectively?
- Have you developed your own cultural awareness?
- Do students have personalities that permit them to open up enough to reveal true achievement?
- Do students see the environment as safe enough to reveal their true achievement?
- Do students understand the need to reveal their true achievement?
- Can accurate records of achievement be kept?

Figure 7.2

Factors to consider when using personal communication as assessment

- Criteria we apply in evaluating answers (often without a great deal of time to reflect)
- Performance records we store (sometimes in memory!)
- Manner in which we retrieve those results for later use
- Interpretations we make of the results
- Various ways in which we use those results

This subjectivity makes it imperative that, as with other assessment methods, you know and understand your achievement target and know how to translate it into clear and specific questions and other probes to generate focused information.

Let's be specific about the three reasons not to take personal communication as assessment too lightly as a source of information and as a teaching strategy. These reasons are (1) the problem of forgetting, (2) the problem of "filters," and (3) the challenge of sampling.

The Problem of Forgetting

The first reason for caution is that we must remain mindful of the fallibility of the human mind as a recording device. Not only can we forget and lose things in there, but also the things we try to remember about a student's performance can change over time for various reasons, only some of which are within our control. This presents validity concerns. We must act purposely to counteract this danger by conducting quality assessments and recording results before they get lost or are changed in our minds.

The Problem of "Filters"

We already have discussed this. We must remain aware of and strive to understand those personal and professional filters, developed over years of experience, through which we hear and process student responses. They represent norms, if you will, that allow us to interpret and act on the achievement information that comes to us through observation and personal communication. If not managed effectively, these filters hold the potential for harming assessment reliability. They can be the source of inappropriate bias.

If we set our expectations of a particular student, not on the basis of a clear understanding of the discipline and the student's current capabilities but rather on the basis of a stereotype unrelated to real academic achievement, we risk doing great harm indeed. For example, if we establish norms of student performance according to gender, ethnic heritage, cultural background, physical appearance, linguistic experience, our knowledge of a student's prior achievement, or any of a variety of other forms of prejudice—all potentially unrelated to actual achievement—we allow bias to creep into assessment, resulting in unreliable scores.

The insidious aspect is that we are hardly ever aware of our own biases. We don't go around saying, "Boys who are athletes never study and don't learn," or "I have a feeling that Sarah can do this, even though she didn't demonstrate it this time." Biases are subtle and operate to reduce the objectivity of the evidence gathered.

We can avoid these problems only by striving to be aware of them and by adhering to sound assessment practices as described throughout this book.

Time for Reflection

As a student, have you ever been on the losing end of a biased assessment where, for some reason, your teacher's inappropriate personal or professional filters led to an incorrect assessment of your proficiency? What was that like? What effect did it have on your learning?

The Challenge of Sampling

As with other forms of assessment, we can make sampling mistakes that invalidate the assessment. One mistake is to gather incorrect information by asking the wrong questions, questions that fail to reflect important forms of achievement. We sample the wrong thing, for example, by asking knowledge recall questions when we really want to get at our students' ability to use that knowledge in a particular manner.

Another mistake is to gather too few bits of information to lead to confident conclusions about proficiency. Our sample is too small.

Still another sampling mistake is to spend too much time gathering too many bits of information. This is a problem of inefficiency. We eventually reach a point of diminishing returns, where collecting additional information is unlikely to change our conclusion about proficiency.

To avoid such sampling problems, we must be crystal clear about targets and purposes and gather just enough information. Remember, any assessment represents only a sample of an ideal assessment of infinite length. The key to successful sampling in the context of personal communication is to ask a representative set of questions, one that is long enough to give you confidence in the generalizations you draw to the entire performance domain.

Example of an Easy Fit.   Mr. Lopez, an elementary teacher I know, tells this story illustrative of a time when sampling challenges were relatively easy to meet:

"I was about to start a new science reading activity on fish with my third graders. As a prereading activity, I wanted to be sure all my students had sufficient background information about fish to understand the reading. So I checked the story very carefully for vocabulary and concepts that might be stumbling blocks for my students. Then I simply asked a few strategic questions of the class, probing understanding of those words and ideas and calling on students randomly to answer. As I sampled the group's prior knowledge through questions and answers, I made mental notes about who seemed not to know some of the key material. There were only three or four. Later, I went back and questioned each of them more thoroughly to be sure. Then I helped them to learn the new material before they began reading."

In this scenario, the performance arena is quite small and focused: vocabulary and concepts from within one brief science story. Sampling by means of personal communication was simple and straightforward, and there are no real record-keeping challenges presented. Mr. Lopez simply verified understanding on the part of the students before proceeding. After that, most records of performance could go on the back burner. Mr. Lopez did make a mental note to follow up with those students who had the most difficulty, but decided that all other records could be "deleted."

Example of a More Challenging Fit.   Now here's a scenario in which the assessment challenges are more formidable: A high school health teacher wants to rely extensively on small- and large-group discussions of health-related social issues to encourage student participation in class discussions. To accomplish this, she announces at the beginning of the year that 25 percent of each student's grade will be based on the extent and quality of their participation in class. She is careful to point out that she will call on people to participate and that she expects them to be ready.

This achievement target is broader than that of Mr. Lopez in two ways: It contains many more elements (the domain is much larger), and it spans a much longer period of time. Not only does the teacher face an immense challenge in adequately sampling each individual's performance, but also, her record-keeping challenge is much more complex and demanding. Consider the record-keeping dilemma posed by a class schedule that includes, say, four sections of eleventh-grade health, each including 30 students! Mental record keeping is not an option: When we try to store such information in our gray matter for too long, bad things happen. Besides, this qualifies as an assessment *of* learning. So the pressure is on to do it right. These are not unsolvable problems, but they take careful preparation to assess. In this sense, they represent a significant challenge to the teacher.

These two scenarios capture the essence of the quality control challenge you face when you choose to rely on personal communication as a means of assessing student achievement. You must constantly ask yourself, Is my achievement target narrow enough in its scope and short enough in its time span to allow for conscientious sampling of the performance of an individual student or students as a group? If the answer is yes, in your opinion, proceed to the next question: Is the target narrow enough in its scope and short enough in its time span to allow me to keep accurate records of performance? If the answer again is yes, proceed. *If the answer to either question is no, choose another assessment method.*

Summary: Avoiding Validity and Reliability Problems

We can avoid problems due to the fallibility of the human mind and bias only by attending to those five ever-present, important, basic attributes of sound assessment as they apply in the context of personal communication. Whether we plan or are spontaneous in our personal communication with students, we must bear these quality standards in mind. Figure 7.3 reviews these standards as they apply to personal communication as assessment.

Understanding Validity: Matching Method to Target

Personal communication-based assessments can provide direct evidence of proficiency in three of our five kinds of targets and can provide insight into the student's readiness to deliver on the other two. This is a versatile assessment option.

Attribute of Quality	Defining Question
Arise from a clear and specific achievement target	Do my questions reflect the achievement target I want my students to hit?
Serve clear purposes	Why am I assessing? How will results be used?
Assure a sound representation of that target	Can the target of interest to me be accurately reflected through personal communication with the student?
Sample performance appropriately	Do I have enough evidence?
Control for unwanted bias	Am I in touch with potential sources of bias, and have I minimized the effects of personal and professional filters?

Figure 7.3
Defining issues of quality for personal communication as classroom assessment

Assessing Knowledge and Understanding

This can be done with personal communication, but you need to be cautious. Obviously, you can question students to see if they have mastered the required knowledge or can retrieve it through the effective use of reference materials. To succeed, however, you must possess a keen sense of the limits and contents of the domain of knowledge. Once again, since you cannot ask all possible questions, especially using this labor-intensive method, your questions must sample and generalize in a representative manner. And remember, knowing and understanding are not the same thing. So you will want to query both.

Assessing Reasoning

Herein lies the real strength of personal communication as a means of assessment. Skillful questioners can probe student reasoning and problem solving, both while students are thinking out their answers and retrospectively, to analyze how students reached a solution. But even more exciting is that you can use questioning to help both of you understand and enhance each other's reasoning.

For example, you can ask students to let you in on their thought processes as they analyze events or objects, describing component parts. You can probe their abilities to draw meaningful comparisons, to make simple or complex inferences, or to express and defend an opinion or point of view. There is no more powerful method for exploring student reasoning and problem solving than a conversation while students are actually trying to solve the problem. By exploring their reasoning along with them, you can provide students with the kinds of understanding and vocabulary needed to converse with you and with each other about what it means to be proficient in this performance arena.

Asking students to "think out loud" offers great promise for delving deeply into their reasoning. For example, mathematics teachers often ask students to talk about their thinking while proceeding step by step through the solution to a complex math problem. This provides a richness of insight into students' mathematical reasoning that cannot be attained in any other way. Further, as students talk through a process, you also can insert followup questions: Why did you take (or omit) certain steps? What would have happened if you had . . . ? Do you see any similarities between this problem and those we worked on last week? When students are unable to solve the problem, tactical questioning strategies can tell you why. Did they lack prerequisite knowledge? Analyze the problem incorrectly? Misunderstand the steps in the process? These probes permit you to find student needs and link your assessment to instruction almost immediately—there is no need to wait for the score reports to be returned!

In a different context, one popular way of assessing reading comprehension is to have students retell a story they have just read. As the retelling unfolds, you are free to ask questions as needed to probe the student's interpretation.

Assessing Performance Skills and Products

In the previous chapter, we established that the only way to obtain direct information about student performance skills or proficiency in creating quality products is to have them actually "do" or "create" and compare their work to established standards of quality.

The great strength of direct personal interaction with students in this category is in the assessment of their oral communication skills—their ability to use the language to convey their ideas. Whether we endeavor to talk with them in English or a foreign language, that interaction can provide evidence of essential performance skills.

However, even in other performance areas, a skilled teacher of "doing" or "creating" (i.e., a teacher who possesses a highly refined vision of relevant skill or product targets), can ask students to talk through a hypothetical performance, asking a few key questions along the way, and know with a certain degree of confidence whether they are likely to be proficient or less than proficient performers. While admittedly an approximation of actual performance, this can save assessment time in the classroom.

In this same performance-related sense, you can ask students strategic questions to examine the following:

- Prior success in performing similar tasks
- Their sense of certainty or uncertainty about the quality of their work
- Knowledge and understanding of the criteria used to evaluate performance (i.e., key skills to be demonstrated or key attributes of quality products)
- Awareness of the steps necessary to create quality products

Based on the results of such probes, you can draw cautious inferences about student competence.

Assessing Dispositions

Herein resides another strength of personal communication as a form of assessment. Perhaps the most productive way to determine the direction and intensity of students' school-related attitudes, interests, values, or motivational dispositions is simply to ask them. An ongoing pattern of honest exchanges of points of view between you and your students can contribute much to creating powerful learning environments.

The keys to making personal communication work in the assessment of student affect are trust and open channels of communication. If students are confident that it's all right to say what they really think and feel, they will do so.

Summary of Target Matches

Personal communication in its many forms can supply useful information to teachers about a variety of important educational outcomes, including mastery of subject matter knowledge, reasoning and problem solving, procedural knowledge that is prerequisite to skill and product creation proficiency, and dispositions. Table 7.1 presents a summary of matches.

To create effective matches between this method of assessment and these kinds of targets, however, you must start with a clear vision of the outcomes to be attained. In addition, you must know how to translate that vision into clear, focused questions, share a common language, open channels of communication with students, and understand how to sample performance representatively. But none of these keys to success is powerful enough to overcome the problems that arise when your interpretive filters predispose you to be inappropriately biased in deciphering communication from students.

Table 7.1
Personal communication: Assessment of achievement targets

Target to Be Assessed	Personal Communication
Knowledge & Understanding	Can ask questions, evaluate answers, and infer mastery, but a time-consuming option
Reasoning Proficiency	Can ask students to "think aloud" or can ask follow-up questions to probe reasoning
Performance Skills	Strong match when skill is oral communication proficiency; also can assess mastery of knowledge prerequisite to skillful performance
Ability to Create Products	Can probe procedural knowledge and knowledge of attributes of quality products, but not product quality
Dispositions	Can talk with students about their feelings

The Many Forms of Personal Communication as Assessment

As with the other three modes, this one includes a variety of assessment formats: questioning, conferences and interviews, class discussions, oral examinations, and journals and logs. We will define each format and identify several keys to its effective use in the classroom.

Instructional Questions and Answers

This has been a foundation of education since before Socrates. As instruction proceeds, the teacher poses questions for students to answer. This activity promotes thinking and learning, and also provides information about achievement. The teacher listens to answers, interprets them in terms of internally held standards, infers the respondent's level of attainment, and proceeds accordingly.

The following keys to successful use will help you take advantage of the strengths of this as an assessment format, while overcoming weaknesses:

- Plan key questions in advance of instruction, so as to ensure proper alignment with the target and with students' capabilities.
- Ask clear, brief questions that help students focus on a relatively narrow range of acceptable responses.
- Probe various kinds of reasoning, as appropriate.
- Ask the question first and then call on the person who is to respond. This will have the effect of keeping all students on focus.
- Call on both volunteer and nonvolunteer respondents. This, too, will keep all students in the game.
- Acknowledge correct or high-quality responses; probe incorrect responses for underlying reasons.
- After posing a question, wait for a response. Let respondents know that you always expect a response and will wait for as long as it takes.

While this last suggestion, allowing time for students to respond, turns out to be surprisingly difficult to do, research reviewed and summarized by Rowe (1978) reveals major benefits for student learning, especially for low-achieving students.

The Nature of Questions

If our objective is to determine what our students know and understand, direct questioning of content will suffice. But if we want to help our students become active strategic reasoners, using their new insights to make meaning, the questions we pose for them are crucial to their success. Table 7.2 suggests some triggers for questions that ask students to apply the various patterns of reasoning described in previous chapters.

Table 7.2
Triggers for reasoning questions

To Tap	Begin the Question with...
Analysis	How do the parts of a _____ work together? How does _____ break down into its parts? What are the components of _____ ? What are the active ingredients in _____ ?
Synthesis	Given what you know about _____ and _____ , what would happen if you _____ ? What two sources of knowledge do you need to combine to solve this problem? What do _____ and _____ have in common?
Comparison	How are these alike? different? Define the similarities between . . . (differences)? How does this correspond to that?
Classification	Into which category does each of the following fit? Group the following and label each category. Match each entry below with its classification.
Induction & Deduction	If this were to happen, then what would result? Using what you know about _____ , solve this problem. What would be the consequences of _____ ? The central idea or theme of the story is what?
Evaluation	State your position on this issue and defend it. Is this a good quality piece of work, in your opinion? Why? Argue in favor of or against _____ .

Think Assessment for Learning

Questions need not always flow from teacher to student. Students can ask themselves key questions and then discuss their answers with you, their teacher. For example, here are some questions that can focus student reflection on their reading experiences:

Understanding	Did I understand what I read?
Ease	Was the reading easy or difficult for me?
Meaning	Did I learn anything from this? If so, what?
Evaluation	Was it well written?
Pleasure	Did I like what I read?

These and similar questions can provide an excellent basis from which to encourage students to think aloud in conversation with you about their reading.

Conferences and Interviews

Some student-teacher conferences serve as structured or unstructured audits of student achievement, in which the objective is to talk about what students have learned and have yet to learn. Teachers and students talk directly and openly about levels of student attainment, comfort with the material the students are mastering, specific needs, interests, and desires, and/or any other achievement-related topics that contribute to an effective teaching and learning environment. In effect, teachers and students speak together in the service of understanding how to work effectively together.

Remember, interviews or conferences need not be conceived as every-pupil, standardized affairs, with each event a carbon copy of the others. You might meet with only one student, if it fills a communication need. Also, interviews or conferences might well vary in their focus with students who have different needs. The following are keys to your successful use of conference and interview assessment formats:

- Carefully think out and plan your questions in advance. Remember, students can share in their preparation.
- Plan for enough uninterrupted time to conduct the entire interview or conference.
- Be sure to conclude each meeting with a summary of the lessons learned and their implications for how you and the student will work together in the future.

One important strength of the interview or conference as a mode of assessment lies in the impact it can have on your student–teacher relationships. When conducted in a context where you have been up front about expectations, students understand the achievement target, and all involved are invested in student success, conferences have the effect of empowering students to take responsibility for at least part of the assessment of their own progress. Conducted in a context where everyone is committed to success and where academic success is clearly and openly defined, interviews inform and motivate both you and your students.

Class Discussions

When students participate in class discussions, the things they say reveal a great deal about their achievements and their feelings. *Discussions* are teacher- or student-led group interactions in which the material to be mastered is explored from various perspectives. Teachers listen to the interaction, evaluate the quality of student contributions, and infer individual student or group achievement. Clearly, class discussions have the simultaneous effect of promoting both student learning and their ability to use what they know.

To take advantage of the strengths of this method of assessment, while minimizing the impact of potential weaknesses, follow these keys to successful use:

- Prepare questions or discussion issues in advance to focus sharply on the intended achievement target.
- Be sure students are aware of your focus in evaluating their contributions. Are you judging the content of students' contributions or the form of their contribution—how they communicate? Be clear about what it means to be good at each.

- Remember, the public display of achievement or lack thereof is risky in the eyes of some students. Provide those students with other, more private, means of demonstrating achievement.
- In contexts where achievement information derived from participation in discussion is to influence high-stakes decisions—assessments *of* learning— keep dependable records of performance. Rely on more than your memory of their involvement.

Think Assessment *for* Learning

As always, remember to consider the learning potential of student involvement in classroom discussion when used as assessment:

- Involve students in preparing for discussions, being sure their questions and key issues are part of the mix.
- Rely on debate or other team formats to maximize the number of students who can be directly involved. Pay special attention to involving low achievers.
- Formalize the discussion format to the extent that different roles are identified, such as moderator, team leader, spokesperson, recorder, and so on, to maximize the number of students who have the opportunity to be deeply involved and thus present evidence of their achievement.

In addition, Figure 7.4 provides an illustration of a student-friendly scoring guide for self-assessment of one's own performance in class discussion situations—that is, a performance assessment in a personal communication assessment context.

Oral Examinations

In this case, teachers plan and pose exercises for their students, who reflect and provide oral responses. Teachers listen to and interpret those responses, evaluating quality and inferring levels of achievement.

In a very real sense, this is like essay assessment, discussed in Chapter 5, but with the added benefit of being able to ask followup questions.

While the oral examination tradition lost favor in the United States with the advent of selected response assessment during the last century, it still has great potential for use today, especially given the increasing complexity of our valued educational targets and the complexity and cost of setting up higher-fidelity performance assessments.

You can take advantage of the strengths of this format by adhering to some simple keys to its successful use, in effect the quality control guidelines listed in Chapter 5 for developing essay assessments:

- Develop brief exercises that focus on the desired target.
- Rely on exercises that identify the knowledge to be brought to bear, specify the kind of reasoning students are to use, and identify the standards you will apply in evaluating responses.
- Develop written scoring criteria in advance of the assessment.

Trait 1: My Understanding of the Topic

I Do This Well—I completely understand what we're discussing.
- I understand the meaning of the "technical" words being used.
- I know exactly which pieces of information I need to make a point.
- I can give good examples of what I mean.
- I can give evidence to support what I say.

I'm On My Way—I think I understand most of what we're discussing.
- I understand some of the ideas, but not all of them.
- I understand many of the "technical" words, but not all of them.
- I can sometimes give examples of what I mean.
- I picked out some of the important information, but I might have missed some.

I'm Just Starting—I'm not sure I understand what we're discussing.
- I'm not sure I understand what everyone else is talking about.
- I don't understand many of the "technical" words being used.
- I'm unsure which examples or information to use to make a point.
- I'm not sure that the information I use is correct.

Trait 2: My Understanding of What Group Work Is About

I Do This Well—I understand the reasons for working in a group and how to get group work done.
- I try to make sure I understand the reasons for the group work—what the group is supposed to accomplish.
- I help make sure that the discussion stays on the topic.
- I understand various ways to get group work done efficiently. For example, I know when it is useful to summarize the discussion, when the group needs additional information or help, when the group needs a leader, when the group needs to make sure all ideas are expressed, and when ideas need to be clearer.
- I know just what information is needed to contribute to the discussion.
- I know when the job of the group is done.
- I try to help make sure the group gets its work done.
- I know when it's useful to work in a group and when it is not.

I'm On My Way—I'm learning the reasons for working in a group and how to get group work done.
- I sometimes understand the goals of group work and sometimes I don't.
- I participate in the group when asked to by others, but I usually don't without being asked.

I'm Just Starting—I'm not sure I understand the reasons for working in a group, nor how to get group work done.
- I don't think I understand why we sometimes work in groups. I don't understand what working in a group is supposed to accomplish.
- I don't understand how to get group work done in an efficient manner.
- I usually don't follow what is going on.
- I get distracted and don't pay attention.
- I let others take responsibility for making sure the work gets done.

Figure 7.4

Self-assessment rubric for group discussion

(continued)

Trait 3: How I Interact with Others

I Do This Well—I know just how to get along with others when working in a group.
- I listen to what others have to say. I don't interrupt.
- When I disagree with someone, I know how to do it so that I don't hurt anyone's feelings.
- I make sure that everyone who wants to has a chance to talk.
- I'm polite.

I'm On My Way—I sometimes get along well with others when working in a group.
- I generally listen to others, but sometimes I get distracted.
- I sometimes interrupt.
- I try not to hurt others' feelings, but I think I sometimes do anyway.
- I understand how to be polite, but sometimes I'm not.

I'm Just Starting—I'm not sure how to get along with the others in a group.
- I think I hurt people's feelings when I disagree with them, but I'm not sure.
- I try to do all the talking.
- I try to never do any talking.
- I don't listen to what others have to say.
- I don't understand what to do to be polite to others.
- I don't understand why everyone needs a chance to talk.

Trait 4: The Language I Use During the Discussion

I Do This Well—I know just how to say things so that others will understand.
- I say things in a way that others in the group will understand.
- I don't use more words than I need to. I know just how much to say to be clear.
- I try to use words that others will understand. I know when I need to use different words to be clear.

I'm On My Way—I sometimes say things in ways that others understand.
- I think I sometimes use more words than needed to make a point.
- I think I sometimes use words that others don't understand.

I'm Just Starting—I'm unsure if I say things in ways that others will understand.
- I try to use big words to impress others.
- I'm not sure how to say things in ways others will understand.
- I didn't realize that I need to pay attention to how I say things.

Figure 7.4
Self-assessment rubric for group discussion *(continued)*

- Be sure criteria separate content and reasoning targets from facility with verbal expression.
- Prepare in advance to accommodate the needs of any students who may confront language proficiency barriers.
- Have a checklist, rating scale, or other method of recording results ready to use at the time of the assessment.
- If necessary, record responses for later reevaluation.

Clearly, the major argument against this assessment format is the amount of time it takes to administer oral exams. However, you can consider assessment *for* learning applications in which you can alleviate part of this problem by bringing students in as partners. If you adhere to the guidelines listed here and spread the work of administering and scoring over many shoulders, you may derive great benefit from oral assessment as a teaching and learning aid.

Journals and Logs: Naturals as Assessments *for* Learning

Sometimes personal communication-based assessment can take a written form. Students can share views, experiences, insights, and information about important learnings by writing about them. You can derive clear and useful information by assigning writing tasks that cause students to center on particularly important achievement targets. Further, you can then provide them with written feedback.

Four particular forms bear consideration: response journals, personal writing journals or diaries, dialog journals, and learning logs. These are infinitely flexible ways of permitting students to communicate about their learning, while at the same time practicing their writing and applying valued patterns of reasoning. In addition, because these written records accumulate over time, you can use them to help students reflect on their improvement as achievers—the heart of assessment *for* learning.

Response journals are most useful in situations where you ask students to read and construct meaning from literature, such as in the context of reading and English instruction. As they read, students write about their reactions. Typically, you would provide structured assignments to guide them, including such tasks as the following:

- Analyze characters in terms of key attributes or contribution to the story.
- Analyze evolving storylines, plots, or story events.
- Compare one piece of literature or character to another.
- Anticipate or predict upcoming events.
- Evaluate either the piece as a whole or specific parts in terms of appropriate criteria.
- Suggest ways to change or improve character, plot, or setting, defending such suggestions.

Teachers who use response journals report that it is an excellent way to permit students to practice applying reasoning patterns, and to increase the intensity of student involvement with their reading. Further, it can provide a means for students to keep track of all the things they have read, building in them a sense of accomplishment in this facet of their reading.

Personal writing journals or *diaries* represent the least structured of the journal options. In this case, you would give students time during each instructional day to write in their journals. The focus of their writing is up to them, as is the amount they write. Sometimes you evaluate the writing, sometimes it is merely for

practice. When you evaluate it, either you, or the student, or both, make judgments. Often young writers are encouraged to use their journals to experiment
with new forms of writing, such as dramatic dialogue, poetry, or some other art
form. Some teachers suggest to their students that they use personal journals as a
place to store ideas for future writing topics. This represents an excellent way to
gain insight into the quality of student writing when students are operating at typical levels of motivation to write well. Because there is no high-stakes assessment
under way, they do not have to strive for excellence. They can write for the fun of
it and still provide both themselves and you with evidence over time of their improvement as writers.

Dialogue journals capture conversations between students and teachers in the
truest sense of that idea. As teaching and learning proceed, students write messages
to you conveying thoughts and ideas about the achievement expected, self-
evaluations of progress, points of confusion, important new insights, and so on, and
periodically give you their journals. You then read the messages and reply, clarifying as needed, evaluating an idea, amplifying a key point, and so on, and return the
journals to the students. This process links you and each of your students in a personal communication partnership.

Learning logs ask students to keep ongoing written records of the following aspects of their studies:

- Achievement targets they have mastered
- Targets they have found useful and important
- Targets they are having difficulty mastering
- Learning experiences (instructional strategies) that worked particularly well
  for them
- Experiences that did not work for them
- Questions that have come up along the way that they want help with
- Ideas for important study topics or learning strategies that they might like to
  try in the future

The goal in the case of learning logs is to have students reflect on, analyze, describe, and evaluate their learning experiences, successes, and challenges, writing
about the conclusions they draw.

Student-Involved Assessment *for* Learning

Because instruction is conducted in large part through personal interaction between
teacher and student, in a very real sense students are always partners in personal
communication-based forms of assessment. Nevertheless, we can list a variety of
concrete strategies for helping this partnership reach its full potential. Consider the
ideas listed in Figure 7.5

- Turn leadership for discussion over to students; they can ask questions of each other or of you (put your own reasoning power on the line in public once in a while).
- Ask students to paraphrase each other's questions and responses.
- Ask students to address key questions in small groups, so more students can be involved.
- Offer students opportunities to become oral examiners, posing questions of each other.
- Ask students to keep track of changes in the depth of their own questions over time, such as through the use of tally sheets and diaries.
- Designate one or two students to be observers and recorders during discussions, noting who responds to what kinds of questions and how well; other teachers can do this too.
- Engage students in peer and self-assessment of performance in discussions.
- Schedule regular interviews with students, one-on-one or in groups.
- Schedule times when your students can interview you to get your impressions about how well things are going for them as individuals and as a group.

Figure 7.5
Ideas for student-involved assessment

Summary: Person-to-Person Assessment

The key to success in using personal communication to assess student achievement is to remember that, just because assessment is sometimes casual, informal, unstructured, and/or spontaneous, this does not mean we can let our guard down with respect to standards of assessment quality. In fact, we must be even more vigilant than with other forms of assessment, because it is so easy to allow personal filters, poor sampling techniques, and/or inadequate record keeping to interfere with sound assessment.

When we attend to quality standards, we use our interactions with students to assess important achievement targets, including mastery of knowledge, reasoning, and dispositions. We also can assess student mastery of knowledge and reasoning prerequisites to performance skills and product development capabilities. But remember, to tap the skills and products themselves, performance assessment is required.

Thus, like the other three modes of assessment, this one is quite flexible. Even though we typically don't refer to personal communication as assessment, if we start with a clear and appropriate vision, translate it into thoughtful probes, sample performance appropriately, and attend to key sources of bias, we can generate quality information in this manner.

So can students. Whether in whole-class discussions, smaller collaborative groups, or working with a partner, students can be assessors, too. They can ask questions of each other, listen to responses, infer achievement, and communicate feedback to each other. Beware, however. The ability to communicate effectively in an assessment context is not "wired in" from birth. Both you and your students must practice it, to hone it as an assessment skill.

Final Chapter Reflection

1. *What are the three most important new insights to come to you as a result of your study of this chapter?*
2. *Which of your previous questions about assessment can you now answer based on your study of this chapter?*
3. *What new questions have come to mind as a result of your study of this chapter that you hope to have answered as your study continues?*

Practice with Chapter 7 Ideas

1. As a practice activity collecting ideas presented through the previous chapters, construct a concept map that shows your current understanding of how the topics shown in Table 7.3 link together.

2. Referring to the text of this chapter as needed, fill in the cells of Table 7.4 in your own words.

Table 7.3
Personal communication as assessment—topics

Selected Response	Essay	Assessment Methods
Performance assessment	Products	Fill in the blank
Constructed response	Dispositions	True/False
Reasoning	Learning targets	Personal communication
Skills	Matching	Knowledge/Understanding
Sampling	Unclear tasks	Sources of bias & distortion
English language learner	Unclear criteria	Problems with test administration

Table 7.4
Communication format strengths and weaknesses

Assessment Format	Strengths as a Source of Evidence of Learning	Weaknesses
Instructional questions and answers		
Conferences and interviews		
Class discussion		
Oral examination		
Journals and logs		

Chapter 8

Assessing Dispositions

CHAPTER FOCUS

This chapter answers the following guiding question:

> Why, when, and how should I assess the dispositions of my students?

From your study of this chapter, you will understand the following:

1. Students' dispositions are motivations, feelings, and desires that inevitably underpin and directly influence academic achievement. Addressed carefully, they can help us maximize student success.

2. As with achievement, we must carefully define these student characteristics in order to assess them accurately.

3. Dispositions vary in their focus, direction, and intensity, and are assessable in these terms in the classroom.

As we start this part of our journey, keep our big picture in mind. Refer to Figure 8.1. In this chapter, we will be dealing in depth with the shaded areas.

School Is Not Just About Academic Achievement

In our opening scenario in Chapter 1, Emily became more than just a good writer. She *felt* like a good writer. The early improvements in her writing gave her the feeling that she could succeed if she kept trying. The direction of this effect was critical. Real academic success preceded, or gave rise to, the motivation or desire to learn more.

From the beginning, I have contended that we can succeed as teachers only if we help our students *want* to learn. Ms. Weathersby succeeded with Emily and her classmates. Motivation and desire represent the very foundations of learning. If students don't want to learn, there will be no learning. If they feel unable to learn, there will be no learning.

	SELECTED RESPONSE	ESSAY	PERFORMANCE ASSESSMENT	PERSONAL COMMUNICATION
Know				
Reason				
Performance Skills				
Products				
Dispositions				

Figure 8.1
Aligning achievement targets and assessment methods

Desire and motivation are not academic achievement characteristics. They are *affective* characteristics. Feelings. Emotions. We have established that achievement is assessable. But are these feelings or dispositions assessable also? Yes, they are. And, from time to time, it will be to both our and our students' advantage if we assess them and use the results to support student learning.

When we assess mastery of subject matter knowledge, we seek to know how much of the material students have learned. When we assess reasoning, we seek to know how effectively students can use that knowledge to solve problems. When we assess performance skills, we evaluate demonstrated proficiencies. When we assess products, we evaluate whether students can create things that meet certain standards of quality. These are things you already know.

When we assess dispositions, we tap the feeling dimensions of students in school, the inner motivations or desires that influence their thoughts and their actions. In this case, we center not on what students know and can do, but on what they feel about key aspects of their schooling; the attitudes, motivations, and interests that predispose students to behave in academically productive ways.

We want our students to become more than competent writers. In the end, we want them to *want* to write. If they fail to see the value of writing, they will not be disposed to use the skills they have acquired. We fall short of our goal of developing competent readers if we fail to impart the great joy of reading. If those feelings are missing, students will not be disposed to make regular reading part of their lives. Indeed, we can do great harm if school leaves students feeling as though they are incapable of learning. Regardless of their actual ability to learn, if they don't perceive themselves as in charge of their own academic well-being, they will not be predis-posed to become the lifelong learners they will need to be in the twenty-first cen-tury. Attitudes about writing, reading, and other academic domains, as well as academic self-concept, are important targets of classroom instruction.

Thus, in this chapter, we deal with the emotional dimension of students in school. Like achievement, dispositions are multidimensional human characteristics, and include such subcategories as attitudes, motivations, and interests. We will dis-cuss the assessment of student affect about many ingredients of school: teachers, classmates, school subjects, extracurricular activities, instructional methods, them-selves as learners, and others.

Our assessment challenge in this case is easy to understand. Feelings about school vary both in their direction (from positive through neutral to negative) and intensity (from very strong to moderate to very weak). Our assessment task is to de-termine both direction and intensity.

With these two features in mind, I can share why I have adopted the label *dis-positions* in this chapter. Our instructional goals for developing student feelings are not value neutral. Often, we hope for strong, positive or negative, feelings in our stu-dents when it comes to learning. We strive to develop learners predisposed to be-have in certain academically productive ways in school. Often, we seek a strong positive work ethic, positive motivation, intense interests, positive attitudes, and a positive academic self-concept; that is, we want them to have a strong sense of in-ternal control over their own academic success.

But in addition, sometimes we seek to develop strong negative dispositions that influence students to behave in certain ways, such as the disposition not to use drugs or not to engage in other unhealthy, unsafe, or inconsiderate behaviors. We can know if we are succeeding only if we are ready to assess student dispositions or af-fect within the context of our own schools and classrooms.

Assessment *for* Learning Involves Student Dispositions

There are those who contend that school should be about academic achievement only, that student feelings or dispositions should be off limits. They feel that attitudes and interests are the responsibility of family, church, and community. In a sense, I must agree. Families and communities differ widely regarding the "proper" attitudes and values to hold. Given those differences of opinion, it becomes very difficult for school leaders to decide which ones to factor into the school curriculum.

One approach to resolving such a dilemma would be to leave the matter of val-ues, attitudes, and such out of the educational equation altogether. Render those unto the family, community, and religious institutions. But there is a compelling rea-son why, as teachers, we cannot do this—why we absolutely must address dis-positions in the classroom. Motivational predispositions go a long way toward determining whether any given student will or can achieve academically.

I have advocated student involvement in classroom assessment throughout this book because it leads to greater student learning. But it is imperative that you understand why it does so. It is because, when applied effectively, the principles of assessment *for* learning help students *feel* like capable learners, feel in control of their own success. They enhance students' confidence and desire to learn.

Dispositions as Means to an End

My point is that we cannot separate dispositions or affect and achievement from one another in the classroom. As teachers, we must know how to help students develop academically empowering dispositions and must be ready to teach them how to use those dispositions to promote their own success.

Students who have positive attitudes about the things they are learning, and feel a sense of internal control of their own academic well-being, are more likely to achieve at high levels than those who are negative, lack desire, and see themselves as victims of a hostile school world. Very often, students fail not because they cannot achieve, but because they choose not to achieve. Often, they have given up and are not motivated to learn. Why? There may be many reasons: They don't understand the work, find it too hard to do, lack prerequisite achievement, and so on. And so they fail, which in turn robs them of (1) the prerequisites for the next learning and (2) a sense that they could succeed if they tried. This can become a vicious cycle, a self-fulfilling prophecy. They feel academically powerless and thus become powerless. This negative academic self-concept drives out of students any motivation to try. This downward spiral can result from the complex interaction between achievement and dispositions. These students become predisposed to fail.

But this spiral also can take a very positive direction. Right from the time students arrive at school, they look to us, their teachers, for evidence of the extent to which they are succeeding. If that early evidence (from our classroom assessments) suggests that they are succeeding, what can begin to grow in them is a sense of hope for the future and expectation of further success down the road. This, in turn, fuels their motivation to strive for excellence, which spawns more success and results in the upward spiral of positive dispositions and academic achievement that every parent and teacher dreams of for their children. These students become predisposed to succeed.

Clearly, many forces in a student's life exert great influence on attitudes, values, interests, self-concept, and indeed on dispositions to try to achieve excellence. Chief among these are family, peer group, church, and community. But schools are prominent on this list of contributors, too, especially when it comes to dispositions to invest the energy required to learn. To the extent that we wish to help students to take advantage of dispositions as driving forces toward greater achievement, it will be important for us to understand and apply the principles of assessment *for* learning:

- Reveal achievement targets to them in rich detail using student-friendly language and examples of good work.

- Show students where they are now in relation to that vision of academic success.
- Show them how to get there from here.
- Provide focused practice relying heavily on descriptive feedback that they can use to see how to do better the next time.
- Permit students to monitor their progress along the way.
- Afford them the opportunity to tell the story of their success, with evidence, as they travel.

In these ways, student-involved assessment can fuel a strong sense of hope for success on every student's part, predisposing them to pursue academic excellence.

Time for Reflection

From a personal point of view, which of your school-related feelings (positive or negative) seem to have been most closely associated with your achievement successes in school? Were there subjects you liked or disliked? Instructors who motivated or failed to motivate you? Positive or negative values that you held? How have your dispositions toward school related to your achievement?

Remain Mindful of Standards of Assessment Quality

During the course of my decades of classroom assessment work, I find a pervasive tendency to take lightly the responsibility to accurately assess student feelings or dispositions. Many seem to assume that, because it is not achievement, we don't have to plan for or conduct rigorous assessments. As a result, many fail to attend carefully to our standards of assessment quality. If your assessments of student dispositions are to be useful, they must do all of the following:

- Arise from a clear vision of the disposition to be assessed. Precisely what disposition will you assess? Have you defined them clearly? We discuss options in the following pages.
- Arise from a clear reason for assessing. How will you use the results?
- Rely on proper assessment methods. Which method provides the most accurate reflection? We discuss options in the following pages.
- Sample appropriately. How can you gather sufficient information to make dependable inferences about student dispositions?
- Control for relevant sources of bias. What factors could bias or distort results and how do you prevent these problems?

The range of available assessment methods is the same as it is for achievement targets. You can opt for paper and pencil methods (selected response or essay), performance assessments, and/or personal communication. While the assessments themselves may look different in format, as you will see, the basic evidence-gathering methodology remains the same.

But There Is One Critical Difference

There is, however, one very important difference between student achievement and student affect that bears directly on differences in the manner in which we *use* assessment. That difference has to do with the reasons for assessing.

It is perfectly acceptable to hold students accountable for mastery of knowledge, reasoning, skill, and/or product targets. In assessment *of* learning contexts, where students are held accountable for learning, we assess to verify that students have met our academic achievement standards.

However, it is *not* acceptable to hold students accountable in the same sense for their dispositions. It is never acceptable, for example, to lower a student's grade because of an attitude that we regard as "negative." Evidence of learning or the lack of it must speak for itself at grading time, regardless of attitudes expressed in class. Nor, conversely, is it acceptable to raise a student's grade just because of a positive attitude or other disposition, regardless of achievement.

Rather, we assess dispositions in the hope of finding positive, productive attitudes, values, sense of academic self, or interest in particular topics so we can take advantage of these—build on them—to promote greater achievement gains.

But if our assessments reveal negative feelings, then we are obliged to strive for educational experiences that will result in the positive dispositions we hope for. In fact, such experiences may or may not succeed in producing the positive motivational predisposition we desire. But if we do not succeed in this endeavor, we cannot place sanctions on students with negative affect in the same way we can for those who fail to achieve academically. We cannot hold them accountable for positive affect in the same way we do for positive achievement.

On the contrary, I think responsibility for school-related student dispositions should rest with us, their teachers. In fact, I hold myself accountable for your dispositions regarding assessment. If I don't help you feel strongly about the critical importance of quality assessment, if you don't leave my classes or complete this book feeling a strong sense of responsibility to create accurate assessments and if you don't feel a strong desire to use them to benefit your students, then *I regard that as my fault.* I must strive to find better ways to motivate you, my students, to act responsibly with respect to the quality of your classroom assessments. I believe you have that same responsibility with your students.

Three Very Important Ground Rules

Before we define and discuss ways to assess dispositions, let me lay out three critically important ground rules for dealing with dispositions in the classroom. Note them well; violate them at your own peril and that of your students.

Ground Rule 1: Remember, This Is Personal

Always remain keenly aware of the sensitive interpersonal nature of student feelings and strive to promote appropriate dispositions through your assessment of them. Assessing feelings of any sort yields vulnerability on both sides. When you assess, you ask students to risk being honest in an environment where honesty on their part has not always been held at a premium. They may be reticent to express honest feelings because of a lack of experience in doing so and because of the risk that you may somehow use the results against them. It takes a teacher who is a true master of human relations to break through these barriers and promote honest expression of feelings in classrooms. One way I have done this is to permit respondents to my queries to remain anonymous. I will offer specific instructions regarding how to foster honesty later in the chapter.

For your part, you risk asking for honesty in a place where the honest response just may not turn out to be the one you had hoped to hear. Positive feedback is wonderful to receive, but negative feedback is never easy to hear and act on. Many avoid this danger by simply not asking. If you ask how students are feeling about things in your classroom, listen thoughtfully to the answers, and act on the results in good faith—the reward will be worth the risk you take. The result will be a more productive student–teacher relationship, a working partnership characterized by greater trust.

Time for Reflection

Under the best of circumstances, teachers become anxious when the time comes to ask students what they think about their teaching. Can you think of specific actions you might take to minimize your personal risk when preparing for, conducting, and interpreting the results of such an assessment? List as many ideas as you can.

Ground Rule 2: Stay in Bounds

Know your limits when dealing with student feelings. There are two important interrelated limits you should be aware of. First, as you come to understand and assess student feelings, you will occasionally encounter students who are deeply troubled, personally and/or socially. Be caring but cautious in these instances. These are not occasions for you to become an amateur psychologist. *If you find yourself in a situation where you feel uneasy with what you are learning about a student or about your ability to help that student deal productively with feelings or circumstances, you may well be reaching the limits of your professional expertise. Listen to your instincts and get help.*

The most caring and responsible teachers are those who know when it is time to contact the principal, a counselor, a school psychologist, or a physician to find competent counseling services for students. Do not venture into personal territory for which you are not trained. You can do great harm if you fail to respond appropriately, even with the most positive intentions.

The second set of limits is a corollary to the first. I urge you to focus your attention on those classroom-level dispositions over which you are likely to (and in fact should) have some influence. When assessing and evaluating student feelings, stick with those feelings as they relate to specific school-related objects: dispositions toward particular subjects or classroom activities, academic interests students would like to pursue in school, personal dispositions as learners in an academic setting, and so on. These have a decidedly school-oriented bent, and they represent values families and school communities are likely to agree are important as parts of the schooling experience

Please understand this: You need not go too far over those classroom-related limits before members of your community may begin to see your actions on behalf of positive, productive affect as invading their turf. Some families and communities are very protective of their responsibility to promote the development of certain strongly held values and will not countenance interference from schools. This is their right.

You must decide how to deal with these limits within your community. Be advised that the conservative approach is to focus in your classroom on those dimensions of affect that we all agree are the legitimate purview of the teacher, dispositions toward school-related matters. As the chapter progresses, you will attain a clearer sense of what this means.

Ground Rule 3: If You Ask, Do Something with the Results

If you care enough to invest in understanding student dispositions and in developing quality assessments in this arena, then care enough to take the results seriously and change your instruction when they suggest a need for change. In other words, don't ask how students are feeling about things just to appear to care. The more you act on these assessment results, the greater the potential that students will share feelings in the future that will allow you to improve the nature and quality of your learning environment. When done well, assessment of school-related dispositions can be a productive classroom activity for students and teachers. It can lead to specific actions on the part of both that promote constructive learning and maximum achievement.

Defining *Affect* as It Relates to Dispositions

To help you make sense of the range of relevant student dispositions, I will follow Anderson and Bourke (2000) and share several kinds of affect that can come into play in the school setting:

- attitudes
- school-related values
- academic self-efficacy
- interests
- academic aspirations
- evaluation or assessment anxiety

These represent significant dimensions of classroom affect that bear directly on students' motivation to learn. They represent students' attributes that predispose them to behave in academically and socially productive ways. In addition, each has been clearly defined in the professional literature, is relatively easy to understand, and can be assessed in the classroom using relatively straightforward procedures.

Attitudes

An *attitude* is a favorable or unfavorable feeling about someone or something. Very simply, if I like a particular teacher, I express a positive attitude about that teacher. If I dislike a school subject, I have learned a negative attitude about it. One does not learn the feeling itself, one learns rather the association between the feeling and a particular focus. And once ingrained, the feeling is consistently experienced in the presence of that object. The focus might be a person, a school subject, or a particular method of instruction. However, they can be unstable in the sense that attitudes can change quickly, especially among young people.

Attitudes vary in direction (favorable to unfavorable) and intensity (strong to weak). The stronger the favorable or unfavorable attitudes, the greater is the likelihood that they will influence behavior.

Obviously, the range of attitudes within any individual is as broad as the array of experiences or objects to which that person reacts emotionally. In schools, students might have favorable or unfavorable attitudes about each other, teachers, administrators, math, science, reading, writing, instructional activities, and so on. It is our hope as educators that success breeds positive attitudes, which then fuel the desire for greater achievement, which in turn breeds more positive attitudes. Thus, certain attitudes predispose students to academic success.

School-Related Values

Our values are our "beliefs about what should be desired, what is important or cherished, and what standards of conduct are . . . acceptable. Second, values influence or guide behavior, interests, attitudes, and satisfactions. Third, values are enduring. That is, they tend to remain stable over fairly long periods of time" (Anderson & Bourke, 2000, p. 32). Values also are learned, tend to be of high intensity, and tend to focus on enduring ideas.

The following are among those values related to academic success:

- Belief in the value of education as a foundation for a productive life
- Belief in the benefits of strong effort in school
- A strong sense of the need for ethical behavior at testing time (no cheating)
- The belief that a healthy lifestyle (for example, no drugs) underpins academic success

These, then, are among the values that influence behavior and predispose students to succeed in school.

Academic Self-Efficacy

No affective characteristic is more school related than this one. It is the evaluative judgment one makes about one's possibility of success and/or productivity in an academic context. In essence, it is an attitude (favorable or unfavorable) about one's self when viewed in a classroom setting. Academic self-concept, write Anderson and Bourke (2000), is a learned vision that results largely from evaluations of self by others over time. Quite simply, those who see themselves as capable learners are predisposed to be capable learners.

There is one part of academic self-concept that is sufficiently important to justify its consideration here. In this case, the characteristic of interest is students' attributions or beliefs about the reasons for academic success or failure (this is referred to in the literature as *locus of control*). One kind of attribution is defined as *internal:* "I succeeded because I tried hard." Another possible attribution is *external,* where chance rules: "I sure was lucky to receive that A!" Yet another external attribution assigns cause to some other person or factor: "I performed well because I had a good teacher." At issue here are students' perceptions of the underlying reasons for the results they are experiencing. These, too, are learned self-perceptions arising from their sense of the connection of effort to academic success.

In school, our aspiration must be to help students see the connection between their efforts and their levels of academic success. This is the basis of my belief in the principles of assessment *for* learning. Those who perceive themselves as being in control of their own academic destiny, and who at the same time see the goal as being within their grasp, are predisposed to succeed. In short, we seek to imbue students with an internal locus of academic control.

Teachers also have to believe that student effort *can* improve their performance with guided practice—that student achievement is *not* totally determined by what they walk in the door with. If *we* don't believe it, our students won't either.

Like other affective characteristics, self-efficacy varies in direction (can do, can't do) and intensity (weak to strong) and is learned. "The learning takes place over time as the student experiences a series of successes or failures" (Anderson & Bourke, 2000, p. 35). At the risk of being repetitive, once again I say that through their involvement in assessment, record keeping, and communication, we hope to help students develop a "can do" perspective in the classroom.

Interests

Let's define an *interest* as a learned preference for some activity, skill, idea, or understanding. This preference influences behavior in that it causes us to pursue its object. Feelings range from a high level of excitement to no excitement at all at the prospect of engaging in, or while engaged in, some particular activity.

A student might be very interested in drama, but completely disinterested in geography. Strong interests, like positive attitudes, can link students to their greater potential for success. In this sense, they too relate to student dispositions. Students learn most effectively and efficiently when they are interested in what we expect them to learn.

Academic Aspirations

In this case, we refer to the desire to learn more—the intent to seek out and participate in additional education experiences. Thus, Anderson and Bourke (2000) write, "We would suggest that aspirations are moderately high intensity affective characteristics . . . the direction of which is 'more' or 'no more'" (p. 30). Aspirations emerge from students' history of academic success or the lack thereof, feelings of self-efficacy or control over that level of success, interests in the topic(s) they are studying, and attitudes about school.

Evaluation Anxiety

Hall and Lindsay (1970) define *anxiety* as "the experience of [emotional] tension that results from real or imagined threats to one's security" (p. 145). This feeling varies from a sense of relaxed safety on one end to extreme tension on the other. When faced with the prospect of having their achievement evaluated, students will experience varying levels of this kind of anxiety, depending on their record of success or the lack thereof and the extent and nature of their preparation to succeed on the assessment.

In the classroom, we can conceive of ways in which anxiety can affect students' behavior. One is as a driving force. It can supply positive energy, motivating students to work hard. This happens when their judgment of the chances of success are high. Alternatively, anxiety can serve as a source of debilitation, fear, and frustration, causing students to give up in hopelessness or cynicism. The systematic application of the principles of assessment *for* learning promotes the expectation of success, reducing evaluation anxiety.

Anxiety also can be a source of feelings of vulnerability, leading students to feel at risk of harm in the face of an assessment. Be advised that, depending on the strength of that anxiety, it can (1) inhibit clear thinking and thus performance on the assessment, thus leading to biased results, or (2) overwhelm the student with a sense of hopelessness, thus inhibiting learning itself. Both are effects to be avoided at all cost.

Dispositions, Student Confidence, and Assessment *for* Learning

Through the preceding chapters, I have suggested that ongoing student involvement in assessment can build their confidence in themselves as learners. Students' confidence builds when evidence of achievement derived from classroom assessment reinforces their belief that they are improving.

Confidence certainly is an affective characteristic. But I do not describe it separately in this chapter because I think it represents the sum of the others listed. Let's consider the positive instance first—the confident learner who anchors one end of a continuum.

The Confident Student

Students who are succeeding typically start with and further develop positive attitudes about what they are learning and about those who are teaching them. Success deepens the value students are likely to attach to education and to its institutions.

Successful students with positive attitudes and strong values are very likely to be confident learners.

Their academic self-concept has its foundations in expectations of future success. They see the relationship between their efforts and their achievement and thus feel in control. They spiral upward from success to success with a "can do" attitude. They are confident enough to take the risks associated with trying new things, because they know that they have the reserves to bounce back if they fail (a rare occurrence for them). They are confident.

As a result, their educational aspirations are high and their anxiety stays at levels that allow them to maintain whatever level of effort they require to succeed.

The Student Who Lacks Confidence

Now let's consider the other end of the confidence continuum. Psychologists who study motivation tell us that students can fall into a classification that they call "failure acceptors" (Covington, 1992). Typically, these students have experienced sufficient failure in the classroom to infer either that they are too dumb to get it or that getting it is just not worth the effort. They took the risk of trying to learn early in their academic lives, did not succeed, were punished for it, lost confidence, and do not want to risk such pain again.

Typically their attitudes about school, school subjects, and their teachers are unfavorable. They place little value in learning. Their academic self-concept is rock bottom. Often they blame their teachers for their lack of success. When they do succeed, they tend to attribute it to luck. Their school life depicts a "can't do" soap opera. Their interests may be strong, but not for participating in academic activities. They aspire to nothing more by way of schooling. Additionally, their level of concern or anxiety about it all appears to be very low. These students are not confident learners.

Between the Extremes, a Chance to Help

Between these two end points we find students whose disposition profiles vary widely. They may be academically positive and productive at some tasks or subjects, while remaining in the doldrums on others. But we know one thing for sure: If our objective is maximum achievement, our goal must always be to move all students in the direction of becoming more confident learners. Anything we do to set goals, instruct, and assess student achievement that has the effect of destroying confidence is, by definition, counterproductive.

We can encourage students to develop confidence by sharing with them appropriate rewards for success. But I am convinced that we cannot turn a weak student into a high achiever through the use of coercion or intimidation. They are so lacking in inner reserves that the threat of pending punishment will cause them to give up in frustration. The use of punishment to cause students to want to learn when they don't believe they can is a dead-end enterprise. It will lead to hopelessness long before it leads to learning.

As teachers, I think our challenge regarding dispositions comes in two parts. *The first is to strive to know the dispositions of our students. The second is to implement confidence-building interventions.* We can do this with student-involved assessments, record keeping, and communication. The trick to using assessment to build confidence is to use it in ways that keep students believing that the target is within reach for them; that is, to instill hope. Then we must help our students succeed as learners. Only then can their confidence begin to grow.

Variations in Dispositions

As mentioned earlier, the various kinds of dispositions vary along some important dimensions: focus, direction, and intensity. They focus on our feelings about specific aspects of the world around us. Some, such as attitudes and values, can focus outside of ourselves. Others, such as academic self-concept and locus of control, focus on our inner views.

Affect also can vary in direction, stretching from a neutral point outward in both directions along a continuum to differing anchor points. Table 8.1 lists those end points.

Table 8.1
The range of dispositions

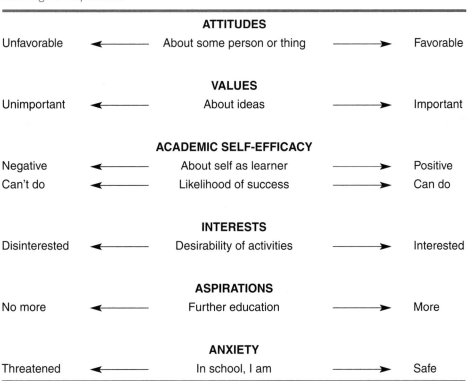

	ATTITUDES	
Unfavorable	← About some person or thing →	Favorable
	VALUES	
Unimportant	← About ideas →	Important
	ACADEMIC SELF-EFFICACY	
Negative	← About self as learner →	Positive
Can't do	← Likelihood of success →	Can do
	INTERESTS	
Disinterested	← Desirability of activities →	Interested
	ASPIRATIONS	
No more	← Further education →	More
	ANXIETY	
Threatened	← In school, I am →	Safe

Source: From *Assessing Affective Characteristics in Schools*, 2d ed. (p. 38) by L. W. Anderson, & S. F. Bourke, 2000, Mahwah, NJ: Lawrence Erlbaum & Associates. Copyright 2000 by Lawrence Erlbaum & Associates. Adapted by permission.

And finally, feelings vary in their intensity, from strong to moderate to weak. As you visualize the continuum for each type of affect, as you move further and further away from neutral, think of feelings as increasing in intensity. In the extremes, feelings become strong.

Bear in mind also that some feelings can be volatile, especially among the young. Such student dispositions as attitudes, interests, and anxiety can quickly change both in direction and intensity for a large number of reasons, only some of which are rational or understandable to adults. On the other hand, values, self-concept dimensions, and aspirations may be more enduring. I mention this to point out that it may be important to sample volatile dispositions repeatedly over time to keep track of them. The results of any one assessment may have a very short half-life.

Given our discussion so far, I'm sure you can understand why our assessment challenge is to gather information on the direction and intensity of school-related feelings. We capture the essence of student dispositions about success in school when we focus on the right-hand column of Table 8.1. It is quite possible to determine how closely students approximate these desired feelings, if we understand and apply some relatively straightforward assessment strategies.

Exploring the Assessment Options

So how do we assess the focus, direction, and intensity of feelings about school-related things? Just as with achievement, we rely on standard forms of assessment: selected response, open-ended written response, performance assessment, and personal communication with students.

In this case, let's group selected response and essay into a single paper and pencil assessment form because the two options represent different ways that questions can appear on a basic affective assessment tool: the *questionnaire*. We can ask students questions about their feelings on a questionnaire and either offer them a few response options to select from, or we can ask them open-ended questions and request brief or extended written responses. If we focus the questions on affect, we can interpret responses in terms of both the direction and intensity of feelings. Examples are coming right up. But first, let's see the other options.

Performance assessment of affective targets is like performance assessment of achievement targets. We conduct systematic *observations* of student behavior and/or products with clear criteria in mind and from them infer the direction and intensity of students' dispositions. So once again, as with open-ended questionnaires, professional judgments form the basis of our affective assessment.

Assessments of dispositions via personal communication typically take the form of *interviews,* either with students alone or in groups. In addition, we can interview others who know the students. These can be highly structured or very casual, as in discussions or conversations with students. The questions we ask and the things we talk about reveal the direction and intensity of feelings.

The remainder of this chapter examines each of these basic assessment options and explores how each can help tap the various kinds of dispositional targets defined previously.

Matching Method to Target

Each method for tapping student dispositions can be cast in many forms and each carries with it specific advantages, limitations, keys to success, and pitfalls to avoid. Let's examine these, then review a few tips for your effective development and use of each. As we go, I will try to illustrate how you can use the various forms of questionnaires, performance assessments, and personal communications to tap the different kinds of dispositions.

We will now consider procedural guidelines that can enhance the quality of questionnaire, performance assessment, and interview planning and design.

Questionnaires

Questionnaires represent one of the most convenient means of tapping important student dispositions if we can find ways to help students provide complete and honest responses. That means focusing on topics that students care about and making sure they know we will act on results in ways that benefit them.

In general, your assessment should not be so long that motivation lags among respondents. And it should not include questions that "lead" them to the response you want to receive. Here are two "out-of-balance" questions that lead respondents:

You really do like math, don't you?

Which response best reflects your attitude toward math?
    a. I love it
    b. I like it a lot
    c. I find it very challenging
    d. I really enjoy it

You should instead ask focused, value-neutral questions:

How confident are you that you can solve this kind of math problem appropriately (fill in some math problem-solving challenge)?

Then offer response options that combine direction and intensity:
    a. Very confident
    b. Quite confident
    c. Somewhat confident
    d. Not confident at all

Within the questionnaire itself, we must strive to ask questions that are relevant, about which students are likely to have an informed opinion. We must avoid ambiguity; ask brief, precise, complete questions; and offer response options that make sense.

Whenever I develop a questionnaire, I strive to combine all of these ideas in a way that enlists respondents as allies, as partners in generating useful information, information that promises to help us all. Sometimes that means permitting responses to be offered anonymously, to reduce the risk to respondents. Sometimes it means promising to share results or promising to act purposefully and quickly based on those results. Sometimes it just means urging them to take the questionnaire seriously, to care as I do about the value of the results for making things better for all. In any event, I try to break down the barriers between us.

Time for Reflection

In the interest of getting honest responses, what specific actions can you take to help students understand the meaning of a "socially desirable response"? This is when students give you the answer they think you want to hear or will be comfortable with, regardless of how they really feel. How can you help them see why truly honest answers are more appropriate under some circumstances?

Selected Response Questionnaire Formats

The major strength of selected response questionnaires is their ease of administration and processing of results. We have a variety of selected response formats to choose from as we design questionnaires. For example, we can ask students the following:

- If they agree or disagree with specific statements
- How important they regard specific things
- How they would judge the quality of something
- How frequently they feel certain ways

The following examples demonstrate possible response options for these kinds of scales. Note that each scale represents both direction and intensity of feelings. Let's see how they apply to our defined kinds of affect.

We might wish to assess student attitudes toward a specific instructional strategy. One way to do this is to present a positive statement and ask if respondents agree:

The group project we did in class yesterday helped me learn more about my leadership skills.
- a. Strongly agree
- b. Agree
- c. Undecided
- d. Disagree
- e. Strongly disagree

Or, we might assess student interest in participating in certain activities with two questions:

Would you like to do more collaborative group projects in the future?
   a. Yes
   b. Undecided
   c. No

How important are such projects to you?
   a. Very important
   b. Important
   c. Undecided
   d. Unimportant
   e. Very unimportant

Other such selected response scales tap the perceived quality of some object or activity:

How would you judge your performance in preparing your term paper?
   a. Excellent
   b. Good
   c. Fair
   d. Poor
   e. Very poor

You might supplement the information derived from the rating by asking students to write a brief paragraph explaining why they selected that rating.

Some questions may determine perceived frequency of occurrence of a particular event:

How frequently do you feel you understand and can do the math homework assignments you receive in this class?
   a. Always
   b. Frequently
   c. Occasionally
   d. Rarely
   e. Never

One of the most common forms of selected response questionnaire items asks students to choose between or among some forced choices. The following examples are designed to help us understand students' locus of control:

If I do well on a test, it is typically because
   a. My teacher taught me well.
   b. I was lucky.
   c. I studied hard.

Or

I failed to master that particular skill because
   a. I didn't try hard enough.
   b. My teacher didn't show me how.
   c. I was unlucky.

Yet another kind of selected response format, one that I use extensively, is a scale anchored at each end by polar adjectives and offering direction and intensity options in between. Here's an example focused on student interest and motivation:

Use the scales provided to describe your interest in learning the school subjects listed. Place an *X* on the line that best reflects your feelings:

Mathematics

Very Interested ___ ___ ___ ___ ___ Completely Uninterested
Very Motivated ___ ___ ___ ___ ___ Completely Unmotivated

Science

Very Interested ___ ___ ___ ___ ___ Completely Uninterested
Very Motivated ___ ___ ___ ___ ___ Completely Unmotivated

An easy adaptation of the selected response format can provide a means of tapping the attitudes of very young students. Rather than using words to describe feeling states, we can use simple pictures:

Given school-related events or activities about which to express their feelings, such as free reading time, for example, you would instruct the students to circle the face that tells how they feel about it.

Using these kinds of scales, students can easily reveal their attitudes, interests, school-related values, academic self-concept, and the like. Further, it is usually easy to summarize results across respondents. The pattern of responses, and therefore the feelings, of a group of students is easily seen by tallying the number and percent of students who select each response option. This can lead to a straightforward summary of results.

Open-Ended Written Response

Another way to assess affect is to offer open-ended questions, to which respondents are free to write their responses. If we ask specific questions eliciting direction and intensity of dispositions about specific school-related issues, we may readily interpret responses:

> *Write a brief paragraph describing your reaction to our guest speaker today. Please comment on your level of interest in the presentation, how well informed you thought the speaker was, and how provocative you found the message to be. As you write, be sure to tell me how strong your positive or negative feelings are. I will use your reactions to plan our future guest speakers.*

Or here's an interesting option—consider combining assessment of affect with practice in evaluative reasoning:

As you think about the readings we did this month, which three did you find most worthwhile? For each choice, specify why you found it worthwhile.

A thoughtful reading of the responses to these kinds of questions will reveal similarities or differences in students' opinions and can help you plan future instruction.

Additional Thoughts About Questionnaires

To maximize the efficiency and value of the results obtained, always connect your questions to direct action. By this, I mean ask only those questions that will provide you with the specific and significant information you need to make your decisions. For each question you pose, you should be able to anticipate the course of action you will take given each possible response: "If my students respond this way, I will do . . . . If they respond the other way, I should instead do . . . ." Discard any query that leaves you wondering what you'll do with the results.

I have one more critical piece of advice: *If you promise respondents that you will gather information anonymously, stick with that promise under all circumstances.* Never try to subvert such a promise with invisible coding or other identification systems. Students need to be caught in that trap only once to come to believe they can trust neither teachers nor administrators. We face a hard enough challenge establishing open channels of communication without having to overcome this kind of obstacle as well.

Observations as Assessments of Dispositions

Student behavior has always been a standard indicator of dispositions. Adhering to classroom rules, for example, is often cited as evidence of a "positive attitude." Tardiness is seen as evidence of a lack of respect for school or as evidence of poor attitude. It has been almost a matter of tradition that teachers observe and reflect on their interactions with students, such as when students appear not to be trying or when they just don't seem to care. Our almost automatic inference is that they are "unmotivated" and "have a bad attitude."

While these inferences may be correct, they also can be dangerous. What if our casual observations and intuitive inferences about the underlying causes of the behavior we see are wrong? What if adhering to the rules comes from a sense of personal vulnerability and reflects a low willingness to take risks? What if tardiness is due to some factor at home that is beyond the student's control, or the apparent lack of motivation is not a result of low self-esteem, but rather an indication that we were not clear in helping that student understand the task to be completed? If our inferences are wrong, we may well plan and carry out remedies that completely miss the point, and that do more harm than good.

This leads me to a very important note of caution: The cavalier manner in which some observe and draw inferences about student attitudes, values, interests, and the like very often reflects a lack of regard for the basic principles of sound assessment. The rules of evidence for observing and judging don't change just because the nature of the target changes. Vague targets, inappropriately cast into the wrong methods, that fail to sample or control for bias lead to incorrect assessments of dispositions just as they lead to incorrect inferences about achievement. The rules of evidence for sound assessment are *never* negotiable.

For this reason, developing performance assessments of dispositions requires that you follow exactly the same basic design sequence used for performance assessment of achievement. You must specify the performance you will evaluate, devise scoring criteria, select a context and task within which to observe, and record and store results dependably.

This does not mean spontaneous observations and judgments are unacceptable. But you must remain vigilant, for many things can go wrong with such on-the-spot assessments. That awareness can make you appropriately cautious about making snap judgments.

When developing affective performance assessments, you face the same design decisions that we spelled out in detail in Chapter 6. They are translated into design questions for the assessment of dispositions in Figure 8.2.

---

1. How shall we define the disposition to be assessed?

   What shall we focus on to evaluate student feelings?

   • A behavior exhibited by the student?

   • A product created by the student?

   What specific performance criteria will guide our observations and inferences about student affect?

2. How shall we elicit performance to be evaluated in terms of the disposition it reflects?

   What will we tell students to do under what conditions, according to what standards of performance?

   How many instances of performance will we need to observe to make confident generalizations about student feelings?

3. What method will we use to record results of our observations?

   Which do we wish to obtain?

   • A single holistic judgment about student affect?

   • Analysis of several aspects of student feelings?

   What record will we create of student affect?

   • Checklist?

   • Rating scale?

   • Anecdotal record?

Figure 8.2
Designing performance assessments of dispositions

I know this list of design questions looks imposing in this context. You might read it and ask, Why be so formal? It's not as if we're conducting an assessment for a final grade or something! In fact, many regard it as instinctive for teachers to observe some behavior and infer almost intuitively about student attitudes, motivations, school-related values, and so on. But this is exactly my point. If you disregard the rules of evidence in conducting assessments based on observation and judgment whether assessing attitudes or writing proficiency, your assessment will almost always produce undependable results. For this reason, it is always important to strive for quality assessment.

Personal Communication as a Window to Student Feelings

Direct communication is an excellent path to understanding student feelings about school-related topics. We can interview students individually or in groups, conduct discussions with them, or even rely on casual discussions to gain insight about their attitudes, values, and aspirations. In addition, if we establish a trusting relationship with students that permits them to be honest with us, we can understand their sense of self-efficacy and even the levels of anxiety that they are feeling.

This method offers much. Unlike questionnaires, we can establish personal contact with respondents, and can ask followup questions. This allows us to more completely understand students' feelings. Unlike performance assessment, we can gather our information directly, avoiding the danger of drawing incorrect inferences. This assures a higher level of accuracy and confidence in our assessment results.

Keys to Success

One key to success in tapping true student dispositions is trust. I cannot overemphasize its critical importance. Respondents must be comfortable honestly expressing the direction and intensity of their feelings. Respondents who lack trust will either tell us what they think we want to hear (i.e., give the socially desirable response) or they will shut us out altogether. For many students, it is difficult to communicate honest feelings in an interview setting with the real power sitting on the other side of the table, because all hope of anonymity evaporates. This can seem risky to them.

Another key to success is to have adequate time to plan and conduct high-quality assessments. This is a labor-intensive means of soliciting information.

In many ways, the remaining keys to success in an interview setting are the same as those for questionnaires:

- Prepare carefully.
- Make sure respondents know why you are gathering this information.
- Ask focused, clear, brief questions that get at the direction and intensity of feelings about specific school-related topics.
- Act on results in ways that serve students' best interests.

In other ways, this assessment format brings with it some unique challenges. Figure 8.3 offers guidelines to help you meet those challenges.

- *Don't overlook the power of group interview.* Marketing people call these *focus groups*. Sometimes students' feelings become clear to them and to you by bouncing them off or comparing them to others. Besides, there can be a feeling of safety in numbers, allowing respondents to open up a bit more.
- *Rely on students as interviewers or discussion leaders.* Often, they know how to probe the real and important feelings of their classmates. Besides, they have credibility in places where you may not.
- *Become an attentive listener.* Ask focused questions about the direction and intensity of feelings and then listen attentively for evidence of the same. Sometimes interviewers come off looking and acting like robots. Sometimes just a bit of interpersonal warmth will open things up.
- *Be prepared to record results in some way.* Often we use tape recorders in interview contexts, but this is certainly not the only way to capture student responses. For example, you could create a written questionnaire form but ask the questions personally and complete the questionnaire as you go. Or, you could just take notes and transcribe them into a more complete record later. In any event, students will appreciate that you asked how they felt, but only if you seem to remember what they said and take it into consideration in your instructional planning.

Figure 8.3
Guidelines for conducting interviews to assess dispositions

Summary: Dispositions Can Help Us Boost Achievement

Our aspiration for students is that they develop positive dispositions about learning and negative dispositions about those things that interfere with it. Our assessment questions are these:

1. Are students developing the positive attitudes, strong interests, positive motivations, positive school values, positive academic self-concept, and the "can do" sense of internal locus of control needed to succeed in school and beyond?
2. Are students feeling safe in school and are they experiencing levels of anxiety appropriate to fuel productive learning but not so high as to be debilitating?

These are affective targets influencing student tendencies to behave in academically productive ways. They vary both in intensity and direction, ranging from strongly positive to strongly negative. Our assessment challenge is to track their intensity and direction.

There are two basic reasons why we should care about student dispositions. First, they have value in their own right. They represent personal characteristics that we value as a society. We want all citizens to feel as though they are in control of their own destinies. Second, student attitudes, motivation, interests, and preferences are closely related to achievement. Those who experience academic success are far more likely to develop appropriate attitudes and values that, in turn, provide the impetus to take the risks associated with seeking further academic success. Thus, we know that affect and achievement support each other in important ways.

Our assessment options in this case are the same as those we use to track student achievement: selected response, open-ended written response, performance assessment, and personal communication. Selected response and open-ended written alternatives take the form of questionnaires. We reviewed several different question formats for use in these instruments. Performance assessments have us observing student behaviors and/or products and inferring affective states. Careful development of these observation-based assessments may help us draw strong inferences about dispositions. Personal communication using interviews, discussions, and conversations can clarify student attitudes and often give us the clearest insights.

We began the chapter with three specific ground rules intended to prevent misuse of assessment in this arena. They bear repeating as final thoughts on this topic.

1. Always remain keenly aware of the sensitive interpersonal nature of student feelings and strive to promote productive dispositions through your assessment of these outcomes.
2. Know your limits when dealing with student affect. Assess school-related dispositions only and get help when you need it.
3. If you care enough to learn about these affective student characteristics and to develop quality assessments of them, then care enough to take the results seriously and change your instruction when needed.

Final Chapter Reflection

1. *What are the three most important new insights to come to you as a result of your study of this chapter?*
2. *Which of your previous questions about assessment can you now answer based on your study of this chapter?*
3. *What new questions have come to mind as a result of your study of this chapter that you hope to have answered as your study continues?*

Practice with Chapter 8 Ideas

1. Listed here are some cultural perspectives that have implications for how, when, or if we assess student dispositions. For each, what are the implications and what would be the proper course of action in contexts where these perspective emerge?
   a. In some cultures, the public expression of private attitudes and concerns is viewed as inappropriate.

   b. When assessing dispositions through nonverbal behaviors that occur naturally in the classroom (e.g., assuming that student eye contact with the teacher represents interest in the content of a lesson) cultural differences among students can interfere with the accuracy of our judgments. In some cultures, a raised

Table 8.2
Disposition questions

A student whose attitude toward science is unfavorable would be likely to say _____. Would this be true of students from all cultures?	**ATTITUDES**	A student whose attitude toward science is favorable would be likely to say: _____. Would this be true of students for all cultures?
How might a student whose culture favors individual achievement above group accomplishment act when taking a test?	**VALUES**	How might a student whose culture favors group collaboration above individual accomplishment act when taking a test?
Negative: How might a student with a negative view of herself as a learner act when faced learning challenging content? *Can't do:* What actions or words would indicate that a student believes he is unlikely to succeed? Might telling words or actions be different in a culture where humility is valued?	**ACADEMIC SELF-EFFICACY**	*Positive*: How might a student with a positive view of himself as a learner act when faced with learning challenging content? *Can do:* What actions or words would indicate that a student believes she is likely to succeed? Might these words or actions be misleading in a culture that requires public expressions of confidence and discourages public admission of uncertainty?
Disinterested: In what ways does a student indicate disinterest? What nonverbal cues do you look for? Is our mental set of "interest" cues limited by our cultural expectations?	**INTERESTS**	*Interested:* How might a teacher interpret a child's interest in reading if, when asked "Darren, would you like to read the next paragraph?" the child will not read aloud? How would this interpretation change if the teacher knew that the child is from a culture where a question such as the teacher asked is viewed as an invitation, not a request, and that it is okay to decline invitations?
Low: When asked about their future academic goals, what are likely responses from students whose aspirations for themselves are low?	**ASPIRATIONS**	*High:* What are some of the things that students with high academic aspirations are likely to say and do?
Threatened: How might a student act who is anxious about speaking in front of a group?	**ANXIETY**	*Safe:* How might a student act who is not anxious about speaking in front of a group?

eyebrow signifies agreement and interest. In others, eye contact with one's elders is considered disrespectful. In still others, silence is a sign that one is in agreement with perspectives being expressed.

   c. Young people in some cultures are expected to express only positive dispositions to those in authority—in the classroom, in the home, and in the community. Inviting such students to fill out a scaled attitude survey is likely to result in high ratings regardless of the student's feelings. It is thought disrespectful of those in authority to do otherwise.

2. Answer the questions and fill in the blanks for each of the kinds of disposition listed in Table 8.2 to reveal how dispositions might be expressed.

3. Let's say you want to tap student attitudes about a particular textbook you are using. Your challenge is to assess the direction and intensity of their most important feelings about the text. Create 5 to 10 bipolar scales for a questionnaire that focus on aspects of the book students might have an opinion about. Here are two examples:

Instructions: Place an X on the space on each scale that best describes your feeling:

Well organized __ __ __ __ __ __ Very disorganized

   Well written __ __ __ __ __ Not well written

Once you have written and administered your questionnaire, how might you use the results in your decision making to benefit students' learning?

PART III

Communicating Assessment Results

We can deliver accurate information about student mastery of important achievement targets (as described in Chapter 2) into the hands of important decision makers to serve important purposes (as outlined in Chapter 1) only if we understand how to assess those targets accurately (Chapters 3 to 8) and then communicate the results effectively. This effective communication is the focus of Part 3. Our investments in clarifying our achievement expectations and in developing sound assessments are wasted if the results don't arrive in users' hands in a timely and understandable manner. This set of chapters introduces the keys to making sure our communication about student achievement "works." As we keep the big picture in mind, Part 3 deals with the shaded box in our standards of sound classroom assessment graphic.

Chapter 9 sets the stage by offering concrete suggestions for effectively managing information about student achievement. Once again in this case you will see the differences between assessment *of* and *for* learning coming into play, as they have direct implications for how we manage achievement information; that is, gather, store, retrieve, and share evidence of learning. Also included in this chapter are basic principles of effective communication that will need careful attention regardless of the mode of communication used. Please note that the standards of sound practice framed here and integrated throughout Part 3 appear in the Appendix as our Rubrics for Judging Classroom Assessment Quality.

Chapter 10 deals with standardized test scores as a means of conveying information about student achievement. You will learn where these scores come from and how to interpret them, as well as their strengths and limitations.

Chapter 11 delves into report cards and grades as communication vehicles. We will explore what should be factored into report card grades and what should not. Sound grading practices are spelled out in specific detail, as are other forms of report cards that provide more detailed descriptions of student mastery of standards.

Chapter 12 details a truly effective way to communicate the detail of student achievement in certain context: portfolios. We will establish that portfolios can be structured in a number of ways to serve different purposes. The key is to know what story the collection of work is to tell.

Finally, Chapter 13 takes us into conferences in which the topic of conversation is evidence of student learning. We will explore three conference formats, two involving students, to discover the strengths, weaknesses, and proper application of each.

In each chapter, we will consider opportunities for student-involved communication of assessment results. Involving students in assessment development during learning helps them understand the terms of their own success. If we involve students in repeated assessment of their own achievement over time, we provide them with the opportunity to watch themselves grow. This permits them to feel in control of their own success and can motivate them to strive for excellence. So it is with student-involved information management and communication. We involve students in collecting and presenting evidence of their own success in order to sustain within them the belief that they will succeed if they keep trying.

Keys to Effective Classroom Assessment

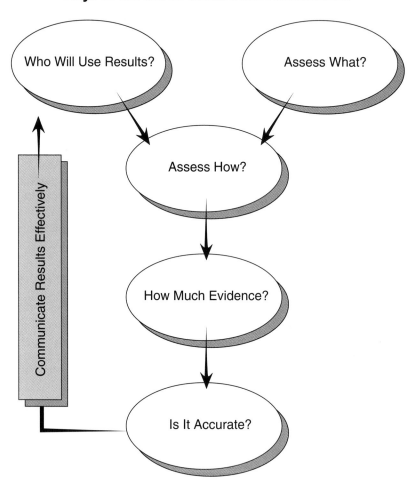

Chapter 9

Managing and Communicating Achievement Information

CHAPTER FOCUS

This chapter answers the following guiding questions:

> What challenges will I face in managing and sharing student achievement information?

> How can I best overcome those challenges?

From your study of this chapter, you will understand the following:

1. Effective management of information within a communication system requires deliberate planning around information gathering, storage, retrieval, summary, and sharing.

2. Effective sharing of information about student achievement requires adherence to several principles that place student and teacher on the same communication wavelength.

The Information Management Challenges

As teachers, we face the challenging task of tracking the mastery of standards by each individual student and students in groups in ways that permit us always to know where they are now in their learning and where we want them to go next. To maintain a clear sense of these we need to manage information about student achievement very carefully. We need systems of information storage and retrieval that are able to do several things.

They must *accommodate the diverse information needs* of a variety of users and uses. Remember the different classroom, instructional support, and policy assessment information users we discussed in Chapter 1? Those lists tell us that we need to use assessment *for* learning; that is, to keep students in touch with their own growth. And we need assessment *of* learning to keep the various adults in the system equipped with the evidence they need to make those instructional decisions that help students learn. To make the right instructional decisions, everyone needs access to evidence of student achievement.

In addition, our classroom assessment information management systems must *accommodate the differences in students' rate of academic development.* Some will march along our continuous-progress curriculum map very quickly. Others will travel much more slowly because of their particular academic challenges. And then there will be everyone in between. As they travel at different rates, they will be completing different assessments—everyone may not be taking the same test at the same time, for example. We must accommodate those real differences among them in their rate of learning. This presents information gathering, storage, retrieval, and summary challenges—in short, information management issues.

Another challenge is presented by our desire to collect and manage information about several *different forms of student achievement* (knowledge, reasoning, performance skills, and product development capabilities) using a *variety of different assessment methods*, each of which yields its own kind of evidence of learning—test scores, performance ratings, or anecdotes—that we wish to retain for later use.

The Conditions Underpinning Effective Information Management

Let's say you've mapped the learning targets you want your students to master within a unit or course of study, developed a corresponding sequence of assessments, and begun to conduct those assessments. Evidence of student learning is accumulating. This information needs to provide the basis for feedback and it needs to inform your instructional decisions to keep students learning. The next task is to deliver that information into the user's hands in a timely and understandable manner. Obviously, effective communication is crucial. The four chapters that follow this one provide specific guidance on the communication options that you have at your disposal: test scores, report card grades, portfolios, and conferences. This chapter is the bridge between the assessment processes described previously and the communication strategies to follow. Here we deal with the effective management of the flood of evidence of learning that comes to you from your assessments.

The Information Management Options

There are several specific factors to consider in planning for effective management as a foundation for effective communication. Planning is crucial—think your system through completely or the flood of information coming to you about the achievement of your students will make you crazy!

As you will see, the assessment context will help you make appropriate system design decisions. Refer to the list of design features provided in Figure 9.1 to help you see the big picture as we go.

The Nature of the Evidence

To begin with, you must decide *what evidence* of student achievement you will gather. This is the information you need to manage. Options include evidence of student mastery of achievement standards themselves, such as state standards, or

1. What will be the evidence gathered?
   - Mastery of enabling targets leading to standards or of standards themselves?
   - Taking what form: scores, performance ratings, samples of work, descriptions of work, or judgments?
   - Gathered by whom: teacher, student, both in partnership?
2. How will the information be stored?
   - In the form of descriptive detail or as a summary judgment?
   - In a gradebook or portfolio (folder) of work?
   - Stored by whom: teacher, student, or both in partnership?
3. How will the information be summarized?
   - Reflecting achievement status or improvement?
   - For individual students or for students in a group (e.g., averaged)?
   - Who will do the summarizing: teacher, student, or both in partnership?
4. How will the information be reported?
   - Results reported to whom?
   - Reported when?
   - In what form?

Figure 9.1
Summary of classroom assessment information management possibilities

evidence of mastery of knowledge, reasoning, skill, or product classroom achievement targets that students attain on their way to meeting state standards. In standards-driven schools, it is best to maintain achievement records, such as your gradebook, organized by standard or enabling target.

In addition, you must determine *how that evidence will be gathered—that is, what assessment method(s) will be used.* This has been the focus of most of the book. The choices are familiar. But let's just take a moment to identify the kind of information each provides, as this has information management implications. The options are selected response, essay, performance assessment, and personal communication-based assessments.

Selected response evidence can include test scores or subtest scores when subsets of items on a test reflect particular learning outcomes. Essay evidence also will take the form of total test scores or ratings of performance on individual essay exercises. Performance assessments can produce profiles of ratings on rubrics, as well as actual samples of student work to be stored as evidence of achievement. Personal communication-based assessments tend to result in impressions, anecdotal evidence, and professional judgments.

Finally with respect to evidence, you must consider *who will gather the evidence.* Will it be you, the teacher, or will your students play a role in evidence gathering?

If not you or your students, will you turn to other teachers or perhaps to students' parents?

Information Storage

As evidence is gathered, it must be used immediately or stored for later use. If the latter, you must consider in *what form the information will be stored.* Several choices are available to you. For instance, you might wish to retain a detailed description of achievement (as with profiles of performance ratings), or maybe even actual samples of student work. On the other hand, the context might permit you to retain just a summary of student performance, either in the form of summary descriptions (such as score averages) or your summary judgments (such as grades). Summarizing information involves its own set of decisions, which we discuss in the next subsection.

You will need to decide *where this information is to be stored.* Will it take the form of entries in your gradebook (handwritten or electronic), or will you rely on a working folder or portfolio of examples? If a portfolio, will it include hardcopy or will you rely on such information management technologies as computer, video, or audio records? A variation on the portfolio theme might be a journal or notebook of work completed.

Finally, you must decide *who will be in charge of storage.* Will you, the teacher, rely on your own system, or will you engage your students? Would you consider having your students' families involved in this facet of information management?

Summarizing Information (or Not!)

Some contexts require only a summary of student achievement information, while others demand greater detail about achievement. So you must decide when to summarize and when not to do so. Your summaries can focus on student *achievement status* at a particular point in time or they can *examine change* in achievement over a period of time.

Another variable in planning to summarize is whether your decision context centers on an *individual student* or the performance of *a group of students* such as an entire class. The summary itself might take the form of a score or group of scores such as a profile of analytical performance ratings. Either might be converted to letter grades, depending on the situation, or to a list of standards or targets mastered.

In any case, you must consider *who will do the summarizing.* Will it be you, your students, your gradebook software, another teacher, parents, or another school official? As you will see, the answer depends on the context.

Reporting Information

In planning for information management in the classroom, also consider the specific reporting requirements: *Who will receive the results?* This, of course, will be a function of user needs. Also consider *the timing of the communication* and *how results will be conveyed.* Will they take the form of test score reports, some form of report card, a portfolio of examples of work, or a conference? We will address each of these options in the four following chapters.

When Planning for Information Management, Context Is Everything

To understand how best to manage all of the information about student achievement that comes to you, you must consider the context. The information management requirements of assessment *for* and *of* learning contexts differ. As we consider these differences, we will follow the outline provided in Figure 9.1.

When assessment is being used to support learning—assessment *for* learning— we intend to inform students about themselves. They join us, their teachers, as important decision makers. We must ensure that they understand what the results mean. Our information management challenge is to *describe* (not judge) achievement in rich detail as it is evolving over time.

But on the other hand, when it comes time to put a grade on the report card or determine if a student has met an important state standard, then we conduct assessments *of* learning. We compare each student's level of achievement to a preset standard. It's time to *summarize* achievement and *judge* its sufficiency.

Evidence gathered during learning, to support the learning (assessments *for* learning), doesn't fit comfortably into contexts where accountability decisions hang in the balance (assessment *of* learning). Neither do assessments *of* learning serve the purpose of helping students grow. I recommend keeping them separate, maintaining separate information management systems. My vision is a classroom driven by a continuous array of assessments *for* learning, most being conducted and used by students themselves—always under the watchful eye of their teacher. They are collected in growth portfolios (described in detail in Chapter 12). These are punctuated by periodic assessments *of* learning—always announced well in advance, so students know when it's time to demonstrate competence so others can see how to help them. Everyone involved sees the synergy between assessments *for* and *of* learning. There are no surprises and no excuses. The evidence always speaks for itself. It reveals achievement or the lack of it and leads, therefore, to appropriate action on behalf of student success.

Information Management in Assessment *for* Learning Contexts

You will recall that, in this context, we are relying on student involvement in classroom assessment, record keeping, and communication as a powerful confidence builder, motivator, and learning tool. We aren't merely checking for learning or assigning grades, rather we use assessment and its results to help students learn more. Another purpose for assessment *for* learning is to help teachers diagnose student needs. Let's consider the information management issues in each context.

Inform Students About Themselves

The Evidence

To begin with, you must decide what evidence of student achievement will be gathered. Previously, we established that classroom-level assessment, when used in support of learning, needs to focus on the knowledge, reasoning, skill, or product classroom achievement targets that students attain on their way to meeting state standards. In this assessment *for* learning scenario, you need to have developed an assessment map that parallels your continuous-progress curriculum map so you and your students can anticipate when each assessment will happen and how it will help them learn to do better the next time.

Since we established that any of our assessment methods can be opened up to permit student involvement, your assessment map can include any of a number of methods. As stated previously, the kinds of evidence you will manage will be determined by the method you select. But in all cases, students will be full partners in gathering the evidence of their own achievement. Whatever methods you use must yield results—scores, ratings, and so on—that students understand. The entire point is to be sure that this evidence reveals to them the change in their achievement over time. Part of your instructional job is be sure they become qualified to understand their own improvement.

Information Storage

As you gather evidence, you will use some of it immediately, and store some for later use. Both are important in this context. Under all circumstances you will want to retain a detailed description of achievement, probably including actual samples of student work. But from time to time you will require summaries of student achievement, for instance, when you and a student discuss "progress to date" with reference to your expectations.

You will need to decide *how this information is to be stored.* In this case, the gradebook can remain closed, or at least contain a separate, clearly identified section for recording assessment *for* learning results. This not about accountability or report card grades. You want students to watch themselves improving over time. You will rely on a working folder or portfolio of evidence. These will include periodic self-reflections by students on changes in their own achievement. This portfolio might include hardcopy or rely on such information management technologies as computer, video, or audio records, depending on the resources made available by your district.

Finally, you must decide *who will be in charge of storage.* In this case, the records are the students' to keep, under your watchful eye and in consultation with you. They build the evidence that tells the story of their own success.

Summarizing Information (or Not!)

The richer the descriptive detail in assessment *for* learning contexts, the sharper will be students' ability to focus on critical improvements in their achievement. But periodically, the evidence will need to be summarized for a status check, such as in preparing for a student-led parent-teacher conference. The story of Emily at the school board meeting in Chapter 1 represented an instance when a descriptive summary was needed. She used two of her own writing samples as the basis for her description of her own improvement in writing. Obviously, the focus always will be on the individual student in this context. It is the student who will be doing the summarizing, again, under your watchful eye.

Reporting Information

Information management in the classroom also includes reporting achievement results to intended users. In this case, the primary users are both you and your students working as a team—learner and coach. You both will need continuous access
to the evidence. That evidence will take the form of actual samples of work, whether
tests or performance assessments. Communication will be based on evidence in
working folders and growth portfolios, and on lots of conferences—with you, classmates, and family—many conducted by the student.

Diagnosing Student Needs

Let's say you want to diagnose your third-grade students' strengths and weaknesses
in the performance domain of reading, another assessment *for* learning context. Evidence from last year's standardized testing suggests that they are having difficulty
learning to read.

The Evidence

The evidence you will gather will center on mastery of reasoning proficiency in the
reading context—a classroom achievement target that students must attain on their
way to meeting state standards in reading. Therefore, you will need to rely on the
appropriate assessment method for the intended target. In this case, you might
choose a personal communication-based strategy in which students read a story
silently and then retell it aloud, while you judge the accuracy of the retelling.

Because designing, developing, and using this assessment requires understanding
of the intended achievement target, and since the assessment is taking place in advance of any student learning, students would have difficulty being partners this time.

Information Storage

The evidence is to be used immediately. But you also want to use it as a baseline
for checking progress later on. You will record your judgments of the accuracy of
each student's retelling on a rating scale immediately after the event. The rating sheet
also provides you space to comment on specific comprehension difficulties to inform helpful ongoing instructional decisions. You will file the evidence sheet in the
working file that you have established for each student.

Summarizing Information (or Not!)

Some contexts require only a summary of student achievement information, while
others demand greater detail about achievement. In this case, you rely on both—a
summary rating of the accuracy of the retelling and notes on comprehension problems. But it is an assessment of achievement at a particular point in time, as initial
helpful decisions must be made at once. In this case, your focus is on the individual
student—not on group performance.

Reporting Information

Information management in this classroom for this purpose requires only that you
have access to the results. The evidence will speak for itself student by student. No

further reporting is required at this time. However, note that you also would regard this evidence as baseline data for tracking student progress over time. That evidence may serve another whole set of users and uses. But that's another scenario.

Information Management in Assessment *of* Learning Contexts

In this case, we assess to *inform others about students*—to provide information needed by the adults in the system who must make the instructional decisions that help them to help students learn or to hold students accountable for their learning. Teachers must *assign grades on a report card.* Still other times, school officials must determine if *students have met requirements* for advancement to the next grade, to graduate, or for other questions of eligibility. These are the sorts of accountability decisions that arise in the lives of students and teachers.

As you read through this section, it will become immediately clear that assessment *of* and *for* learning contexts require fundamentally different information management systems.

Assigning Report Card Grades

The Evidence

The focus within each grading period will be on gathering evidence of student mastery of preestablished knowledge, reasoning, skill, or product classroom achievement targets that underpin state standards for a particular subject and grade level. We will rely on the targets-by-methods matrix to tell us what assessment method to use for each evidence-gathering episode. A map of planned assessments *of* learning will be needed to guide us along the way, paralleling the assessment *for* learning map that we developed to help students improve.

In this case, it will be you, the teacher, who gathers the evidence used to determine the report card grade. The process of establishing expectations, designing and using accountability assessments, and assigning report card grades is your professional responsibility. Chapter 11 addresses this matter in detail.

Information Storage

As you gather evidence, you will store it for later use in summary form, such as test scores or performance ratings, or will immediately transform it into letter grades for each test or assignment. In any event, extensive detail or samples of work are unnecessary here.

Evidence will take the form of entries in your gradebook (handwritten or electronic), which must remain under your control because of the accountability focus.

Summarizing Information

For purposes of assigning report card grades, the evidence must reflect your best estimate of each individual student's level of achievement at the end of the grading period—as the grade is assigned. This might be reflected in performance on a final assessment *of* learning or a summary (typically an average) of numerous smaller assessments you conduct during the grading period. For reasons spelled out in Chapter 11, I strongly recommend against basing report card grades on amount of improvement during the grading period.

Reporting Information
A composite estimate of student achievement is mapped onto a grade scale: A, B, and so on. You establish the achievement requirements for attaining each grade and communicate them to students at the beginning of the grading period, to permit students to clearly understand the meaning of each grade.

Other Assessment *of* Learning Contexts

Assessment *of* learning in the form of report card grades takes place to inform specific decisions made by adults to guide student learning. Other such instances include the following:

1. Determine eligibility for promotion or graduation.
2. Determine eligibility for special education programs or resources.
   - For advanced study
   - For remedial study
3. Select scholarship recipients.
4. Evaluate the effectiveness of a particular instructional intervention.

In these and similar assessment *of* learning cases, the information management requirements are clear. Evidence must be gathered by the teacher or another school official to reflect student mastery of specific standards as reflected in a few strategic assessments. The summary judgments to be made typically do not require access to a great deal of detail about achievement. Storage in the form of scores or ratings is not demanding, but, depending on the specific situation, summarizing evidence can be challenging. For instance, in grading contexts, assigning weights to various pieces of evidence requires some thought—as you will see in Chapter 11. But in this case, as with all others, you must adhere to the basic principles of effective communication:

- Message sender and receiver must mutually understand the achievement standard(s) in question.
- The evidence must be accurate.
- The symbols used to convey information (such as letter grades) must have the same meaning for message sender and receiver.
- The message receiver must be open to hearing and acting on the information provided.

In the next four chapters, we explore how to be sure we always meet these standards. Figure 9.2 summarizes the differences between information management in assessment *for* and *of* learning contexts.

Planning Factor	Assessment *for* Learning	Assessment *of* Learning
Remember the decision to be made	Is the student progressing?	Have standards been mastered?
Evidence to be gathered	• Focus on enabling classroom targets • Form of evidence depends on method • Student involved in assessment	• Focus on required standards • Form is summary judgments of mastery • Gathered and judged by the teacher
Information storage	• Store descriptions of performance • May include actual work samples • Might rely on portfolios of evidence • Student and teacher partner in storage	• Store final judgments of proficiency • Stored and maintained by the teacher, typically in a gradebook
Summarize?	• No, maintain the details in evidence, with some summary to see improvement over time • Focus on improvement • Student involved	• Primarily summary judgments by the teacher • Focus on status at a point in time
Reporting to	• Student • Teacher • Parent	• Agents of accountability • Program planners • Other teachers • Students • Parents

Figure 9.2
Information management differences between assessment *for* and *of* learning

The Challenges to Effective Information Sharing

As you can see, preparing to communicate effectively about classroom assessment results requires thoughtfully planned information management. But that's just part one of the effective communication equation. Part two requires that we carefully consider the principles of effective communication. To see what this means, let's start with a brief analysis of some important barriers to effective communication, followed by a discussion of how attending to sound communication principles helps us overcome these barriers.

The Risk of Accountability

As a teacher, I always risk having my performance on the job evaluated on the basis of the achievement of my students. If my students learn, both they and I am judged to have performed effectively. Everyone wins. But what if my student achievement is very low? And what if students fail, not as a result of my actions, but for reasons beyond my control such as learning disabilities or poor home environment? Then as an educator, I might be unfairly blamed.

To keep from being victimized by this, I may conclude that it is safer for me to remain vague about achievement expectations. I might cloak my assessments of student success and grading procedures in unfathomable complexity, so no one can really figure out what went on in my classroom. In this way, I can put forth a convincing case for having taught well, regardless of the underlying reality. If I wish, I can escape any real accountability for student learning, minimizing the risk by hiding behind a smoke screen of assessment and grading complexity.

Why, you might ask, would a teacher think this way? Well, just consider the practicalities. For example, teachers who are clear and public about their achievement targets might open themselves to unnecessary hassle. Some parents or other taxpayers might disagree with and want to challenge the achievement standards. If I want to avoid that confrontation, I might remain vague about those expectations.

Worse yet, what if classroom assessments consistently reveal a lack of achievement? My own students and their families might turn on me, portfolios in hand, demanding that I provide them with more effective help. In short, I stand to lose control, to lose power, to lose my sense of personal professional safety. If I feel vulnerable about any of this, why go through it when I can just hide in my gradebook with no one the wiser?

On the other hand, if I am a confident teacher whose goal is to help the highest possible proportion of my students attain the highest possible levels of academic achievement, my reasoning would be completely different. The reason I would need to communicate openly would be very clear. I cannot reach my teaching goals unless I take this risk. Consider, for example, which students are more likely to succeed academically:

- Those striving to hit clearly defined standards of excellence, or those for whom those standards remain a mystery?
- Those who see a clear path to success, or those for whom that path remains a mystery?
- Those who get to take advantage of effective communication to watch their work improving, or those who are forced to remain in the dark about their learning due to absence of feedback or inability to interpret the feedback they receive?

I think the answers are clear. As a teacher working for student success, I must risk being open to public review of my success in teaching.

The Challenge of Too Little Time

Perhaps the most prominent internal barrier to best practice from the teacher's point of view is the lack of time to communicate well. As a teacher, several specific time issues might trouble me deeply. For instance, the past decade has seen an explosion in the scope of the school curriculum, with new targets being added and old targets acquiring greater complexity. This broadening of the curriculum means I have more to assess and more to communicate about. I might simply feel that I don't have time to cover it all.

Further, many of the new communication methods advocated these days, such as portfolios, conferences, and narrative reports, seem very labor intensive. Whenever student achievement is being assessed and communicated about, I am the only laborer in this classroom and must do all the work.

The bottom line might be that all of this talk about effective communication can leave teachers frustrated about the apparent lack of concern for their workload. Better to keep it simple, even if the results might be imperfect.

In the chapters that follow, we will discuss specific time- and labor-saving strategies for assessment, record keeping, and communication.

What if the Receiver Can't or Won't Hear the Message?

Another troubling barrier to effective communication can be the lack of willingness or ability of the message receiver(s) to hear or accept the message being delivered. Obviously, this is rarely a problem when the message is positive, when grades or test scores are high, or when sincerely felt words of praise are flowing forth. But it is a problem when the message is about disappointing student achievement. For example, students simply may avoid or dismiss the feedback or parents simply may not show up for parent-teacher conferences. The "turnoff" can happen for any of a number of reasons, most of which have to do with the receiver's self-concept or view of the message sender.

Sometimes it's difficult to remain mindful of the conditions under which individuals may actually listen to and accept negative information about themselves. For instance, students may need to hold certain attitudes and perspectives to be able to receive and act on such messages. They may need to see themselves as key players in the search for information about their own achievement. They may need assistance in developing a sufficiently strong academic self-concept so they can acknowledge their shortcomings and not feel defeated. Further, students must see the person who provides the feedback as credible, honest, and helpful. And finally, they must come to see the benefits of the message very quickly, so they can muster the resources needed to act purposefully. These are challenging standards to meet.

From the other point of view, as the givers of the feedback, we must be able to present it constructively, delivering a clear, focused, and understandable message. We must be able to communicate our acceptance of students while critiquing their achievement. Even more importantly, we must help students understand that we share a common mission: greater achievement for them.

Clearly, it is no simple task to communicate to students that they have missed the target but still have the hope of success and reason to stay motivated. But as teachers and communicators, that is exactly what we must do.

Removing the Barriers

Classrooms and schools simply cannot function effectively in the service of student learning unless decision makers (students, teachers, parents, etc.) receive timely and accurate information about achievement in understandable terms. Therefore, we must be explicit and public about our achievement targets, assess and communicate with precision and maximum efficiency, and communicate in ways that keep students listening and trying. We have at our disposal several ways to do this:

- Make a commitment to communicate effectively in the service of greater student achievement.
- Take the risk of going public about achievement expectations in student and family-friendly terms.
- Become students ourselves of how to assess and communicate in ways that most efficiently remove the time barrier. This book is about how to do this.
- Formulate messages that deliver information about achievement—whether evidence of success or a lack of it—in ways that keep students believing that effort is still justified. We know how to do this—again, this book is about how.

We either communicate effectively or we waste our accurate assessments and fail at our mission to maximize student learning.

The Communication Options

While the ways of communicating about student achievement are varied, we can group them into categories: test scores, report cards, portfolios, and conferences. I introduce them here so you can keep them in mind as you learn more about achievement targets and assessment methods, and I devote a complete chapter to each after we study those methods.

Test Scores

When we assemble items, whether multiple choice or essay, into a test and then administer that test, the resulting score represents information about student achievement. Such scores can derive from standardized tests, such as state assessments or districtwide tests, or they can arise from classroom assessments. We use these to communicate effectively only when we have satisfied conditions as discussed previously.

Also remain cognizant of the fact that, with test scores, we might be communicating about the achievement of an individual student or we may summarize scores over many students and communicate about group achievement. In either case, conditions for effective communication must be satisfied.

Report Cards

In schools, we communicate about student achievement in a variety of ways. Without question, the flagship means of communicating is report cards. But we also use other communication vehicles when we require greater detail.

Regarding report cards, we assign grades to tests, assignments, and projects. We then summarize those component grades into a summary grade for the report card. Finally, we summarize individual course grades into grade point averages. When we attend to specific principles of effective communication, we can use such grades to communicate efficiently.

When we need to share more detail, we have other options available. Narrative reporting, for example, offers greater precision and the opportunity to address levels of detail unavailable when using only grades. When we devise report cards to reflect achievement expectations in the form of specific competencies, which teachers check or rate as having been mastered or not, we rely on narratives—words and sentences—to convey meaning from message sender to receiver. As always, we need agreed-on targets, accurate information, mutually understood vocabulary, and openness to communicate.

Portfolios of Student Work

Another way to communicate about learning is through collections of samples of student work. Each sample conveys useful information about the level of proficiency demonstrated. If we sample student work over time, centering on evidence of improvement, we build a growth portfolio that tells one kind of story about achievement. If students gather samples of their work that they particularly like—celebration portfolios—we tell another story. Further, portfolios of student work can provide evidence of achievement status in relation to a specified set of achievement expectations, thus providing a basis for certifying and communicating about required levels of competence.

Conferences About Student Achievement

An excellent way to convey rich detail about student achievement is by talking about it. When student and teacher meet to review and evaluate a piece of student work, they strive to communicate effectively. Also included here are peer conferences, parent-teacher conferences, and student-involved parent or parent-teacher conferences. If evidence has been assembled of student learning and a message sender seeks to convey that evidence in a timely and understandable manner to a message receiver, they can review, discuss, or talk about that evidence. But they can do it effectively only if the conditions for effective communication are satisfied.

Summary of Options

The challenge is to transport evidence of a student's current level of achievement from one party (the assessor) to another (the decision maker) in a timely and understandable manner. We have several tools at our disposal to accomplish this transfer: we can condense it into a concise summary form, such as a score or grade, or we can retain and convey richer detail. Which option we choose is a function of the user's information needs. But under any circumstances, we must prepare to communicate effectively *long before* the time comes to convey the information.

Time for Reflection

Some users need the detail about student achievement that is provided, for example, by the careful review of a growth portfolio, while others need only the summary of achievement information provided by a letter grade on a report card. Who might be someone who needs the detail and why? Who might be someone for whom the summary would suffice and why?

The Conditions Underpinning Effective Information Sharing

If you are to communicate effectively about student achievement, both you, the message sender, and the receiver must understand the specific achievement target(s) about which you wish to communicate. Then, as we have established, you must gather dependable information about student achievement and must translate this performance information into symbols that the receiver will understand and interpret accurately. And finally, you must manage the communication environment to ensure that the message receiver is open to hearing and acting on the message. If any of these conditions is not satisfied, you simply won't communicate effectively. Here is how to make these conditions work for you.

Agreeing on the Focus of the Communication

Both message sender and receiver must be aware of the relevant achievement standards or classroom targets if they are to avoid miscommunication. If you, the teacher, hold one set of expectations about the attributes of good writing and a parent, for example, holds a different vision of excellence, then the grades you send home on a report card about student performance in writing are likely to be misunderstood. This is true regardless of sender, receiver, or context. If the report card labels a grade as "Reading," and you mean comprehension while the parent thinks it means oral reading fluency, then miscommunication will result. If the standardized test score is labeled "Science", and the test items tapped science reasoning, while you think the score reflects science knowledge—or worse, have no idea what the score actually reflects—then miscommunication will result in inappropriate instructional decisions. A necessary condition for effective communication is that as message sender you must take steps up front to help the message receiver understand the knowledge, reasoning, skills, products, or dispositions in question.

Gathering Accurate Evidence

Given a common vision, to communicate effectively you must transform your targets into quality assessments; that is, assessments capable of producing accurate information about student achievement. As you know, each assessment must do the following:

- Rely on a proper method.
- Sample achievement appropriately with high-quality exercises.
- Control for all relevant sources of bias and distortion.

You can communicate effectively only if you can depend on your assessment results to reflect student achievement accurately.

Using Symbols with Shared Meaning

Assessment results can take many different forms. They can be test scores, letter or number grades, descriptions, or actual examples of student work demonstrating proficiency, among other things. For communication to "work," both you and your message receiver must have the same understanding of whatever symbols are used.

Managing the Communication Environment

You must also thoughtfully manage the interpersonal communication environment. You must be ready to share information with your message receiver(s) in an environment conducive to hearing and understanding each other. Such an environment is characterized by the following:

- You both must understand and agree up front on the expected consequences of communicating. If communication is to work in the desired ways, you must know what this means both from your and your receiver's points of view.

Planning for Effective Information Management
  • Identify the evidence to be collected.
  • Develop plans for storing and retrieving evidence.
  • Decide if and how evidence will be summarized.
  • Plan for reporting results to users.

Planning for Effectively Communicating Achievement Information
  • Agree on the achievement standards or targets.
  • Ensure accurate assessment.
  • Rely on symbols that mean the same thing to all involved.
  • Be sure the interpersonal environment is open to good communication.

Figure 9.3
The basics of effective information management and communication

- There must be a designated time, place, and set of circumstances where you both attend, without distraction, to the information being shared.
- As message sender, you must check to be sure that the receiver both understands the information shared and knows what to do with the results.

Figure 9.3 summarizes the basics of effective information management and communication.

Customs to Rethink

As you build your communications environment, be aware of customs and traditions that may be restrictive, and that may not serve either you or your students well.

Think Communication *for* Learning

As you visualize lines of communication in school settings, it is tempting to see the teacher at the center of the network, conducting assessments, entering the results in a gradebook, and delivering information to those who need it—most often students and their parents. Our habit is to think of teachers as message senders and others as message receivers. And to be sure, if you follow the guidelines for effective communication described here, this can be an effective way to share achievement information.

However, you are mistaken if you assume that this represents the only or even the most effective way to deliver messages about student success. We have an array of additional communication options at our disposal, many of which can be distinctly more productive, depending on the context.

Rely on Complete Definitions

It has become the custom in our most visible communication systems, such as report cards and test score reports, to define our achievement targets very simply, using such one-word labels as *reading, mathematics, spelling, science,* and so on, with no accompanying information about underlying meaning. Typically, we have assumed that both message senders and receivers understand and agree on the meaning of each label. But what if this is an invalid assumption? The message is lost.

There is a way to avoid this risk. We can devise more inclusive communication systems that still value reading, math, spelling, science, and other domains of achievement but that describe them in richer detail, permitting us to share more precise information about student success. We accomplish this by building communication around specific standards and classroom-level achievement targets, not generic labels.

For instance, *reading* is far more than a generic label. The word actually refers to a complex process made up of component parts, all of which must come together for readers to construct meaning from text. In this context, relevant assessment questions would include the following:

- Are readers able to use context to determine word meaning?
- Can they comprehend and monitor their own understanding?
- Are they able to alter reading strategies to fit the reading context?

We can assess to gather answers to such questions, and we can devise information management systems to reflect the extent to which students have demonstrated the component proficiencies in each academic subject area, if we wish. Such systems are likely to be far more useful than simple labels and associated grades for helping students to achieve ever-higher levels of proficiency.

Share the Meaning

Unfortunately, one of our longstanding assessment customs has been to keep the target a secret from students. It seems to be somehow seen as cheating to tell students exactly what we want them to achieve. But we know that students learn far more when we open lines of communication so all participants—students, teachers, and (to the extent possible) parents—share a common understanding of the relevant vision of success. Only when all individuals involved actually understand that vision can they communicate about its attainment. Further, if students can play even a small role in setting the target (under our leadership), we can gain considerable motivational, and therefore achievement, benefits.

More Assessors and Communicators

Our traditional communication systems have relied on test publishers and teachers to be the assessors. In open, inclusive systems, everyone shares responsibility for assessing and interpreting results, but under the teacher's leadership. All three key players in classroom assessment—students, teachers, and parents—understand the meaning of academic success, the standards to meet, and the meaning of assessment results. This is the whole idea underpinning our principles of assessment *for* learning.

Our traditions also have made teachers directors of communication, with all information emanating from them and going to students and parents. In more inclusive communication, teachers, students, and parents trade responsibility for delivering information to others. Sometimes students take charge, sending information to teachers and parents. Sometimes parents deliver information to students and teachers. Still other times, teachers run the show. Sometimes, members of the network team up to inform the others. Information about student achievement can pass in all directions—always in support of learning.

More Detail in the Communication

Our primary communication symbols traditionally have been grades and test scores. Effective communication systems might rely on these, too, but in a context of deeper mutual understanding of what they mean. More importantly, however, such systems use other forms of communication, such as descriptions, pictures, examples conveyed in portfolios, narratives, lists of standards and targets attained, and so on.

Our traditions have us relying on report cards, test score reports, and parent-teacher conferences as primary vehicles for sharing achievement information. To be sure, when used appropriately, such vehicles help us convey meaningful information. But we also can rely on more complete written reports, conferences that involve students, and portfolios as treasure troves of information about and reflections on student achievement, again, all used in support of learning.

Summary: Communication Is Key to Achievement

Think about effective communication as conveying useful and accurate information (Chapter 3) about student mastery of important learning targets (Chapter 2) from the information gatherer to its intended user (Chapter 1), to help that person decide what to do next. So we need to prepare purposefully, share our information carefully, and follow up to be sure the message was understood.

Remember from Chapter 1 that a number of people need access to dependable information about students to do their jobs, including classroom-level users as well as users at levels of instructional support and policy. These are important people whose decisions determine

student well-being. We need to communicate effectively.

We prepare well by agreeing in advance (between message sender and receiver) precisely what achievement we wish to communicate about, by gathering accurate achievement information, by developing a shared vocabulary, and by building an interpersonal environment amenable to an honest exchange of information.

We also prepare carefully by anticipating what can go wrong that can keep the message from getting through and by heading those problems off at the pass. We do this by satisfying the conditions as discussed and by taking the risk of always being open and honest about student learning—by acknowledging what is really happening, not merely what we wish were happening.

The foundation of good communication is effective information management. Standards of good management vary as a function of the context. In assessment *for* learning contexts, we rely on student-involved assessment, record keeping, and communication at least some of the time as a means of helping students feel in control of their own success and needing access to the best possible information about their own level of performance. In assessment *of* learning contexts, where the purpose is to verify that learning has occurred, we teachers typically are the managers of summary information about mastery of established standards.

Final Chapter Reflection

1. *What are the three most important new insights to come to you as a result of your study of this chapter?*
2. *Which of your previous questions about assessment can you now answer based on your study of this chapter?*
3. *What new questions have come to mind as a result of your study of this chapter that you hope to have answered as your study continues?*

Practice with Chapter 9 Ideas

1. Read the following letter from a frustrated parent. Which of the necessary conditions, barriers, and so on described in this chapter may have come into play here to create the problems? What possible solutions come to mind?

Dear Superintendent Lopez:

My daughter Natalya's fourth-grade teacher, Mary, is a wonderful, kind person with a lot of creativity. Natalya loves her. But many of us parents are about to go crazy from not being able to tell what's going on in class. We haven't gotten a single thing returned so far this year to gauge how our kids are doing.

We've been working closely with Mary and have a good relationship—so far. I'm worried about hurting her feelings or having her feel threatened by us (or other parents), but I'm not sure what to do next.

First of all, the school district changed its elementary report card this year. On the positive side, it is more closely aligned to the district curricular frameworks, and, ultimately, to state academic achievement standards. The parent's guide you gave us to outline the expectations from the curricular frameworks is not perfect (it's probably confusing to most parents), but it's much better than anything we've ever had in the past. For example, it delineates various levels of reading and math achievement and approximately where students should be at various grade levels in school (for example, at Reading Level 3 by third to fifth grades). I'm okay with that. But we were offered no examples of what work looks like at those various levels, so it's still way too abstract. I'm not sure that the teachers themselves were even trained with any concrete examples, so it appears they are still going on "intuition" more than anything else.

I don't know how you chose the rating scale (although I hear from a friend that it's also used in another district) to describe Nayalya's achievement, but it's bound to lead to confusion. The scale goes 4–3–2–1–X. Well, of course, that looks a lot like the 4.0 grade scale used by high schools and colleges. It's a stretch for parents to NOT associate 4 with A, 3 with B, 2 with C, etc. I don't know if the intent was to loosely map the grades that way:

> *4–Exceeds standards for this grade*
>
> *3–Meets standards for this grade–proficient*
>
> *2–Does not meet standards but making progress*
>
> *1–Does not meet standards/not progressing*
>
> *X–Not covered this reporting period*

Now here's the rub. The only assessment that our teacher could show us was an initial districtwide test she did with Natalya on reading and mathematics. The reading assessment showed that Natalya was 6.5 grade equivalent overall (8.5 in comprehension), but her marks on the report card were all "3" for reading. What on earth does that mean? When my husband tried to ask the teacher gently

what it would be like for someone to get a "4," she really couldn't say. The teaching intern offered that it might be a student who had picked multiple books off the Newbery reading list, made regular trips to the library (which Natalya does), etc.

In any case, Natalya ended up with all "3's" on her report card. Yet, not three weeks ago we had received a letter from the Highly Capable Program director saying that Natalya had been recommended by her teacher for the program—which requires students to be operating at about 2 years ahead of grade level. What gives? HELP!!

2. Select a course of study in your college program in which you are or were enrolled. Analyze that course according to the principles of effective communication. Does (did) the instructor communicate effectively with you?

3. Think of a situation in your educational past in which the principles of effective communication were violated. What went wrong—what specific principles were not met? What impact did this have on you and your educational experience? Now think of another context in which effective communication reigned. What happened and what was the effect? Contrast the two and draw implications for your classroom.

4. Assume you are building an information management system to support student-led parent-teacher conferences. What might the active ingredients look like in that system—evidence, storage, summary (or not), and reporting?

Chapter 10

Communicating with Standardized Test Scores

CHAPTER FOCUS

This chapter answers the following guiding question:

> What role should periodic large-scale standardized tests play in communicating about student achievement?

From your study of this chapter, you will understand the following:

1. The scores these tests produce can provide valuable information to some very important decision makers, although they are of limited value day to day in the classroom.

2. As professional educators, it is our responsibility to see that standardized tests are administered and used appropriately.

As you read this chapter, continue to keep in mind our big classroom assessment picture. Standardized tests represent one way to gather and communicate information about student achievement to some assessment users. Typically, they meet the once-a-year information needs of policy makers and curriculum and program planners.

Tests That Produce Comparable Results

Thus far, we have focused exclusively on assessments teachers develop or select for use in their particular classrooms. In this chapter, however, we will veer away from that track to explore the world of large-scale standardized achievement tests. We will study their purposes, the complex array of assessment forms used, and how to interpret and use test results. We will consider the techniques test developers use to create quality assessments, and we'll compile a list of responsibilities that teachers and administrators who administer, interpret, and use standardized testing must fulfill.

These once-a-year tests are not likely to be of much specific diagnostic or instructional value to classroom teachers. They are assessments *of* learning that are too infrequent, broad in focus, and slow in returning results to inform the ongoing array of day-to-day decisions. But this does not mean that these tests are without value in improving schools. They can communicate valuable information about students' achievement status to other decision makers. So I have included this chapter specifically to address the classroom teacher's primary standardized testing question: As a classroom teacher, what should I do in response to unrelenting demand from politicians, school administrators, and the community to "raise those test scores"?

The purpose of this chapter is to provide you with enough background information about large-scale standardized assessment to permit you to understand how such assessments fit into the big assessment picture in general and into your classroom in particular.

The Meaning of Scores

First, it is important to understand that the educational system in the United States has included a strong standardized test tradition for the better part of a century. The idea in standardized testing is to have large numbers of students respond to the same or similar sets of exercises under approximately the same conditions. Thus, test exercises, conditions of test administration, scoring procedures, and test score interpretation are "standardized" across all examinees. As a result, users can interpret the scores to mean the same for all examinees and thus can compare them across students and classrooms.

Comparable scores can inform some important decisions. For example, special education teachers can use them to identify relatively strong or weak students, so limited resources can be channeled to them. Scores on some standardized tests, averaged across students within schools or districts, communicate about strong and weak programs. Here again, the objective is to funnel resources to those places where they will do the most good.

Standardized tests are developed and published to assess both students' achievement and their aptitude or intelligence. This chapter is limited to the consideration of achievement tests only. Fundamental and deep-seated disagreements among learned scholars about the definition of intelligence, as well as their concern over the dangers of intelligence testing, cause me to exclude them from this book. If you wish to accommodate individual differences in student learning, I recommend individualizing on the basis of *prior achievement*, not intelligence.

Often, school districts participate in several layers of standardized achievement testing, from districtwide testing to statewide to national and sometimes even to international programs. Some districts may administer a dozen or more different standardized testing programs in a given year for different purposes involving different students. Some districts test every pupil at every grade, while others sample students or grade levels.

Some standardized tests produce scores that are *norm referenced;* they communicate in a manner that permits us to compare a student's achievement to that of other students who took the same test under like conditions. Scores on these tests can communicate information about how students rank in achievement.

Some standardized tests yield scores that are *criterion referenced;* they communicate how each student's test score compares, not to other students, but to a preset standard of acceptable performance. These kinds of scores permit us to detect which specific achievement standards students have and have not met; that is, to determine individual strengths and weaknesses in achievement.

Professional test publishers develop standardized tests, either to sell directly to schools or under contract for a local, state, or national educational agency. Tests are available to cover virtually all school subjects across all grade levels. Further, they can involve the use of any of our four basic forms of assessment, although historically most have relied on selected response formats because they can be automatically scanned and scored with great efficiency. This permits relatively inexpensive scoring of very large numbers of tests. Recently, we have seen a major increase in reliance on essay and performance assessment formats too, as test publishers strive to align their tests with more complex forms of achievement targets. This is a healthy development.

The Various Layers of Standardized Testing

From the beginning of our standardized testing traditions in the United States in the first part of the last century, we have evolved into a school culture that has increasingly relied on centralized assessment of student achievement, resulting in the layers of standardized testing programs that we see in place today.

College Admissions Testing

This level of testing began modestly in the 1920s and 1930s with a few local scholarship testing programs, which relied on essay tests to select winners. Thus, right from the outset, quality tests were those that could differentiate among levels of student achievement. These differences would serve to rank examinees for the award of scholarships.

These local applications were so effective that they gave rise to our first national college admissions testing programs, the College Boards (also known as the SATs). While the earliest tests relied on essay assessment, in the 1930s the huge volume of national testing soon forced a change as the College Board turned to multiple-choice testing technology as a more efficient format. With this change dawned the era of selected response testing for sorting purposes.

Then in the 1940s, the second college admissions test appeared on the scene, the ACT Assessment Program. Recently, ACT veered away from our traditions of relying on college admissions tests merely to sort for selection by making the ACT Assessment a standards-based examination. Each test in the battery (English, Mathematics, Reading, Science) is made up of test items reflective of a published set of academic achievement standards. This helps educators factor those standards into their instruction, thus setting students up for higher levels of ACT success. You can find those standards deconstructed into classroom-level achievement targets, as well as student-involved assessments *for* learning, in the guide *Promoting Student*

Success: Connecting ATI Classroom Assessment to the ACT Assessment (ACT & Assessment Training Institute, 2002).*

Districtwide Testing

Beginning in the 1940s, several test publishers were selling standardized versions of selected response tests to schools for use at all grade levels. The test user guides were careful to point out that scores on these tests were intended to serve as one additional piece of information for teachers to use to supplement their classroom assessments and help sort students into proper instructional treatments. Remember this purpose; it is a critical issue in the whole historical picture.

The most commonly used form of assessment in districtwide programs is the commercially published, norm-referenced, standardized achievement test battery. Test publishers design, develop, and distribute these tests for purchase by local users. Each battery covers a variety of school subjects, offering several test forms tailored for use at different grade levels. Users purchase test booklets, answer sheets, and test administration materials, as well as scoring and reporting services. It is not uncommon these days for districts with their own response sheet scanning technology to also purchase test scoring software from the publisher to analyze their own results.

The unique feature of these tests is the fact that they are nationally "normed" to facilitate test score interpretation. This simply means that the designers administered the tests to large numbers of students before making them available for general purchase. Test results from this preliminary administration provide the basis for comparing each subsequent examinee's score. I explain exactly how this is accomplished later in this chapter.

In addition, however, most test publishers now report at least some criterion-referenced information on score reports. Items in the battery that test the same standard are collected into a small test within a test, allowing the publisher to generate a score for each student reflecting that student's mastery of each specific standard. Again, I will show you such scores later in the chapter.

Statewide Testing

In the 1960s, in the midst of a time of social upheaval in the United States, society began to raise serious questions about the effectiveness of schools. There emerged the sense that schools (and the educators who run them) should be held accountable for more than just providing quality opportunities to learn, for more than just sorting students according to achievement. Rather, they should also be held responsible for producing real student learning and for ensuring that all students attain certain specified levels of achievement.

In response to the challenge that schools might not be "working" (that is, to evaluate their programs) administrators were forced to turn to their only source of believable student achievement data: scores from commercially available standardized objective paper and pencil achievement tests.

---

*This public service guide can be downloaded as a .pdf file directly from http://www.assessmentinst. com/resources.html

This represented a profoundly important shift in society's perceptions of these tests. They would no longer be seen as just one more piece of information for teachers. Now they would be seen as standards of educational excellence. Understand that the underlying testing technology did not change. These were still tests designed to sort students based on assessments of very broad domains of content. All that changed was our sense of how the tests should be used. They came to be seen as the guardians of our highest academic expectations, a use their original developers had never intended.

Educational policy makers across the land began to believe that society could achieve major improvements in school effectiveness if we broadened the scope of our application of standardized tests. We moved rapidly beyond just districtwide testing to statewide testing applications.

We began the decade of the 1970s with just a handful of such tests and ended with nearly 40 states conducting their own testing programs. As of this writing (early 2004) virtually every state conducts its own program. Significantly, many states opted to develop their own tests to be sure they focused on important academic standards in that state. They tended to move from tests designed to sort to tests reflecting student attainment of specific achievement targets (that is, from norm-referenced to criterion-referenced tests).

National Assessment

Beginning in the late 1970s and extending into the 1980s and 1990s, we added the National Assessment of Educational Progress (NAEP) in the hope that testing achievement at ever more centralized levels would somehow lead to school improvement in ways that other tests had not.

NAEP is a federally funded testing program that periodically samples student achievement across the nation to track the pulse of changing achievement patterns. These biannual assessments gauge the performance of national samples of 9-, 13-, and 17-year-olds, as well as young adults, reporting results by geographic region, gender, and ethnic background. Results are intended for use by policy makers to inform decisions. Since its first test administration in 1969, NAEP has conducted criterion-referenced assessments of valued outcomes in reading, writing, math, science, citizenship, literature, social studies, career development, art, music, history, geography, computers, life skills, health, and economics. NAEP assessment procedures have used all four assessment methods, with selected response methods dominating.

International Assessment

Periodically, the United States, Canada, and other nations around the world collaborate in competitive assessments specifically designed to determine the relative standing of nations with respect to student achievement. Content and assessment experts from around the world meet for the following purposes:

- Define achievement targets common to the participating nations' collective curricula.

- Design exercises that pose problems that make sense in all particular cultures.
- Translate those exercises into a range of languages.
- Devise scoring criteria reflecting differing levels of proficiency.

Given the cultural and linguistic diversity of the world, you can anticipate the challenges in conducting such an assessment.

National Every-Pupil Testing

In 2001, with the signing of the No Child Left Behind Act into law, President George W. Bush launched the first-ever national every-pupil examination system in the history of the United States. This law requires every state to administer annually a standardized achievement test in reading and mathematics to every student in grades 3 to 8. Results are to be reported by both school and district and desegregated by ethnic group. In all reporting categories, results must reflect "adequate yearly progress" or the school is labelled "failing." States are free to establish their own academic achievement standards, develop their own assessments, and define "adequate yearly progress" in their context. But the accountability for achievement is clear—for all students, including every ethnic subdivision of the student population. States judged not to be in compliance with testing requirements risk losing federal educational funding.

The Result: Troubling Contradictions

You can see the pattern of practice that has emerged since the 1930s. The conventional wisdom has held that, if we just find the right level at which to test and exert the proper level of threatening consequences for low test scores, schools will improve. Throughout this evolution, standardized testing has been troubled with apparent contradictions arising out of a general lack of understanding of these tests, both within and around our school culture. Let me illustrate.

As a society, we have placed great value on standardized tests. We assign great political visibility and power to the results they produce at local, state, national, and international levels. The paradox is that, as a society (both within and outside schools), we seem to have been operating on blind faith that educators are using them appropriately. As a society, almost to a person, we actually know very little about college admission testing, national assessment, state testing, or local assessment programs. It has been so for decades. This blind faith has prevented us from understanding either the strengths or the important limitations of standardized tests. As a result, the discrepancy is immense between what most educators and the public think these tests can do and what they actually are capable of delivering.

We have tended to ascribe a level of precision to test scores that they simply do not have. Many believe we can use standardized test scores to track student acquisition of new knowledge and skills so precisely as to detect deviations from month-to-month norms; so precisely that we can use them to predict success at the next grade level, in college, or in life after school. But standardized tests typically are not the precision tools or accurate predictors most think they are. Typically, they do not produce high-resolution portraits of student achievement. Rather, they are designed to produce broad general indicators of that achievement. This is their often-misunderstood heritage.

Over the decades, some have noticed these problems and concluded that we should do away with standardized tests, arguing that the problems meant that the tests were of poor quality. In fact, standardized tests generally do a good job of assessing a limited range of kinds of achievement—those that can be tapped with multiple-choice test items and very brief essays. This includes mastery of content and some kinds of reasoning. So their coverage is very limited—not performance skills or product development capabilities beyond writing proficiency.

Our long-term societal habits of assigning great power to standardized tests, ascribing unwarranted precision to the scores they produce, striving to make them instructionally relevant, and generally misunderstanding them even while attacking them have conspired to create a major dilemma in education today. We have permitted these tests to form the basis of a school accountability system that is incapable of contributing to much-needed school improvement efforts. Sadly, our general lack of understanding of these tests has prevented us from achieving the real accountability that we all desire.

Addressing the Contradictions: A Guiding Philosophy

One challenge we face as a school culture and as a larger society is to keep these standardized tests in perspective in terms of their potential impact on student learning. They do inform policy- and program-level users once a year in productive ways. But the plain and simple fact is that *large-scale assessment results will have much less impact on student learning than will your classroom assessments.* Yet our allocation of resources, media attention to scores, and political emphasis on standardized tests would lead one to believe just the opposite is true. In this regard, our priorities are grossly out of balance.

If we are to establish a more balanced set of assessment priorities, we must give far greater attention to (1) promoting communitywide understanding of the limitations of standardized tests to ensure their proper use, and (2) establishing and maintaining the quality of classroom assessments. A balanced perspective encourages effective use of all assessment tools we have at our disposal. This includes standardized tests. In the hands of informed users who know and understand both the strengths and limitations of these tests, they can contribute useful information to educational decision making. Besides, they are so deeply ingrained in our educational fabric that our communities have come to expect periodically to see scores from these tests.

This leads me to the following statement of beliefs: We should continue the limited use of standardized tests where relevant to inform programmatic and policy decisions. At the same time, we must be absolutely certain each and every user of assessment results (from the classroom to the living room to the boardroom to the legislature) is thoroughly schooled in the meaning and limitations of the scores. In short, we must balance assessment *of* and *for* learning.

Standardized Test Development

While standardized tests may differ in coverage from publisher to publisher, they all rely on the same basic development process. I explore that process here, so you may appreciate how much work developers must do, and how dedicated to quality local, state, and national large-scale tests they must be.

Step 1: Clarify Targets

Typically, standardized test developers begin with the thoughtful study of the valued achievement targets they wish to assess—the academic achievement standards that students are to master. In terms of our five attributes of sound assessment, therefore, these tests typically arise from very clear targets.

Step 2: Translate Targets into Assessments

Developers of large-scale standardized tests typically know how to match their target with a proper assessment method. In the past, they have relied on selected response formats because these have allowed them to easily tap their valued knowledge and reasoning targets. Now, however, these same test publishers are beginning to turn also to performance assessments, to tap more complex skill and product targets.

Selected Response

The most popular mode of assessment in this context by far is and always has been selected response. It is relatively easy to develop, administer, and score in large numbers. When the achievement targets are content mastery and/or certain kinds of thinking and problem solving, its great efficiency makes this the method of choice for large-scale test developers. Its major drawback, as you know, is the limited range of targets test developers can translate into these formats.

Essay

Historically, this option has been infrequently used in standardized testing in the United States. Recently, however, this has begun to change. Short answer essays have begun to appear in the content-area exams, such as science and social studies, of state assessments. This popularity arises directly from the fact that, these days, state proficiency standards typically include reasoning and problem-solving targets. Document scanning technology and computer-driven paper management systems have permitted test scoring services to evaluate written work with great dependability and efficiency. These services have developed the ability to scan student essays, train raters to score them dependably, and present those scorers with student essays online for rating. The result is a powerful test-scoring technology.

Performance Assessment

This option is the focus of much current discussion and exploration in large-scale assessment, although cost is a major downside factor. The assessment research and development community is exploring applications in writing, mathematics problem solving, science, reading, foreign languages, the arts, interdisciplinary programs, and other performance areas. The great strength of this methodology is its ability to capture useful information about student performance on complex targets. Its limitations are the cost of sampling and scoring. This is a labor-intensive option when large numbers of examinees are involved.

Personal Communication

This option is rarely used in large-scale standardized testing due to cost. One-on-one standardized testing is simply too expensive. But perhaps one day that will change. By having students "think aloud" about what they have read, reading specialists tell us we can gain insight into student comprehension. Math and science assessments also could take advantage of this idea. By having students reason out loud as they solve complex problems and respond to carefully crafted questions, assessors can gain insight into students' reasoning and into their ability to communicate effectively.

Step 3: Develop Test Items

When assessment plans are ready, test construction begins. Some developers use their own inhouse staff of item writers; others recruit qualified practicing teachers to create exercises. In either case, item writers are trained in the basic principles of sound item construction. Further, once trained, item writers must demonstrate an appropriate level of proficiency on a screening test before being asked to contribute to test development.

Typically, test publishers write two or three times more test exercises than will appear on the final test. In doing so, they are guided by a sampling plan or test blueprint that ensures sound sampling of the intended targets.

Step 4: Assemble Test and Control for Bias

Once items have been written, qualified test development experts, content-area experts, and members of minority groups review the exercises for accuracy, appropriateness, and bias. Poor-quality or biased exercises are replaced. This review and evaluation removes possible extraneous sources of bias and distortion.

To uncover and eliminate other potential problems, the next step in test development is to pretest or pilot test the items. Developers recruit classrooms, schools, or districts to administer the exercises under conditions as similar as possible to those in which the final test will be used. Their objectives are to find out if respondents interpret exercises as the authors intended and to see how well the exercises "function." Test developers also want to know how difficult the items are and how well they differentiate between those who know and do not know the material. All of this helps them retain only the most appropriate exercises for the final test.

Then, yet another external review takes place. Test item development experts, content-area experts, and representatives from various minority groups again examine the final collection of test items to ensure quality, equity, and appropriateness.

Step 5: Administer Trials to Establish Norms (Norm-Referenced Tests)

The result of this creation, selection, and review of items is a broadly focused, high-quality new test. But the work doesn't stop there. Many test development plans call for administering the final test as a whole for further quality control analysis and, in the case of norm-referenced tests, to establish norms for score interpretation.

As soon as a test is ready, the publisher launches a national campaign to recruit school districts to be part of the "norming sample." The aim is to involve large and small, urban and rural districts in all geographic regions, striving to balance gender and ethnicity; in short, to generate a cross-section of the student population in the United States.

Even though thousands of students may be involved, these norm groups are volunteers. For this reason, they cannot be regarded as systematically representative of the national student population. Thus, when we compare a student's score with national norms, we are *not* comparing them with the actual national student population, but rather to the norm group recruited by that test publisher for that particular test.

Because of the voluntary nature of norm group selection, different test publishers end up recruiting different districts to norm their particular tests. Because none is necessarily equivalent to the national student population nor to any norm group used by another publisher, norm-referenced scores attained on different test batteries cannot be meaningfully compared to one another.

Norm-referenced standardized tests are revised and renormed regularly to keep them up to date in terms of content priorities, and to adjust the score scale. This is necessary because, as the test remains on the market, districts align their curricula to the material covered. This is how they meet the accountability challenge of producing high scores. Over time, more and more students will score higher on the test. To adjust for this effect and to accommodate changes in the student populations, test publishers renorm their tests to adjust the score scale downward.

Setting Standards of Acceptable Performance (Criterion-Referenced Tests)

As states have established statewide achievement standards and transformed them into criterion-referenced state assessments, an important issue has come to the fore: How do we decide if a student's score is "high enough" to be judged competent? This is a critically important issue when decisions such as grade-level promotion, high school graduation, or the award of certificates of mastery hang in the balance.

Typically, these "cutoff scores" are established by pooling the collective opinions of teachers, administrators, parents, representatives of the business community—a cross-section of society within that state. The processes employed to accomplish this are too complex to describe here. But suffice it to say that this test scoring technology is very well developed and is very precise when carried out by experts.

Once those cutoff scores or standards are established, then each new test developed for use in subsequent years can be "equated" to the original to ensure comparability of score meaning, even though it might use different test items. This is important to ensure equity of opportunity for students regardless of the year when they happen to be tested. Again, for our purposes, it's not important that you know how this is done. I just want you to know that it *is* done.

Interpretation of Commonly Used Test Scores

Standardized tests that rely on selected response items can report any of a variety of kinds of scores. We will review these in two contexts in this section by explaining how each score is derived and suggesting how educators may use each score to understand and interpret test performance. One context is the standards-referenced score typically used in statewide testing programs and in some district testing programs. The other context is with published, commercially available, norm-referenced standardized achievement test batteries like those often used in districtwide testing programs.

It is imperative that you understand what these different kinds of scores mean and do not mean because it will be your responsibility to interpret them to the parents of your students or to your students themselves. It is *your* responsibility to promote clear understanding.

Scores Reported on State Assessments

State assessments typically are designed to reflect student mastery of specific academic achievement standards. State departments of education hire professional test developers to translate their standards into test items that yield evidence of student mastery of those standards. This process can yield either of two kinds of scores: evidence of student mastery of each standard or a composite score reflective of student mastery of an array of standards.

Mastery of Each Standard
When the evidence is to take this form, the test developer will include enough items on the test for each standard to permit a determination of each student's mastery of it. The number of items will vary as a function of the scope of the standard. Simple, focused standards will require a smaller sample of performance to yield a dependable result. The student must answer a certain number or percentage right to be judged to have mastered that standard. In any event, interpretation is straightforward

and criterion referenced: Did each student provide evidence of having met each standard? I prefer this kind of score to the one I discuss next because it is more precise.

Composite Mastery Score

Our standardized testing traditions have focused on assessing student mastery of material in broad domains. You will see in the next subsection, for example, commercial tests report scores labeled "reading," "math computation," and so on. Each test includes a set of items that samples these domains broadly.

This kind of thinking also has carried over into many state assessments. Test developers will pool all of the individual academic achievement standards into a broad set and build the test to lead to a conclusion about student master of that "domain"—reading, math, and so on. Then a cutoff score is established, identifying the number of items the student must answer correctly to be judged to have mastered this domain of standards. In fact, often, multiple cut scores are calculated: mastered, nearly mastered, and clearly did not master, or words to that effect. The contention is that, because standards drove test development, this represents a standards-referenced examination.

I have always regarded this option as imprecise and far less useful than the score described previously, which centered on each student's mastery of each standard. It can lead to misinterpretation. A student might perform at a very low level on standards within a set and still score high enough on the test to be judged competent. In that instance, the results are undependable.

Scores Reported on Commercial Norm-Referenced Tests

In this case, you can encounter five different kinds of scores. Each provides a different perspective on student achievement.

Raw Score

This is the easiest score to explain and understand. When students take a test, the number of items they answer right is called their *raw score*. In the standardized test context, this forms the basis of all the other scores. In other words, all other scores are derived from it, as you will see. It is the foundation of any communication arising from a standardized test.

Percent Correct

This score is as familiar and easy to understand as the raw score. *Percent correct* reflects the percent of test items the examinee answered correctly: raw score divided by total test items. This is the kind of score we use in the classroom to promote a common understanding and interpretation of performance on classroom tests. As the total number of items changes from test to test, we can always convert raw scores to percent correct and obtain a relatively standard index of performance.

There are two reasons why this kind of score is important in the context of standardized tests. First, this is the kind of score large-scale test developers use to determine mastery of objectives for a criterion-referenced score report. Score reports often label these *objective mastery scores* or something similar. This is exactly like the state assessment score described previously. Examinees are judged to have mastered the objective if they answer correctly a certain percentage of the items covering that objective. The exact cutoff varies at around 70 to 80 percent correct across standardized tests.

The second reason for addressing this kind of score is to differentiate it from percentile score or percentile rank. Very often, test users confuse percent correct with percentile scores. *They are fundamentally different kinds of scores bringing completely different interpretations to the meaning of test performance.* To understand the differences, we must first understand each.

Percentile Score

The *percentile score* (or *percentile rank*) represents the essence of a norm-referenced test score. This score tells us what percent of the norm group a student with any given raw score outscored. A student with a percentile rank of 85 outscored (scored higher than) 85 percent of the examinees in that test's original norm group. They allow us to see how each student's score ranked among others who have taken the same test under the same conditions. Did the student score higher than most? Lower? Somewhere in the middle?

Table 10.1 shows you how a student's raw score can be converted to a percentile score. It describes the performance of our norm group on a new test. We will study this table column by column to describe this conversion.

Column one tells us we will be analyzing student performance on a 30-item test. The maximum number correct is 30 and is the score at the top of the column. Possible raw scores range from 0 to 30. However, in truth, no students will score at or even anywhere near zero. If items on a multiple-choice test offer four response options, even a student who guesses will be right a quarter of the time. So a pure guessing score will be 25 percent of 30, or 7 or 8 points. Only a very few of the most poorly prepared and unlucky students (poor souls!) will score lower than that. So there are no percentiles reported for scores under 7.

Column two tells us how many students in our 1,500-person norm group (see "Total" at the bottom of the column) actually got each raw score. For instance, 20 students scored 25 on the test, 70 scored 13, and so on.

Column three presents the percentage of students who got each raw score. Look at raw score 20. One hundred fifty students actually achieved this score, which represents 10 percent of the total of 1,500 examinees in the norm group.

Column four is where it begins to get tricky. This column presents the percentage of students who scored at or below each raw score. Start at the bottom of the column. What percent of students attained a raw score of 7 or lower? One-half of one percent. Move up the column. What percent of students attained a raw score of 17 or lower? 38.5 percent—the sum of all the percentages for raw scores 0–17: .5 + .5 + .5 + .5 + 1.5 + 2.5 + 4.5 + 5.5 + 6 + 8 + 8.5 = 38.5. So, a student who attains a raw score of 17 scored equal to or higher than 38.5 percent of those in the norm group.

Now on to percentile scores—see column five. For each raw score, by definition we need to know *what percentage of those who took the test scored lower than*

Table 10.1
Understanding percentile scores

(1) Raw Score	(2) Number of Students	(3) Percent of Students	(4) Cumulative Percent	(5) Percentile Score
30	10	0.5	99.5	99
29	10	0.5	99.0	99
28	20	1.5	98.5	97
27	20	1.5	97.0	96
26	30	2.0	95.5	94
25	20	1.5	93.5	92
24	40	2.5	92.0	90
23	60	4.0	89.5	86
22	80	5.5	85.5	80
21	120	8.0	80.0	72
20	150	10.0	72.0	62
19	180	12.0	62.0	50
18	170	11.5	50.0	39
17	130	8.5	38.5	30
16	120	8.0	30.0	22
15	90	6.0	22.0	16
14	80	5.5	16.0	11
13	70	4.5	10.5	6
12	40	2.5	6.0	4
11	20	1.5	3.5	2
10	10	0.5	2.0	2
9	10	0.5	1.5	1
8	10	0.5	1.0	1
7 (Chance)	10	0.5	0.5	0
6				
5				
4				
3				
2				
1				
Total	1,500	100		

that score. Look at raw score 26. These students outscored everyone with scores of 25 or lower. We see that 93.5 percent of examinees attained a score of 25 or lower. If we round to whole numbers, then the percentile score for a raw score of 26 is 94. Anyone attaining a raw score of 26 outscored 94 percent of those in the norm group; thus, a raw score of 26 converts to a percentile score of 94.

Test publishers calculate each of these conversions and then place them in the computer. From that point on, all students who get a certain raw score have

Table 10.2
Understanding stanines

Stanine	Percent of scores	Percentile range	Descriptor
9	4	96–99	well above average
8	7	89–95	
7	12	77–88	above average
6	17	60–76	
5	20	40–59	average
4	17	23–39	
3	12	11–22	below average
2	7	4–10	
1	4	1–3	well below average

its corresponding percentile score printed on their score report. So, for example, a raw score of 29 reflects a level of achievement on this test that is higher than 99 percent of the examinees in the norm group. This will remain true as long as this test is in use.

When test publishers norm a test, they create conversion tables for their national norm group, and typically also offer percentile conversions based on geographic region, gender, race/ethnicity, and local performance only. This means that exactly the same kind of conversion table is generated for students who are like one another in these particular ways.

You can see why the percentile is a norm-referenced score. It provides a straightforward comparison of student-to-student performance as the basis for score interpretation.

It also should be clear how percent correct and percentile differ. The former refers scores back to the number of items on the test for interpretation, while the latter compares the score to those of other examinees for interpretation. Their points of reference are fundamentally different.

Stanine

A student may also be assigned a stanine score based on percentile rank. *Stanine* simply represents a less precise score scale, each point of which can be interpreted quite easily (Table 10.2). In this case, the percentile scale is divided into nine segments, each of which represents a "standard nine" or, abbreviated, stanine. When interpreted in terms of the general descriptors listed in the right-hand column on Table 10.2, this score is easy to understand. A student who attains a stanine of 3 on a test is interpreted to have scored below average in terms of the performance of the norm group.

Grade Equivalent Scores

This score scale represents yet another way to describe the performance of a student in relation to that of other students. The basis of the comparison in this case is students in the norm group at specified grade levels.

Let's say a test publisher is norming a newly developed 40-item test of fifth- and sixth-grade math. It administers its test to large numbers of students in those two grades at the very beginning of the school year. Each student receives a raw score ranging from 10 to 40. On further analysis of test results, let's say that the average score for fifth graders is 23, while sixth graders score an average of 28 correct. With this information, as represented graphically in Figure 10.1, graph A, we can begin to create our conversion table. The first two conversions from raw to grade equivalent scores are those for the average raw scores. Because 23 was the average score for fifth graders, we assign that raw score a grade equivalent of 5.0. Because 28 was the average raw score of sixth graders when we administered our test, it is assigned a grade equivalent of 6.0. That accounts for 2 of the 30 raw score points to be converted. What about the rest?

Under ideal circumstances, the best way to convert the rest would be to administer our new test to students each month, so we could compute averages for them and complete more of our conversion table. Unfortunately, however, real schools will never permit that much test administration. Besides, the cost would be astronomical.

So, as an alternative, we can simply assume that students grow academically at a steady and predictable rate between grade levels. By connecting the two dots (averages) with a straight line that depicts that steady rate of growth, we create a mathematical equation that allows us to convert the scores between 23 and 28 to grade equivalents, as in Figure 10.1 graph B. By projecting each raw score point over to the straight line on the graph and then down to the corresponding point on the grade scale, we find the grade equivalent to assign to each raw score.

But what about scores above and below this grade level? How shall we convert these? We have two choices: (1) administer the new test to students at higher and lower grade levels, compute averages, and complete the table; or (2) rely on our assumption that students grow at a predictable rate and simply extend our line down from 23 and up from 28. Option 2 is depicted in Figure 10.1 graph C, where a raw score of 40 converts to a grade equivalent of 8.5.

Once the conversion table is completed and read into the computer, henceforth any student who attains a given raw score will be assigned its corresponding grade equivalent. Thus, the grade equivalent score reflects the approximate grade level of students in the norm group who attained that raw score.

The strength of this kind of score is its apparent ease of interpretation. But this very strength also turns out to be its major flaw. Grade equivalent scores are easily misinterpreted. They don't mean what most people think they mean. Here is an example of what can go wrong:

Let's say a very capable fifth-grade student scores a perfect raw score of 40 on our new math test. As you can see from Figure 10.1, graph C, this will convert to a very high grade equivalent score. For the sake of illustration, that score is 8.5. An uninformed person might see that and say "We must start this fifth grader using the eighth-grade math book at once!"

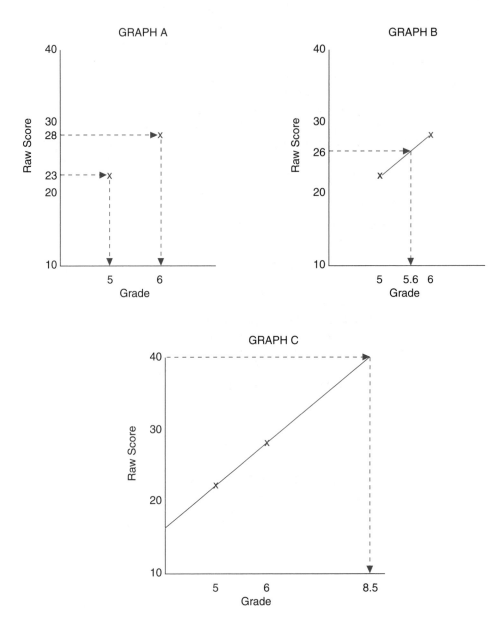

Figure 10.1
The derivation of grade equivalents

This is an incorrect conclusion for two reasons. First of all, no information whatever was gathered about this student's ability to do seventh- or eighth-grade math.
All that was tested was fifth- and sixth-grade math. No inference can be made about
the student's proficiency at higher-level work. Second, eighth graders have probably
never taken the test. The score represents an extrapolation on the part of the test

Table 10.3

Test score summary

Score	Meaning	Strength	Caution
Raw	Number of items answered correctly; range=0 to number of items (points) on the test	Provides the basis of all other scores	Difficult to interpret by themselves in a norm-referenced context; can't be used to compare scores across tests
Percent correct	Percent of total test items answered correctly; range=0% to 100%	Easy to understand; can communicate mastery of specific objectives	Sensitive to test length—short tests yield huge % jumps between scores. Can't compare across tests
Percentile	Percent of students in norm group that the examinee outscored; range=0 to 99 percentile	Permits clear comparison to other similar students; can serve to compare scores across tests in same battery	Often confused with percent correct; cannot be averaged
Stanine	Divides scores into 9 broad categories	Permits a broad grouping of students by score	Too imprecise to detect small differences in achievement; cannot be averaged
Grade equivalent	Compares performance on the test to that of students at various grade levels who took the same test	Provides interpretive reference to grade levels	Often misinterpreted; does not refer to grade-level competencies. Cannot be averaged

score analyst as to how eighth graders would be likely to score if they had taken the test of fifth- and sixth-grade math. Thus, again, no reliable conclusion can be drawn about any connections to eighth-grade math.

The bottom line is that grade equivalent scores are not criterion-referenced scores. There is no sense in which the grade equivalent score is anchored to any body of defined content knowledge or skill mastery. It is only a comparative score referring a student's performance back to the typical performance of students at particular grade levels in the norm group. Our fifth grader is just very good at fifth- and sixth-grade math—probably a whole lot better than most fifth and sixth graders.

Table 10.3 provides a concise summary of the various kinds of scores we have discussed.

Real-World Test Score Interpretation

Now let's apply these definitions to interpreting a real score report. Refer to Figure 10.2, an individual student score profile for *Terra Nova,* a standardized test product of CTB McGraw Hill of Monterey, California. Note that it reports both norm-referenced scores (at the top) and criterion-referenced information on student performance on objectives (at the bottom).

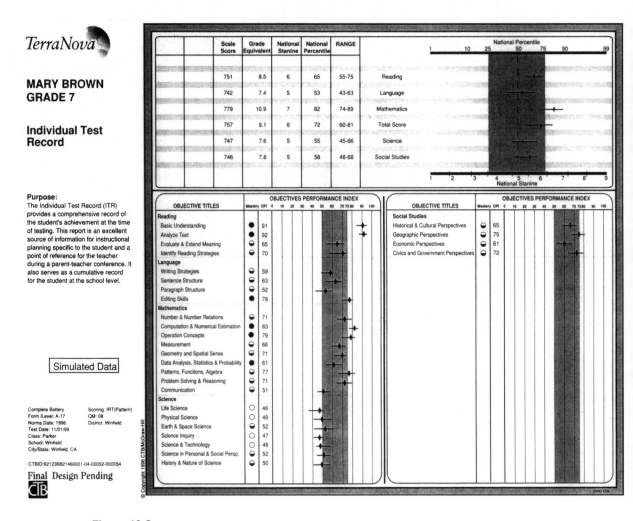

Figure 10.2
Sample score report
Source: Copyright © 1996 by CTB/McGraw-Hill, Inc. Reprinted by permission.

In the top section, we see the headings "Grade Equivalent," "National Stanine," "National Percentile," and "Range." (For our purposes, we can disregard the first column, "Scale Score." This is a technical score not useful in the classroom.) So in the top section, in Reading, Mary Brown, a seventh grader, demonstrated a grade equivalent score of eighth grade, fifth month and a national stanine of 6. In the percentile column, we see that Mary outscored 65 percent of the students who took the test during norming. Further, see the "Range." If Mary took this test lots of times, we would expect her score to vary up or down slightly, to fluctuate between the 55th and 75th percentile—due to errors of measurement—those factors that come up day to day that make all test scores slightly unstable.

The reference to "National" for these scores is important, because it means that the norms were based on the performance of all students from across the nation who participated in test administration during norming. Sometime score reports will list "State" percentiles. That simply means that we interpret each student's score in terms of those who took the test within our state during norming. In addition, school districts also can request norm-referenced scores comparing each student's performance to their classmates within their own community. These are called "Local" norms. Neither state nor local norms appear on the report in Figure 10.2.

The "Objectives Performance Index" section of the profile tells us what objectives Mary was judged to have mastered based on her performance on individual items. Here's how to interpret these scores, according to *Terra Nova's* guidelines for teachers:

> Each objective is measured by a minimum of four items. The Objectives Performance Index provides an estimate of the number of items that a student could be expected to answer correctly if there had been 100 items for that objective. The OPI is used to indicate mastery of each objective. An OPI of 75 and above characterizes Mastery. An OPI between 50 and 74 indicates Partial Mastery, and an OPI below 50 indicates Non-Mastery. The two-digit number preceding the objective title identifies the objective, which is fully described in the Teacher's Guide to *Terra Nova*. The bands on either side of the diamonds indicate the range within which the student's test score would fall if the student were tested numerous times. (CTB/McGraw-Hill, 1996, p. 2)

Implications for Teachers

So what does all of this mean for those concerned primarily with classroom assessment? For you as a teacher, it means understanding that you have a three-part responsibility with respect to standardized tests.

Responsibility 1: Protect the Well-Being of Your Students!

Your first and foremost responsibility is to keep your students free from harm. First, make sure they have the opportunity to learn to hit the achievement targets reflected in whatever standardized tests they take. Second, ensure that the scores reported for your students are accurate—that they reflect each student's real level of achievement. Third, you must do everything you can to be sure all students come out of large-scale assessment experiences with their academic self-concepts intact. Let's consider several specific things you can do to fulfill these professional obligations.

Prepare Your Students by Providing an Opportunity to Learn

Do all in your power to gather information about and to understand the achievement targets to be assessed in upcoming standardized tests. If a state assessment is pending that reflects state standards, it is your job to know what those standards are and how they apply to your students. Remember the very important lesson you learned in Chapter 2 on achievement targets. Deconstruct each state standard into the enabling knowledge, reasoning, performance skill or product development targets that form the scaffolding leading up to that standard. Plan instruction and assessment *for* learning to bring students up that scaffolding in ways that let you and them know they are progressing appropriately over time.

If a published test is to be administered, consult the teacher's guide or the user's materials for that test to know precisely what knowledge, reasoning, performance skill, or product targets it will be assessing. Again, make these the focus of instruction.

Another lesson from Chapter 2 on achievement targets needs reaffirming here: Be sure you yourself are a master of the achievement targets your students will be expected to master. Be sure you have the vision of success, then share that vision with your students in terms they can understand.

Strive for Accurate Results

When asked to administer standardized tests, take the responsibility seriously and follow the prescribed instructions. This contributes to the quality of the results. You must follow accepted standards of ethical practice. Anything you may do to cause students to misrepresent their real levels of achievement has the potential of doing harm to them, to you as a professional, and to the integrity of the educational community as a whole. If you are opposed to a particular set of standardized testing practices, bring all of your assessment literacy tools to bear during the debate. That is your right and your responsibility. But when assessment begins, adhere to prescribed procedures so users can accurately interpret the results.

Sometimes ensuring accuracy demands more than merely following prescribed test administration procedures. Some students bring physical or intellectual handicaps to the testing environment that require you to adjust test administration procedures to obtain accurate scores for them. Most often these days, test publishers or state testing agencies will issue guidelines for such accommodations. One such list is presented in Figure 10.3. Note that adjustments can be made in setting, timing, scheduling, presentation, and response. As a general rule of thumb, accommodations allowed at testing time are the same as accommodations made during instruction as listed in the student's individualized education program (IEP).

Is it clear to you why such adjustments are necessary in some cases? If some students take the test under standard conditions, the result may well be a score that misrepresents what they know and can do. These accommodations permit us to get past those physical or intellectual challenges to use their strengths to permit us to

Examples of Setting Accommodations

Conditions of Setting	Location
Minimal distractive elements (e.g., books, artwork, window views)	Study carrel
Special lighting	Separate room (including special education classroom)
Special acoustics	Seat closest to test administrator (teacher, proctor, etc.)
Adaptive or special furniture	Home
Individual student or small group of students rather than large group	Hospital
	Correctional institution

Examples of Timing Accommodations

Duration	Organization
Changes in duration can be applied to selected subtests of an assessment or to the assessment overall.	Frequent breaks, even during parts of the assessment (e.g., during subtests)
Extended time (i.e., extra time)	Extended breaks between parts of the assessment (e.g., between subtests) so that assessment is actually administered in several sessions
Unlimited time	

Examples of Scheduling Accommodations

Time	Organization
Specific time of day (e.g., morning, midday, afternoon, after ingestion of medication)	In a different order from that used for most students (e.g., longer subtest first, shorter later, math first, English later)
Specific day of week	Omit questions that cannot be adjusted for an accommodation (e.g., graph reading for student using Braille) and adjust for missing scores
Over several days	

Figure 10.3

Example of assessment accommodations to meet special needs

Source: Adapted from *Testing Students with Disabilities* (pp. 47–58) by M. L. Thurlow, J. I. Elliott, and J. E. Ysseldyke, 1998. Thousand Oaks, CA: Sage Publications. Copyright 1998. Adapted by permission of Sage Publications.

see students' real achievement more clearly. But we have to be sure that such accommodations don't alter the target being assessed, thus leading to inaccurate measurement.

Encourage Student Self-Confidence

Prepare your students to participate productively and as comfortably as possible in large-scale testing programs. Take time to be sure they understand why they are taking

Examples of Presentation Accommodations

Format Alterations	Procedure Changes	Assistive Devices
Braille edition	Use sign language to give directions to student	Audiotape of directions
Large-print version	Reread directions	Computer reads directions and/or items
Larger bubbles on answer sheet	Write helpful verbs in directions on board or on separate piece of paper	Magnification device
One complete sentence per line in reading passages	Simplify language, clarify or explain directions	Amplification device (e.g., hearing aid)
Bubbles to side of choices in multiple-choice exams	Provide extra examples	Noise buffer
Key words or phrases highlighted	Prompt student to stay focused on test, move ahead, read entire item	Templates to reduce visible print
Increased spacing between lines	Explain directions to student anytime during test	Markers to maintain place
Fewer number of items per page	Answer questions about items anytime during test without giving answers	Dark or raised lines
Cues on answer form (e.g., arrows, stop signs)		Pencil grips
		Magnets or tape to secure papers to work area

Examples of Response Accommodations

Format Alterations	Procedure Changes	Assistive Devices
Mark responses in test booklet rather than on separate page	Use reference materials (e.g., dictionary, arithmetic tables)	Word processor or computer to record responses
Respond on different paper, such as graph paper, wide-lined paper, paper with wide margins	Give response in different mode (e.g., pointing, oral response to tape recorder, sign language)	Amanuensis (proctor/scribe writes student responses)
		Slantboard or wedge
		Calculator or abacus
		Brailler
		Other communication device (e.g., symbol board)

Figure 10.3
Example of assessment accommodations to meet special needs (continued)

these tests and how the results will be used. My next suggestion may startle you, but take it seriously. If the scores are complex or technical in nature, such as percentiles or state assessment mastery scores, do not report them to students. If the scores can't help students in any purposeful way to make productive decisions about their own learning do not give them the scores. Under these circumstances, the scores will do more harm than good. But if you do report them, be sure students know what the scores mean and do not mean—how they will and will not be used. Provide practice with the kinds of test item formats they will confront, so they know how to deal with and feel confident with those formats. This includes practice with accommodations in place for special education students.

Communicate with parents about the importance of keeping these tests in perspective. Be sure they know the meaning of the scores. And above all, be positive and encouraging to all before, during, and after these assessments and encourage parents to do the same. All of these steps help students become "test wise." Positive talk can send students into uncomfortable testing circumstances knowing that you are on their side—and that helps.

Responsibility 2: Community Awareness

As a classroom teacher, you can and should strive to promote understanding within your community of the role of standardized testing and the meaning of test results. Members of the school board, parents, citizens, and members of the news media may need basic assessment literacy training to participate productively in the proper use of results. Only when they, too, understand the meaning of sound assessment will they be in a position to promote the wise use of these tests.

Responsibility 3: Maintain Perspective

Be constantly mindful of when standardized tests are likely to contribute useful information and when they are not. You can do this only if you understand the meaning of test results and how that meaning relates to the reasons for testing. In my opinion, we have entirely too much standardized testing being conducted merely as a matter of tradition, with no sense of purpose. Always insist on attention to purpose: What are the specific decisions to be made, by whom, and what kind(s) of information do they need? Will the test provide useful information?

We must all constantly urge those who support, design, and conduct standardized testing programs to keep these tests in perspective in terms of their relative importance in the larger world of educational assessment. We must constantly remind ourselves and others that these tests represent but a tiny fraction of the assessments in which students participate and that they have relatively little influence on day-to-day instruction.

Summary: Meeting the Challenges of Standardized Testing

Our purpose in this chapter has been to understand and learn to negotiate the challenges presented by standardized testing to teachers and those in positions of instructional support.

We reviewed the array of assessment purposes introduced in Chapter 2, emphasizing again the place of standardized testing in the larger context of educational assessment. These tests serve both policy and instructional support functions. They tend to be of little specific value to teachers, because classroom demands require greater frequency of assessment and higher-resolution pictures of student achievement than the typical standardized test can generate. The one part of the score report teachers are likely to find useful are the criterion-referenced scores reflecting student mastery of specific objectives. While once a year is not frequent enough to be comprehensive, at least teachers get some detail with these scores.

We studied the various levels of standardized testing, from local to state to national to college admission testing, pointing out that all four assessment methods are used at various levels. We discussed their history, and the mechanics of their development.

Next, our attention turned to understanding and interpreting commonly used standardized test scores: raw scores, percent correct, percentile, stanine, and grade equivalent. These and other such scores are safe and easy to use when users understand them. But, by the same token, they can be easily distorted by the uninformed. Your challenge is to become informed.

We ended with a quick summary of your professional responsibilities, emphasizing that your concern first and foremost should be for the well-being of your students. Under all circumstances, we must demand accurate assessment of the local curricula. Each of us should strive to be an activist with a voice of reason in this arena. Only then will we be able to use this form of assessment productively.

In the previous chapter, we established certain conditions that must be satisfied to achieve effective communication: mutual understanding of the targets tested, accurate scores, and an interpersonal communication environment amenable to productive sharing. When using standardized tests as the means of gathering information and communicating about learning, we maximize the chances of success if all of the following are true:

1. Both message sender and receiver understand the nature of the achievement targets reflected in the exercises of the test; they know and understand what was and what was not tested.
2. The tests are developed by professionals who have the technical credentials to create tests that provide dependable information; tests developed in the absence of this expertise are likely to be of inferior quality.
3. The interpersonal communication environment is open to good communication:
   - Everyone involved knows what the scores can and cannot be used for, and uses them accordingly.
   - Message sender(s) and receiver(s) share a common language; in this case, both know what the scores mean and how to interpret them correctly.
   - Opportunity is created by message senders where they and all receivers are compelled to attend to the test scores being shared.
   - During this time message, senders ask receivers to restate in their own words what the scores mean and what their implications are.

Final Chapter Reflection

1. *What are the three most important new insights to come to you as a result of your study of this chapter?*
2. *Which of your previous questions about assessment can you now answer based on your study of this chapter?*
3. *What new questions have come to mind as a result of your study of this chapter that you hope to have answered as your study continues?*

Practice with Chapter 10 Ideas

1. Assume that your careful analysis of commercially available standardized tests reveals that only one-half of the items in any subtest covers material specified in your curriculum at the specified grade levels you had planned to test. That is, the best overlap you can get between what you want to test and any available test is 50 percent. This means that you will not have taught one-half of the material tested during the year you test it. Yet your school board and administration compel you to choose and administer a test anyway. How should you proceed? What should you do to maximize the value of this assessment and minimize harm to students?

2. Mark True or False for each of the following questions.* Explain your reasoning. After you have done so, check your answers against the scoring key that follows the quiz:

T   F   1. Tim is a sixth grader. He obtained a grade equivalent score of 9.2 in reading. This means that Tim scored well above average sixth graders in reading.

T   F   2. Tim's grade equivalent score of 9.2 in reading means that Tim could well be put in a class of ninth graders for material in which reading skills were important.

T   F   3. Juanita is a sixth grader. She got a percentile score of 70 in reading on a published standardized test. This means that Juanita got 70 percent of the items correct.

T   F   4. Susie, a third-grade student, scored at the 30th percentile in arithmetic at the end of the school year. According to school grading policy, scores below 65 percent are regarded as failing. Therefore Susie should be retained for another year in arithmetic instruction so that she will not be handicapped in the future.

T   F   5. Mary is a sixth grader who received a stanine score of zero on her standardized test in math. This means that Mary's score is very low compared to other sixth graders.

T   F   6. Each stanine range contains 10 percent of students.

T   F   7. Mr. Rivera wondered about his student, Elena, whose stanine score in reading comprehension went up from the fourth stanine to the sixth stanine. That big a difference is important.

Answers to Test Score Quiz

1. **True.** A grade equivalent score is the average performance of students on the test at each of several grade levels. A sixth grader who has gotten a grade equivalent of 9.2 has performed like a ninth-grade student on the sixth grade test. Therefore, he has performed above average for students in his grade.

2. **False.** A grade equivalent of 9.2 means that Tim does as well as ninth graders on sixth-grade work. It does not necessarily mean that he can do ninth-grade work.

3. **False.** Percentile scores indicate the relative standing in a group, not the percent of items that are correct.

---

*Adapted from John R. Hills, *Hill's Handy Hints* (n.p.), 1983, Washington, DC: National Council on Measurement in Education. Copyright 1983 by the National Council on Measurement in Education. Reproduced with permission of the publisher.

4. **False.** Scores at the 30th percentile are really not far below average. The 30th percentile means that the student has scored better than 30 percent of similar students taking the test. Usually no more than a few percent of a class are failed, say 3 or 4 percent, not anywhere near 30 percent. Besides, a nationally standardized test may not accurately sample the arithmetic skills covered in Susie's class.

5. **False.** There is no such thing as a stanine score of zero. There has been a scoring error.

6. **False.** The first and ninth stanine of each have about 4 percent of student scores; the second and eighth about 8 percent; the third and seventh about 12 percent; the fourth and sixth about 16 percent; the fifth about 20 percent. Envision a bell-shaped curve.

7. **True.** When scores differ by two stanines, we tend to think of there being a real difference, not an error of measurement. A difference that large is unlikely to be an accident so it deserves further investigation. Perhaps Elena has benefited from some effective teaching, or she may have become more motivated, or she may have found more time to read, or something in her life that was impeding her progress may have been removed.

3. Pretend you are explaining standardized test scores.

Part A: How would you explain the following to a parent? Prepare a written set of responses:

a. Raw scores, percent correct, percentile, and grade equivalent
b. When each score should be used
c. The implications of such scores for your instruction

Part B: Now pretend you are explaining them to your students. What would you say about each of the items in Part A? Again, write out your responses.

Part C: Do your responses suggest to you that you understand how to communicate about standardized test scores? Comment on your sense of self-confidence in this arena.

4. Turn to Figure 10.2 or another standardized test score report provided by your professor and answer the following questions:

- Identify as many different kinds of scores as you can and discuss their meaning.
- What do you understand from this report? Is there anything you do not understand? If so, how might you secure clearer understanding?
- What are the possible implications for instruction of these results? That is, where did students perform well? Less well?
- What prerequisite proficiencies do students need to develop to be ready to take a test like this? What do the scores mean if those skills are absent? What should a teacher do in that instance?

Chapter 11

Communicating with Report Cards

CHAPTER FOCUS

This chapter answers the following guiding question:

> How can I communicate about student achievement using report cards in a manner that helps my students find success?

From your study of this chapter, you will understand the following:

1. Historically, we have assigned report card grades based on evidence and teacher judgment about student ability, achievement, effort, compliance, and attitude. This practice has done far more harm than good in building effective lines of communication.

2. There is one best way to develop report card grades. In fact, in a standards-driven educational environment, there is only one acceptable way.

3. As professional educators, it is our ethical and pedagogical responsibility to understand and apply only acceptable grading practices.

4. Grades represent just one of several ways to communicate using report cards. Other options include lists of competencies, narrative reporting, and continuous-progress reporting.

Report Card Grading

We begin our exploration of report cards with a comprehensive treatment of grading issues. The key issues revolve around the following:

- What student characteristics should we factor into a report card?
- What sources of evidence are appropriate to tap in determining a student's grade?
- How should we combine evidence gathered over time into the composite index that will form the basis of the grade?
- How should we convert that composite picture of achievement into a grade?

Each hides troubling dilemmas within it, and thus poses real dangers to students' confidence and to their ultimate academic success.

Grades are by no means the only way to share information about student achievement using report cards. Some report card designs convey much greater detail about student achievement. Sometimes that detail is crucial to sound decision making. So, after we address grades, I will present examples of useful alternatives.

Grading, What's a Teacher to Do?

As a teacher for many years, I experienced great anxiety about the appropriateness of my grading practices. I wondered whether there was a right way and whether I was grading my students that way. I constantly questioned myself:

- Why do I have to assign grades anyway? What's the purpose?
- Exactly what distribution of grades am I to assign? How many As, Bs, and so on?
- Should I grade on a curve (comparing students to each other) or use preset cutoff scores (everyone with a 90% average or above gets an A)?
- Should my grades reflect absolute achievement at one point in time or improvement over time?
- Should I hold all students to the same standard or can I adjust my grading expectations for special needs students?
- Should I grade just on ability, effort, and attitude? What other factors, if any, should I consider?

My list of questions, uncertainties, and concerns seemed endless. What teacher has not wondered about these same things?

If we are to use grades as an effective means of communication, each of us must come to terms with these issues. The goal of this chapter is to help you do just that.

Understanding Our Current Grading Environment

To answer questions such as those posed here, we have to think about the evolving school environment within which we grade students. Five key dimensions of that environment warrant our careful reflection:

1. Grades as communicators versus motivators
2. A continuing expectation of grades
3. The changing mission of schools
4. Evolving achievement targets
5. Changing student needs

Grades as Communicators versus Motivators

First, we must decide what we want to accomplish with grades. One major barrier to the use of report card grades as effective communication about achievement is our use of them as rewards and punishments to manage student behavior. Frequently, those two purposes come into direct conflict with one another.

For instance, let's say a teacher uses homework grades as a motivator to compel students to practice because this teacher believes that those who do so learn more. He warns students that failure to turn in any homework assignment will be entered as a failure in the gradebook. All incomplete assignments turn into Fs when it's time to compute that final grade.

Now let's say there are two students in this class, both of whom have developed a very high level of mastery of the material. Each has an outstanding record on all tests, quizzes, and projects. Yet one student has consistently failed to complete practice assignments and so has accumulated many Fs for homework in the gradebook.

At report card grading time, the message sender (the teacher) sends out word (via grades) that one student has been assigned an A, while the other is assigned a D (the result of averaging in all those Fs). The resulting communication problem becomes apparent when we realize that both students learned the same amount. The message receivers (parents, other teachers, etc.) have no basis on which to distinguish the differences in messages. They won't know or understand the subtleties of meaning hidden within the message and may draw inappropriate conclusions about each student's achievement. The result of a grading policy designed to promote greater effort will be miscommunication about one student.

This is precisely why I argue that one simple set of five little letter grades cannot shoulder the responsibility for being both (1) our primary way of sharing information about student achievement, and (2) our primary means of motivation. We must pick a purpose.

I advocate using grades as communication about achievement. Everyone needs effective communication about this to ensure sound decision making. But not every student responds to the threatened punishment of failing grades by redoubling their efforts. Some respond by giving up in hopelessness or cynicism. For them, grades don't work as motivators. For them, we have better options. We can do a much better job of helping many students want to learn by using student-involved assessment, including portfolios with student self-reflection on their improvement. This, then, is the grading philosophy that we will explore in this chapter.

A Continuing Expectation of Grades

The second dimension of our current grading environment that commands our attention is the fact that a huge majority of parents and communities still expect their children to be assigned report card grades in school, especially at junior high and high school levels. They know, as we should too, that grades will play a role in decisions that influence students' lives. This may not remain true forever, because we are constantly confronting the limitations of grades as a communication system. But it is true now and will be for the immediate future, at least. This means our challenge is to do the very best job we can of assigning accurate, interpretable grades.

To be sure, we are currently experiencing greater freedom to explore other communication options. We will consider many alternatives, including portfolios, checklists, rating scales, narratives, and student-led conferences, in the following chapters.

In the meantime, we must address grades and grading in all of their various forms. Elementary teachers often say to me, "We don't grade our students. We use check, check plus, and check minus." Or, "We use O for outstanding, S for satisfactory, and U for unsatisfactory. So we don't have to worry about grades." Of course, in a very real sense, these are grades, too, and the ideas covered in this chapter apply in these contexts also. *Grading* is the process of abstracting a great deal of information into a single symbol for ease of communication. The only things that change in the instances just cited are the symbols used; the underlying issues remain the same.

The Changing Mission of Schools

In the 1990s, grades took on a new meaning. Schools used to be considered effective if they produced a dependable rank order of students at the end of high school. We discussed this in earlier chapters. As long as there was a valedictorian and everyone had a "rank in class," few questioned the effectiveness of the school's functioning. Grades formed the basis of this sorting and selecting.

However, during the 1980s and 1990s, as the demands of both our society and the economy changed, we came to understand the inadequacy of this definition of effective schools. The demand for higher levels of competence for larger proportions of our students brought about a demand for schools driven by expectations of high achievement, not merely a rank order.

This change in mission carries implications for our grading practices. For decades in the American educational system, we have been demonstrating how it is possible to rank students dependably without knowing much about the quality of the assessments or sound grading practices. This is evidenced by the historic lack of teacher training in assessment and grading.

The troubling fact is that *it is possible to obtain a dependable rank order of students at the end of high school, even if the accumulated assessments and grades are individually undependable.* Here's how this can happen: Over four years and many courses, if classroom assessments are unreliable, some teachers will overestimate real student achievement, while others will underestimate it. When these inaccuracies are averaged into a composite grade point average at the end of four years, these errors of measurement (some too high and some too low) will tend to cancel each other out and the result will be a relatively dependable estimate of each student's overall achievement. Thus a class rank based on this four-year composite will, in fact, sort accurately according to achievement.

But this changed in the 1980s and 1990s, as society began to realize the limitations of schools that merely rank students. We have come to understand that, while we can assign grades and sort students dependably without quality classroom assessments and sound grading practices, *we cannot ensure the highest level of competence for all students without them.* Here's why: As students ascend through ever-higher levels of competence, seeking ultimately to meet graduation standards, each unit and course of study provides prerequisites for those that follow. If the individual assessments and grades assigned along the way are undependable, both teachers and students are likely to fall victim in their decision making to the resulting misinformation. Teachers, for instance, may misdiagnose student needs, fail to discover ineffective teaching practices, and misinform subsequent teachers about a student's current level of competence. Misinformed students may not allocate study time and energy appropriately, may lose confidence in themselves, or may make inappropriate educational or vocational plans.

In short, when schools are driven by a desire for competence for all students, the ongoing mismeasurement of student achievement (which was no problem with a rank-order mission) becomes a formula for disaster. Thus, with a mission of ensuring competence, we are forced to assess and grade accurately.

Evolving Achievement Targets

We also are experiencing rapid changes in our collective vision of the meaning of academic success. Two facets of our evolving expectations are important from a grading point of view. First, our range of expectations is expanding with the addition of technology, health-related, and teamwork achievement targets, among others. Second, the complexity of our expectations is increasing as researchers help us understand more clearly what it means to be a good reader, writer, math problem solver, computer user, and team member, to mention a few. These changes make it necessary for teachers to gather, store, retrieve, summarize, grade, and otherwise communicate about far more achievement targets today than ever before. In short, the information-processing challenges faced by the typical classroom teacher are immense. This means that we must also address grading practices from a perspective of efficiency.

Changing Student Needs

In addition, we must deal with the grading implications of mainstreaming special needs students. The typical teacher is facing a much broader range of academic abilities than ever before. As our society becomes more ethnically diverse, this challenge intensifies. We must plan and conduct assessments and assign grades in classrooms where individual students are working toward attaining fundamentally different achievement targets. If each student succeeds at a personally appropriate level, each deserves an "A." But how do we communicate the differences among those As? Is it even conceivable to individualize these communication systems to promote understanding and sound decision making? This reality places immense pressure on our traditional report card grading practices. I will explain in this chapter how to deal with this issue.

Communicate About What?

If we are to devise report card grading approaches that meet our communication needs in achievement-driven schools and that contribute to a supportive, productive, and motivating environment, the first issue we must confront is: What do we wish to communicate about? We must decide which student characteristics should be factored into report card grades.

Traditionally, most teachers have considered several factors, among them the following five:

- *Achievement*—Those who learn more receive higher grades than those who learn less.
- *Aptitude*—Those who "overachieve" in relation to their aptitude, intelligence, or ability receive higher grades than those who fail to work up to their potential.
- *Effort*—Those who try harder receive higher grades.
- *Compliance*—Those who follow the rules receive higher grades than those who don't.
- *Attitude*—Those who demonstrate more positive attitudes receive higher grades than those with negative attitudes.

It is likely that teachers will define these in different terms in assigning grades. It is interesting to speculate on the interpretability of a single letter grade when the message receivers and interpreters don't know (1) which of these elements the grader deemed important, (2) how they defined each, (3) how or how well they assessed each, and (4) what weight they gave each factor in grade computation. If we expect to communicate effectively about student achievement via grades, we must regard all of these unknowns as deeply troubling. But this is just the tip of the iceberg when it comes to describing the challenge of communicating through grades.

To illustrate what I mean, join me now in a thoughtful analysis of the role in the grading process of each of the five listed factors. Here are the issues in a nutshell:

- Should *achievement* be a factor in grading? That is, if two students have demonstrated fundamentally different levels of attainment of your achievement expectations, should you assign them different grades?
- Should you consider students' *aptitude, intelligence,* or *ability* when grading? That is, let's say two students have demonstrated exactly the same level of achievement, and let's say that level is right on the line between two letter grades. But you regard one as an overachiever in relation to ability and the other an underachiever, not having worked up to potential. Is it appropriate to assign them different grades?
- Is it appropriate to consider a student's level of *effort,* seriousness of purpose, or motivation in grading? That is, let's say two students have demonstrated exactly the same level of achievement and, again, that level is right on the line between two letter grades, but you regard one as having tried very hard while the other has not tried hard at all. Is it appropriate to assign them different grades?
- If you establish rules and deadlines with which you expect students to *comply,* should students who violate them be assigned lower grades? For instance, say you have two students, both of whom demonstrate the highest level of achievement on major tests and assignments, but one is delinquent in completing work. Should that student's grade suffer?

- Is it proper to factor students' *attitudes* into the grade? Again, given two students equal in actual achievement and on a grade borderline, one of whom has exhibited a positive attitude in class and one a distinctly negative attitude, is it appropriate to assign them different grades?

Time for Reflection

Please Note: *The reflections in this chapter represent particularly critical aspects of your learning. I am going to make some very provocative assertions in the following discussion. They are intended to elicit a response from you. You need to be a critical consumer of the ideas that I offer. This chapter's "Times for Reflection" will help you in this regard. Please take time to think them through. Before reading on, think about and take a personal position on each of the five questions listed. If possible, discuss your views with colleagues or classmates. Continue only after you have answered each of the five questions with a yes or no.*

To figure out the best answers to these questions, conduct a thoughtful analysis of arguments for and against weaving each of these factors into a grade. Then compare these two sets of arguments to draw conclusions regarding which should win out, arguments for or against, given that our purpose is to communicate effectively.

Achievement as a Grading Factor

If we use achievement as one basis for determining students' report card grades, in effect, our contract with students says that those who learn more (that is, master a larger amount of the required material, hit a larger proportion of the valued targets, progress further, or produce higher-quality work) will receive higher grades than those who learn less. This has long represented the foundation of grading.

Arguments For

One obvious reason this factor has been so prominent in grading is that schools exist to promote student achievement. In that sense, it is the most valued result of schooling. If students achieve, they are being set up for future success and schools are seen as working effectively. Grades have represented our index of success.

Besides, students are expected to achieve in life after school. School is an excellent place to learn about this fundamental societal expectation.

These are all compelling reasons why we traditionally have factored achievement into the report card grade, most often as the most prominent factor. Who would question the wisdom of grading in this way? Are there reasons not to factor in achievement?

Arguments Against

Not really. Given that achievement is the mission of school, we must communicate about it and grades represent one possible vehicle.

But to be sure, some dangers deserve our attention, if only to remind us of our assessment responsibilities. For example, what if we define achievement in complex terms that are difficult to assess well and we inadvertently mismeasure it? Or, what if we grade student performance based on a very important term-length homework assignment that a student, in fact, did not do but rather was done by a well-meaning parent instead? In both cases the grade will misrepresent real student achievement. Those who read the grade later on will draw incorrect inferences about student achievement and would make inappropriate decisions.

Or, what if we lack sufficient assessment expertise in the valued target to adequately evaluate student achievement of it? Again, mismeasurement is likely and the grade might not reflect real achievement.

Or, in a more serious and more likely dilemma, what if each teacher has a different definition of the meaning of successful achievement, assesses it differently, and assigns it a different weight in her/his grade computation? Now our attempts to communicate about achievement are full of noise and static, not clear, meaningful signals. When this happens, grades become uninterpretable.

But these do not represent arguments against grading on achievement. Rather they tell us that we had better know what we are doing when we do it.

Resolution

In this case, the decision is straightforward. In effect, there are no compelling arguments against factoring achievement into report card grades. But we must confront the dangers and eliminate all of them.

If there is a danger of mismeasurement due to the complexity of targets, we can either simplify them, or we can participate in professional development to help us to (1) refine our vision of the target to capture its complexity, and (2) devise more accurate assessments. These actions can help us prevent inadvertent mismeasurement of achievement.

If problems arise because some teachers hold different definitions of achievement, we can meet to compare definitions. By airing differences of professional opinion, we can find the common ground on which to build sound grading practices.

Thus, if we purposefully develop and implement practices that remove objections by setting clear and specific targets that are within all students' reach, and use sound assessments, we can find ample justification for including achievement in report card grades.

Aptitude as a Grading Factor

Remember the issues here: Assume two students demonstrate exactly the same level of achievement, and that level happens to be right at the cutoff between two grades. If you judge one student to be an overachiever in relation to ability, aptitude, or intelligence, and judge the other to be an underachiever, is it appropriate to assign them different grades? In other words, is it appropriate to factor a judgment about students' aptitude into the grading equation?

Arguments For

If we consider intelligence, ability, or aptitude in the grading equation, we hold out the promise of an appropriate level of success for every student. Those who can learn more and faster can be expected to do so. For those who learn more slowly, we can take that fact into account in determining their grade. This is encouraging to students. As they gain a sense of their own efficacy, we hope they will be motivated to try harder. What teacher is not energized by the promise of individualized achievement targets set to match the capabilities of individual students, thus ensuring each student at least the chance of academic success?

Besides, if we can identify those underachievers, we can plan the special motivational activities they need to begin to work up to their fullest potential. And we do so with no grading penalty to the perennial low achiever. This is a win-win proposition!

These are compelling arguments indeed. Factoring aptitude or ability into the grading process makes perfect sense. Who could argue against it?

Arguments Against

In this case, there are important counterarguments. For example, the definition of *aptitude* or *intelligence* is far from clear. Scholars who have devoted their careers to the study of intelligence and its relationship to achievement do not agree among themselves as to whether each of us has one of these or many, whether this is a stable or volatile human characteristic, or whether it is stable at some points in our lives and unstable at others. Not only do they disagree fundamentally about the definition of these characteristics, but they also are at odds regarding how to assess them (Gardner, 1993; Sternberg, 1996).

Given these uncertainties among experts, how can we, who have no background whatever in the study of intelligence, presume to know any student's aptitude or intelligence? That is not to say that all students come to school with the same intellectual tools. We know they do not. But it is one thing to sense this to be true and quite another matter to assume that we possess enough refined wisdom about intelligence to be able to measure it dependably, turn it into a single quantitative index, and then factor it in when computing report card grades.

Given the absence of training in aptitude assessment, even if teachers were to come up with a dependable definition (which they cannot), then they would face the severe difficulty of generating the classroom-level data needed to classify students according to their aptitude. Remember the key attributes of a sound assessment: clear targets, proper method, representative sampling, and control of bias. Each would have to be met for an attribute called *aptitude,* separately from achievement!

Even if we were able to resolve those problems (which we cannot), we would face another insurmountable dilemma. Each teacher would need a formula for deciding precisely how many units of achievement are needed per unit of aptitude to be labeled an over- or underachiever, and that formula would have to treat each and every student in exactly the same manner to assure fairness. *We do not possess the conceptual understanding and classroom assessment sophistication to enable us to do this.*

A brief comment is in order about aptitude as something separate from achievement. It is tempting to use students' records of prior achievement as a basis from which to infer ability, intelligence, or aptitude. But achievement and aptitude are not the same. Many things other than intellectual ability influence achievement, such as home environment, school environment, and dispositions. *Inferring level of ability from prior achievement is very risky. Resist this temptation.*

Besides, what if you label a student as an underachiever on the record and you are wrong? That student may be misclassified for years and suffer dire consequences. Such a wrong label may well become a self-fulfilling prophecy.

Even if the label is justified, is there not a danger of backlash from the student labeled as being a bright high achiever? At some point, might this student ask, How come I always have to strive for a higher standard to get the same grade as others who have to do less? Consider the motivational implications of this!

And then there is the possibility, if we consider aptitude when grading, that the same level of achievement attained by two students in the same class could deserve different grades, especially in borderline cases. I know of no one who wants to try to explain *this* one to those students or their parents.

And finally there is the same "signal–noise" dilemma we faced with achievement. Because different teachers define intelligence or ability or aptitude differently, assess it differently, and factor it into the grade computation equation differently, those who try to interpret the resulting grade later cannot hope to sort out those teachers' intended messages. This adds only confusing noise to our communication system.

Resolution

There are compelling arguments for and against factoring this student characteristic called aptitude into report card grades. Which shall win?

Time for Reflection

How do you sort out the arguments for and against? Take a position and articulate your defense before reading on.

The standards by which we judge the appropriateness of factoring intelligence into grades are the same as those we used for achievement. To justify incorporating it, we must be able to take concrete and specific action to overcome all arguments against it. Can we devise a definition of aptitude that translates into sound assessment and that promises to treat each student equitably? Perhaps someday, but not today. We lack a defensible definition and the measurement tools needed to know students' intelligence. We can't even say for sure whether it's a stable human characteristic. There is no place for aptitude, ability, or intelligence in the report card grading equation. For now, these problems are insurmountable.

But, you might ask, what about all of those compelling arguments in favor of this practice? What about our desire to individualize so students and teachers can be motivated by the potential of success? What about the hope this practice seems to offer to perennial low achievers? Must we simply abandon these hopes and desires?

The answer is a clear and definite, No! We must individualize on the basis of a student characteristic that we can define clearly, assess dependably, and link effectively to learning. I submit there is a far better candidate, a candidate that meets all requirements while not falling prey to the problems we experience in struggling with aptitude or intelligence. That individualizing factor is students' *prior achievement.*

Think of it this way: If we know where a student stands along the continuum of ascending levels of competence, then we know from our carefully planned continuous-progress curriculum what comes next for that student. Thus, we can tailor instruction to help that student move on to that next step in mastery of knowledge, demonstrated reasoning proficiency, performance of required skills, and/or creation of required products. Each student's success in hitting those next targets, then, becomes the basis for the report card grades we assign. Think of it as a contract between teacher and student where all agree on targets at the outset and then monitor progress continually together, until success is achieved.

Effort as a Grading Factor

Remember that, in this case, the issue is framed as follows: Assume two students demonstrate exactly the same level of achievement, and that level happens to be right on the borderline between two grades. If one student obviously tried harder to learn, demonstrated more seriousness of purpose, or exhibited a higher level of motivation than did the other, is it appropriate to assign them different grades? Does level of effort have a place in the report card grading equation?

Arguments For

Many teachers factor effort into their grading for apparently sound reasons. They see effort as being related to achievement: Those who try harder learn more. So by grading on effort, in effect, they believe that they are driving students toward greater achievement.

Besides, as a society, we value effort in its own right. Those who strive harder contribute more to our collective well-being. School seems an excellent place to begin teaching what is, after all, one of life's important lessons.

A subtle but related reason for factoring effort into the grade is that it appears to encourage risk taking, another characteristic we value in our society. A creative and energetic attempt to reach for something new and better should be rewarded, even if the striving student falls short of actual achievement success. And so, some think, it should be with risky attempts at achievement in school.

This may be especially important for perennial low achievers, who may not possess all of the intellectual tools and therefore may not have mastered all of the prerequisite knowledge needed to achieve. The one thing within their control is how hard they try. Even if students are trapped in a tangle of inevitable failure because of their intellectual and academic history, at least they can derive some rewards for trying.

Thus, there are compelling reasons, indeed, for using effort as one basis for grades. Could anyone argue against such a practice?

Arguments Against

In fact, we can. One such argument is that definitions of what it means to "try hard" vary greatly from teacher to teacher. Some definitions are relatively easy to translate into sound assessments: Those who complete all homework put forth effort. But other definitions are not: Trying hard means making positive contributions to the quality of the learning environment in the classroom. To the extent that teachers differ in their definition, assessment, and manner of integrating information about effort into the grading equation, we add noise to our grade interpretation. Message receivers simply have no way to uncover the subtleties of the teacher's intended message.

Besides, some teachers may say they want students to participate in class as a sign of their level of effort. But who most often controls who gets to contribute in class? The teacher. How, then, do we justify holding students accountable for participating when they don't always control this factor?

Further, students can manipulate their apparent effort to mislead us. If, as a student, I know you grade in part on the basis of my level of effort and I care what grade I receive, I promise that I can behave in ways that make you believe that I am trying hard, whether I am or not. How can you know if I'm being honest?

From a different perspective, effort often translates into assertiveness in the learning environment. Those who assertively seek teacher attention and participate aggressively in learning activities are judged to be motivated. But what of naturally quieter or more timid students? Effort is less likely to be visible in their behavior regardless of its level. And this also may carry with it gender and/or cultural differences, yielding the potential of systematic bias in grades as a function of factors unrelated to achievement. Members of some groups are enculturated to avoid competition. Gender, ethnicity, and personality traits have no place in the report card grading equation.

And finally, factoring effort into the grade may send the wrong message to students. In real life, just trying hard to do a good job is virtually never enough. If we don't deliver relevant, practical results, we will not be deemed successful, regardless of how hard we try.

Besides, from the perspective of basic school philosophy, what is it we really value, achieving, or achieving and knowing how to make it look like we tried hard? What if it was easy?!

Resolution

The balance scale tips in favor of including effort in the computation of report card grades only if we can eliminate all arguments against including it.

Time for Reflection

Given the arguments of both sides, what is your position? How does the scale tip and why?

First, as a matter of general principle, we must decide what we value. If we value learning, then we must define it and build our reporting systems to share information about student success in learning. If we value effort too, then again we must arrive at a mutually acceptable definition and must devise appropriate assessment tools and procedures. If we value both, why must we combine them into the same grading equation? It's not complicated to devise reporting systems that present separate information on each.

Continuing the theme of what we value: As noted previously, what do we care about, learning, or learning and making it look hard? What if it's easy for some students? What if I don't need to put forth much effort to learn? What if I don't have to practice anymore because I've got it? What if I can demonstrate mastery without doing hours of homework assignments? Why am I to be penalized for this? *However we define and assess effort, there can be no penalty for those who need little effort to learn.* Besides, what do you think will happen to their motivation (desire to learn) if we do?

Let's examine the other side as well. Let's say, as a student, I do need to practice a lot to learn and I don't take responsibility for doing so. Will that fact (my lack of effort) be reflected in my lack of achievement? Certainly it will. I won't learn much. If you factor my level of effort into the report card grade in addition to achievement, are you not in effect counting effort twice?

After we define effort, we must assess it well. As we have established, the assessment must arise from a clear target, rely on a proper method of assessment, sample effort in a systematically representative manner, and control for all relevant sources of bias that can distort our assessment and mislead us. But if we use behavioral indicators of students' level of effort and most of the "trying hard" behaviors take place outside of our presence (i.e., at home), how can we know that we are sampling well or controlling for bias?

For example, here's one form of bias that is hard to overcome: When students set out purposely to mislead us with respect to their real level of effort, they can seriously bias our assessment. This may be impossible to eliminate as a problem. If we see 30 students per day all day for a year and some are misleading us about their real level of effort, we may well see through it. But as the number approaches and exceeds 150 students for one hour a day and sometimes only for a few months, as it does for many middle and high school teachers, there is no way to confidently and dependably determine how hard each student is trying.

Think about that issue of student motivation. Let's say that you gather undependable evidence and conclude that a student is not trying hard and, in fact, this is incorrect. That is, in the truth of the world, that student is giving maximum effort but you conclude the opposite. What message does that send to the student? What effect is this turn of events likely to have on her desire to try hard and learn? Also, consider the other error. What if you say that a student is trying hard and, in fact, he is not? What message does this send and what impact is that message likely to have?

Moreover, if effort influences the grades of some, equity demands that it have the same influence on all. The assessment and record-keeping challenges required to meet this standard are immense, to say the least.

But a more serious challenge again arises from the personality issue. Less aggressive people are not necessarily trying less hard. Quiet effort can be diligent and productive. As teachers, we really do have difficulty knowing how much effort most students are putting forth. And we have few ways of overcoming this problem, especially when most of the effort is expended outside the classroom.

If you can define effort clearly, treat all students consistently, and meet the standards of sound assessment, then gather your data and draw your inferences about each student's level of effort. Just be very careful how you use those results at report card grading time. This is a minefield that becomes even more dangerous when you combine effort and achievement data in the same grade. *I urge you to report them separately,* if you report effort outcomes at all.

Want Better Ways to Motivate? Think Assessment *for* Learning

We grade on effort to motivate students to try hard. We feel that if they try hard, they will learn more. For those students who care about their grades, this may work. But if we are to understand other ways to motivate, we must also consider those cases in which our leverage has lost its power. We discussed this in Chapter 1. How shall we motivate those students who could not care less what grade we assign them, those who have given up and who are just biding their time until they can get out? For them, grades have lost all motivational value. If you think they are going to respond to our admonitions that they try harder so they can raise their grade, you are being naïve.

Consider this hypothetical situation: What would you do to encourage students to come to school and participate with you in the learning experiences you have designed for them if you could no longer use grades and report cards as a source of reward and punishment to control them?

Now consider these options: You might strive to learn students' needs and interests and align instruction to those. You might work with students to establish clear and specific targets so they would know that they were succeeding. In short, you could try to take the mystery out of succeeding in school.

You could be sure instructional activities were interesting and provocative, keep the action moving, always keep agreed targets in mind. You would share decision-making power to bring students into their learning as full partners, teaching them how to gauge their own success. In short, you would strive to establish in your students an internal locus of control over their own academic well-being. If they participate, they benefit, and they know this going in.

These ideas will work better as motivators than saying to students, "If you make it look too easy, I will lower your final grade," or, "If you convince me you are trying hard, I will raise your grade." The message we must send is, "Hard work leads to higher achievement. Higher achievement leads to good grades." This is a tough love message. In effect it says, "Trying hard may or may not be important for you, but either way it's never good enough. Just doing the work does not get good grades. The only thing that gets good grades is the *learning* that comes from doing the work." Achievement standards never merely ask that students "try hard to become good writers." They always demand that students "become good writers." In a standards-driven environment, it's achievement that counts.

Compliance as a Grading Factor

The question in this case is, What role should adherence to school and classroom rules play in determining students' report card grades? If two students have demonstrated exactly the same level of achievement, but one disobeys the rules, should that student's grade be lowered?

Arguments For

Of course it should. Consider the kinds of compliance that we absolutely must demand. What if students fail to come to school? The law says they must attend. If they're not in school, how can they learn? The threat of reduced or failing grades can compel attendance, as well as punctuality. Students are expected to learn important lessons of personal responsibility. Fail to show up on the job after school and you get fired. We can use grades to teach this lesson.

Another problematic behavior that we can control with the threat of grade reduction is cheating. If you cheat on a test, you get a zero. When averaged in at the end of the term, this will have the effect of radically reducing the final average and grade. This punishment will deter cheating and, again, teach another important life lesson.

Besides, without factoring compliance into grading, how do we manage the classroom? Deadlines would mean nothing. If students thought they didn't have to get homework in on time, they'd never do it. Then we'd have no evidence on which to base their grade. Or they'd hand it in late all at once and our grading workload would become overwhelming. If we can't issue sanctions for misbehavior by connecting compliance with the rules to their grade, students would be out of control. We're talking about one of the teacher's most powerful classroom management tools here.

In real life, society expects us to follow the rules—to obey our agreed-on laws. It's the way we preserve the social order. Schools are supposed to be conveying to young people the lessons of behavior in a civil culture. Connecting grades to behavior helps us in that effort.

Compliance with the rules leads to greater student learning in at least two ways. First, as the teacher, I know better than my students do what is best for them. Learning is maximized when they follow my plan—comply with my wishes. If they deviate, learning suffers. Second, a well-managed, compliant class permits everyone to benefit the most. If one or two students fail to follow the rules, everyone's learning suffers. We should not permit that to happen. It's not fair to the others.

Finally, although students are not in control of the academic ability that they bring to school, they are in complete control of whether they follow the rules and meet deadlines. If they wish to influence the grades they receive, this is one concrete way for them to do it.

Arguments Against

Before citing the counterarguments, I need to establish that it is very important for students to obey school and classroom rules. Not only can those rules affect student learning, but they can protect their safety and well-being.

But surprising as it may seem, that's not the issue in this case. When behaviors like truancy, tardiness, cheating and the like come up, they inflame the rhetoric. I mentioned them in citing "arguments for" for just that reason. I wanted to show you how easy it is to draw your attention away from the essential issue. These behaviors are counterproductive and need to be addressed. But the question is, How? If our desire is to punish students in the hope that we can extinguish the undesirable behaviors, then what is the most appropriate way to punish? Is lowering report card grades the best way?

If we do issue sanctions in the form of lowered grades, then the accuracy of the information about student achievement contained within the grade suffers and miscommunication is assured. Let me explain how. Let's say a student has taken four of five exams during a grading period and averaged 93 percent correct across all of them. Then this student is accused of cheating on the fifth exam and is given a zero in the gradebook. To add to the intrigue of this case, let's say that this student had mastered the material of that last exam and could have attained another very high score. If we wanted to communicate accurately about the achievement of this student we would assign an A on the report card to deliver a message to all message receivers of almost total mastery of the material.

However, when we factor the zero into the average, the result is 74 percent (93 times 4 on the first four exams plus zero on the fifth exam equals 374, divided by 5 equals 74), or a C on the report card. The effect is a complete misrepresentation of the student's level of achievement. Miscommunication. We have no way to let the various message receivers know the subtle message hidden in this grade. Is it wise to completely sacrifice any hope of accurate communication simply to punish alleged dishonest behavior? Are there other punishment options that don't result in such a profound communication breakdown?

Besides, once again we must consider the noise that is introduced into our communication system if every teacher defines standards of compliance differently, gathers evidence of different sorts, and gives compliance issues different weight when determining their particular grades. The message receiver will always have difficulty determining what the report card grade is supposed to mean. Miscommunication will result.

Finally, we have to be very careful about the messages our grading practices send to our students. Sometimes adult life presents us with situations where it might be wise to challenge established rules. While I would never advocate violation of accepted codes of behavior, if our nation's forefathers and mothers had merely obeyed the prescribed rules, where would our country be today? Obviously, I am not encouraging rebellion. But we must help our students keep perspective regarding the meaning and role of compliance.

Time for Reflection

How do you sort out these arguments for and against? Take a position and articulate your defense before reading on.

Resolution

To be sure, as mentioned previously, violation of some school or classroom rules is unacceptable. Sometimes, stiff penalties should be imposed.

However, I believe that the decisions that will be made based on the achievement information contained in report card grades are too important to permit that information's accuracy to be sacrificed by lowering grades as punishment for behaviors unrelated to actual achievement. Besides, there is strong legal precedent for this perspective. The courts have consistently disallowed grading policies that, for example, permit grade reduction for poor attendance. When the use of grade reduction as punishment has the effect of distorting the student's academic record, we violate the student's constitutional guarantees to equal access to future educational opportunities. By factoring things other than achievement into a report card grade, such as compliance with the rules, we distort and thus misrepresent the student's true academic record. According to the rulings of several federal district courts, this is unjust (Bartlett, 1987).

Let me hasten to add that the courts also have upheld the school's right to administer punishment for violating the rules. It's just that the punishment cannot lead to a distortion of the student's record of achievement. The courts compel us to separate the punishment, whatever that is, from our grading practices.

In the case of cheating cited here, the school is justified in administering fair punishment. But that punishment cannot have the effect of reducing the student's grade. The only acceptable action is to administer another fifth exam, average the resulting score with the other four, and assign the grade indicated by that average.

We have many appropriate punishment options at our disposal that don't distort the record and violate student rights, including detention, limiting access to desirable activities, community service, and so on. There is no need to sacrifice the accuracy of our communication.

Attitude as a Grading Factor

You understand the problem: Two students attain exactly the same level of achievement. Their semester academic average is on the cutoff between two letter grades. One has constantly exhibited a positive attitude, while the other has been consistently negative. Are you justified if you assign them different grades?

Arguments For

A positive attitude is a valued outcome of school. Anything we can do to promote it is an effective practice. People with positive attitudes tend to secure more of life's rewards. School is an excellent place to begin to teach this lesson.

Besides, this just may be the most effective classroom management tool we teachers have at our disposal. If we define *positive attitude* as treating others well, listening to the teacher, interacting appropriately with classmates, and the like, then we can use the controlling leverage of the grade to maintain a quiet, orderly learning environment.

And, once again, this represents a way for us to channel at least some classroom rewards to perennial low achievers. As with effort, attitude is within students' control. If they're "good," they can experience some success. Sounds good, let's make it part of the grading equation!

Arguments Against

It is seldom clear exactly which attitudes are supposed to be positive. Are students supposed to be positive about fellow students, the teacher, school subjects, school in general, or some combination of these? Must all be positive or just some? What combinations are acceptable?

How shall we define a positive attitude? As teachers, we value different human characteristics. Is it positive to accept an injustice in the classroom compliantly, or is it positive to stand up for what you think is right? What is the important value here?

Is it positive to act as if you like story problems in math, when in fact you're frustrated because you don't understand them? The definition of "positive attitude" is not always clear.

Further, if students can manipulate their apparent effort, so can they manipulate their apparent attitude. Regardless of my real feelings, if I think you want me to be positive and if I care about that grade, you can bet that I will exhibit whatever behavior you wish. Is dishonest game-playing a valued outcome of education?

Assessment also can be a source of difficulty in this case. It takes a special understanding of paper and pencil assessment methodology, performance assessment methods, and personal communication to evaluate affective outcomes such as attitudes, as you saw in Chapter 9. The rules of evidence for quality assessment are challenging, as you will recall from our earlier discussion of the assessment of affect. So mismeasurement is a very real danger.

Oh, and as usual, to the extent that different teachers hold different values about which attitudes are supposed to be positive, devise different definitions of positive, assess attitudes more or less well, and assign them different weights in the grading equation, we factor even more noise into our communication system.

Some pretty tough problems . . .

Time for Reflection

Once again, are you for or against? Make your stand and then read on.

Resolution

To decide which side of the balance sheet wins out here, we must determine which use of attitude information produces the greatest good for students. Let's say we encounter an extremely negative attitude on the part of one student about a particular school subject. Which use serves that student better: Citing your evidence of the attitude problem (gathered through a good assessment) and telling that student they had better turn it around before the end of the grading period or their grade will be lowered? Or, accepting the attitude as real and talking with the student honestly and openly about the attitude and its origins (using high-quality assessment of this disposition through personal communication) in an honest attempt to separate it from achievement and deal with it in an informed manner?

The power of attitude data lies, not in its potential to help us control behavior, but in helping us promote more positive learners and learning environments. If we go through the following difficulties:

1. Defining the attitudes we want to be positive (and this can be done)
2. Devising systematic, high-quality assessments of those attitudes (which can be done, too)
3. Collecting representative samples of student attitudes (an eminently achievable goal)

and then we fail to use the results to inform instructional design, choosing only to factor the results into grades, we have wasted an immense opportunity to help students.

If we enlist students as partners, they are likely to be even more honest with us about how they feel about their learning environment, thus providing us with even more ammunition for improving instruction. But if you think for one moment students are likely to be honest with us in communicating attitudes if they think the results might be used against them at grading time, you are being naïve.

Although we might be able to overcome the difficulties associated with defining attitudes for grading purposes, and can overcome the assessment difficulties attendant to these kinds of outcomes, I personally think it is bad practice to factor attitudes into report card grades.

Summary of Grading Factors

In an era of standards-driven schools, if report card grades are to serve decision makers, they must reflect student attainment of the specific knowledge, reasoning, skill, and product creation achievement targets leading up to state or local standards. Only then can we teachers, for example, know where students are now in relation to where we want to take them. For this reason, grading systems must include indicators of student achievement unencumbered by other student characteristics, such as aptitude, effort, compliance, or attitude. This is not to say that we should not report information about factors other than achievement, if definition and assessment difficulties can be overcome, which is no small challenge. But under any circumstances, aptitude or intelligence or ability have no place in grade reporting.

Grades can help us communicate effectively about student success in meeting our achievement expectations only if we do the following:

● Clearly define these expectations in each grading context for a given grading period.
● Develop sound assessments for those outcomes.
● Keep careful records of student attainment of the achievement expectations over the grading period.

In the next section, we explore these procedures in detail.

Gathering Achievement Information for Grading Purposes

If report card grades are to inform students, parents, other teachers, administrators, and others about student achievement, then we must clearly and completely articulate and assess the actual achievement underpinning each grade. To be effective, we must spell out the valued targets before the grading period begins. Further, we must lay out in advance an assessment plan to systematically sample those targets. While it sounds like a great deal of preparation to complete before teaching begins, it saves a great deal of assessment work during instruction.

1. Begin the grading period with a comprehensive set of achievement expectations.
2. Transform that "big picture" into an assessment plan describing evidence-gathering tactics.
3. Develop and administer the specific assessments as instruction unfolds.
4. Summarize assessment results into a composite index of achievement for each student.
5. Convert the composite into a grade.

Figure 11.1
Steps in report card grading

Let's analyze an effective and efficient five-step plan for gathering sound and appropriate achievement information for grading purposes. Figure 11.1 summarizes the key steps.

Step 1: Spelling Out the Big Achievement Picture

To complete a picture of the valued achievement targets for a given subject over a grading period, gather together all relevant background information: appropriate state or local achievement standards, the local written curriculum, and text materials for your intended units of instruction. From these, answer four questions (they will sound very familiar!):

1. What is the subject matter *knowledge* that students are to master? Outline the big ideas and essential concepts that you want students to know and understand. Write them out.
2. What patterns of *reasoning* and problem solving are they to master? Specify each of them in writing.
3. What *performance skills,* if any, are students to demonstrate? What things do they need to be able to do? List them.
4. What *products,* if any, are they to create and what are the attributes of a good one? Outline them.

Think about these things on a unit-by-unit basis and then glean an overall picture of them. Within and across units, develop a sense of the relative importance of these four targets in your overall expectations. Write down those priorities, with relative emphasis in the form of percentages that add to 100.

By the way, I do not list disposition targets here, not because they are unimportant, but because, as discussed, they should not play a role in report card grading decisions.

The targets you select for students obviously will form the basis of your actual assessments and instruction. For now, simply create a general outline of the important elements of your big assessment picture, spelled out in your own words, across units. In short, immerse yourself in this and force yourself to set priorities within and to impose limits on it.

As you prepare to present each unit of instruction, you will need to provide your students with (1) student-friendly descriptions of your expectations, and (2) the opportunity to learn to hit each of the achievement targets you have set out for them. There should be one-to-one correspondence between targets and instruction. For each target, you should be able to point to its coverage in your instructional plans.

Step 2: Turning Your Big Picture into an Assessment Plan

Once you are clear about your targets, your assessment and report card grading challenge is clearly drawn. The next question is, How will you assess to accumulate evidence of each student's attainment of those targets? Remember, this is an assessment *of* learning decision-making context. Taken together, the assessments that you use over time must help you determine, with confidence, what proportion of the total array of achievement expectations each student has met. In other words, what specific assessments (selected response, essay, performance, personal communication) will provide you with an accurate estimate of how much of the required material each student has mastered? You need an assessment plan to determine this.

You don't need the assessments themselves, not yet. Those come later, as each unit of instruction unfolds. But you do need to know how you will take students down the assessment road, from "Here are my expectations" to "Here is your grade," making sure both you and they know how they are progressing all along that road. The assessment plan that you start the grading period with needs to satisfy certain conditions:

- It must list each assessment you will conduct for grading (assessment *of* learning) purposes within each unit of instruction, detailing the expected achievement target focus of each, approximately when you expect the assessment to take place, and what assessment method(s) you will use.
- Each assessment listed in the plan needs to supply an important piece of the puzzle with respect to the priority targets of the unit and grading period within which it occurs.
- Each assessment must accurately represent the particular targets(s) it is supposed to depict (i.e., each must be a sound assessment according to our five quality standards).
- The full array of assessments conducted across units over the entire grading period must accurately determine the proportion of your expectations that each student has attained.
- The entire assessment plan must involve a reasonable assessment workload for both you and your students.

A Reality Check
These conditions may be easier to meet than you think. The report card grading challenge is to gather just enough information to make confident grading decisions and

no more. Ask yourself: How can I gather the fewest possible assessments for grading and still generate an accurate estimate of achievement? I believe that most teachers spend entirely too much time gathering and grading too many assessments. Some feel they must grade virtually everything students do and enter each piece of work into the record to assign accurate report card grades. This is simply not true. With planned, strategic assessments, you can generate accurate estimates of performance very economically.

I also see many teachers operating on the shotgun principle of grading: Just gather a huge array of graded student work over the course of the grading period, and surely somewhere, somehow, some of it will reflect some of the valued targets. While this may be true in part, this approach is at best inefficient. Why not plan ahead and minimize your assessment work?

If you can zero in on the key targets and draw dependable inferences about student mastery of them with a few unit assessments and a final exam or project assignment, that's all you need to produce report card grades that reflect student achievement.

Assessments *for* Learning, But Not for Grading

Let's be sure to remember that we don't assess in the classroom merely for the purpose of assigning grades. We established that fact very early. We also assess to diagnose student needs, provide students with practice performing or evaluating their own performance, and track student growth as a result of instruction. In fact, sometimes we assess just to boost student confidence by helping them see themselves growing.

Generally, it's a bad idea to factor into the report card grade student performance on assessments intended for purposes other than grading. Self-assessment is used for diagnosing needs and to see how to do better the next time. We don't grade students when they are evaluating their own needs or trying to discover the keys to their own success. Practice assessments are for polishing skills, overcoming problems, and fine tuning performance. We shouldn't grade students when they are trying to learn from their mistakes. Students need time simply to explore new learnings, time to discover through risk-free experimentation, time to fail and learn from it without the shadow of evaluative judgment.

Experienced teachers who read this might say, "If I don't assign a grade and have it count toward the report card grade, students won't take it seriously, they won't do it!" Trust me. Once students come to understand that practice helps, but performance on subsequent assessments is what counts for the grade, they will learn to practice, if they need to. They must take responsibility for developing their own sense of control over their success. This is exactly the point we have made repeatedly when speaking of developing an internal sense of responsibility for one's own success.

While it might take some time to break old dependencies, once students come to understand that good grades are not the rewards for doing work but are rather a signal of their success at achieving through studying effectively, they will practice as needed, especially if that practice can take place in a supportive, standards-based and success-oriented classroom.

Let's say a student fails to practice on interim assignments and performs poorly on the assessment that counts for the grade. As a teacher, how do you respond? One option is to say, "I told you so," and let it go so you can move on to the new stuff. Another response is, "I guess you found out how important practice is, didn't you? Nevertheless, I value your learning whenever it occurs. Do you want to practice now and redo the assessment? If you do, I will reevaluate your performance, no penalties. But that reevaluation will need to fit into my schedule."

Be a Merchant of Hope

Your job as a teacher is to set appropriate targets that reflect your assigned teaching responsibilities. Then agree with your students and your supervisor that you will do everything ethical within your power to maximize student success in hitting those targets. You are not the best teacher you can be until all of your students succeed.

We already have established that this was not always our perspective. When the mission of schools was to sort students by achievement, grades served as the basis for the ranking. We used grades to compare students. We graded on a curve, with only a few students getting As, Bs, and so on, regardless of their absolute achievement.

But remember, in standards-driven schools *there is no such artificial scarcity of high grades.* If you want to see students rapidly become hopeless failure acceptors, just set up an environment in which they actually learn a great deal but still receive low grades. In a healthy, success-oriented classroom, if everyone succeeds, everyone receives a high grade. The more students believe they can succeed, the more seriously they will practice in preparation for the assessments that contribute to their grades.

Step 3: From a Plan to Actual Assessments

Therefore, you begin the grading period with your assessment plan in hand. What next? You then need to devise or select the actual assessments for each unit, being sure to follow the development guidelines specified in earlier chapters. You will need to create and conduct each assessment, evaluating and recording the results as you go.

In each case where you have knowledge and reasoning targets to assess via selected response or essay assessments, you need to devise those specific assessments around precisely defined categories of knowledge and reasoning. You can capture these in lists of objectives, tables of specifications, propositions, and finally the test exercises themselves, which you may assemble into assignments, quizzes, and tests.

When assessing skill and product outcomes, you need to assemble performance criteria, tasks to elicit performance, and rating scales or checklists. Each component assessment fills in part of your big picture.

All assessments must align exactly with your vision of student competence. Although you may develop some in advance, to save time later, you may develop others during instruction. I know this sounds like a great deal of work, but remember five important facts:

1. This sharply targeted grading approach is not nearly as much work as the shotgun approach.
2. It affords the conscientious teacher a great deal more peace of mind. When your students obviously are succeeding, you will know that you have been successful.
3. In between your periodic assessments *of* learning for grading purposes, your students can play key roles in your assessments *for* learning, thus turning nearly all of that assessment time and energy into productive learning time and energy.
4. Student motivation to learn is likely to increase; "no surprises, no excuses" leads to a success orientation.
5. The plans you develop now remain intact for you to use or adapt the next time you teach the same material, and the time after that. Thus, development costs are spread out over the useful life of your plan and its associated assessments.

A Comment on Assigning Grades to Individual Assessments and Assignments

Because it is common practice to assign grades to the component assessments, such as assignments, during the grading period, not just at report card time, we need to reflect for a moment on this meaning of "grading." Think of your achievement expectations as a mosaic, with small tiles (each component assessment) coming together to tell the overall story. In fact, each component assessment represents its own small mosaic in the sense that it too is made up of its own small tiles, the exercises (e.g., test items) used to sample student achievement. If in the end you wish to draw conclusions about the proportion of your overall set of expectations each student has met, then each component assessment must help you see what proportion of its targets each student has mastered. When you combine all component assessment results at grade computation time (i.e., combine all of the tiles that are individual assessment grades into the mosaic), you create the overall picture of student achievement you need. I'll share an example later in the chapter to illustrate.

Given the mosaic metaphor, it should be clear to you why step two, building an assessment plan, is so critical. How do you plan instruction to help students master the mosaic if you don't know in advance how the overall picture comes together? Or even more importantly, how do you help them practice hitting targets not yet specified? This has been our theme throughout this text. It is relevant in grading too. At no point during the grading period should either you or your students have any question about what grade they are achieving at that point in time. Both you and they should know how much of the big picture has been covered as well as how much they have mastered, based on component grades.

Further, at no point should students feel that they can no longer influence the grade they receive. A high school student I know at one point informed her parents that her algebra teacher told her two weeks before the end of the semester that she was going to get a C on her report card regardless of how she did on the final exam.

Would you care to speculate how much algebra she learned after that announcement? Only students who possess some hope of succeeding are likely to succeed.

When you have carried out your assessment plan and collected the records, the time has come to generate a composite index of achievement for conversion to a grade. Incidentally, teachers have discovered that they can easily store, retrieve, and summarize grading records and convert them to actual grades using their personal computers. Software packages are available that can serve as your gradebook and much more. As you explore and evaluate these packages, be sure that the grading practices they apply are consistent with the guiding principles and procedures described in this chapter.

Step 4: Summarizing the Resulting Information

At the end of the grading period, your record from your assessment plan should tell you about each student's performance on each standard. This constitutes a portrait of how well each student mastered the targets that made up your big picture. The question is, how do you get a grade out of all of this information?

I urge you to rely on a consistent computational sequence for all students that you can reproduce later should you need to explain the process or revise a grade. Such a sequence helps to control for your personal biases, which may either inappropriately inflate or deflate a grade for reasons unrelated to actual achievement.

Please note that I am not opposed to a role for professional judgment in grading. As we established in earlier chapters, that role comes in assessment design and administration. We need to minimize subjectivity when combining indicators of achievement for grading purposes. Let the evidence speak for itself.

Combining Achievement Information

To derive a meaningful grade from several records of achievement, again, *each piece of information gathered should indicate the proportion of the targets each student has mastered.* If we combine them all, we should obtain an estimate of the proportion mastered for the total grading period. Remember the mosaic? Two relatively simple ways to achieve it are the percent method and the total points method:

Percent Method.   Convert each student's performance on each contributing assessment into a percentage of total possible points on that assessment. If you convert everything to the same percent scale, then both record keeping and later averaging become much simpler. For instance, if a selected response test has 40 items, and a student answers 30 correct, enter 75 percent in the record. But be careful with performance assessment. If a student scores all 4s on six 5-point performance assessment rating scales, that totals 24 of 30 possible points, or 80 percent. However, for reasons explained later in the chapter, I recommend against this grade computation practice. While several analytical scales can be combined in this manner, I recommend treating them differently in grading. Based on your professional judgment, what profile of ratings must a student demonstrate to deserve an A, a B, and so on? You set those profiles.

Beware of holistic ratings too. Let's say you are rating student performance on a single 4-point holistic scale. Only five percentage scores are available for conversion: 100 percent (4 of 4), 75 percent (3 of 4), 50 percent, 25 percent, or 0 percent. There is simply not enough precision in such a scale to permit meaningful conversion to percents or grades.

If the individual assessment results recorded as percentages are averaged across all assessments for a whole grading period, then the result should indicate the proportion of the total array of expectations for that grading period that each student has mastered. In effect, translating each score to a percentage places all on the same scale for averaging purposes and permits you to combine them in an easily interpreted manner, in terms of intended targets.

With this procedure, if you wish to give greater weight to some assessment results than to others, you can accomplish this by multiplying those scores by their weight before adding them into the overall computation. For instance, if some are to count twice as much as others, simply multiply their percentages by two (count it twice) when summing to arrive at an average. Here's an example: Let's say you administer three tests during a grading period, all of which contribute to the grade. But one test (number 3) covers a much broader curriculum segment than do the other two. You weigh it at twice the value of the other tests. The result is a higher grade that is more reflective of student mastery of the overall achievement expectations.

Time for Reflection

Under what conditions might you assign some assessment results a greater weight than others in your grading?

With this system of record keeping and grade computation based on percentages, everyone involved can know at any particular point in time how their scores, to that date, relate to expectations to date. This permits students to remain aware of and in control of their success. Some teachers also ask students to assign their own grade as a means of promoting student self-evaluation. If information gathering, storage, and retrieval systems are working effectively, there should be total agreement between teacher and students at all times about what grade students are earning.

Total Points Method.   Another way to combine information is to define the target for a grading period in terms of a total number of points. Students who earn all or most of the points demonstrate mastery of all or most of the valued targets and earn a high grade.

In this case, each individual assessment contributes a certain number of points to the total. If you carefully plan this so the points earned on each assessment reflect their fair share of the big picture, then at the end of the grading period you can simply add up each student's points and determine what percentage of the total each student earned. That percentage of total points, then, represents the proportion of valued targets attained. Just remember that the assessments that result in the largest number of points will contribute the most to the determination of the final grade.

This fact makes differential weighting possible. Just be sure that you assign a large number of points to those assessments (such as final exams or large projects) that cover the largest proportions of the valued targets and fewer points to the assessments (such as daily assignments) that are narrower in focus.

Either of these options provides an acceptable basis for clearly communicating via report card grades about student achievement. But be careful, difficulties can arise! We discuss next some of these difficulties, and offer ways to handle them.

Some Practical Advice

Unless you carefully develop and summarize assessments, the result may be misleading about the proportion of the total achievement picture that students have mastered. Let me illustrate.

Using the Most Current Information.   Let's say your strategic assessment plan includes five unit assessments and a comprehensive final exam that covers the entire set of targets for the grading period. A particular student starts slowly, scoring very low on the first two unit assessments, but gains momentum and attains a perfect score on the comprehensive final exam, revealing, in effect, subsequent mastery of the material covered in those first two unit assessments.

The key grading question is this: Which piece of information provides the most accurate depiction of that student's real achievement at the end of the grading period, the final exam score or that score averaged with all five unit tests? If the final is truly comprehensive, averaging it with those first two unit assessments will result in misleading information.

If students demonstrate achievement at any time that, in effect, renders past assessment information invalid, then you must drop the former assessment from the record and replace it with the new—even if the new information reflects a lower level of achievement. To do otherwise is to misrepresent that achievement.

Grades and Heterogeneous Grouping.   There is another difficult challenge to address: How do we grade different students in the same classroom who are striving to attain fundamentally different targets? As we try to mainstream special needs students and students from diverse cultural and linguistic backgrounds, this becomes a critical issue. It is critical because I think I just described *every* classroom.

In a classroom of mixed ability, for instance, one student might be working on basic math concepts, while another is moving toward pre-algebra. If both hit their respective targets, each deserves an A. But those A's mean fundamentally different things. How is someone reading the report cards of these two students to be made aware of this critical difference?

If we report the grade alone, they cannot. We are doomed to miscommunicate. In my opinion, this single problem renders simple letter grade-based communication systems inadequate to meet our communication needs in a standards-driven educational environment. The only solution I can find for this problem is to add greater detail to the reporting system, by identifying the achievement targets covered by the grade reported. Without that detail, we cannot communicate about individual differences in the grades assigned within the same classroom.

Grading on Status versus Improvement.   This one is just a bit tricky: Should students' report card grades be based on achievement status at the end of the grading period or how much they have improved during that period? To find resolution, we need to turn to our distinction between assessment *of* and *for* learning.

Remember, assessment *for* learning is all about helping students watch themselves improve. We always want them to be in touch with where they are now in relation to where they started and where we want them to be. We established early in the text that, during assessment *for* learning time, we want the gradebook closed. It is not about accountability. It is about growing.

But report card grading is all about accountability. It is assessment *of* learning time—show what you know. We want to report achievement status at a particular point in time—the end of the grading period. What proportion of achievement expectations did each student master?

First, we use assessment to support learning, then we use it to verify learning. Report card grading represents an instance of the latter.

If we introduce the idea of improvement into an assessment *of* learning context, things get confusing very quickly. For instance, the issues framed in the previous subsection on heterogeneity emerge. If students start at fundamentally different places and grow at fundamentally different rates, improvement profiles are going to vary all over the place. We introduce the risk of unfair sanctions for those who gain less because of their challenges. But these aren't the only students to be concerned about. Think also about the student who begins already at a high level, leaving less room to gain. How will we treat that student in this case?

The best practice, I believe, is to set expectations based on actual starting points for students; that is, on their IEP for students with special needs and on relevant state standards for all others. Then base report card grades on each student's approximation of those expectations at the end of the grading period.

Having so stipulated, let me now backtrack slightly. If you find evidence of learning in an assessment *for* learning context that reveals a new level of attainment than was shown on a previous assessment *of* learning, rely on that more current evidence in making the grading decision. The wall between assessment *of* and *for* learning need not be made of stone. But it does need to be pretty strong.

Time for Reflection

Given this guideline, if a special education student is "mainstreamed" into a regular classroom, is it possible for that student to receive an A on the report card—even though other students are hitting much higher targets? Collect your thoughts on this and we will return to it later.

What About Borderline Cases?   Another common problem arises when a particular student's academic average is literally right on the borderline between two grades and you just don't know which way to go. Some teachers allow factors unrelated to achievement to push the grade one way or the other. We addressed the unacceptability of that approach previously. A better way to determine such grades is to collect one or two significant pieces of achievement data during grading that overlap other assessments, thus double checking previous information about achievement. Hold these assessments in reserve, don't factor them into your grades. Then, if you need "swing votes," use them to help you decide which grade to assign. This keeps unrelated factors out of both the grading decision and the communication system.

Grading in a Cooperative Learning Context.   In cooperative learning environments, questions often arise about how to assign grades. The rule is this: Report card grades must provide dependable information about the actual achievement of the student to whom they are assigned. This means that, even in contexts where students cooperate during learning, at least some assessments must yield a clear and unencumbered indication of how well each individual student mastered the desired learning target. These are assessments *of* learning that happen after learning is supposed to have occurred. Only evidence derived in this way should contribute to determining a report card grade.

Dealing with Cheating.   Let me address this one more time: A student cheats on a test and, as punishment, is given a zero in the gradebook, to be averaged with other assessments to determine the semester grade.

     The problem in this instance is that the zero may systematically misrepresent that student's real achievement. *This is not acceptable under any circumstances.* Consequently, you must separate the grade and the discipline for cheating. You should retest the student to determine real levels of achievement and enter that retest score into your gradebook. Cheating should not be punished via grade reduction if you are to communicate accurately.

Awarding "Extra Credit."   Some teachers try to encourage extra effort on the part of their students by offering extra credit opportunities. You must be very careful of the message you send here. If grades are to reflect achievement, you must deliver the consistent message that *the more you learn, the better your grade.* If extra credit work is specifically designed to provide dependable information that students have learned more, then it should influence the grade assigned. But if students come to believe that merely doing the work, whether or not it results in greater learning, is sufficient to attain a higher grade, then it is counterproductive. To communicate effectively, grades must reflect the amount learned—not how much work was done to accomplish the learning.

The Matter of Unsound Grading Policies.   Sometimes, district policy can cause serious grading problems. For instance, some districts link grades to attendance. A policy might specify that more than five unexcused absences in a given grading period must result in an F for the student, regardless of actual achievement. In the case in which a student has mastered enough of the material to receive a higher grade, this policy leads to the purposeful misrepresentation of actual student achievement, and is unacceptable. Administrative policies that mislead anyone about academic achievement and that interfere with report card grading must be abandoned if we are to communicate accurately about student attainment.

Prior Notice.   One final critically important guideline to follow is to be sure all students know and understand in advance the procedures you will use to compute their grades. What assessments will you conduct, when, and how will you factor each into your grading? What are students' timelines, deadlines, and important responsibilities? If students know their responsibilities up front, they have a good chance of succeeding.

The Bottom Line

In developing sound grading practices for use in communicating about achievement, logic dictates that you start with a clear vision of targets, translate it into quality assessments, and always remain mindful of that big achievement picture for a given grading period. Then you must follow this simple rule (another part of the art of classroom assessment): *Grades must convey as accurate a picture of a student's real achievement as possible. Any practice that has the effect of misrepresenting actual achievement of agreed standards is unacceptable.* Figure 11.2 presents a summary of guidelines for avoiding the problems we have discussed here.

- Grade on achievement of prespecified targets only, not intelligence, effort, attitude, or personality.
- Always rely on the most current information available about student achievement.
- Devise grades that reflect achievement status with respect to preset targets rather than improvement.
- Decide borderline cases with additional information on achievement.
- Keep grading procedures separate from punishment.
- Change all policies that lead to miscommunication about achievement.
- Advise students of grading practices in advance.
- Add further detail to grade report when needed.
- Expect individual accountability for learning even in cooperative environments.
- Give credit for evidence of extra learning—not for doing extra work if it fails to result in extra learning.

Figure 11.2
Practical guidelines for avoiding common grading problems

Step 5: Converting Composite Achievement Scores to a Grade

Once you have attained an average or total set of points or some other overall index of student achievement for the grading period, you face the final and in some ways most difficult decision in your grading: What grade do you report?

Over the years, some districts and schools have opted simply to report that final achievement average as a percentage score. This has the benefit of permitting the record to convey the maximum amount of available information about a student's achievement. In doing so, no useful information is sacrificed by converting it to another scale. That's good.

But most districts require teachers to convert the academic achievement average or point total to a letter or number grade, from A to F or from 4.0 to 0. This has the effect of sacrificing a great deal of available information. For instance, a range of scores, say the 10 points between 90 to 100 percent, are all transformed into just 1 point on the grade scale, and in effect, are made equal.

The key question is, How do you convert a composite index of student achievement into an accurate report card grade? Traditionally, we have accomplished this in one of the following ways:

- Grading in terms of preset performance standards
- Assigning students grades according to their place in the rank order of class members

In an era of achievement or performance-driven education, only the first option makes sense. Let's explore each and see why.

Grading with Preset Standards

Grading in terms of preset standards says, Here are the assessments that represent the achievement targets; score at this level on them and this is the grade you will receive. A set of percentage cutoff scores is determined and all who score within certain ranges receive that designated grade:

90–100 = A

80–89 = B

70–79 = C

etc.

If two important conditions are met, this method maximizes the opportunity for success for students. Those conditions are (1) that students possess the prerequisites to master the required material, and (2) that assessments accurately represent the targets on which you will base the grade.

One advantage of this system is that the meaning of the grade is clearly couched in the attainment of intended achievement targets. Another is that it is computationally simple; you need only know how to compute percentages and averages. Still another strength is that grades can work effectively in the context of a continuous-progress curriculum. As students master prerequisites for later, more advanced work, as indicated by high grades, teachers can know that they are ready for the next stage. A fourth advantage is that grading in terms of preset standards increases the possibility that all students can succeed, if they achieve. And finally, from your perspective, if you as a teacher become more effective over time, greater student success will be reflected in a greater proportion of higher grades.

However, grading in terms of predetermined percentage cutoff scores is not without its limitations. For instance, the cutoff scores themselves are arbitrary. There is no substantive or scientific reason why 90 to 100 percent should be considered an A. This cutoff, and those used to assign other grades, represent social conventions adopted over decades. As a result, cutoffs vary from district to district, school to school, and even teacher to teacher. The range for an A in some places may be 94 to 100 percent, for example. Although these differences cannot be eliminated, we can acknowledge the lack of precision they imply. Just be sure everyone knows what conventions of communication (cutoff scores) you are using.

Comparative Grading, "On a Curve"

The tactic of assigning grades based on students' place in the rank order of achievement scores within a class is commonly referred to as "grading on a curve." In its classic application, the teacher uses the composite index of achievement for each student to rank students from the highest to the lowest score. Then, counting from the top, the teacher counts off 7 percent of the students on the list. These students receive As. Then the next 24 percent receive Bs, and so on down to the bottom 7 percent of students, who are assigned Fs.

Another variation on this method is to tally how many students attained each score and then to graph that distribution to find natural gaps between groups of scores that appear to permit division into groups of students to whom you can then assign different grades.

These ranking methods have the strength of yielding a grade that is interpreted in terms of group performance. They also have the effect of promoting competition among students: Students will know that their challenge is to outscore the others.

But in a context in which high achievement is the goal, the limitations of such a system become far more prominent than the strengths. The percentage of students receiving each grade is not a matter of science. Again, the cutoffs are arbitrary, and once grades are assigned and recorded on the transcript, no user of that grade information will necessarily know or understand the system of cutoffs used by the grader.

Besides, it's not clear what group should be ranked for grading purposes. Is it all students in the same class at the same time? In the same school? In the same district? In the same semester or year? Over the years? The answers to these questions can have major implications for the grade a student receives. For instance, if a student happens to fall into an extremely capable cohort, the results might be vastly different from how they would be if that same student just happens to be part of a generally lower-achieving group. Consequently, issues of fairness come into play.

Further, this system produces grades that are unrelated to real achievement. A class could, in fact, learn very little but the grade distribution could still convey the appearance that all had performed as expected. Alternatively, in a high-achieving group, some who actually learned a great deal but scored below the highest achievers might be doomed to receive a low grade.

And again, from your point of view as a teacher, even if your instruction improves markedly over the years, and helps more and more students master the important material, the distribution of grades will appear unchanged. That would frustrate anyone!

Teachers who develop success-oriented partnerships with students have no use for grading on a curve. They know they are not the best teacher they can be until every student attains an A by demonstrating the highest possible achievement on rigorous, high-quality assessments.

Report Cards That Deliver Greater Detail

As schools have become more standards driven in mission and in their planning and delivery of instruction, interest also has increased on reporting achievement results in greater detail. Here are some examples of how local educators are making that interest operational.

Standards-Based Reporting

One currently popular way to report greater detail about student achievement in preparation for conferences is to assemble an extended list of specific achievement standards or competencies and to indicate the extent to which students have mastered each. An example from Lincoln Elementary School, Madison, Wisconsin, appears in Figure 11.3. Note that each academic discipline is allocated one section of the report. Then each of these is subdivided into statements about student work. The teacher rates each, from "Excellent" to "Needs Improvement." This form presents over 80 different pieces of information about student achievement.

Another commonly used way of sharing greater detail about student achievement is to devise performance continua along which student achievement might vary. For example, part of the Juneau, Alaska, School District primary-grade reporting system

LINCOLN ELEMENTARY SCHOOL—GRADE 5

Student _____

Teacher _____ Principal _____ Quarter 2 3 4

E = Excellent   S = Satisfactory   P = Making Progress   N = Needs Improvement

READING PROGRAM

Materials Used: _____

___ Reads with understanding
___ Is able to write about what is read
___ Completes reading group work accurately and on time
___ Shows interest in reading

Reading Skills

___ Decodes new words
___ Understands new words

Independent Reading Level:
Below   At Grade Level   Above

LANGUAGE ARTS

___ Uses oral language effectively
___ Listens carefully
___ Masters weekly spelling

Writing Skills

___ Understands writing as process
___ Creates a rough draft
___ Makes meaningful revisions
___ Creates edited, legible final draft

Editing Skills

___ Capitalizes
___ Punctuates
___ Uses complete sentences
___ Uses paragraphs
___ Demonstrates dictionary skills

Writing Skill Level:
Below   At Grade Level   Above

MATHEMATICS

Problem Solving

___ Solves teacher-generated problems
___ Solves self-student-generated problems
___ Can create story problems

Interpreting Problems

___ Uses appropriate strategies
___ Can use more than one strategy
___ Can explain strategies in written form
___ Can explain strategies orally

Math Concepts

Understands Base Ten
Beginning Developing Sophisticated

Multiplication, Basic facts
Beginning Developing Sophisticated

2-digit Multiplication
Beginning Developing Sophisticated

Division
Beginning Developing Sophisticated

Geometry
Beginning Developing Sophisticated

Overall Math Skill Level:
Beginning Developing Sophisticated

Attitude/Work Skills

___ Welcomes a challenge
___ Persistence
___ Takes advantage of learning from others
___ Listens to others
___ Participates in discussion

It Figures
Is working on: _____

Goal:
Is working on achieving goal: _____

SOCIAL STUDIES

___ Understands subject matter
___ Shows curiosity and enthusiasm
___ Contributes to class discussions
___ Uses map skills
___ Demonstrates control of reading skills by interpreting text

Topics covered: Individual cultures, Columbus—first English colonies

SCIENCE

___ Shows curiosity about scientific subject matter
___ Asks good scientific questions
___ Shows knowledge of scientific method
___ Uses knowledge of scientific method to help set up and run experiment(s)
___ Makes good scientific observations
___ Has researched scientific topic(s)

I Wonder
Is currently working on _____

WORKING SKILLS

___ Listens carefully
___ Follows directions
___ Works neatly and carefully
___ Checks work
___ Completes work on time
___ Uses time wisely
___ Works well independently
___ Works well in a group
___ Takes risks in learning
___ Welcomes a challenge

HOMEWORK

___ Self-selects homework
___ Completes work accurately
___ Completes work on time

PRESENTATIONS/PROJECTS

HUMAN RELATIONS

___ Shows courtesy
___ Respects rights of others
___ Shows self-control
___ Interacts well with peers
___ Shows a cooperative and positive attitude in class
___ Shows a cooperative attitude when asked to work with other students
___ Is willing to help other students
___ Works well with other adults (subs, student teacher, parents, etc.)

ATTENDANCE

	1st	2nd	3rd	4th
Present				
Absent				
Tardy				

Placement for next year: _____

Figure 11.3

Reporting specific competencies attained

Source: From "Reporting Methods in Grades K–8" by K. Lake and K. Kafka, 1996 (p. 104). In T. Guskey (ed.), *ASCD Yearbook: Communicating Student Learning.* Alexandria, VA: Association for Supervision and Curriculum Development. Copyright 1996 by ASCD. Reprinted by permission of the publisher.

is depicted in Figure 11.4 detailing the reading continuum. Similar rating scales are available for writing targets. Note once again that specific proficiencies are listed. Then various levels of performance are described. It is along these continua that student achievement is profiled. One interesting feature of this reporting is the progress that can be reported during the year. This kind of reporting, backed up by a writing portfolio, can provide an excellent basis for student, parent, and/or teacher discussion at a conference.

Dealing with the Practicalities

As you consider these options, remember that their successful implementation requires that teachers collaborate in developing the achievement targets, creating the performance rating system, and implementing the communication system. It must represent the collective wisdom and teamwork of many experienced professionals. This backing and commitment is required to make such a-system work.

Another important key to successfully using this communication system is that teachers must be trained to make dependable ratings of student performance. This training takes time and effort. Resources must be allocated to make it possible. However, these costs are minimized to the extent that the teachers who are to use the system play a role in its development.

This system provides a high level of detail about student achievement. Although users report that the performance criteria become second nature and easy to rate with practice and experience, we would be naïve to think such records are easy to create and deliver at conference time. Because the report is detailed, communicating results can be time consuming.

Narrative Reporting

Another way to forge a stronger communication link between school and home is to use narrative descriptions of student learning. Narrative descriptions of student achievement must be carefully crafted to reflect a clear vision of achievement, clear criteria and standards, and a vivid sense of how this student relates to those expectations. Such written descriptions and samples of student work, in addition to grades and scores, communicate a great deal about student achievement.

Dealing with the Practicalities

The major drawback of these reports, obviously, is the time required to prepare them. High student–teacher ratios may render this option impractical for many teachers. However, if the narrative is intended for delivery to parents, could students and teachers work as partners to compose the letter? Shared work results in positive achievement for the student; shared planning and preparation of the narrative assists the teacher; open and effective student-involved communication goes to families; and everyone shares credit for doing a good job! Sounds like a win-win-win situation.

In addition, as always, we must center the narrative message on the relevant achievement targets. We must take care to transform those targets into rigorous assessments and write about specific achievement results. In other words, we must maintain

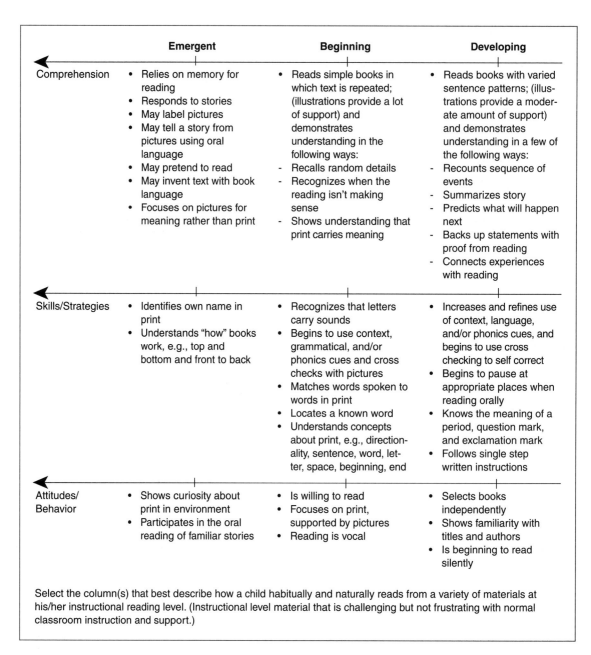

	Emergent	Beginning	Developing
Comprehension	• Relies on memory for reading • Responds to stories • May label pictures • May tell a story from pictures using oral language • May pretend to read • May invent text with book language • Focuses on pictures for meaning rather than print	• Reads simple books in which text is repeated; (illustrations provide a lot of support) and demonstrates understanding in the following ways: - Recalls random details - Recognizes when the reading isn't making sense - Shows understanding that print carries meaning	• Reads books with varied sentence patterns; (illustrations provide a moderate amount of support) and demonstrates understanding in a few of the following ways: - Recounts sequence of events - Summarizes story - Predicts what will happen next - Backs up statements with proof from reading - Connects experiences with reading
Skills/Strategies	• Identifies own name in print • Understands "how" books work, e.g., top and bottom and front to back	• Recognizes that letters carry sounds • Begins to use context, grammatical, and/or phonics cues and cross checks with pictures • Matches words spoken to words in print • Locates a known word • Understands concepts about print, e.g., directionality, sentence, word, letter, space, beginning, end	• Increases and refines use of context, language, and/or phonics cues, and begins to use cross checking to self correct • Begins to pause at appropriate places when reading orally • Knows the meaning of a period, question mark, and exclamation mark • Follows single step written instructions
Attitudes/Behavior	• Shows curiosity about print in environment • Participates in the oral reading of familiar stories	• Is willing to read • Focuses on print, supported by pictures • Reading is vocal	• Selects books independently • Shows familiarity with titles and authors • Is beginning to read silently

Select the column(s) that best describe how a child habitually and naturally reads from a variety of materials at his/her instructional reading level. (Instructional level material that is challenging but not frustrating with normal classroom instruction and support.)

Figure 11.4

Juneau primary reading continuum

Source: From the Juneau, Alaska, School District. Reprinted by permission.

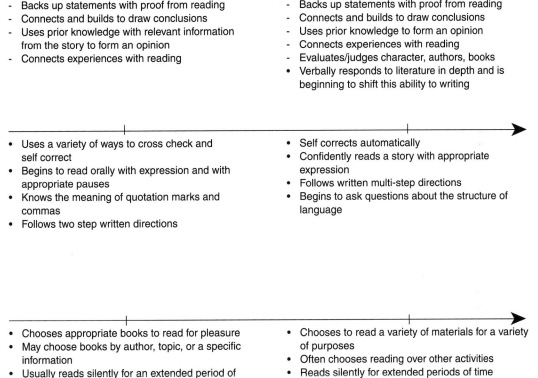

Expanding	Transitional
• Reads books with long descriptions, challenging vocabulary; (illustrations provide low support) and demonstrates understanding in several of the following ways: - Remembers sequence of events - Summarizes story - Predicts what will happen next - Backs up statements with proof from reading - Connects and builds to draw conclusions - Uses prior knowledge with relevant information from the story to form an opinion - Connects experiences with reading	• Reads books with long descriptions, challenging vocabulary (illustrations provide very little or no support) and demonstrates understanding in most of the following ways: - Remembers sequence of events - Summarizes story - Predicts what will happen next - Backs up statements with proof from reading - Connects and builds to draw conclusions - Uses prior knowledge to form an opinion - Connects experiences with reading - Evaluates/judges character, authors, books • Verbally responds to literature in depth and is beginning to shift this ability to writing
• Uses a variety of ways to cross check and self correct • Begins to read orally with expression and with appropriate pauses • Knows the meaning of quotation marks and commas • Follows two step written directions	• Self corrects automatically • Confidently reads a story with appropriate expression • Follows written multi-step directions • Begins to ask questions about the structure of language
• Chooses appropriate books to read for pleasure • May choose books by author, topic, or a specific information • Usually reads silently for an extended period of time, sometimes vocalizing when text is difficult • Reads lengthier material	• Chooses to read a variety of materials for a variety of purposes • Often chooses reading over other activities • Reads silently for extended periods of time • Recommends books to others

Figure 11.4
(continued)

a clear focus on achievement. To use this option productively, users must regard these reports as far more than "free writing time," when they can say whatever comes to mind about the student. The issue in narrative reports is, What does it mean to be academically successful, and how did this student do in relation to those expectations?

The only way this communication can become practical for a teacher is with careful planning and record keeping. At the time of the writing, all relevant information to be factored into the report must be readily available. The framework for the report must be completely spelled out. And to the extent possible, modern information processing technology should be brought to bear. For example, you might develop a template for narrative reporting on your personal computer. Within this general outline, then, you might merely need to enter essential details.

Remember, however, that narrative reporting places a premium on being able to write well. Teachers or students who have difficulty communicating in writing will find a narrative system frustrating to use and will not use it well.

Continuous-Progress Reporting

Teachers in Victoria, Australia, have devised yet another reporting scheme that develops a continuous record of student progress through a series of specifically defined and progressively linked targets (Ministry of Education and Training, Victoria, 1991). They call these records *profiles* and describe them as follows:

> Profiles are a means of reporting on a student's progress and achievement in key areas of learning. Profiles consist of a series of short descriptive statements, called indicators, arranged in nine levels of achievement called bands. These describe, in order of difficulty, significant skills and knowledge that students must learn to become proficient. A student's progress can be charted over these bands. English Profiles show student progress and achievement in the key areas of reading, writing and spoken language. (p. 7)

The spoken language bands are identified in Figure 11.5, from A at the beginning to I on the high-performance end. Figure 11.6 illustrates one parental reporting form used, the English Profile, focusing on spoken language bands B and C. Note that it highlights the band the student is working on at the time of reporting, and includes prior and following proficiencies for context. Teachers enter brief comments for the record regarding student progress and achievement.

Dealing with the Practicalities

This reporting overcomes some, but not all, of the shortcomings of the systems described previously. First, it minimizes the amount of narrative teachers must enter. This saves time. Second, it reduces the range of achievement targets and levels over which teachers must comment, focusing on the particular forms of achievement students are working on. This, too, saves time. Third, a concrete record of progress is generated, with cumulative reports of bands of achievement. This helps with interpretation. Fourth, this is quite a comprehensive and carefully articulated communication system, with the span of achievement covered ranging from elementary levels through high school. This makes the system valuable in contexts where students are expected to make continuous progress in acquiring an interlaced series of outcomes across grade levels.

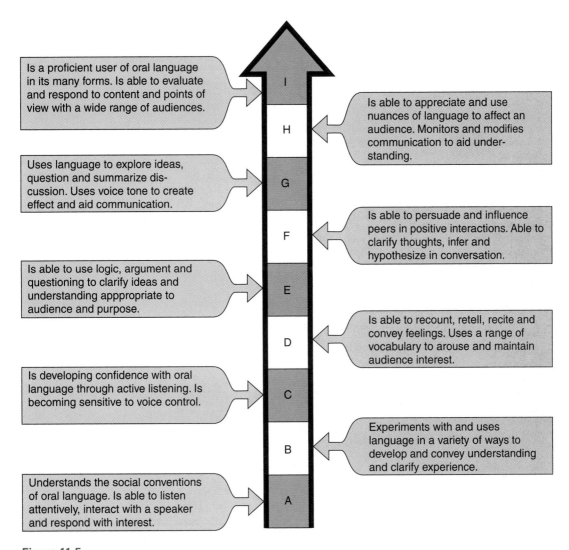

Figure 11.5

The spoken language bands

Source: From *English Profiles Handbook* (n.p.) by the Schools Program Division, Ministry of Education and Training, Victoria, Australia, 1991. Reprinted by permission of the publisher.

But there remains the challenge of defining, sharing, and being able to dependably assess the various levels of achievement reflected in the bands. These will take considerable investment. Their development and implementation across the curriculum requires that teachers meet across grade levels from primary grades through high school to articulate a continuous-progress curriculum, to divide up responsibility for helping students make smooth transitions through the various levels of proficiency.

But imagine the nature and quality of the open, inclusive, student-involved communication environment we could achieve with such bands in place and with

ENGLISH PROFILE—SPOKEN LANGUAGE

School _____   Class _____

Name _____

Language Spoken at Home _____

Teacher's Assessment
Contexts and Comments   Date

SPOKEN LANGUAGE BAND B

Use of Oral Language
Makes short announcements clearly. Tells personal anecdotes in discussion. Retells a story heard in class, preserving the sequence of events. Accurately conveys a verbal message to another person. Responds with facial expressions. Responds with talk when others initiate conversation. Initiates conversation with peers. Holds conversation with familiar adults. Asks what unfamiliar words mean. Uses talk to clarify ideas or experience.

Features of Oral Language
Reacts (smiles, laughs, etc.) to absurd word substitutions. Demonstrates an appreciation of wit. Reacts (smiles, laughs) to unusual features of language (such as rhythm, alliteration or onomatopoeia).

SPOKEN LANGUAGE BAND C

Use of Oral Language
Makes verbal commentary during play or other activities with concrete objects.

Speaks confidently in formal situations (e.g., assembly, report to the class).

Explains ideas clearly in discussion.

Discusses information heard (e.g., dialogue, news item, report).

Based on consideration of what has already been said, offers personal opinions.

Asks for repetition, restatement, or general explanation to clarify meaning.

Features of Oral Language
Sequences a presentation in a logical order.

Gives instructions in a concise and understandable manner.

Reads aloud with expression, showing awareness of rhythm and tone.

Modulates voice for effect.

Nods, looks at speaker when others initiate talk.

Figure 11.6

English Profile—Spoken Language

Source: From *English Profiles Handbook* (n.p.) by the Schools Program Division, Ministry of Education and Training, Victoria, Australia, 1991. Reprinted by permission of the publisher.

everyone able to accurately assess student progress through them. Imagine the power of a portfolio system (including extensive use of student self-reflection on their improvement as achievers) when used in conjunction with such a continuous-progress curriculum. And finally, imagine the learning power brought to bear if the *student* is the primary record keeper.

Summary: Communicating with Report Cards

As in all aspects of assessment addressed in this book, the key to effective report cards is for you, the teacher, to be master of the material your students are to learn. This permits you to translate your clear and appropriate targets into rigorous, high-quality assessments, which, in turn, you can convert to information that you may report in detail or combine into fair and equitable grades.

The reference point for interpreting a report card grade should always be the specific material to be learned, *and nothing else.* Students deserve to know in advance how you will accomplish this in their class, and they need to know the standards you expect them to meet. If you are assessing characteristics other than achievement, you must follow appropriate rules of sound assessment, and should report results separately from achievement grades.

Teachers must carefully plan for gathering information for report card grades. In times when grades served only to rank students, it didn't seem to matter what those grades actually meant. Today, however, we need to produce meaningful communication about student attainment of ascending levels of ever-more-advanced competencies.

This requires a clearly stated set of grading priorities. These achievement expectations are most productively set when a faculty meets across grade levels and across classrooms within grade levels to determine the building blocks of ultimate competence and to integrate them into their classrooms, systematically dividing up responsibility for learning.

You must, however, take responsibility for assembling a strategic assessment plan for generating the information to determine which of your students attain the desired targets. You must then translate that plan into quality assessments throughout the grading period.

As you conduct assessments and accumulate results, you must take care to record as much detail about student achievement as is available. To be sure, nearly all of this useful detail ultimately will be sacrificed in our obsession to describe the rich complexity of student achievement in the form of a single letter grade. But don't give up the detail until you absolutely must. And when report card grading time arrives, share as much of the detail as you can with your students, so they understand what is behind the single little symbol that appears on the report card. Then boil the richness of your detail away only grudgingly.

Remember two final guidelines: (1) You need not assign a grade to absolutely everything students produce. It's acceptable to sometimes simply use words and pictures to convey your judgment. Allow time to learn (explore and grow) in between grades—assessment *for* learning. (2) Your challenge is not to rank students in terms of their achievement. Although not all students will learn the same amounts or at the same rates and a ranking may naturally result from your work, the student's next teacher needs more information than a place in the rank order to know what to do next to assist. Remember, as teachers, our goal is to communicate in ways that help students learn and feel in control of their own success.

When you need to communicate greater detail when using a report card–based communication system, consider the alternatives of sharing your information about student achievement via a checklist of competencies attained, a written narrative report, or a continuous-progress reporting system.

Final Chapter Reflection

1. *What are the three most important new insights to come to you as a result of your study of this chapter?*
2. *Which of your previous questions about assessment can you now answer based on your study of this chapter?*
3. *What new questions have come to mind as a result of your study of this chapter that you hope to have answered as your study continues?*

Practice with Chapter 11 Ideas

1. Consider the entries in the gradebook from Chris Brown's science class shown in Table 11.1. Note particularly the information collected in the Miscellaneous category as footnoted, the manner in which missing items are dealt with, and the grading scale used. Please answer the following questions:
   a. Do the final letter grades awarded fairly reflect the results from which they are derived? Why or why not?
   b. What grades would you assign for each student?
   c. What grading issues arise from this case, both with respect to sound grading practices and the principles of effective communication?
   d. What should Chris do in the future to avoid these problems?
2. Please read the following newspaper story. Using the principles and guidelines discussed in this chapter, identify as many apparent violations in achievement reporting referenced in this editorial as

you can. What remedy would you recommend for each suspected violation?

Report Card Stew—Case Study

By Linda Cagnetti, Cincinnati Enquirer, Forum, Sunday, November 30, 1997*

If men are from Mars and women are from Venus, the men and women who create report cards must be from a more distant galaxy. As some of the report cards reviewed in our Forum section today demonstrate, schools and parents are sometimes not on the same planet at grading time.

First of all, they're no longer called report cards; they're "progress reports." Students don't pass or fail they are now "recommended for promotion" or "assigned to the same level." Ds and Fs are replaced with "areas of concern" or "needs

*Copyright 1997 Cincinnati Enquirer. Reprinted by permission.

Table 11.1

Gradebook page

NAME	LAB REPORTS										TOTAL LABS	TEST/EXAMS			TOTAL TESTS	MISCELLANEOUS*					TOTAL MISC.	FINAL TOTAL	FINAL GRADE	
																1	2	3	4	5			%	Letter
Out of	10	10	10	10	10	10	10	10	10	10	100	50	50	100	200	20	20	20	20	20	100	400	%	Letter
Robin	6	6	6	6	5	6	6	7	6	6	60	33	39	81	153	15	15	12	0	10	52	265	66	C
Kay	2	3	5	5	6	6	7	8	9	10	61	11	29	86	126	15	13	18	10	10	66	253	63	C
Marg	10	10	A	10	10	10	A	10	A	A	60	50	A	100	150	0	0	0	0	15	15	225	56	D
Jim	9	8	9	8	9	10	9	10	8	9	89	24	24	49	97	20	17	17	20	20	94	280	70	B
Peter	10	10	9	8	8	7	7	6	6	5	79	45	36	32	113	20	10	15	10	5	60	252	63	C
Lorna	10	10	10	10	10	10	10	10	10	10	100	32	29	59	120	20	20	20	20	20	100	320	80	A
John	8	8	8	8	9	9	8	9	10	8	84	32	30	57	119	20	8	7	0	5	40	243	61	C

A = Absent = 0 (for Lab Reports and Tests/Exams)

*Miscellaneous: 1–Attendance; 2–Care of Equipment; 3–Attitude/Participation; 4–Notebook; 5–Reading Reports (4 × 5 marks)

Letter Grade Legend (in Ontario): A = 80%–100%; B = 70%–79%; C = 60%–69%; D = 50%–59%; F = 0%–49%

Source: From How to Grade for Learning: Linking Grades to Standards, by Ken O'Connor. © 2002 by SkyLight Professional Development. Reprinted by permission of LessonLab, a Pearson Education Company, www.lessonlab.com.

317

more time to develop." Behavior is now "social habits."

Most of these kinder-gentler report cards are computer generated, with check-marked "comments" such as "pleasure to have in class," or "uses self control." None look alike; each district and sometimes each school, designs its own.

Reactions from parents vary. Some say they're much better than the old-fashioned, too-simple ABC versions. Others find them ridiculous. Most parents are simply bewildered.

"I don't have a clue what half of this means," one parent told us. "I'm not sure how my child is doing, but, hey, they say this is progress."

Kentucky Enquirer *columnist Karen Samples recently wrote about the [recently]-reformed report cards from a dozen or so districts in [several] counties, along with [traditional] ones. It's quite a smorgasbord. Some cards are easy to understand with both letter and number grades; others are overwhelming and mystifying.*

Schools are working hard to communicate more to parents about new standards. Good idea. But more doesn't automatically translate to better. For example, the common-sense alarm buzzes when you read that an elementary student is graded on 72 different skills, and the explanations are so fuzzy that a college-educated parent is befuddled.

Smoke-and-mirror report cards are another example of the gap between what education reformers believe is important and what ordinary people want. No wonder Joe and Jane Public don't feel public schools belong to them anymore.

Student report cards are the most basic and precious link between schools and *parents. When they're reduced to meaningless symbols and babble, educators deserve an old-fashioned, unequivocal F for failure.*

3. A group of teachers, school administrators, and parents attended a workshop on grading. A parent asked if the educators in the room would explain what's in a letter grade of B on a report card and how it differs from an A or C. Participants were asked to answer the following specific questions:

   ● What should a grade tell us about students?
   ● What are the factors that are actually used to determine students' grades?

Here are the brainstormed answers of the educators present:

What should grades tell us about students?	What factors are actually included in grades?
What things they know and can do	Attendance and lateness
Why they have improved during the marking period	Behavior/attitude
What their strengths are and the things they need to work on	End of marking period test scores
Whether they can solve real-world problems	Homework
What level their work is	Family status
How well they behave	Ability
Whether they are ready to move on	Appearance
How they help one another	Personality
Whether they've reached a standard	Teacher attitude toward the student
How well they can apply what they know	Portfolios

Answer the following questions:

1. Do you agree with the first list—what grades should tell us?

2. Would this list of factors actually provide the information needed to tell us what these educators believe grades should tell us? Think particularly about sound assessment practices, sound grading practices, and effective communication as you answer.

3. What changes are needed in each list to form a foundation for effective communication about achievement? Why?

Chapter 12

Communicating with Portfolios

CHAPTER FOCUS

This chapter answers the following guiding question:

How can my students and I communicate effectively about their achievement using portfolios—that is, through collecting samples of their work and their own self-reflections about the quality of that work?

From your study of this chapter, you will understand the following:

1. The power of a portfolio communication system resides in its potential for student involvement in record keeping and communication.

2. Portfolios come in many forms, all of which can serve you well if you keep your purpose in mind as you select from among the options.

3. The challenge of portfolios resides in the need to weave them into day-to-day classroom practice in practical ways. But careful planning can remove any roadblocks.

Portfolio Defined

A *portfolio* is a collection of student work assembled to provide a representation of student achievement. The representation conveyed, as you might anticipate, is a function of the context: the purpose for assessing and communicating and the achievement target(s) about which we wish to communicate. Thus, the range of possible applications of portfolios in the classroom is wide indeed, as you shall see in this chapter.

The best depiction of the portfolio concept that I have seen is as follows (adapted from Arter & Spandel, 1992, p. 36):

A *student portfolio* is "a purposeful collection of student work that tells a story about the student's efforts, progress, or achievement" in one or more academic disciplines. The portfolio's communication potential and instructional usefulness are enhanced when students participate in selecting content; when the selection of material to include follows predetermined guidelines; when criteria are available for judging the merit of the work collected; and when students regularly reflect on the evolving quality of their work.

Just as artists assemble portfolios of their work to convey their talents and journalists assemble samples of their work to represent their writing capabilities, so too can our students collect examples of their work to tell their school achievement story.

The essential difference between report card grades and portfolios as ways of communicating is that, with grades, we aspire to the most efficient way to share information and care little about details, whereas, with portfolios, we abandon concern for efficiency and seek to maintain the detail. Each can meet the information needs of intended users depending on the context.

What Role for Portfolios?

Based on our discussion of report card grades in the previous chapter, it should be clear to you that we condense a great deal of information into one single little symbol when we assign them. Over an entire semester or year, as teachers, we gather a great deal of detail about student achievement. Visualize a large ball full of information on student mastery of content, reasoning proficiencies, skills, and product development capabilities. To assign a grade, we must force that big ball through a narrow-diameter pipe. When it comes out the other end as an A, B, or C, all of the detail is gone.

But here's the problem: some decision makers need that detail to do their jobs—to make their decisions. For instance, let's say I am a teacher receiving new students on their journey to excellence as math problem solvers and all I receive from their previous teacher is a letter grade next to the word "Math" on a report card. That level of specificity tells me nothing about each student's strengths or weaknesses. Based on the report card grade alone, I have no idea what comes next. I need greater detail in this communication.

Or say I'm a parent. My ability to understand, appreciate, and support my child's growth is enhanced if I have access to details regarding that growth, or its lack. A single report card grade only tells me a small part of the story.

This is where portfolios can help. Typically, they contain details in the form of examples of student work with student reflections on the quality of that work. As a teacher or parent, if I can study those work samples, read the student's reflections, and have that student talk me through the portfolio, describing growth during the past year, I get a clear view of that individual's growth and current needs.

In this chapter, we will explore this communication option, with the goal of having you know and understand the following:

1. Why this record-keeping and communication option has become so popular
2. The challenges that accompany the use of portfolios
3. The active ingredients that go into a sound portfolio system
4. The range of possible uses of portfolios to both improve communication and enhance student achievement
5. How to manage many of the practicalities of using portfolios in the classroom

The Emergence of Portfolios

The portfolio idea as it is being played out in schools these days brings with it a mixed bag of strengths, limitations, and possible applications. Without question, it is a very powerful and popular example of inclusive, student-involved communication at work in the classroom. By the same token, portfolios can lead to counterproductive and frustrating work for both students and teachers if we don't use them wisely. Let's consider these pluses and minuses.

Benefits for Teachers and Students

If done well, portfolios permit teachers to do the following:

- Track student achievement over time to reveal improvement or the lack thereof. In this sense, they can be diagnostic.
- Afford students an excellent context within which to take responsibility for maintaining and tracking their own files and records of achievement. This assessment *for* learning application teaches a critical life skill.
- Help students learn to reflect on and see their own improvement as achievers. This involvement, as we have established previously, has real motivational power.
- Provide important insights into students' academic self-concepts, academic interests, and sense of their own needs.
- Provide excellent opportunities for students to practice their reasoning proficiencies, analyze their own work, compare work over time, draw inferences about their growth or needs, and learn evaluative or critical thinking skills.
- Document student attainment of required district or state standards in an assessment *of* learning context.

For all of these reasons, teachers experienced in using portfolios find them to be engaging for both themselves and their students.

The Challenges

With all of this encouragement, it's tempting simply to dive in and start developing and using student portfolios. But wait, there's more. Portfolio specialists Spandel and Culham (1995) remind us of three myths about portfolios that you would do well to keep in mind as you study this idea for your classroom.

Myth 1: Creating Portfolios Automatically Makes You a Better Teacher
They advise us that it's not that simple. Without a student-involved assessment environment in place, that is, without a strong foundation underpinning the portfolio structure, this way of communicating will not automatically lead to better teaching.

That means we must start with clear targets, organized for continuous progress and feeding into quality assessments (i.e., sound sampling of skills and control for bias and distortion), with students as full partners in assessing and assuming responsibility for their own learning. Only then can portfolios help you become a better teacher.

Myth 2: Portfolios Are Easy to Manage if You're an Organized Person
Being organized helps, to be sure. Over time, teachers report that they become more organized about their portfolios and therefore more comfortable using them. But the lessons they learn along the way are critical to their success. Even if you're organized, it's hard work. It takes time and patience to work into this idea. If you have difficulties early on, it is not because you are disorganized. As one teacher put it, when she first started implementing this idea in her classroom, her students "had portfolios." Now, years later, her students "do portfolios" in her classroom (Austin, 1994). By the time you finish this chapter, you will know what she means and understand what it takes to use them successfully.

Myth 3: Portfolios Make Learning Easy for Students
"On the contrary," Spandel and Culham (1995) tell us, "portfolios offer students a whole new set of challenges: planning, time management, comparing, analyzing, and learning to understand how to learn. What is equally true is that students can potentially gain great insight from the experience, insight equivalent to the effort they put into it" (p. 14). Our challenge as teachers is the same in this case as it has been throughout: Help students see the personal value of assuming responsibility for their learning.

Maintaining Perspective

The immense popularity of portfolios and their rapid evolution have led in some instances to an unfortunate narrowing of perspectives. As you think about and plan for possible applications of portfolios in your classroom, be cautious of the following perspectives.

Portfolios and Performance Assessment

It is common to find the concepts of "portfolios" and "performance assessment" closely linked in current professional literature. When artists assemble portfolios of their work, they collect the artistic products they have created. When journalists collect samples of their articles, they too gather their work into a coherent whole. These are products. That's one kind of performance assessment. Thus, it is tempting to speak of a portfolio as relying only on performance assessment as the source of its information of student achievement. Resist that temptation. You have four forms of assessment in your repertoire: selected response, essay, performance assessment, and personal communication. We have said consistently that they are all potentially valuable contributors to the story we tell about student achievement. They all can appear in portfolios. Additionally, portfolios can hold many other types of artifacts, such as photos, letters, rough drafts, schedules, lists (such as of books read), and other evidence relevant to telling a complete story of achievement status or growth.

Time for Reflection

What would you include if you were to develop a portfolio that told the story of who you are as an educator right now—say, as a job application portfolio?

Portfolios and Life Skills

The popular culture associated with portfolios often requires that they focus on "real-life skills" that stretch beyond the academic proficiencies of school. Some hold that portfolios should be married to the concept of "authentic" assessment of skills required in the adult world.

Be advised that this is far from the only or even the most valuable application of portfolios. Opportunities abound in classrooms for portfolios to tell powerful stories about emerging academic proficiencies, such as math problem solving, beginning writing skills (including spelling and grammar), social interaction skills, knowledge and understanding of science, and others. These are the academic foundations that ultimately will underpin students' life skills and for this reason they are important. Portfolios can contribute to student success in developing these too, inside the academic world.

The Need for Accurate Assessments

The trend that concerns me most about portfolios is the tendency of many users to think that, just because they're using portfolios, they're assured a rich and accurate portrait of student achievement. I have met teachers, administrators, and policy makers who seem to feel that the mere presence of portfolios somehow ensures quality schools, regardless of how well they implement the idea. This is potentially very dangerous. Because any portfolio is really a collection of relevant artifacts, each provides part of the mosaic of student achievement. For this reason, *it is essential that each contributing assessment provide valid and reliable information* about the part of the story it is intended to represent. Just as high-quality assessments give meaning to report card grades, so too do they permit portfolios to tell rich and compelling stories about student academic growth and development.

The Keys to Successful Use

First and foremost, you and your students must concentrate on building your portfolios in ways that account for the necessary conditions for effective communication that we framed in Chapter 9. This aspect of portfolio construction underpins *every* aspect of their purpose and use.

Sharp Focus on Targets

The effective use of portfolios requires that we apply them in a disciplined way. I have come in contact with several local and even state education agencies that like the portfolio idea so much that they simply order teachers to start one for each student. Envision what I call the universal, all-encompassing, "mega-portfolio." Starting in primary grades, teachers accumulate evidence of achievement. Then each teacher along the way adds more, as the child's school story unfolds. Visualize a file folder that then becomes a file drawer, then a file cabinet, and then a closet full of material. Soon we've evolved to a room-sized collection, leading ultimately to the student driving a tractor-trailer across the stage at high school graduation!

Sound foolish? Of course it does. And I take little solace from technology buffs who tell us not to worry about volume of "stuff" because we can digitize it all and place it on a computer chip the size of your thumbnail. Imagine an "electro-mega-portfolio," still completely devoid of purpose. This lack of focus arises from a lack of understanding or discipline on the part of those who would conceive of such plans. If we start with no focus, no story to tell, no purpose, no clear achievement targets, we end up with a useless and unmanageable portfolio.

To understand how to avoid this, we must visualize a different scenario. We must begin each portfolio application with a clear sense of the target(s) in question. During their schooling, students will develop and use many portfolios, each associated with a different target. Some will reflect math competence, some reading and writing, and others science skills. Some will be more structured, some less. Some will be more student involving, some less. Some will deal with knowledge targets, others with reasoning, still others with skills or products. Their content will vary. But we hope what will remain in students' minds is a sense that they are in control of their increasing academic competence—a strong and growing academic self-concept. My vision has teachers using portfolios flexibly and opportunistically to communicate information about student achievement and develop a sense of academic well-being. Over the years, most of these portfolio collections will end up in students' hands after serving their purpose. But everyone of them will focus on its own unique and crystal clear set of achievement expectations.

Accurate Assessments

By this point, we don't need to add detail about how quality assessments form the foundation of an effective communication system. We have long since defined our five quality control criteria and discussed how to meet those standards. As we accumulate evidence of student achievement in a portfolio, we must continue to meet those standards. We can use selected response assessments, if they fit the context, to collect some of that information. Essay and performance assessments obviously represent viable options, too, in the hands of qualified users.

I know of a school in which teachers record students struggling to speak a new language and then continue to collect recorded segments on that same audiocassette over the years as each student's proficiency increases. They wrap the cassettes as gifts and present them to their students at graduation along with their diploma. If they have developed high-quality, student-involved assessments, students not only hear themselves improving over time, but also can articulate precisely what it is that makes each new addition to the recording better than those that preceded it. Quality assessments placed in student hands encourage achievement.

Form Follows Purpose

To merge effectively into instruction, portfolios must be specifically designed to serve a purpose. There needs to be a reason for telling the story. Thus, we must plan to collect materials that can tell that story. Those plans provide students and teachers with specific guidelines for selecting work for the portfolio. Guidelines will vary according to the purpose and target. Spandel and Culham (1995) provide us with a productive way to think of this by suggesting several structures for portfolios. These are not mutually exclusive categories, and you may blend them to fit the occasion. These structures are the celebration portfolio, the time sequence or growth portfolio, the project portfolio, and the status report portfolio.

The Celebration Portfolio

A portfolio can be used as a keepsake, which you invite students to create as a personal collection of favorite works and special academic mementos. They might use this to communicate to families the things they are most proud of or to show positive examples of their learning experiences or classroom activities.

In this case, students' guidelines for portfolio selection are driven by this purpose: What do I think is really special about my work and why? This is a wonderful place for young students to begin their portfolio development experience by just collecting favorite pieces of work. They may then begin to categorize and cull for the really special works. The only evaluations are made by the students, according to their own vision of what's "special." No one else's standards have a place here. This is critically important.

Students can use this experience to begin to identify the attributes of special classroom work and to generate personal insights about their own meaning of quality. Over time and through interaction with us, their teachers, and with classmates. We can help them expand their sense of what represents "good work." In this sense, the celebration portfolio can begin to put students in touch with their own strengths and interests, and can help them learn to make choices.

Time for Reflection

If you did a celebration portfolio of your years as an educator, what might you put in? List some things you would enter. Next to each, specify why you would include it. Then, try to capture in a few sentences the story you are trying to tell.

The Growth Portfolio

Another reason to build a portfolio is to reveal changes or accomplishments in a student's academic performance over time. Two classroom applications of this idea warrant discussion, the growth portfolio and the project portfolio.

In the growth portfolio, the creator (storyteller) collects samples of work over time to show how proficiency has changed. When this is the purpose, guidelines for selection dictate assembling multiple indicators of the same proficiency, such as samples of writing or selections of artwork. As you recall, in the opening scenario in Chapter 1, Emily shared a sample of her writing from the beginning of the year for the school board to review and critique. Then she wowed them with another sample from the end of the year that revealed how much more proficient she had become. These writing samples came from her writing portfolio—a growth portfolio.

In this case, the evaluation criteria need to be held constant over time. Emily was able to discuss specific improvements in her work included in her portfolio over the year because the writing criteria—word choice, organization, sentence structure, voice, and so on—remained the same for each writing activity. This gave her a yardstick by which to see her writing progress to higher levels of competence. The motivational power of a growth portfolio can be immense when students get to see their own improvement.

The Project Portfolio

Alternatively, the storyteller might depict the completion of steps in a project conducted over time. When this is the purpose, guidelines for selection dictate that the storyteller provide evidence of having completed all necessary steps in a quality manner. For example, students completing a major science project might show how they arrived at a hypothesis, how they assembled the apparatus for gathering the needed data, how they conducted the tests, the test results, and their analysis and interpretation of those results. A project portfolio is an ideal format to use to describe such work carried out over an extended period.

The evaluative judgments made in this case are based on two sets of performance criteria. The first reflects the steps students must have completed within a specified time frame. These typically provide highly structured guidelines for what to collect as proof of work completion. They teach students lessons about the necessity of planning a task and sticking to a timeline. You might also hold students accountable for periodically reviewing progress with you.

The second set focuses on the quality of work completed at each step along the way. These, of course, demand that students not merely provide evidence of having done the activity, but also provide evidence that they did it well.

One final comment regarding growth and project portfolios: The span of time covered can range from a brief several-day project to one lasting a full year or longer, depending on the context. These are very flexible.

The Status Report Portfolio

Yet another story to tell by means of a portfolio can be that of having met certain established academic standards. In this instance, the student must make a case within the portfolio for having attained certain levels of proficiency. Therefore, the intended achievement targets determine the guidelines for content selection.

Several applications of this portfolio are relevant in school. As students progress through a continuous-progress curriculum in math, for example, you might maintain a portfolio depicting each student's current achievement status. Then at any point in time, decision makers could check this record and know what comes next. In this case, when a sample of student work is collected that reveals a new high level of achievement, the old evidence previously held in the portfolio—now outdated—would be discarded. If there is any portfolio format that might accompany a student across grade levels over the years, this is it.

In another application, in some districts students present a portfolio of evidence of having attained certain essential proficiencies in order to qualify for graduation. Indeed, some states require such evidence to earn a certificate of mastery.

In a much simpler context, we might ask students to assemble evidence of having mastered all requirements for completing a particular course. Or, we might review a status report portfolio to make a course placement decision, such as, What is the next natural course in this student's progression of math instruction?

In all cases, the guidelines for selecting material will probably be highly structured and driven by specific academic requirements that provide evidence that students have mastered prerequisites and are ready to move on.

Summary of Purposes and Portfolio Designs

Clearly, the concept of a "mega-portfolio" (a monster file of academic stuff devoid of purpose and structure) makes no sense in assessing student achievement or helping students succeed. However, if we formulate careful guidelines for selection around focused stories to tell, we can use portfolios advantageously to integrate our students deeply into teaching and learning.

We can use them with celebration portfolios in early grades to start students evaluating their own work. We can also help students track their own academic development over time. Sometimes this might center on the growth of a particular set of proficiencies. Other times, it might track the completion of a set of required projects. Either way, the student's achievements are the focus of the story.

And finally, we can tap the portfolio idea to describe students' achievement status—standards met, courses completed, and requirements satisfied, descriptions that inform our decisions about appropriate next steps.

The possible combinations and permutations of these portfolio options in the classroom are seemingly infinite. Also remember, both the time span covered and amount of material collected for any particular portfolio may vary from a little to a great deal, depending on the learning context and the teaching strategy, thus making this a flexible communication approach.

Think Assessment *for* Learning: Criteria for Judging Quality

As you well know by now, we need to establish criteria by which to evaluate students' progress, whether judging the merit of writing, charting the expansion of scientific knowledge, or recording increased proficiency in speaking a foreign language. Portfolios can handle a range of target possibilities, relying on a variety of assessment formats.

To illustrate, if a student-teacher team decides that the best evidence of student attainment of a particular target is a score on a multiple-choice test, then the criteria used to judge merit is a high score on the test. If an essay test most accurately reflects the target, then once again, a traditional test score provides the needed information. However, with performance assessments, the applied criteria must reflect proficiency on the skills of interest or reflect the extent to which the student has met quality product standards.

Consequently, we must decide in advance and share with our students how we and they will judge merit. I continue to press the point that students can hit any target that they can see and that holds still for them. Obviously, this is equally important with portfolios, and is the essential way to link assessment and instruction.

By the way, some teachers have found it productive to develop and share with their students criteria for judging the merit of the portfolio as a whole. These often center on such attributes as whether the evidence collected reflects the right target(s), whether the evidence shows growth, the organization of the evidence and self-reflections, and the quality of the self-reflections. In fact, one teacher I know begins the year with students analyzing portfolios of varying quality, so they can play a role in establishing the criteria for evaluating the portfolios they will build during the coming year.

Involving Students in Selecting Portfolio Items

Let's say you are assembling a job application portfolio. Clearly it would be important for you to take responsibility for selecting the material to be included, for two reasons. First, you know yourself best and can best ensure the telling of a complete and accurate story. Second, selecting the content allows you to present yourself in the most positive light called for in this competitive situation.

Our students are driven, Covington (1992) tells us, by a desire to maintain and to present to the world a sense that they are academically capable. We support and encourage that positive self-image by involving students in recording their own story through their portfolios. But to make this work, they must also actively participate in selecting the work for the portfolio.

In the celebration portfolio described previously, the story is essentially the student's to tell. But there also is much room for student involvement in the growth, project, and status report options. Notice that I am not saying that the student selects everything, nor does their teacher. We're talking partnership here. Here's how one teacher friend of mine handles this: Her sixth graders maintain files of all work completed, one for each discipline. When it comes time to assemble the representative work for their growth portfolios in preparation for the periodic student-led parent conferences (discussed in detail in the next chapter), students and teacher work as a team to select work.

Davies, Cameron, Politano, and Gregory (1992) advise us that we can maximize the benefits of student involvement in selection by having them describe what they selected and why they selected it. They recommend using a cover sheet for each portfolio entry to capture this information. Figure 12.1 presents an example.

When I chose to include this example of my writing in
my portfolio I remembered that . . .

FICTION	NON-FICTION
• has a good story	• gives information
• uses interesting language	• groups information under
• has a beginning, a middle, and an end	main headings
• uses a variety of sentences, both	• has a table of contents
simple and complex	• has diagrams or pictures to give
	additional information

I also know that it is important that my work is neat and
that it has been edited for spelling and sentence structure.

The piece of work I have chosen is...

It shows...

I want you to notice...

Please give me one compliment and ask me
one question after you read my selection...

I put this in my portfolio on _____ _____
                                    [date]   [signature]

Figure 12.1

Summary sheet for student use in describing portfolio selections

Source: From *Together is Better: Collaborative Assessment, Evaluation and Reporting* (p. 79) by
A. Davies, C. Cameron, C. Politano, and K. Gregory, 1992. Winnipeg, MB: Peguis Publishers Ltd.
Reprinted by permission.

Periodic Student Self-Reflection

Of all the dimensions of portfolios, the process of self-reflection is the most important. If we are to keep students in touch with their emerging academic selves, we must share our vision of what it means to succeed in understandable terms. We must provide them with a vocabulary to use in communicating about it and keep them in touch with the accumulating evidence of their own proficiency. One way to hold them accountable for achieving a clear sense of themselves as learners is to have them write or talk about that accumulating evidence. With portfolios, this has come to be known as *student self-reflection*.

Clearly *students who learn to evaluate their own achievement become better achievers through the process*. They maintain contact with their own evolving strengths and weaknesses. Figure 12.2 provides an example in two parts, another of Emily's essays, "Visions of Hope," and her reflection on the quality of her work. In this essay, she assumes the persona of a prisoner who uses her art to maintain perspective. Please read the essay carefully first, then the self-reflection. Note that Emily continues to apply the six analytical writing assessment score scales presented earlier. Here is more evidence that Emily is in touch with her own writing proficiency.

Helping Students Learn to Reflect

Sometimes it's helpful to initiate students into self-reflection by posing some simple questions for them to reflect about, such as the following (adapted from Arter & Spandel, 1992):

- Describe the steps you went through to complete this assignment. Did this process work and lead to successful completion or were there problems? What would you change next time?
- Did you receive feedback along the way that permitted you to refine your work? Describe your response to the feedback offered—did you agree or disagree with it? Why? What did you do as a result of this feedback?
- What makes your most effective piece of work different from your least effective? What does your best work tell you about where you have improved and where you need further work?
- What are the strengths of your work in this project (or this series of works)?
- What aspects still need more work? What kind of help will you need?
- What impact has this project had on your interests, attitudes, and views of this area?

These and other related questions can be very helpful in beginning self-reflection. It's human nature to experience some difficulty being constructively analytical and self-critical, at least at first. As we established earlier, this is risky business for most, and especially for those with a history of academic failure. Research reminds us that students will go to great lengths to maintain a positive internal sense of academic ability, even to the point of denying or being unable to see, let alone face, the flaws in their work (Covington, 1992). For this reason, guided practice is a necessity.

It may be helpful for your students to see you model the process by reviewing, analyzing, and self-evaluating some of your own work. Or, consider having

VISIONS OF HOPE

I call my picture "Visions of Hope." If I'm caught with this picture, I'll be killed. But it's worth it if people outside see it. I want them to know what life was like in the camp and how we kept our hopes up.

You may be wondering how I got the materials I used in this picture. It wasn't easy. I got the materials for the prisoner figures from old pieces of uniforms that had been torn off. This was one of the easier things to get. Uniforms get torn all the time from hard work. All the people look alike because to the Nazis it doesn't matter what you look like—only what you can do. To the Nazis we are all just numbers, without faces and without names.

The buildings in the picture are black to represent evil and death. Most of the buildings, aside from the barracks, you would enter but never come out again alive. I got this cloth from an old blanket that had worn thin from overuse. The Germans didn't care if we were cold or uncomfortable, so they didn't make any real effort to mend things. Everything in our world badly needs mending, too, including our spirits.

Inside the smoke of death coming out of the smokestacks you will see the Star of David. This star represents hope. Hope for life and for living. We will never totally die as long as our hope lives on.

My picture has two borders. One is barbed wire. It symbolizes tyranny, oppression, and total loss of freedom. The barbs are shaped like swastikas to represent the Nazis, Hitler and hate. This is a symbol of true evil.

The other border, outside the barbed wire, represents all the hope and dreams that are outside the camp. The flowers, sun, moon and bright colors were all things we took for granted in our old world. Even though we can see the sun through the clouds and smoke, we can't enjoy it anymore. The feathers represent the birds we barely see or hear inside the camp. We miss the cheeriness of their voices. The tiny brown twigs are as close as we come to the trees we remember. I got the bright cloth from a dress. When new prisoners come to the camp they must take off their own clothes and put on the hated prison outfits. All the nice clothes are sent to Germans outside the camps. My job is to sort through the clothes and pick out the nice things that will be sent away. When I saw this beautiful cloth, I tore off a piece and saved it for my picture.

I hope someone finds this and remembers that we always kept our hopes alive even when they took away everything else. They could never take our hope.

Figure 12.2
Sample of student writing and author's self-reflection
Source: "Visions of Hope," a sample of writing and self-reflection by N. Spandel. Reprinted by permission.

the whole class collaborate as a team to compose a hypothetical self-reflection on a particular project. This is the best way I know to show students that your classroom is a safe place within which to risk trying. Either success or problems point the direction not to a judgmental grade, but to a specific path to each student's improvement.

REFLECTION

This piece has always been one of my favorites. It shows not only what I can do as a writer, but as an artist as well. I knew very little of the Holocaust before working on this project. It was almost impossible for me to believe how brutal people could be. It both frightened and horrified me. In my written piece and my picture, I tried to capture that horror but also the courage which kept many people going. I also tried hard to imagine how it would really feel to be imprisoned, locked away from the things and the work and the people I loved. I don't know if anyone can really imagine this without living it, but this project made me think.

In **Ideas and Content,** I gave myself a 5. I thought my ideas were clear, and I thought I created a vivid picture of an artist trying to keep his work alive.

I would also give myself a 5 in **Organization.** My opening does a good job of leading the reader into my paper, especially with the dramatic and honest statement: "If I'm caught with this picture I'll be killed." I want the reader to know right away what is at stake.

My **Voice** is not as strong as I would have liked it to be. It is hard to take on the voice of another person. I am pretending to be someone else, not myself. I guess I just haven't had enough practice at this. Also, my natural voice tends to be humorous, and clearly, this is the most serious of topics. Anyway, I just did not find quite the voice I wanted, and I gave myself a 4.

I gave myself a 5 in **Word Choice.** The language is simple and natural. I did not try to impress the reader with words they might not understand. Also, I tried to capture the mood of what it would be like to live in a concentration camp and think how the people who lived there might talk. What words would they use?

My **Sentence Fluency** was pretty strong. You will notice that I vary my sentence beginnings a lot. That's one of my strengths. It's smooth, whether you read it silently or aloud. I think a few sentences are a little short and choppy, though. Some sentence combining would help. So I rated myself a 4 on this trait.

In **Conventions** I would rate myself a 5. I have always been strong in this trait. Conventions are fairly easy for me, if I think about them, especially with the aid of a computer. I can catch most grammatical errors, and I use a spell checker. I also read through my paper when it's finished to make sure it sounds just right. Rating myself on these traits is very helpful. It allows me to see how I'm doing as a writer, and to see my work as it really is. I think the traits give you a way of teaching yourself.

Figure 12.2
Sample of student writing and author's self-reflection *(continued)*

Attributes of Good Self-Reflection

In effect, self-reflection is a kind of student performance. Therefore, it too can be the focus of an evaluation. When asked to reflect on their work, students unschooled in the process will respond emotionally by saying, "I hate it," or, "I think it's really good." Typically, they will be at a loss as to what else to say. They will be unable to muster evidence to substantiate their judgment. But when schooled in appropriately applying the right performance standards and when they feel safe enough to be honest in making and defending their judgments, they will assert control over the evaluation and speak openly about issues of quality.

Remember the strategy discussed in the performance assessment chapters of having students contrast samples of outstanding and poor-quality performance to uncover key differences? Consider involving older students (mature middle schoolers and high schoolers) in a similar process to discover the key elements of an effective self-reflection. To minimize the risk to students, show them anonymous high- and low-quality self-reflections of some of your work and have students do the contrasting, devising criteria for evaluating their own reflections. Plan to engage students over time in refining their visions of a good self-reflection as needed.

For those who need more specific guidance, consider these key dimensions. But remember, their relevance will vary with the activity (adapted from Arter & Spandel, 1992):

- *Coverage*—Does the reflection address all relevant criteria? Make a checklist of them, and work with the students to review their self-reflection and check them off.
- *Accuracy*—Are students developing an accurate sense of their achievement or growth? Compare your evaluations with theirs. Discuss similarities and differences of perspective.
- *Specificity*—Does the reflection include examples to support points made in the self-reflection? Work with students to identify or develop them.
- *Integration*—Have students appropriately synthesized important insights into broader conclusions about their achievement? Work with them to be sure they understand how to draw this inference (excellent practice using an important form of reasoning).
- *Revelation*—Does self-reflection bring students to new insights about their learning? Discuss these new insights with your students.

Time for Reflection

Let's say you wanted to develop a set of five analytical rating scales, one for each of the attributes of a student self-reflection listed in the preceding text. Further, you want each to include three rating points: (1) Outstanding Reflection, (2) Mid-Range Reflection, and (3) Poor Quality Reflection. What would those rating scales look like? Please take a few moments to draft them. Also think for a moment about how you might involve your students in their development as a means of helping them enhance their understanding of self-reflection.

Dealing with Some Practicalities

As I work with teachers exploring classroom applications of portfolios, several questions seem to come up over and over. I recently sat down with Ms. Weathersby, Emily's teacher and a skilled and experienced user of portfolios, to discuss them.

"Ms. Weathersby," I began, "how does your district use portfolios?"

"We start small," she responded. "Our primary-grade teachers start with a simple celebration portfolio to ease their students into the process. We ask them to answer questions like, What do you like about this piece? What do you think you might be able to improve?

"In the elementary grades, we have them explore simple growth portfolios, keeping the targets simple and the criteria constant. Then in middle and high school we introduce the status report portfolio. I use the growth one, but our students must assemble a status report, too, during high school."

"The long-term experience with repeated applications must help," I commented.

"It makes the process much easier for students to learn and manage. I have really noticed a difference in my students' comfort level when they come to my class with prior portfolio experience. Those who began with them very early plunge with confidence into my project assignment."

"I've seen Emily's growth portfolio. How did you get started?"

Ms. W. thought for a second, and then replied, "We thought Em did a fine job at the board meeting. She's a perfect example of what happens when the growth portfolio works well, and it works well a lot.

"The way several colleagues and I got started was that we wanted to do student-led parent conferences. We needed the portfolio to help students prepare evidence of their achievement to share with parents. My particular application of the idea is a writing growth portfolio. Over the grading period, each student has to complete all the assignments and keep a portfolio of evidence of the nature and quality of their work."

"How much time does it take?"

"It varies," she said. "It depends on coverage. As the scope of the target and time span of the portfolio increase, so does the time commitment. But as students mature and gain experience, they learn to handle most of the work and to enjoy it. You can see that in Emily. The greater role the students play, the more feasible the idea becomes."

"You teach high school and face 150 students a day in different classes, yet the idea really is feasible for you?"

Ms. W. was very clear about this. "You bet! But you have to be collaborative about it. As I said, my assessment for my English classes requires my students to complete a series of writing assignments. Their work must meet certain standards of quality. I expect each student to keep a growth portfolio containing evidence of having completed all of the steps in the assignment. I count on heavy student involvement in all phases of the work."

"Can students really manage their own portfolios? What if they cheat?" I asked.

"They can manage it, as long as I provide leadership and insist on those timelines.

"Cheating always becomes an interesting topic in my classes. In other classrooms, students can copy someone else's test paper, sneak in a crib sheet, have someone else do their homework for them, and even change grades on assignments before returning them to the teacher. In my years of teaching, I've seen it all.

"But do you know what really minimizes cheating? The weekly written self-reflection I require. Students first share them with their study teammates, then put them in their portfolios, where I get to read them. If you don't know where you are in your own development and don't know what you're talking about, it's impossible to bluff. It stands out like a sore thumb."

"You've made cheating irrelevant, in effect," I observed.

"My students know that I expect to see increasing quality over time on their part. It's as if each self-reflection is more demanding than the one preceding it. Everyone seems to acknowledge that there are no excuses in this classroom. It may sound crazy, but I think you're right, they believe that cheating makes no sense in here. There's no percentage in it. In fact, pretty quickly, they see that it hurts them more than it helps.

"Besides, my students quickly learn through the grapevine that they simply can't bluff in the conference with their parents and me at the end of the project, where any attempt to misrepresent their own achievement will be transparent. I ask tough questions in front of their families. They know they're responsible for providing good answers. And you know, I can see the pride in their eyes when they deliver quality."

"How do you convert portfolio work to a grade?"

"We work as a class to devise a set of grading criteria," she replied. "Before anyone starts, I share examples of good and bad work from past classes, and we work as a team to identify the differences between them. We establish and define our keys to success, and formulate performance rating scales. Those are all things that Emily told you about.

"I base their grade on the quality of the final products at the end of the grading period. We agree on the target in advance, and we define levels of proficiency that equate to different grades—you know, what their profile of ratings must look like to earn an A, a B, and so on. No one gets credit for just doing work. It's the learning that comes from doing the work that counts."

Next, I asked, "Who owns the portfolios?"

"My students keep the growth portfolio. When our purposes have been served, they take them home.

"However, the district is experimenting with a graduation portfolio. That requires a record of evidence of student achievement of a specified set of expectations for high school graduation. This might take on the stature of an official transcript. If it does, then this portfolio would become part of the student's permanent record."

"Where do you store all of these portfolios?"

"With their owners—my students. They can be responsible for this. If they wish, they can use a file cabinet in my room. But, the agreement is that each portfolio is private property.

"I have heard that there are some electronic portfolio software packages now on the market. We've begun to investigate this option for the district for the future."

"Thanks, Ms. Weathersby."

About Those Electronic Portfolios

As Ms. W. points out, there are some promising products available for storing student portfolios. A number of computer software developers have created and are refining packages that permit classroom teachers to help students develop electronic portfolios. These purport to allow easy entry of traditional academic records (student background, grades, etc.), as well as actual examples of student work, including everything from written products to color videos with sound. Easy retrieval also is possible using networked personal computers. Teachers who have access to these information management systems report immense time savings. Contact the technology experts in your school or district to learn more about the available options.

Summary: Communicating with Portfolios

Portfolios offer ways to communicate about student achievement in greater detail than is permitted by report card grades. In this case, the communication arises out of collecting and displaying actual examples of student work. Unlike grades, portfolios can tell a detailed story of a student's achievement. This does not mean that they should replace grades, but rather that we should see them as serving different purposes—different users and uses.

Portfolios have gained immense popularity in recent years because of their potential as a teaching tool that offers many opportunities for student involvement. Portfolios can help teachers diagnose student needs and reveal improvement over time. They can encourage students to take responsibility for their own learning, track that learning, and gain an enhanced sense of academic progress and self-worth. Portfolios help students learn to reflect on their own work, identify strengths and weaknesses, and plan a course of action—critically important life skills. And finally, they give students opportunities for practicing important and useful reasoning and problem-solving skills.

But with all these pluses, they take very careful planning and dedication to use well. The hard work can pay off with immense achievement and motivational dividends if we implement them in calculated small steps. See the big picture, but move toward it in baby steps, one step at a time. Unfortunately, many have drowned in the sea of student papers collected to serve a policy maker's mandated "mega-portfolio" system. We can avoid such problems by preparing carefully.

Specifically, this means the following:

- Collect evidence of student attainment of clearly articulated achievement targets.
- Gather dependable evidence so as to create an accurate picture.
- Use portfolios in a communication environment that lends itself to open sharing by doing the following:
  a. Be sure everyone understands the portfolio's purpose.
  b. Develop a shared vocabulary for discussing levels of proficiency.
  c. Provide plenty of opportunities to interact with students about achievement.
  d. Regularly check to be sure students are in touch with and feeling in control of their own progress.

The possibilities of student involvement in this kind of communication are limited only by the imagination of the users, meaning you and your students. They can play key roles in identifying the story to be told, devising guidelines for the selection of work to go into the portfolio, devising criteria for judging merit, applying those criteria, reflecting on their own achievement status or growth over time, and communicating to others about their success in learning.

Final Chapter Reflection

1. *What are the three most important new insights to come to you as a result of your study of this chapter?*
2. *Which of your previous questions about assessment can you now answer based on your study of this chapter?*
3. *What new questions have come to mind as a result of your study of this chapter that you hope to have answered as your study continues?*

Practice with Chapter 12 Ideas

1. Create a chart, labeling each line with one of the four types of portfolios discussed in this chapter: celebration, growth, project, and status report. Add four columns headed by these questions: What story will the portfolio tell? What evidence must it contain? How will we evaluate the information? How does this portfolio type connect to our instruction? Referring to the text, within each cell of this four-by-four chart, briefly answer each question for each portfolio type.

2. Compare and contrast report card grades and portfolios as means of communication about student achievement. How are they alike? How are they different? What do those similarities and differences tell you about the information users each is likely to serve well?

3. Listed here are several reasons to design and build portfolios. Classify each as calling for a celebration, growth, project, or status report portfolio:
   a. Student-led parent-teacher conference
   b. Certify competence for high school graduation
   c. Collect personal favorites
   d. Science fair
   e. Tracking progress toward math standards

   f. College admissions
   g. Encourage students to keep reading
   h. Identify academically challenged or gifted students

4. Assume that you are an educator applying for new job. However, instead of completing the normal application form, you decide to submit a portfolio as your application. You identify the job and context that would be right for you. What would you put in your portfolio? Identify each entry and your rationale for its inclusion. What story do you want to tell and why? When you have completed this task, answer the following questions:
   a. Of the four kinds of portfolios described in this chapter, which kind is this?
   b. In the job application and candidate selection process, who sets the scoring criteria? Therefore, in preparing your story, with whom would you like to speak in advance? Why?
   c. What would you do if they wouldn't tell you what you wanted to know? What if they told you they really hadn't identified selection criteria? Or what if you spoke to several members of the selection committee and they each identified different performance

criteria? How would you feel in each of these cases and what would you do?

d. What if the purpose for your portfolio was different? For instance, what if the purpose was for you to build your own personal celebration portfolio of your career as an educator? Would you include different ingredients? Why?

e. What generalizations would you draw about the importance of purpose in structuring portfolios?

5. If you were to replace your parent-teacher conferences with student-led parent conferences, what type of portfolio would you have students develop? Why? If you were helping students to prepare portfolios to certify completion of high school graduation requirements, what kind would you help them develop? Why?

6. We have established that the attributes of a quality portfolio include a sharp focus on achievement targets, accurate assessments, and selecting a portfolio format that fits the context and opportunities for student involvement. If you were to devise a simple rubric for the evaluation of a colleague's portfolio plan in these terms, what would that rubric look like?

Chapter 13

Communicating Through Conferences

CHAPTER FOCUS

This final chapter of our journey through the realm of classroom assessment answers the following guiding question:

> How can my students and I communicate effectively with each other and their families about their achievement through the use of various conference formats?

From your study of this chapter, you will understand the following:

1. As with report cards and portfolios, certain conditions must be satisfied if we are to confer effectively about student achievement.

2. We have choices—we can team students, parents, and teachers in a variety of combinations to meet our communication needs. Each conference format brings with it strengths and challenges.

Let the Conference Begin

"The tablecloths are out, cookies arranged, lemonade cooling, and I'm eating supper—frozen yogurt." Terri Austin, a sixth-grade teacher from Fairbanks, Alaska, begins to tell us what it's like in her classroom the evening of student-parent conferences. Let's listen to the rest of her story.

> It's 5:45. Will they come? No matter how many times I do this, I always wonder if families will show up.
>
> At 5:50, Frank and his mom arrive early. He's all polished, clean shirt and hair combed. As she sits at a table by the window, he quickly finds his portfolio, joins her and begins.
>
> At 6:00, the room fills quickly, Ruth and her mother drink lemonade while looking at the class photographs on the bulletin board.
>
> Chuck says, "Pick a table, Mom." She picks one with a purple tablecloth. Chuck smiles and says, "Oh yeah, you like purple. Would you like some refreshments?" After his mother and brother are seated, Chuck goes to pick up cookies and drinks.
>
> Dennis and his father come in. Dennis's father is still in his military uniform. They find a table by the window. As Dennis shares his work, his father smiles. The father leans closer to Dennis, so they see the paper at the same time.

With his mother sitting across from him, Chuck goes over each paper very carefully. Occasionally, she looks over Chuck's head and smiles at me.

Greg and his mom speak Spanish as they look at the papers together.

Darrin's father rushes in with his family trailing behind. His father asks, "Mrs. Austin, what time are we?" "I scheduled the time wrong," Darrin apologizes. I say, "It's OK. There are no set times. Just find a table and begin." They stop at the refreshment table as Darrin finds his portfolio.

I hear Greg explaining his summary sheet in Spanish.

Steve, his mom, and an unknown lady and child arrive. At the end of the conference, I find out the woman is a neighbor who heard about "Steve's portfolio" and wanted to see it. So Steve invited her to his conference.

Darrin's mom catches my eye and smiles. She listens to Darrin read [one of his papers].

On their way out the door, I talk with Hope's family. They are very pleased with Hope's work. Her mom has tears in her eyes as she tells me how proud she is of Hope.* (Austin, 1994, pp. 66–67)

Thus, Terri introduces us to the idea of student-led parent conferences. In this case, we combine the strengths of student-teacher conferences and parent-teacher conferences into a rich and engaging learning experience for students. Terri and her students spend a great deal of time both preparing information about student achievement and preparing to share it with parents. These personal conferences with families add a depth of communication about student growth and development over time that is unattainable with any of the other communication options.

After the conferences, Terri checked with her students to see if they thought the hard work and preparation were worth it for them. She was startled at the strength of student feelings:

ANNE	I think it really does make a difference. It's definitely easier because you know the outcome of the conference and you don't get the jitters and all worried wondering about the outcome. It teaches you responsibility. You also learn while you're getting ready. I admit it is hard but you are also satisfied knowing you can prepare a conference like a teacher can.
DAVE	Yes, it does make a difference. It is fun and a new experience. I learned patience and responsibility. I learned to tell the truth and to talk about my grades.
SAMANTHA	I have learned that I could explain myself and my grades. It also teaches me to take my time. I learned that I could do more things if I tried because I thought I never could have done them. I also learned that it is a better way to get in touch with your parents.
PHILIP	I learned I can find trust within my grades and show responsibility as in how to make the most of my grades.
MARY	It's scary sometimes.

*Excerpts on pp. 340–342 reprinted by permission from *Changing the View: Student-Led Parent Conferences* by Terri Austin. Copyright © 1994 by Terri Austin. Published by Heinemann, a division of Reed Elsevier, Inc., Portsmouth, NH. All rights reserved.

AARON	It's a very good method.
RICK	I know a lot more about what's going on. Otherwise I don't know what the teacher has said about me. I feel a lot more comfortable doing this. I know my grades and my papers, I seem to know what's going to happen and how I'm doing in school. I'm fair to myself.
DAVID	I learned that I do things that I've never done before and that I can make mistakes sometimes.
MRS. A	Would you recommend this type of conference to other students and teachers?
	[Everyone agrees they would.]
MRS. A	What do you think? Should we continue this procedure for the rest of the year?
	[All agree they should.]
MELISSA	Yes. I think parents understand things better when their child answers their questions. Also, we know the answers to all the questions. Maybe a teacher-parent conference wouldn't answer all the questions. (Austin, 1994, pp. 27–28)

Any doubt about the power of Terri's way of setting clear goals, compiling evidence of goal attainment in portfolios, and preparing students to share information about their own achievement is erased when we read this kind of comment from a parent:

> The transformation of Jason as a student has been remarkable, from an F and C student to an A and B student. We cannot help but believe that a great deal of the credit must go to the manner in which class materials are presented and the curriculum is organized. Jason certainly has become more focused on his capabilities rather than his limitations. The general emphasis on responsibility for one's own actions and performance has also been most beneficial. Jason was a very frustrated young man in [his former school] and has had a tendency to place blame on others rather than accepting responsibility for his own choices. The last portion of this year has brought welcome changes in this respect. Though not always the most conscientious student, he puts forth serious effort on his studies and assumes responsibility for the results of his efforts. We believe that the "writing classroom" environment has been crucial to Jason's educational development, self-examination and personal growth. (Austin, 1994, p. 48)

I hope this vignette encourages you to explore open, inclusive, student-involved ways of communicating. In this final chapter I will share an array of ideas for communicating about student achievement that stretch far beyond our traditional teacher-centered report card grades and parent-teacher conferences. But remember, my point is not to negate those ways of sharing information; rather, it is to offer additional possibilities.

Be advised from the outset that these alternative means of sharing information do not represent panaceas that promise to deliver us from our communication challenges. Each option presents its own unique strengths and challenges. And, to be sure, each requires every bit as much work. However, I believe that we can markedly increase our positive impact on students' achievement by using conference formats intelligently.

In addition, never lose sight of the fact that conferences, just like report cards and portfolios, require the use of high-quality assessments as the basis for gathering accurate information about student achievement. *No one has succeeded as yet in inventing a communication alternative capable of converting misinformation into accurate information.*

Necessary Conditions

As in the previous three chapters, before we delve into the topic of conferences, let's do one final review of the keys to effective communication. If conferences are to be conducted in a productive manner, the following conditions must be satisfied:

We must be crystal clear and up front with our students about the achievement expectations we hold for them. Those expectations should fit into a continuous-progress vision of student growth, both within and across grade levels. And we ourselves must be confident, competent masters of the targets that they are supposed to hit. Without this, we can neither assess nor communicate.

Our assessments of student achievement must be accurate. Dependable information lays a solid foundation for effective communication. Inaccurate information lays a foundation of shifting sand.

To communicate effectively, the interpersonal environment must be right. That is, all who are involved must

- Understand what we are trying to achieve by means of our communication about student achievement.
- Use a common language to convey meaning.
- Take time to be in the moment when information is being shared—take the opportunity to share thoughts about and reactions to the information being presented.
- Check back with each other to be sure everyone understood and felt able to use the achievement information shared.

Our students must be deeply involved in assessing their own achievement over time, so they can understand the meaning of success, watch themselves grow, and develop the vocabulary needed to communicate effectively about their own success.

It is only with these pieces in place that we can meet with each other to share insights into individual students' learning.

Conference Formats That Enhance Communication

We're going to explore three practical conference formats:

- Student-teacher conferences
- Traditional parent-teacher conferences
- Student-led parent conferences

In the first format, *teacher and student* share a common vision and definition of academic success that allows them to share focused discussions of the student's progress. Some teachers are using these strategies to transform their classrooms into workshop settings. I'll share an example.

The second format brings *parents and teacher* together to share information on student achievement. While this kind of conference has long been a standard part of schooling, we'll put some new spins on the idea to bring students into the process.

The third, *student-led* parent conferences, takes advantage of the benefits of the other two formats, adding some special pluses of its own. It represents the capstone of an assessment *for* learning environment. Further, it overcomes many of their weaknesses, although it brings its own challenges. With this approach, as we learned from Terri Austin at the beginning of the chapter, the primary responsibility for communicating about expectations and progress shifts from teacher to student. We'll explore some practical guidelines for using this option, review benefits to students and parents, and share some reactions from users.

Student-Teacher Conferences

A classroom learning environment turns into a workshop when the teacher shares the vision of achievement with students and then sets them to work individually or in small groups in pursuit of the designated target. In this setting, the teacher becomes a consultant or coach, working one on one or with groups to improve students' performance. This permits individualization that works very well when students are at different levels of achievement, such as in the development of their math or writing proficiencies. Much of the communication between teacher and student occurs in one-on-one conferences between them.

These conferences give students personal attention. Besides, students who are reticent to speak out in class often will come forth in a conference. As a result, that two-way communication so essential to effective instruction can take place. And finally, the conference provides an excellent context in which to provide specific descriptive feedback. Teachers can provide commentary on student performance and students can describe what is and is not working for them.

To understand the dialogue that can emerge from this idea, read the example of student writing shown in Figure 13.1. A conference is about to take place between the teacher, Ms. Weathersby, and the student focusing on this work. Ms. W. has been holding conferences with her students since the beginning of the school year. It is now January. She tries to confer with each student every 2 to 3 weeks, and, though it takes a fair amount of time, she feels that the payoff is worth it. The dynamics of the conferences are changing a bit. In the beginning, she had to ask lots of questions. Now, students usually come to a conference with things to say.

Jill, the student, has never been an exceptional writer. Until recently, she didn't like to write and wrote only when forced. She didn't like talking about her writing, and her most frequent comment was, "I can't write."

At first, she didn't want to speak about her writing. The last two conferences, however, have been somewhat different. Jill is beginning to open up. She is writing

My Dog

Everyone has something important in their lives and the most important
thing to me, up to now, has been my dog. His name was Rafe. My brother
found him in an old barn where we were camping in a field near my
grandpa's house. Somebody had left him there and he was very weak and
close to being dead. But we nursed him back to health and my mom said
we could keep him, at least for a while. That turned out to be for ten years.

Rafe was black and brown and had a long tail, floppy ears, and a short, fat
face. He wasn't any special breed of dog. Most people probably wouldn't of
thought he was that good looking but to us he was very special.

Rafe kept us amused a lot with funny tricks. He would hide in the shadows
and try to spook the chickens but they figured out he was just bluffing so
he had to give up on that one. When Rafe got hit by a truck I thought I
would never stop crying. My brother misses him too, and my mom, but no
one could miss him as much as I do.

Figure 13.1
Sample of Jill's writing
Source: From *Creating Writers: Linking Assessment and Writing Instruction* (p. 105) by V. Spandel and R. J. Stiggins; 1990. Published by Allyn & Bacon, Boston, MA. Copyright © 1990 by Pearson Education. Adapted by permission of the publisher.

more on her own. She keeps a journal. She is still, however, reluctant to voice opinions about her own writing; she looks to her teacher for a lead. (Be sure to read Figure 13.1 before continuing.)

"Pretty terrible, huh?" Jill asks Ms. Weatherby.

"What do you think of it?" Ms. W. asks, tossing the question back to her. She doesn't answer right away, but her teacher doesn't break the silence. The seconds tick by. Ms. W. waits.

"I don't like the ending," Jill volunteers at last.

"Tell me why."

"Well, it just stops. The whole thing just doesn't tell how I really feel."

"How do you feel?"

She thinks for a minute. "Oh, it isn't like I miss him all the time. Some days I don't think about him at all. But then—well, it's like I'll see him at the door, or I'll see this shadow dashing around the side of the barn. Sometimes when we cook out, I think about him because he used to steal hot dogs off the grill, and one time my dad yelled at him when he did that and he slipped and burned one of his feet real bad."

"Now there's the real Jill and Rafe story beginning to come out! You're telling me about Rafe in your real personal voice and I sense some of your feelings. When you wrote about Rafe, did you speak like that? Let's read part of your writing again."

After doing so, Jill comments, "Pretty blah, not much me!"

"If you did write like you were speaking, how do you think it might read?"

"Like a story, I guess."

"Try it and let's see what happens. Talk to me about Rafe in your own personal voice. Besides, stealing hot dogs off the grill conjures up a funny picture, doesn't it? Those are the kinds of mental pictures great stories tell. When I can picture what you're saying, that's 'ideas.' You're giving the story some imagery and focus that I like very much. What kind of imagery do you see in this writing?"

They scan the piece again. Jill says in a low voice, "No images here—just facts."

"How about if you think up and write about some of those personal things you remember about Rafe?"

"Do you think I should?"

"Well, when you were talking, I had a much better sense of you in the story—of how much you missed your dog and how you thought about him."

"I think I could write about some of those things."

"How about if you give it a try, and we'll talk again in about a week?"

"How about the spelling, punctuation, and sentences? Were those okay?" Jill asks.

"Let's leave that 'til later. Think about the ideas, the organization, the voice. We'll come back to the other."

"I don't want any mistakes, though," Jill confesses.

"But is this the right time to worry about that?"

"I don't know; I just don't want to get a bad grade."

"Okay," Ms. W. nods. "Suppose we agree that for now, we'll just assess the three traits I mentioned: ideas, organization, and voice."

"That's all?"

Ms. W. nods again. "And if you decide you want to publish this paper in the school magazine, then we'll work on the rest."

"We can fix the other stuff then, right?"

"You will have time to fix it, yes."

Time for Reflection

In your opinion, what are the keys to making conferences like this work? What are some of the barriers to effective conferences? How might you remove these barriers?

Dealing with the Practicalities

Those who have turned classrooms into workshops tell us that conferences need not be long. We can communicate a great deal of information in just a few minutes. However, thoughtful preparation is essential. It is best if both students and teacher examine student work beforehand with performance criteria in mind and prepare focused commentary.

Good listening is essential. If you prepare a few thoughtful questions in advance, you can draw insight out of students, triggering their own self-reflection. Effective conferences don't rely on traditional, one-way communication. Rather, they work best when teachers share both the control of the meeting and the responsibility for directing the communication.

Over time, and with experience in conferences, it will become easier to open the dialogue because both you and your students will become more at ease with each other. Over time, students also will become more familiar with your expectations. They will develop both the conceptual frameworks and vocabulary needed to communicate efficiently with you about their progress. So begin with modest expectations and let the process grow.

Parent-Teacher Conferences

I would be remiss if I failed to insert the traditional parent-teacher conference into our discussion of effective ways to communicate. During our school years, most of us became the "odd person out" of these meetings. We were left wondering, What did they say about me? Further, many experienced teachers who have been on the other side of the desk and who obviously know what was said, wonder if they said the right things and if they were understood.

Analyzing the Benefits

Parent-teacher conferences offer three specific advantages over report card grades as means of communication. They permit us to do the following:

1. Retain and share a sufficiently high level of detail to provide a rich picture of student achievement. In effect, they provide a personal way to share the checklists, rating scales, and narratives discussed previously.
2. Ask followup questions to determine if we have succeeded in communicating. We can provide additional detail and explanation as needed to be sure the message gets through. Parents can ask questions to eliminate uncertainty.
3. Plan jointly with families to blend school and home learning environments for maximum productivity. In some cases, that means we can find out what may be going wrong with a student's home environment and urge adjustments in that environment.

But these advantages should not lead us to infer that conferences should replace report cards or any other record-keeping or communication option. Rather, we can use our various communication options in combination, where part of our conference time is used to explain grades, checklists, ratings, or other symbols, for example.

Anticipating the Challenges

Of course, challenge number one is time. Parent-teacher conferences take a great deal of time to prepare for and to conduct. Every family must get its share of one-on-one time with you. For junior high and high school teachers working with large numbers of students, again, this option may not be feasible, especially given the number of courses students take at one time.

Challenge number two is that of devising a jargon-free, family-friendly vocabulary and interpersonal manner to use in describing student achievement to parents. If we pile on a great deal of technical language delivered in an aggressive style, we will have difficulty connecting.

Challenge number three is encouraging parental participation in the conferences. Some families care more about their children's grades than do others. Some have busy lives, and competing priorities always seem to win. Some parents feel vulnerable in parent-teacher conferences, especially if things aren't going well in school for their child. There is always the chance in their minds that you might accuse them of failing to support your teaching efforts. Even though you know you would never do that, they don't know it for sure.

Challenge number four is helping students to come through conference time with academic self-concepts intact. This can be risky stuff for our students. If they're left wondering what was really said about them—as they usually are—the effect can be uncertainty, frustration, and even anger. At the very least they may be left with the impression that they aren't important enough in this communication equation to warrant a role.

For any one or all of these reasons, if we use parent-teacher conferences as our means of message delivery, we can be in danger of failing to communicate effectively with students and with some families.

Dealing with the Practicalities

We can meet these challenges and take maximum advantage of this conference format if we follow some simple, straightforward procedures:

STEP 1: Establish a clear and complete set of achievement expectations.

STEP 2: Transform those expectations into quality assessments and gather accurate information.

STEP 3: Carefully summarize that information for sharing via grades, checklists, rating scales, narrative, portfolios, or test scores.

STEP 4: Conduct a student-teacher conference to review all of this material before conducting the parent-teacher conference. This permits students to understand the message to be delivered. In fact, imagine a classroom in which this step was unnecessary because steps 1 to 3 were carried out with full student involvement. With targets clarified and shared, students involved deeply in accumulating achievement evidence, and students as partners in developing the portfolio that will be the topic of discussion at the parent-teacher conference, everyone shares. The motivational and achievement benefits of such a partnership are considerable.

STEP 5: Schedule and conduct the parent-teacher conference. By the way, imagine the ongoing communication link that we might forge with parents if we had our continuous progression of achievement targets organized into bands like the previous Australian illustration (see Figures 11.5 and 11.6). We'd have concrete ways to show parents both how their children are doing with respect to our expectations and, if necessary, in relation to other students of like age or grade.

STEP 6: Ask for a written followup reflection from parents presenting their impressions of the achievement and progress of their children.

Student-Led Parent Conferences

Of all the communication possibilities available to us, this one excites me the most, because it places students at the heart of the process. Notice immediately that I did not label this "student-involved parent-teacher conferences." I used the label "student-led" to emphasize the need to both give students the opportunity to tell, and to hold students accountable for telling, at least some of the story of their own achievement.

This is a more complex communication option than either of the other two conference formats. However, the payoff for the added work can be impressive, to say the least. In fact, I regard this conference format to be the biggest breakthrough to happen in communicating about student achievement in the past century.

Exploring the Benefits
Among the positive effects reported by teachers who use this idea are the following:

1. *A much stronger sense of responsibility for their own learning among students.* When students understand that, down the road, they (not you) will be telling their own success (or lack of success) story, they realize that there is no escaping accountability. They realize very quickly that, if they have nothing to share at that meeting by way of success, they are going to be very uncomfortable. This can be a strong motivator. And once they have some positive experience with this process and develop confidence in themselves, they become even more motivated to do well at it.
2. *A much stronger sense of pride when they do have a success story to share at conference time.* It feels good to be in charge of a meeting in which you're the star of a winning team.
3. *A different and more productive relationship between students and their teachers.* When that conference takes place, if the student has nothing by way of success to share, the student won't be the only one who will be somewhat embarrassed. In this sense, students and teachers become partners in the face of a common challenge. Both must succeed together. This alliance can boost student achievement.
4. *Improved student–parent relationships.* Many families report that their conversations about student achievement extend far beyond the conference itself—sometimes weeks beyond. Often what emerges from the meeting is a sense of mutual interest in student projects, along with a shared language that permits ongoing interaction. School–family partnerships can flourish under these circumstances.
5. *An active, involved classroom environment built on a strong sense of community.* Students take pride not only in their own accomplishments and their ability to share them, but also in the opportunity to help each other prepare for and succeed at their conferences. A team spirit, a sense of community, can emerge and this can benefit the motivation and achievement of all.
6. *A reduction in relevance or value of cheating.* Not only is it difficult to misrepresent one's achievement when concrete evidence will be presented at the conference, but also, students seem less interested in cheating. What can emerge is a greater sense of honor and honesty related to their heightened sense of responsibility for and pride in actually achieving.

7. *The development of important leadership skills.* Coordinating and conducting a student-led parent conference requires that the student schedule the meeting, invite participants, handle the introductions, organize and present information to the group, and follow up to discern meeting results. These are important life skills.

8. *Greater parental participation in conferences.* Virtually all schools report that a far higher percentage of parents show up to be part of conferences when students are the leaders. You can probably anticipate why this might be the case. If you are a parent, which invitation is more likely to bring you to a meeting: a mimeographed note from your child's teacher stuck to the refrigerator with a date and time filled in, or your child standing in front of you looking up with those eyes reminding you that the conference is tomorrow and she will be in charge and "You're going to be there, right?"

Also, remember that some parents' school experiences were less than positive and, for some, things may not be going well in their adult lives. In their minds, there is a danger that, if they come to a parent-teacher conference, you might accuse them of being a bad parent. For this reason alone, they might avoid the meeting. When they know that their child is to lead the meeting, this risk seems to be reduced in their minds. For this reason among others, virtually all users of this conference format report a major jump in the proportion of parents who participate.

Facing the Challenges

At the same time, this idea of student-led conferences is not without its downside risks. For example, it's not easy for some teachers to share control with students. This requires a trust teachers typically don't grant to their students. When we give up control in this way, we cannot always be absolutely sure what will happen. If difficulties arise, they arise in a fishbowl and some pretty important people will see them. That's scary.

Further, it should be clear that the presentation of student-led conferences is just the tip of a pretty big iceberg. *You buy the whole environment or none of it.* Effective communication is possible only if the conference arises from a student-involved classroom assessment *for* learning environment. We cannot simply plug in student-led parent conferences in a traditional teacher-centered assessment environment, where students have little idea what the expectations are or how they are doing with respect to those targets. I recently spoke with a parent who's third-grade daughter "got caught" between two adults talking about her. The child was scared before and during the event, according to her mom. She had no idea what was happening, was given no responsibility in planning for the meeting, was asked to answer questions she was totally unprepared to address, and had a completely negative experience. This was a good idea badly implemented and one mother was left very cold about the whole concept. *We must set students up to succeed at the conferences or such conferences are not worth conducting.*

Another challenge is finding the time to prepare for and manage such conferences. Most teachers plan for at least 30-minute conferences. This is especially difficult for junior high or high school teachers, who might face 150 students a day. First, be careful about how you think about time used in this context. There is a strong tendency to think of it as time lost to instruction. Nothing could be further from the truth. The time spent preparing to confer turns into highly focused teaching and learning time.

Beyond this, we need to creatively manage the logistics of holding conferences. Many teachers report that they can have students conducting several at one time, once those students have experience running conferences. In addition, high school teachers I know limit conferences to one or two courses per grading period, thus spreading them across four quarters of the year. In fact, one teacher I know asks that conferences last at least one hour, with only the first 30 minutes taking place in the classroom. The remainder is to take place at home, and students are responsible for reporting back in writing about how the rest of the conference went. To a person, her students report that conferences stretch far beyond the required hour.

But perhaps the most difficult challenges faced by those who would place students in charge of these conferences arise when the student comes from a dysfunctional family. The easiest version of this problem occurs when parents simply fail to show up. More difficult versions have parents showing up and becoming abusive in any of a number of ways.

Time for Reflection

How might we plan conferences in collaboration with our students in ways that maximize the chances that parents will show up? Further, if parents or other invited guests fail to arrive for the conference, how might we handle this in a manner that keeps the student's ego intact? Think about this for a moment before reading on.

Some teachers I know cover the very rare occurrence of parents failing to show up by having a backup "listener" available on conference day. It might be a former teacher, the principal, a custodian, or counselor. The only requirement is that the listener be someone the student knows and whose opinion the student cares about. When this condition is satisfied, students can present enthusiastically and take pride in their achievements. It's okay to reschedule too, if the listener scheduled cannot make it.

Keys to Success

We overcome these challenges only by attending to some simple fundamental conditions. To make this idea work, we need the following:

- Students who feel confident, safe, and trusting enough to take the risk of describing their own growth to their parents

- Students who have had time to learn about, to prepare for, and to practice their leadership roles
- Teachers who are willing to take the risk of stepping aside and letting their students take charge, just as a coach helps players learn the game and then places them on the field or court to play the game themselves
- Achievement targets that have been clearly and completely defined, woven into instruction, and used as the basis for an open and honest ongoing communication system
- Accurate, student-involved assessments filling the portfolios that tell the story
- Both teacher and students who share a common language for talking about attainment of each important achievement target

When these conditions are satisfied and students take the lead in evaluating their learning, many good things occur. For example, because students and teacher must work closely together to prepare for the conference, it builds a greater amount of individual attention into instruction. As evidence of success is compiled, a sense of being in control emerges for students, spurring them to greater heights—especially in the hope that they might be able to achieve those last-minute gains that will impress their parents even more. Parents acquire new understanding of their children, and of the teacher. This gives students a greater sense of their own importance in the classroom.

Time spent planning and preparing for student-led parent conferences becomes high-quality teaching and learning time. Students work to understand the vision of success, master the language needed to communicate about it, learn to describe their achievements, and evaluate their own strengths and weaknesses. Is this not the essence of a productive learning environment? Besides, as they prepare for the meeting, students might organize demonstrations, set up exhibitions, and/or develop other documentary evidence of success. It is difficult to envision more engaging student learning experiences.

Dealing with the Practicalities

Here are the steps in conducting a student-led parent conference:

STEP 1: Establish the relevant achievement targets, be sure all students and parents are aware of them, and plan instruction around their achievement.

STEP 2: Convert those expectations into quality assessments and use those assessments to help students build portfolios of quality evidence of their own achievement. Note that these can be either growth or status report portfolios, depending on your wishes. You don't have to rigorously control the evidence gathering. Your students can take the lead—if they're prepared.

STEP 3: While the evidence is building, keep the channels of communication open with the student's family. This might involve the use of a "take-home" portfolio or journal that students use to keep their parents informed of progress during instruction. Ask parents to respond to you in writing about their impressions of the progress or about any concerns they may have.

STEP 4:   As conference time approaches, convene a student-teacher conference to assemble the conference portfolio. Work as a team to select the samples of student work that you will use to tell the desired story.

STEP 5:   Model a student-led conference for your students. Role play a good one and a bad one, so they can see what makes them work well. Be absolutely sure students know their role (as leader), your role (as coach), and their parents' role (as interested listeners and questioners). Be sure your students understand that we strive for a natural conversation among conferees—an interaction about accomplishments that includes examples, questions, answers, and sharing.

You might consider engaging your students in collaborating to develop performance criteria for a good conference. Remember from performance assessment design?

- Brainstorm important elements of a good conference.
- Cluster them into major categories.
- Label and define the categories.
- Analyze and compare conferences of vastly diferent quality (have your students role play good and bad conferences).
- Devise rating scales or checklists to capture the essential differences between the two.

Your students can be partners with you in building criteria for good student-led conferences. Then you can team up to plan conferences that meet your agreed standards of excellence.

STEP 6:   Provide opportunities for students to practice their conference presentations in teams using the performance criteria developed in step 5 to provide feedback and offer suggestions for improvement.

STEP 7:   Establish the time period during which the conferences are to take place. Permit students to select their own specific presentation time. Make them responsible for inviting participants, and for following up the invitation to be sure all are informed.

STEP 8:   When the event happens, be sure students welcome all participants, handle introductions, review the objectives of the meeting, coordinate meeting events, handle followup communications, and summarize results. If you have prepared carefully, conferences should unfold productively with few surprises.

STEP 9:   Offer parents an opportunity for an additional one-on-one meeting with you, the teacher, if they wish—just in case there are any personal, family, or risky issues that need attention. In my experience, virtually all parents will decline, but it is good to offer. Incidentally, one teacher I know frames the conference this way: It will last 30 minutes, with the student leading the first 20 minutes. The final 10 minutes is intended for teacher and parents alone, unless the parents invite the student to remain. Almost all do.

With a combined 35 years of teaching experience, we have rarely found a more valuable educational process than student-led conferences. During preparation the students experienced goal setting, reflected upon their own learning, and created a showcase portfolio.

Once underway, the conferences seem to have a life of their own. We, the teachers, gave up control and became observers, an experience that was gratifying and revealing. It validated our growing belief that students have the ability to direct their own learning and are able to take responsibility for self-evaluation. For many of our students, we gained insights into individual qualities previously hidden from us in the day to day classroom routine.

Students blossomed under the direct and focused attention of their parents. In this intimate spotlight, where there was no competition except that which they placed on themselves, they stepped for a moment into the adult world where they took command of their own convergence as well as their own development. Parents were surprised and delighted at the level of sophistication and competence their children revealed while sharing personal accomplishments.

In order to refine and improve this process, we surveyed both students and parents. Parents were emphatic in their positive response to student-led conferences, with most requesting that we provide this type of conference more often. Students, even those at risk and with behavior problems, overwhelmingly responded with, "We needed more time; a half an hour was not enough."

Figure 13.2
Teacher commentary on experiences with student-led conferences
Source: By Harriet Arnold and Patricia Stricklin, 1993, Central Kitsap School District, Washington. Reprinted by permission of the authors.

STEP 10: Solicit a followup written review from parents. You might develop a simple questionnaire to help them. Such a questionnaire might, for example, offer them the opportunity to suggest future learning targets for their child. Students can take responsibility for collecting this feedback and can be partners in its interpretation and use.

STEP 11: Debrief your students on the entire experience. Discuss it as a group or have students evaluate the experience by writing about it. What facets worked? What needs improvement? Be sure you and they learn the important lessons this process teaches both about academics and students' personal reactions.

At the time of this writing, virtually every teacher I have spoken with across the continent who has carefully prepared for and conducted student-led parent conferences has found it to be a compellingly positive experience. In fact, a surprising number have told me that it was a career-altering and powerfully rejuvenating experience. Figure 13.2 shares the thoughts of two sixth-grade teachers on their experiences with student-led conferences. Figure 13.3 presents a concise summary of the key points made in this section about student-led parent conferences.

Benefits

1. Stronger sense of accountability among students
2. Stronger sense of pride in achievement among students
3. More productive student-teacher relationship
4. Improved student-parent relationship
5. Stronger sense of classroom community
6. Reduced cheating
7. Development of leadership skills among students
8. Greater parental participation in conferences

Challenges

1. The uncertainty of sharing control with students
2. The need to adopt a completely student-involved philosophy
3. The amount of time required to prepare and present conferences
4. The logistical challenges of organizing for conferences
5. The difficulties that can arise with dysfunctional families

Keys to Success

1. Students willing and able to risk
2. Teachers willing and able to step aside
3. Clear targets known to all
4. Accurate student-involved assessments
5. A shared language for talking about targets and their achievement
6. A commitment of time to learn, prepare, and practice

Figure 13.3
Student-led parent conference in a nutshell

A Final Thought About Your Communication Challenge

If you want your students to use feedback about their achievement as the basis for academic improvement, they need to have continuous access to timely and understandable information about their current achievement. When that evidence affirms learning, confidence and effort grow. When the evidence reveals a lack of success, acceptance of the message can be difficult. Students can and often do find ways to brush these messages aside, to rationalize them, to discredit the source, or to find some other way to escape. Call this human nature. The problem is, however, that in a learning community, such avoidance is immensely counterproductive.

You must be mindful of conditions you must satisfy for students to really listen to and accept negative information about themselves. You must find ways to help your students see themselves as key players in the search for information about their own achievement. In addition, students need assistance in developing a sufficiently strong academic self-concept so they can acknowledge their shortcomings and not feel defeated. In other words, they must always believe that success is within reach if they keep trying. Someone once said, "Confidence gives us the freedom to be patient with our failures." Confidence comes only from some level of success in learning. It is your responsibility to help students find that success.

Further, students must see the provider of the feedback as credible, honest, and helpful. The feedback must be descriptive and must reflect attributes of their academic performance—not attributes of them as learners. Only then can they see how to do better the next time.

And finally, they must come to see the benefits of the message very quickly, so they can muster the resources needed to act purposefully. They must see that if they act purposefully on the feedback they receive, they will move their work closer to the desired level of quality.

From the other point of view, the giver of the feedback (you) must be able to present it constructively, delivering a clear and focused message using understandable language. You must be able to communicate your acceptance of students while critiquing their achievement. They must know that you are evaluating their achievements, not them as people. Even more importantly, you must help students understand that you share a common mission: their academic success.

Clearly, it is no simple task to communicate to students that they have missed the target but still have the hope of success and reason to stay motivated. But as a teacher-communicator, that is exactly what you must do. The suggestions offered in previous chapters for clearly defining the meaning of academic success, assessing it well, and involving students throughout, then transforming the results into quality information, are intended to help you fulfill this most important of your teaching responsibilities. As long as students continue to see the target as being within reach and as long as they see their own progress, they will keep trying.

Summary: Finding Effective Ways to Communicate

We explored three communication systems that rely on direct contact among students, teachers, and parents. One turns the classroom into a workshop by using regular ongoing conferences to exchange information between teachers and students. Another is the traditional parent-teacher conference, preceded by a student-teacher conference covering the same material. The third places students in charge of their parent conferences. All require that students understand expectations well enough to be able to converse about them. They also permit students the opportunity of gathering and communicating relatively detailed information about their own achievement. Proficient assessors and communicators rapidly become better performers.

We must continue to explore, develop, and implement these kinds of communication systems as our achievement targets become more numerous, complex, and individualized. Implementation will be made easier as modern information-processing technology evolves and we learn new ways to apply it to the art of assessment. In the meantime, for the immediate future, we will most often use these alternatives in conjunction with or parallel to report card grading systems.

The methods of conveying information reviewed in this chapter hold the promise of allowing students to tell their story about their own academic success. That, in and of itself, represents one of the most powerful learning experiences we can offer them.

The End of Our Studies Together

As educators, our job is to teach ourselves out of a job. By this, I mean that we must take our students to a place where they don't need us anymore. Any students who leave school still needing to rely on their teachers to tell them they have done well have not yet learned to hit the target, because they cannot see the quality of their own performance. We must turn our achievement expectations and performance standards over to our students, to make them independent of us. Only then can we assure ourselves that we have helped our students become the lifelong learners they will need to be in the new millennium.

Covington (1992) advises us that, "Indeed, at its best, education should provide students with a sense of empowerment that makes the future 'real' by moving beyond merely offering children plausible alternatives to indicating how their preferred dreams can actually be attained" (p. 3). I submit that we can fulfill this mission only if we rely on student-involved classroom assessment combined with student-involved record keeping and student-involved communication.

This ends our journey together through the realm of classroom assessment. By way of saying farewell, let me reiterate the checklist of principles of assessment *for* learning that I presented in Chapter 1. As you reread them now, remember, physicians have a creed that says, "Above all, do no harm." Let's adopt an educators version of that creed: *Above all, do nothing to destroy confidence.* I hope you will be able to say that the following things are true of your instruction:

1. I understand and can articulate *in advance of teaching* the achievement targets that I want my students to hit.
2. I inform my students continuously about those targets *in terms that they can understand.*
3. I transform those targets into classroom assessments that I am certain *will yield accurate evidence* of student achievement.
4. I understand the relationship between assessment and student motivation and, in my classroom, we use assessment *to build* (and not to destroy) *student confidence.*
5. I consistently *act on classroom assessment results,* as needed, to revise instructional plans.
6. The feedback that my students receive is *frequent and descriptive* (versus infrequent or merely judgmental) providing a basis for improvement.

7. My *students are actively involved* in assessing their own achievement.
8. My students *actively communicate* with others about their achievement status and improvement over time.
9. My students *can describe the achievement targets* they are trying to hit, even though they can't hit them yet.

Please accept my best wishes for a successful career in teaching and classroom assessment.

Practice with Chapter 13 Ideas and Final Text Activities

1. Reread the conference in this chapter (pp. 344–346) between Jill and Ms. W. about Jill's piece on Rafe. Then answer the following questions:
   - What conditions of effective communication as described in Chapter 9 were demonstrated by this interaction?
   - What was Ms. W. doing well?
   - What questions would you like to ask either participant about their communication and why?
   - How might this communication have been improved, if at all?

2. Following is a case study in student-led conferences. Please read it and then respond to the questions that follow.

The High School Faculty Debate on Student-Led Conferences

A high school principal has just returned from a national conference on assessment full of excitement about an innovative new idea—student-led parent conferences—and he has put the topic on the agenda for the next faculty meeting. After introducing it and discussing some of its positive aspects, the principal invites the faculty to comment.

One teacher was negative about the idea based on his experience at a previous school. There, students assembled portfolios that included all subjects and met with their parents in homeroom at year's end to review their achievement. Conferences were 20 minutes, so it took a long day and evening to complete them all.

For this teacher, such conferences just didn't work. First, 20 minutes was not enough to cover six different subjects. Further, students didn't know what work to place in their portfolios or how to share it, so the meetings turned out to be very brief discussions of the report card grades— completely from the student's point of view. Finally, homeroom teachers were not equipped to answer parents' questions in subjects other than their own, so parents' needs were not satisfied. All in all, it was a disaster and was abandoned after one try.

Another teacher offers a different experience. She had one student who seemed full of academic potential but didn't seem to care about school. Her only comment was, "If my parents don't care, why should I?" When the teacher called the parents it became obvious that there had been a severe breakdown in communication in the family.

In a risky move, the teacher bet the student that her parents did care and that she could prove it. During the next grading period, the two of them assembled a growth portfolio showing the student's improvement. Further, the teacher asked her to think about how she might present herself as an improving student and to write biweekly self-reflections about the work in her portfolio. As the term ended, the teacher requested the student to invite her parents in for a special student-parent-teacher conference. The conference was a success for all.

In response to these comments, the principal makes a proposal: The faculty could institute student-led conferences to bolster three initiatives already in place. First, twelfth graders are required to complete special senior projects. Second, the guidance staff has all college-bound students assemble "college admissions portfolios." Finally, students are required to complete a certain number of community service hours and assemble evidence of the productivity of their work. All three might provide an excellent basis for a school-and communitywide end-of-year acknowledgement of a productive school year.

Specifically, he proposes a three-day "School Success Celebration." Senior projects might culminate in "showcase" student-led conferences in which students

present their work for review and discussion. College admissions portfolios might be shared with parents or review boards. Community service portfolios might be presented in a group session.

The principal asks for volunteers to see if this is feasible and useful.

Questions:

1. Analyze each of the teacher's experiences with student-led conferences, applying the standards of effective communication. Why might their experiences been different?

2. What do you think is motivating the principal here? How good is the celebration idea from the perspectives of the students, teachers, and community? What would it take for this idea to play out successfully?

3. Make a two-by-two chart crossing students and teachers on one dimension with benefits and problems on the other. Use it to evaluate the pluses and minuses of this idea. What judgment does this analysis lead you to?

APPENDIX

Rubrics for Judging Classroom Assessment Quality

Rubrics for Judging Classroom Assessment Quality

Standard of Quality	Still Needs Work	Well on Its Way	Ready to Go
The intended user(s) and use(s) of the assessment are clear.	No purposes are stated, nor can they be inferred from the context; it is not clear why the assessment is being conducted. There are too many users and uses; it would be impossible to satisfy all the stated purposes in a single assessment. The purpose is inappropriate—the evidence to be gathered cannot inform the user or use.	Users and uses can be implied, but are not explicitly identified. Users and uses are stated, but there is some uncertainty about the appropriateness of the assessment for them.	The intended users and uses are clearly identified; it is clear that this assessment can help them.
The valued student learning target(s) are clear and appropriate.	The learning targets around which the assessment is to be built are not stated, so there is no basis for evaluating assessment exercises or scoring procedures. Targets are broad and/or vague with little attempt at clarification. There is little apparent connection to district or state standards. Targets don't reflect best thinking in the field.	Learning targets are listed, but sometimes the connection to state or district standards is not clear. Some of the goals represent best thinking in the field, others do not.	Learning targets are stated, clear, and easy to find. They are important—worth the assessment time devoted to them. For example, targets reflect the best thinking in the field.
A proper assessment method has been selected.	The method(s) used is/are not capable of properly reflecting the achievement target(s) in question.	When multiple methods are used in an assessment, sometimes the proper method is selected, sometimes an improper method is used.	The method(s) chosen is/are capable of properly reflecting the achievement target(s) to be assessed.

362

The assessment samples achievement using enough high-quality exercises and scoring procedures.	**Sampling:** There are not enough assessment tasks to cover the material to be learned. Some exercises reflect achievement targets not included in the set to be assessed. There are too many tasks included to yield an efficient assessment, making the assessment grossly inefficient. **Sound Exercises and Scoring:** Enough of the selected response, essay, performance assessment, or personal communication exercises and tasks violate standards of good quality that the assessment will not yield accurate information about student achievement. Scoring keys or guides contain errors or other characteristics that will cause scores or ratings to misrepresent student achievement.	**Sampling:** In some cases there are too many or too few tasks or exercises to get an efficient estimate of student learning, yet some outcomes are sampled well. The assessment reflects most, but not all, of the stated learning targets, or reflects learning of some goals not stated. **Sound Exercises and Scoring:** At least a few of the exercises or scoring schemes violate accepted standards of quality in ways that may negatively impact the accuracy of results.	**Sampling:** There are neither too many nor too few tasks or exercises, but just enough to get a stable estimate of learning, and the tasks cover the learning target(s) (domain) well. There is a clear match between stated learning goals and items on the assessment. **Sound Exercises and Scoring:** All or nearly all of the exercises, tasks, and scoring procedures meet standards of good practice sufficiently well that the assessment is likely to yield accurate results.
Relevant sources of bias have been minimized.	Assessment results may misrepresent the achievement of students in some gender, ethnic, or linguistic subgroups due to characteristics of the assessment or the manner of its use. Extreme evaluation anxiety may keep some students from demonstrating their actual level of learning. Distractions in the assessment environment may cause students to lose focus and not demonstrate their actual level of attainment. Failure to accommodate the unique needs of students with learning disabilities may cause inaccurate assessment of their achievement. Cheating or other unethical behavior may lead to an overestimate of actual student achievement.	The danger remains that some of the potential sources of bias listed may distort results, but results can be understood in an unbiased manner if explained with certain caveats. Or, the majority of causes of bias have been addressed, minimizing distortion. Or, the likely impact of any distortion on instructional decisions within the assessment context is minimal.	Accommodations for diverse student characteristics are made, minimizing any distortions in final judgment of student learning. Thus, cultural or gender differences, anxiety, distractions, disabilities, or unethical behavior are unlikely to interfere with students' ability to accurately demonstrate their level of attainment.

Standard of Quality	Still Needs Work	Well on Its Way	Ready to Go
Results are communicated effectively.	**Information Management:** No systems have been created to store, retrieve, or summarize results appropriately; little attention has been paid to the level of detail of records, how they will be stored, or by whom. **Reporting:** No attention has been given to who needs access to results, in what form, or when. No accommodation is made for differentiated information management or reporting depending on the assessment *of* and *for* learning environment.	**Information Management:** There is some awareness of the need to compile and summarize information, but the level of detail stored and summarized and by whom, as well as the unique requirements of the assessment context, needs further attention. **Reporting:** Information about student achievement is shared in a manner that complies with school requirements; but the real information needs of possible users working in different contexts needs further attention.	**Information Management:** Systems are in place to store information about student achievement at the proper level of detail to fit the context; it is clear how those records are to be stored and by whom. **Reporting:** Procedures are in place to deliver information about student achievement into the hands of intended users in a timely manner and in a form that they will understand and be able to use. Both information management and reporting systems reflect a clear awareness of differences between assessment *of* and *for* learning contexts.

References

ACT & Assessment Training Institute. (2002). *Promoting student success: Connecting ATI classroom assessment and the ACT Assessment.* Iowa City, IA & Portland, OR: Authors.

Anderson, L. W., & Bourke, S. F. (2000). *Assessing affective characteristics in schools,* 2nd ed., Mahwah, NJ: Lawrence Erlbaum & Associates.

Arter, J., & Spandel, V. (1992). Using portfolio of student work in instruction and assessment. *Educational Measurement: Issues and Practice, 11*(1), 36–44.

Austin, T. (1994). *Changing the view: Student-led parent conferences.* Portsmouth, NH: Heinemann.

Bartlett, L. (1987). Academic evaluation and student discipline don't mix: A critical review. *Journal of Law and Education, 16*(2), 155–165.

Black, P., & William, D. (1998). Inside the black box: Raising standards through classroom assessment. *Phi Delta Kappan, 80*(2), 139–148.

Covington, M. (1992). *Making the grade: A self-worth perspective on motivation and school reform.* New York: Cambridge.

CTB/McGraw-Hill, Inc. (1996). *Terra nova: The only one.* Monterey, CA: Author.

Davies, A., Cameron, C., Politano, C., & Gregory, K. (1992). *Together is better: Collaborative assessment, evaluation and reporting.* Winnipeg, MB: Peguis.

Gardner, H. (1993). *Frames of mind: The theory of multiple intelligences.* New York: Basic Books.

Hall, C. S., & Lindsay, G. (1970). *Theories of personality,* 2nd ed. New York: John Wiley & Sons.

Meisels, S. J., Atkins-Burnett, S., Xue, Y., & Bickel, D. P. (2003). Creating a system of accountability: The impact of instructional assessment on elementary children's achievement test scores. *Educational Policy Analysis Archives, 11*(9), 1–19.

Ministry of Education and Training, Victoria. (1991). *English profiles handbook: Assessment and reporting student progress in English.* Melbourne, Australia: Author.

Paul, R. (1995). *Critical thinking: How to prepare students for a rapidly changing world.* Santa Rosa, CA: Foundation for Critical Thinking.

Rowe, M. B. (1978). Specific ways to develop better communication. In R. Sund & A. Carin (Eds.), *Creative questioning and sensitivity: Listening techniques,* 2nd ed. Upper Saddle River, NJ: Merrill/Prentice Hall.

Shepard, L. A. (1997). *Measuring achievement: What does it mean to test for robust understanding?* Princeton, NJ: Educational Testing Service.

Spandel, V., & Culham, R. (1995). *Putting portfolio stories to work.* Portland, OR: Northwest Regional Educational Laboratory.

Sternberg, R. J. (1996). Myths, countermyths and truths about intelligences. *Educational Researcher, 25*(2), 11–16.

Stiggins, R. J., & Conklin, N. F. (1992). *In teachers' hands: Investigating the practice of classroom assessment.* Albany, NY: SUNY Press.

Index